X Window Inside and Out

Levi Reiss
Joseph Radin

X Window Inside & Out

Osborne **McGraw-Hill**

Berkeley New York St. Louis San Francisco
Auckland Bogotá Hamburg London Madrid
Mexico City Milan Montreal New Delhi Panama City
Paris São Paulo Singapore Sydney
Tokyo Toronto

Osborne **McGraw-Hill**
2600 Tenth Street
Berkeley, California 94710
U.S.A.

For information on translations and book distributors outside of the U.S.A., please write to Osborne **McGraw-Hill** at the above address.

The following statement appears in M.I.T.'s X documentation:

X Window Inside & Out

1234567890 DOC 9987654321

ISBN 0-07-881796-X

To our wives and children: Noga, Sami, and Maya Reiss; and Sara, Gal, and Nurit Radin.

Publisher

Kenna S. Wood

Acquisitions Editor

Jeffrey M. Pepper

Associate Editor

Emily Rader

Technical Editor

Otto Gygax

Project Editor

Judy Ziajka

Copy Editor

Paul Medoff

Proofreader

Linda Medoff

Indexer

Valerie Robbins

Computer Designer

Stefany Otis

Illustrator

Marla Shelasky

Quality Control Specialist

Bob Myren

Cover Designer

Mason Fong
Bay Graphics Design, Inc.

Contents At a Glance

Contents

Acknowledgments

A computer book is never the sole product of one or two authors, and *X Window Inside and Out* is no exception. We wish to thank the excellent Osborne/McGraw-Hill team for their multifaceted efforts whose fruits you hold in your hand. Jeff Pepper not only signed us and helped mold our proposal, he also provided valuable comments during the writing and rewriting. On a day-to-day basis, Emily Rader was in constant contact with us. "This should take only a few minutes" often stretched into what seemed like hours, but every page shows the value of her input. Special thanks go to Judy Ziajka and Paul Medoff for manuscript preparation and copy editing. Their multiple clarifications helped us all. Thanks also to Linda Medoff, proofreader, whose eagle-eye attention caught so many errors and inconsistencies, large and small. Otto Gygax had the heavy task of technical reviewer. We want to thank him for his many minor and occasionally major corrections. We wish to convey our appreciation to the design team and Stefany Otis for a beautiful text, designed with you, the reader, in mind. Heartfelt credit goes to David Flack and Allen Southerton of *UNIX World* and Dr. Gerald Karam of Carleton University for their valuable suggestions and aid with this project. We thank Barbara LoFranco and the Santa Cruz Operation for providing us with the industry-leading software on which we ran all the programs. Final appreciation goes to our wives, Noga Reiss and Sara Radin, for their infinite patience and important input in all stages of the process. On many occasions, if they didn't like it, you don't see it. As is customary, the authors acknowledge their sole responsibility for any errors.

Introduction

X Window does windows. It is *the* software tool for developing graphical user interfaces (GUIs) on workstations. X Window is to UNIX systems what MS Windows is to MS-DOS systems with an important difference: X Window systems are the industry-accepted standard for UNIX windowing. This standardization has far-reaching consequences: Graphical user interfaces developed on one computer can be run on completely different computers. X Window systems can provide common output for networked workstations, mainframes, minicomputers, and microcomputers.

The continuing decline in microcomputer prices has put X Window systems within reach of literally millions of computer users. For example, all programs appearing in this book were developed and tested on an IBM-compatible 33-MHz 486 computer, with 8 megabytes of memory and a 110Mb hard disk. Such a computer is hardly an entry-level platform, but no longer beyond most budgets for new equipment. A slower but feasible development platform is a similarly equipped 25-MHz 386 computer. The operating system used was implemented with UNIX System V Release 3.2, the industry leader for UNIX on personal computers, the SCO Open Desktop Personal System Release 1.1.0 with the Open Desktop Development System Release 1.1.0. Development software included X Window Version 11, Release 4, with OSF/Motif toolkit and the C programming language. The use of alternative development systems such as the recently released DESQview/X multitasking environment by Quarterdeck Office Systems may reduce hardware requirements. Functioning X Window applications will run on ATs and XTs.

About This Book

All programs in this book were written using the C programming language and appropriate X Window features and will run under the UNIX operating system. They were tested under both UNIX V and BSD. Moderate C programming language experience is a prerequisite. The first program includes generous reminders for readers whose C is a bit rusty. Except for the last program in the book, the programs do not require advanced knowledge of UNIX.

This book is addressed to two very different categories of users. Many have no previous experience with X Window programming. They may or may not have previous experience in programming GUIs as well. Our advice to such readers is to brush up on your C language programming skills if necessary, turn on your computer, roll up your sleeves, and get started. You will probably want to run every program in this book.

Other users have previous X Window programming experience that they want to consolidate. These users may be able to pick and choose among the chapters. They, too, will want to turn on the computer and roll up their sleeves. Both categories of users will want their system documentation within reach.

Successful completion of this book means that you will be able to apply X Window systems to develop graphical user interfaces, applying the three levels of X Window systems described in the next section. While the level of programming is beginning to intermediate, the last chapter presents a relatively advanced application that you can modify to meet special requirements. You will be able to pick up any of the system's numerous manuals and fly (or, in some cases, crawl) with it. We venture to say that you'll have some fun doing so.

How This Book Is Organized

The book is divided into three sections and several appendices. The beginning section, composed of four chapters, introduces the X Window system and includes a completely dissected, functioning program. The middle section, composed of six chapters, describes X Window functions and illustrates them with functioning programs that can be run and modified on your UNIX system. The final section, Chapter 11, presents a fundamental application, integrating X Window functions, C language functions, and UNIX system calls to build a graphical user interface. The chapter concludes with a description of advanced X Window functions. A discussion of each of the chapters and appendices follows.

Chapter 1, "Introducing the System," describes the need for X Window systems and defines their basic requirements, components, and characteristics. It introduces the three levels of X Window programming: Xlib, C language functions that carry out fundamental tasks; Xt Intrinsics, a standard toolkit that is easier to use for applications; and OSF/Motif, the proprietary toolkit used in this text. The chapter explains when to use each of these levels. It concludes by comparing and contrasting X Window systems to other windowing systems such as Microsoft Windows.

Chapter 2, "Hello World," presents and explains in full detail a functioning program similar to the well-known C language Hello World program. In contrast to the four-line C language program, the source code of the X Window program is over two pages long.

Chapter 3, "Basic Concepts and Terminology," defines and discusses fundamental hardware and software aspects of X Window systems. For example, it illustrates X Window's approach to client/server architecture and introduces the six categories of server resources. It concludes by acquainting you with events, the cornerstone of the X Window system.

Chapter 4, "Windows and Windowing Techniques," examines in great detail X Window's definition and handling of windows. It covers window geometry, temporary and permanent features, and the relationships among windows and introduces Xlib window processing functions.

Chapter 5, "Toolkit Concepts and Techniques," introduces in great detail the two upper levels of X Window programming: the Xt Intrinsics toolkit and the proprietary OSF/Motif toolkit. It discusses widgets, the building block of toolkit programs. It returns to the Hello World program introduced in Chapter 2 and presents two versions of this program using the Motif applications structure. The chapter concludes with an extensive examination of the toolkit approach to X Window programming and its underlying concepts.

Chapter 6, "Text," is devoted to theoretical and practical aspects of generating text in X Window programs. The chapter includes six functioning programs that illustrate various features of text processing.

Chapter 7, "Keyboard," is devoted to theoretical and practical aspects of keyboard handling in X Window programs. The chapter includes two functioning programs that illustrate various features of keyboard manipulation.

Chapter 8, "Mouse," is devoted to theoretical and practical aspects of manipulating the mouse in X Window programs. The chapter includes three functioning programs that illustrate various features of mouse handling.

Chapter 9, "Pixmaps, Bitmaps, and Images," is devoted to theoretical and practical aspects of processing pixmaps, bitmaps, and images in X Window programs. The chapter includes two functioning programs that illustrate various features of handling pixmaps, bitmaps, and images.

Chapter 10, "Color and Graphics," is devoted to theoretical and practical aspects of processing color and graphics in X Window programs. The chapter includes six functioning programs that illustrate various features of graphics output.

Chapter 11, "Complete Fundamental Application and Advanced Features," consists of a complete basic X Window program integrating Xt Intrinsics, OSF/Motif, C language functions, and UNIX system calls to build a graphical user interface that provides the capabilities of the UNIX operating system to users unfamiliar with UNIX. The chapter concludes by presenting advanced X Window programming features.

Appendix A, "Xlib," lists the contents of the Xlib.h header library in the X Window system and explains its use.

Appendix B, "Xutil," lists the contents of the Xutil.h header library in the X Window system and explains its use.

Appendix C, "Intrinsic.h," lists the contents of the Intrinsic.h header library in the X Window system and explains its use.

Appendix D, "OSF/Motif Widgets," lists and describes the major widgets available with the OSF/Motif toolkit used in this text.

Appendix E, "X Window Programming Errors," lists and describes many common errors encountered by X Window programmers of all levels of experience. The time saved by a single reference to this appendix might well pay for the book.

A glossary provides definitions of terms important to X Window users.

Conventions Used in This Book

The text respects standard conventions for the X Window system, the C programming language, and the UNIX operating system. All function names appear in boldface; Xlib functions start with the letter X, and C language functions are identified as such. Parameters, variables, identifiers, fields, elements, and arguments appear in italics. Boolean operators appear in uppercase. New terms appear in italics when they are first defined.

Programs Disk Offer

Why work your fingers to the bone typing the source code for the various examples? You're bound to make typos and waste precious hours looking for your errors. The authors offer a floppy disk containing the complete source code for all programs in the text for $29.95. Just fill in the order blank on the next page and mail it, along with your payment, to the listed address.

Please send me _____ copies, at $29.95 each, of the programs in *X Window Inside and Out* on a UNIX-format floppy disk (3 1/2 inches).

Orders inside U.S. and Canada only: Checks must be drawn on a U.S. bank. Please add $5.00 per disk for shipping and handling.

_____

Name

_____

Address

_____   _____   _____

City   State or country   ZIP

(_____)_____
Telephone number

Send check or money order payable to:

Levi Reiss and Joseph Radin
P.O. Box 41067
Ottawa, Ontario K1G 5K9
CANADA

This offer is subject to change or cancellation at any time.

CHAPTER

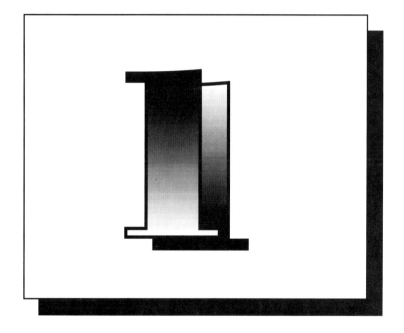

Introducing the System

Welcome to the *X Window system* (also called X Window and sometimes erroneously referred to as X Windows). In the course of the last few years this system has become the standard software tool for developing *graphical user interfaces* on *workstations*. A graphical user interface (*GUI*) can be briefly defined as a computer/user interface that runs in graphics mode. Workstations are desktop computers with computational and graphics facilities that are more powerful than high-end microcomputers.

Because of X Window's device independence, graphical user interfaces developed on one computer can be run on completely different computers. X Window systems often provide common output for networked workstations, mainframes, minicomputers, and microcomputers. Before examining X Window systems in detail, let's consider the need for windowing systems and GUIs.

Each major advance in computer hardware has led to significant progress in how end users and computer specialists interact with the computer. This progress results in a less stressful, more productive workplace.

Some individuals still remember the age of punch-card processing, roughly speaking, the 1950s, 1960s, and early 1970s. At that time most nontechnical people were forced to choose between two unsatisfactory options: either running a very limited set of computer programs or relying on computer specialists to help them access needed data. Programmers considered themselves lucky if they could test a program three or four times a day. Standard output consisted of wiggly lines containing poorly shaped numbers and letters, uppercase only.

Gradually, cathode-ray terminals (CRTs) replaced keypunches and card readers. An ever-expanding group of users applied CRTs to extract needed information from the mainframe computer located in the next room or across the continent. Programmers developed and tested programs interactively, engaging in dialogue with the computer. Computer output facilities advanced as well. Viewing results no longer meant a walk down the hall to the printer. Many CRTs offered new features such as lowercase letters. But to paraphrase Henry Ford, with a standard CRT, you can have any kind of font you want, as long as it's "Computer." Even today, many CRTs attached to mainframe computers cannot generate graphics.

The effects of the microcomputer revolution surround us. Who has not seen dazzling screens and flashy brochures printed by relatively inexpensive computer systems? The very success of the microcomputer revolution has engendered new problems. Long-time IBM-compatible microcomputer users know from bitter experience the difficulty in transferring files from one package to another. The knowledge acquired by mastering your spreadsheet's print function has been, until recently, virtually useless for printing a document via your word processor. In fact, changing word processors has traditionally meant learning to print all over again.

Software developers, as well, keenly feel the pinch of compatibility problems. Graphics software is hard to write and harder to debug. A program that draws a line on the screen must manage two separate but related pieces of hardware: the video controller and the video monitor. A program written for one IBM-compatible graphics standard will not display correctly using other graphics standards for the same computer. Converting traditional graphics programs to run on the Macintosh, workstations, or mainframe computers may be more trouble than it's worth.

Older IBM-compatible microcomputers use either Hercules (monochrome) or CGA (color) graphics. In 1987, IBM introduced the PS/2 line of microcomputers equipped with VGA graphics. To a large extent VGA graphics have replaced Hercules, CGA, and another IBM graphics standard called EGA. Toward the beginning of the 1990s VGA became the entry-level graphics standard for IBM compatibles.

The highest resolution available in VGA is 640×480; a single screen is divided into 640 horizontal and 480 vertical points. Each addressable point is called a *pixel*. Graphics systems capable of handling 800×600 resolution are common. These are often known as Super or Extended VGA, but neither the nomenclature nor the technical specifications are standard. Two different standards exist for 1024×768 graphics systems, commonly used with computer-aided design and desktop publishing systems. At the time of this writing, a price barrier exists at 1024×768 resolution. Higher-resolution graphics systems are relatively expensive and are not standard. On the other hand, a typical workstation screen resolution is 1152×900, and higher resolutions are common.

Developers of traditional graphics programs must be prepared to count pixels (literally thousands of them) and be familiar with arbitrary codes for patterns and colors. *Porting* (converting) a graphics application from one computer to another can take months. Problems resulting from this technical hurdle, caused largely by different graphics standards, helped microcomputers such as Digital Equipment Corporation's Rainbow and Texas Instruments' Professional lose market share to IBM compatibles. The X Window system addresses these problems.

X Window System

The X Window system has become a standard hardware-independent windowing system. It is a tool for developing both monochrome and color high-resolution graphical systems. A schematic illustration of the X Window system is shown in Figure 1-1.

 X Window System

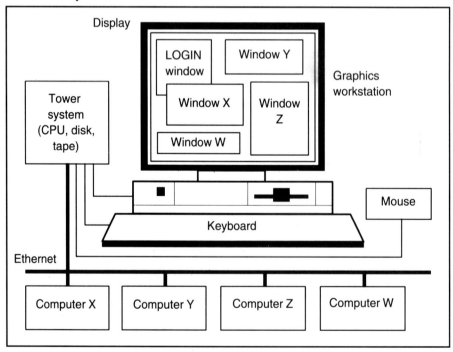

History and Need

In 1984, the Laboratory for Computer Science at the Massachusetts Institute of Technology (MIT) in Cambridge, Massachusetts, launched Project Athena, lead by Robert Scheifler and Jim Gettys. Like many other organizations, both commercial and nonprofit, MIT juggled a wide assortment of CPUs, terminals, and operating systems. The Project Athena goal was straightforward. Programs must be available interactively to users at any station, anywhere on campus. The starting point was a Stanford University windowing system known as W.

The X Window system first became available to developers with version 10.4 in 1986. Major computer vendors, including Digital Equipment Corporation (DEC), International Business Machines (IBM), American Telephone and Telegraph (AT&T), Sun Microsystems, and Hewlett-Packard, have funded the development of the X Window system on an ongoing basis. During its short life the X Window system has been constantly upgraded. At the time of this writing the most recent version is X11R5 (Version 11 Release 5).

Hardware

X Window systems run on a variety of common hardware devices. The output unit is a graphics screen, usually with at least VGA resolution. The most commonly used input devices are the keyboard and the mouse. Other input units include trackball, digitizing tablet, and touchscreen. Various processing options are described in the following sections.

Workstations

The vast majority of workstation manufacturers actively support X Window systems. The importance of this market is underscored by considering that as of December 1991, a single company d7clivered almost one-half million workstations. The continuing decline in workstation prices and increase in individual and group computing requirements means an ever-growing role for workstations, and consequently for X Window systems.

X Terminals

Most organizations cannot afford $5000 or more to equip each desktop with a full-blown workstation. An increasingly popular alternative is an *X Terminal.* X Terminals are diskless graphical computer terminals that run a single program, the X Window server program introduced later in this chapter.

The rapid expansion of the X Window marketplace has led to the development of a wide variety of X Terminals, some of which rival workstations for memory and CPU. Because X Terminals do not have disks, they are less expensive than corresponding workstations.

Other advantages of X Terminals are reduced hardware and software maintenance compared to workstations running X Window systems. X Terminals offer increased control by the information systems department and protect the installation's investment in mainframe computers.

X Terminals have potential disadvantages. They cannot process data when and where it is generated. The low-end models tend to be slow. In the eyes of critics, X Terminals represent a step back to the world of time sharing.

Microcomputers

The question arises, "If X Window systems are so wonderful, can I use them on my microcomputer?" The answer is, "It depends."

A virtual requirement is high-resolution graphics. Super VGA is certainly preferable to VGA or Hercules. Processing requirements may make the 1024×768 resolution too slow. Color is a matter of choice but if you choose color make sure that the colors are attractive and varied. (Today's users tend to consider 16 colors a bit boring.)

The minimum processor is an 80386 or equivalent (for example, a 68030). (Patient AT users may find the waiting time acceptable for simple graphics.) A large, fast hard disk is an absolute necessity. The X Window system is not a DOS system; don't even think of squeezing it into a corner of your 40-megabyte (Mb) hard drive. Plan on devoting at least a 110Mb drive to the X Window system and its environment, including UNIX. Check your manuals to determine the necessary configuration for your X Window implementation and the facilities you require.

As discussed in detail in this chapter, X Window systems include two tasks: running the user application and handling the graphics. Unless you have a true multitasking operating system, your microcomputer cannot service both the user application and the graphics. A single DOS-based microcomputer can handle either of these functions; it cannot handle both.

UNIX and other multitasking operating systems often drive large microcomputer systems. For example, the Santa Cruz Operation's Open Desktop, shown in Figure 1-2, has become the leading high-end microcomputer UNIX operating system. This package provides full X Window facilities. You may expect that many packages will provide partial or full X Window support for large microcomputers in the future.

All examples in this book were developed on an IBM-compatible 486/33 MHz microcomputer with a 1024 × 768 color graphics monitor running SCO Open Desktop Personal System Release 1.1.0 with the Open Desktop Development System. 1.1.0 running on UNIX System V Release 3.2; X Window Version 11, Release 4, with the OSF/Motif toolkit; and the C programming language. Don't worry; the use of different hardware or a different X Window implementation will not affect your understanding. This flexibility is really the point of X Window.

The SCO Open Desktop window

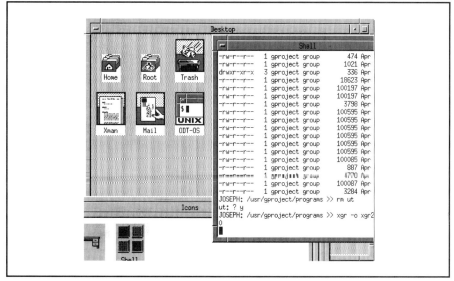

Client/Server Architecture

The heart of the X Window philosophy is the *client/server architecture.* The client/server architecture is the X Window system model by which *clients*, or application programs, communicate with *servers*, or display units over a network. The client/server architecture is shown in Figure 1-3. This section examines in detail the X Window client/server architecture components and then compares this architecture to the client/server model found in other computer systems.

Client

Basically, the client is the application program. Unlike traditional graphics programs, X Window clients do not directly communicate with

FIGURE 1-3   Client/server architecture

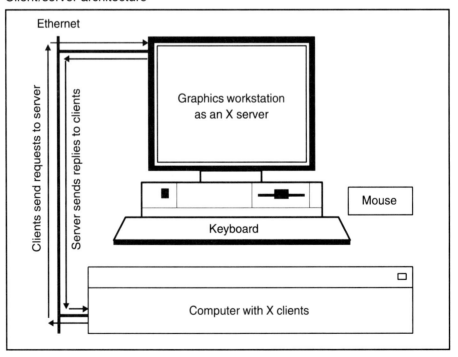

the user. The client obtains user input such as a keypress or click of a mouse button from the server, the other half of the client/server architecture. The client executes X Window commands that request the server to draw graphics. Several clients may be attached to a single server.

Server

In simple terms, the server is the display unit, which may be composed of multiple physical screens. The server performs several related functions:

❏ It passes user input to attached clients. Common examples of user input are pressing a key, clicking a mouse button, and changing the pointer location. This input is unscheduled—any type may occur in any order.

❏ It decodes client messages, such as information requests and the moving of one or more windows. A formal X Window language expresses these requests.

❏ It maintains complex data structures. The server's handling of these structures reduces client storage and processing needs and diminishes the amount of data transmitted over the network.

Connection

An essential part of X Window systems is the physical link between the client (application program) and the server (display). Networking protocols describe the format and order of data and control bytes that compose a message sent from one network point to another. X Window developers need not know the networking protocol actually used. Three commonly used networking protocols for data transfer between the server and the clients are TCP/IP, developed by the University of California, DECNet, developed by Digital Equipment Corporation, and STREAMS, developed by AT&T. X Window was written to make the use of these and other network protocols transparent to the user.

Ethernet is a widely used local-area network communications technology. It supplies the physical communications channel between the clients and the server. It transmits data at an effective rate of 1 million bits per second. Compare this speed to a typical connection between a graphics terminal and a mainframe computer at 19,200 bits per second. The X Window link can transfer data more than 50 times as fast (if the collision rate, which slows data transmission, is low over the Ethernet link).

Relation to Traditional Client/Server Systems

Many people are familiar with the terms "client" and "server" as associated with other types of computer systems. For example, a local area network file server stores files and centralizes file management operations for users (clients). A printer server queues user printer requests. In these cases, the server is located on a remote, often heavy-duty computer, and the client is the user. X Window systems reverse the component locations—the server is located at the user's computer or X Terminal, and the client is located on a remote, often heavy-duty computer. Both traditional client/server systems and X Window systems apply the division-of-labor principle to centralize key operations in the server, enabling the client to focus on the application at hand.

Software

Specialized software is needed to send appropriate data and control bytes from the client to the server and vice versa. Chapter 2, "Hello World," demonstrates the complexity of displaying a single window on the user screen. The first sample program is about two pages long. X Window flexibility comes at a price.

This text shows you how to program X Window systems. It introduces the three levels of programming, ranging from coding C language calls that directly access the X network protocol to commercially available packages that resemble the Microsoft Windows graphical user interface. These three programming levels are illustrated in Figure 1-4. Which programming level should you use? The answer is simple: A typical X Window program may use all three programming levels in varying degrees, depending on the exact nature of the task.

Levels of programming

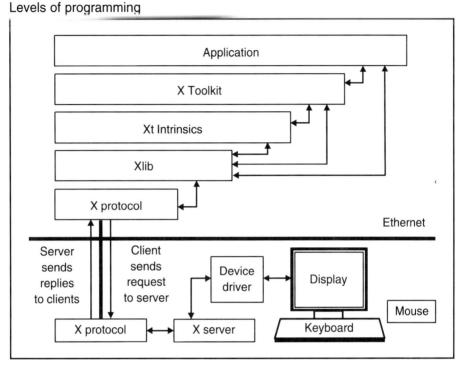

Xlib Functions

X Window system client/server communication is accomplished through a network protocol, called the *X protocol.* The X protocol defines the exact bytes required to perform all X Window operations, including drawing a window, moving a window, or reacting to the click of a mouse button. Programming with the X protocol is extremely arduous—this bare-bones language offers few facilities to help the programmer.

The X protocol is similar to the machine language that actually drives a given computer processor. Few people write programs in either machine language or X protocol. They don't need to. Just as assembly languages provide the power of machine languages at a greatly reduced effort, *Xlib* functions provide the power of X protocol with much less pain.

Xlib is a library of over 300 C language functions used to generate X protocol. This book assumes a working knowledge of the C programming language.

An example of an Xlib function is **XCreateSimpleWindow**. In spite of its name, this function is not particularly simple. When applying this function in an X Window program, the programmer must supply nine specific parameters that handle values such as the window's size, position, and border width.

Xlib functions are a starting point for learning how X Window works. Chapter 2, "Hello World," presents a complete X Window program composed of Xlib functions. While it is essential to master Xlib functions to know how the X Window system works, you will usually want to program with higher-level commands, using Xt Intrinsics or proprietary toolkits.

Xt Intrinsics

X Toolkit Intrinsics, also known as *Xt Intrinsics*, enable programmers to create and use standard onscreen building blocks, called *widgets*, such as menus, scroll bars, buttons, and dialog boxes. Meticulous use of widgets simplifies the X Window programming process. Perhaps more important, it gives the application a standard "look and feel" and consequently makes the application easier to use.

Xt Intrinsic functions start with a capital X followed by a lowercase t. For example, the Xt Intrinsic function **XtWindow** returns the ID of the window associated with a given widget. Do not jump to conclusions when comparing the Xlib function **XCreateSimpleWindow** with the Xt Intrinsic function **XtWindow**. These two functions do not perform the same actions.

Proprietary Toolkits

The uppermost programming level for X Window systems is proprietary. Software houses develop their own toolkits as extensions of the Xt Intrinsics toolkit. *Proprietary toolkits* include custom features that promise attractive output, ease of use, and rapid application development. A *window manager* is a special client responsible for manipulating windows on the screen. The X Window system comes with two window managers: uwm and twm. Proprietary toolkits apply their own window manager, which may be more sophisticated. Chapter 4, "Windows and Windowing Techniques," discusses window managers in greater detail.

Each proprietary toolkit produces a trademark graphical user interface, enabling developers to create a series of applications with a standard look and feel. A warning is in order: It takes considerable skill to produce a truly user-friendly interface, even for a simple application, much less for a series of applications. No matter how powerful the toolkit, sloppy programming remains sloppy programming.

Mastery of X Window programming requires learning three interrelated products: Xlib, Xt Intrinsics, and the chosen proprietary toolkit. Equally important, the programmer must also know when to use each of these products.

OSF/Motif The Open Software Foundation (OSF) is a consortium founded in 1988 by major hardware vendors, including IBM, DEC, and Hewlett-Packard. The OSF/Motif toolkit, often called Motif, is the most widely used X Window proprietary toolkit. The Motif window manager mwm handles the details of window creation and processing. It provides an attractive interface similar to Microsoft Windows. Figure 1-5 illustrates sample windows for OSF/Motif.

FIGURE 1-5

Typical Motif graphical user interface

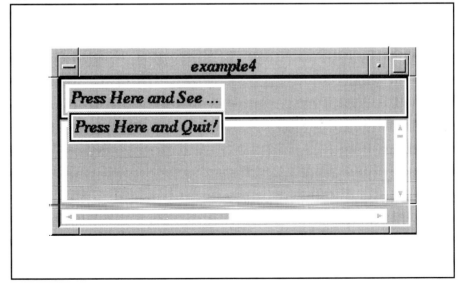

Motif functions start with a capital X followed by a lowercase m. For example, the Motif function **XmCreatePopupMenu** places a popup (temporary) menu on the screen at a location specified by another Motif function.

This text presents OSF/Motif toolkits exclusively. However, it is important to be familiar with competitive software. The product selection process is lengthy and has major implications for X Window developers.

Open Look   The major competitor to OSF/Motif is the Open Look graphical user interface distributed by American Telephone and Telegraph (AT&T) and Sun Microsystems. Sun's version includes functions that ease conversion of previous Sun applications to the X Window system. Figure 1-6 illustrates sample windows created with the Open Look graphical user interface. Table 1-1 shows current vendor and third-party support for Motif and Open Look toolkits.

Other Implementations   Quarterdeck Office Systems, the distributor of best-selling memory management programs for both MS-DOS and

Typical Open Look graphical user interface

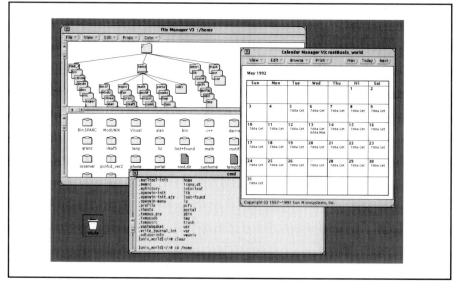

TABLE 1-1 Availability of Motif and Open Look

Vendor	Motif	Open Look
IBM	V	T
Digital Equipment Corp.	V	T
Hewlett-Packard	V	T
UNISYS	V	
Sun Microsystems	T	V
Solbourne	V	V
Compaq	V	
Dell	V	
Prime	V	
Data General	V	
Silicon Graphics	V	
MIPS	V	
NCR	V	
AT&T	V	V
Wang	V	
NEC	V	
Hitachi	V	
Commodore		V

V - Vendor supported   T - Third-party supported

Source: Mike Burgard, "Who's Winning the GUI Race?" *UNIXWORLD*, August 1991

MS-Windows computers, has announced DESQview/X. This package is designed to turn a high-powered microcomputer into a complete X Window client and server for network applications. Competitive micro-computer products are available.

Other Windowing Systems

This introductory chapter concludes by examining other popular windowing systems and comparing and contrasting them to the X Window system. Before examining particular implementations, it is essential to determine the objectives of such systems.

History and Objectives

End users and computer specialists both found early computer systems difficult to operate. Over the years a multitude of businesses and research organizations have applied developing technology to make computers easier to use. Many tools and techniques of modern computing stem from work dating back to the 1980s. Key examples include object-oriented programming, the Apple Macintosh, and the graphical user interface with the mouse. Let's now look at typical components of GUIs and then compare actual implementations to X Window systems. Graphical user interfaces should provide the following facilities:

❑ Extensive use of standard visual-control elements such as *icons* and *scroll bars*. Icons are symbolic representations of objects, such as a garbage can to signify deletion of a file. Scroll bars allow the user to scroll data appearing in a window.

❑ Direct manipulation of onscreen elements: for example, clicking a mouse to drag a document margin to the desired width, rather than entering a calculated value.

❑ Consistency across applications and platforms. Users learn to print once. When they know how to print one document, they know how to print others, independent of the application software and computer system used.

❑ Simultaneous multiple applications. For example, a user can edit a document and recalculate a worksheet at the same time. With a little spade work, as the computer recalculates the worksheet, the updated version automatically appears in the document.

❑ Attractive, easy-to-use system. A happy user is a more productive user. Ideally, users can customize the GUI to suit their working style, rather than adapting their own working style to accommodate the GUI's way of doing things.

Implementations

No presently available graphical user interfaces actually meet all the preceding objectives. Several popular GUIs meet many of them, however.

Macintosh Finder

The Apple Macintosh is one of the original computers developed with a graphical user interface. Because the GUI philosophy was part of its original design, many people feel that the Macintosh will always be easier to use than IBM compatibles. This is not the place to enter into the IBM-Macintosh debate. People in the market for easy-to-use microcomputers should consider the Macintosh. However, the Macintosh Finder does not offer the windowing power and flexibility of X Window systems. Incidentally, both a version of UNIX and standard X Window systems are available on the Macintosh.

Microsoft Windows

Microsoft Windows, also known as MS-Windows, has effectively become the standard GUI for IBM-compatible microcomputers. First released in November 1985, sales of this product skyrocketed when version 3.0 was released in May 1990. Hundreds of popular DOS applications now run in this environment. The suggested configuration for running MS-Windows is a 286 or, preferably, a 386 or 486 computer with at least 2Mb of memory for users running a single program at once and at least 4Mb for task-switching applications. At least VGA graphics are required. Figure 1-7 illustrates the Microsoft Windows graphical user interface.

Typical Microsoft Windows graphical user interface

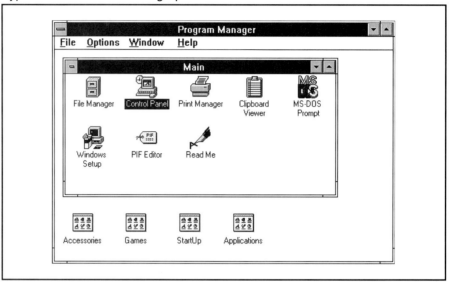

OS/2 Presentation Manager

In April 1987, IBM launched the PS/2 series of microcomputers, many of which run under the OS/2 operating system. Presentation Manager (PM) was the standard GUI for early releases of OS/2. Its look and feel is quite similar to that of MS-Windows. The future impact of OS/2 and PM is unclear, partly because of the ever-changing relationship between Microsoft and IBM.

Quarterdeck Office System DESQview

Strictly speaking, DESQview is not a GUI because it does not run in graphics mode. However, it provides an alternative to MS-Windows for both XT-class and larger microcomputers. DESQview accepts both mouse and keyboard input. It provides windowing and multitasking features, and will even run MS-Windows. An announced version called DESQview/X promises to run X Window systems on IBM-compatible microcomputers.

NeXTstep

The NeXT computer developed by Steven Jobs, one of the two inventors of the Apple, sports a sophisticated windowing system called NeXTstep. The NeXTstep system contains several interesting features such as Display PostScript, a MIDI interface for producing music, and a huge optical disk, invaluable for multimedia applications. All programs appearing in this book were tested on a 68040-based NeXT computer.

Similarities and Differences

X Window systems and microcomputer GUIs have the same basic objective: making the computer easier to use. They both provide graphical elements, such as windows and scroll bars, for user interaction. Proprietary toolkits such as OSF/Motif transform X Window systems into GUIs. In fact, OSF/Motif widgets have been designed to resemble MS-Windows.

Important differences exist between X Window systems and microcomputer-based GUIs. X Window systems developers who limit themselves to Xlib and Xt Intrinsics may create their own look-and-feel interface, rather than working with someone else's conception of an ideal interface. X Window systems are usually based on engineering workstations, a step up from powerful microcomputers. They may be used with X Terminals and computers of all sizes ranging from AT compatibles to supercomputers. Finally, X Window systems are designed with computer networking in mind. One server can display graphics generated by several networked computers.

Key Points

What Is the X Window System?

The X Window system (also called X Window and sometimes erroneously referred to as X Windows) has become the standard software tool for developing graphical user interfaces (GUIs) on workstations. Because of X Window's device independence, graphical user interfaces developed on one computer can be run on completely different computers.

continues . . .

X Window System

The X Window system has become a standard windowing system independent of hardware and operating system. It is a tool for developing both monochrome and color high-resolution graphical systems.

Hardware

X Window systems run on a variety of common hardware devices. The output unit is a graphics screen, usually with at least VGA resolution. The most commonly used input devices are the keyboard and the mouse. The vast majority of workstation manufacturers actively support X Window systems. An increasingly popular alternative is an X Terminal, a diskless graphical computer terminal that runs a single program, the X Window server program. X Window systems are also available on higher-end microcomputers. The Santa Cruz Operation's Open Desktop has become the leading high-end microcomputer UNIX operating system. This package provides full X Window facilities.

Client/Server Architecture

The heart of the X Window philosophy is the client/server architecture. The client/server architecture is the X Window system model by which clients, or application programs, communicate with servers, or display units over a network.

Unlike traditional graphics programs, X Window clients do not directly communicate with the user. The client obtains user input such as a keypress or click of a mouse button from the server, the other half of the client/server architecture. The client executes X Window commands that request the server to draw graphics. Several clients may be attached to a single server.

continues . . .

*Key Points
(continued)*

In simple terms, the server is the display unit, which may be composed of multiple physical screens. The server performs several related functions: It passes user input to attached clients. It decodes client messages, such as information requests and the moving of one or more windows. It maintains complex data structures, reducing client storage and processing needs, and diminishes the amount of data transmitted over the network.

Connection

An essential part of X Window systems is the physical link between the client (application program) and the server (display). Networking protocols describe the format and order of data and control bytes that compose a message sent from one network point to another. X Window developers need not know the networking protocol actually used. Three commonly used networking protocols for data transfer are TCP/IP, DECNet, and STREAMS.

Software

Specialized software is required to send appropriate data and control bytes from the client to the server and vice versa. X Window system client/server communication is accomplished through a network protocol, called the X protocol. Mastery of X Window programming requires learning three interrelated products: Xlib, Xt Intrinsics, and the chosen proprietary toolkit. Equally important, the programmer must also know when to use each of these products.

Xlib is a library of over 300 C functions used to generate code that conforms to the X protocol, which has a complex set of requirements. Xlib greatly reduces the pain of X programming.

continues . . .

Xt Intrinsics is a toolkit provided by X Window that provides building blocks, such as menus, scroll bars, and dialog boxes, to help produce consistent application interfaces.

Proprietary third-party toolkits provide their own extensions to the X toolkit and usually add their own window managers. The most widely used of these is the OSF/Motif toolkit, provided by the Open Software Foundation (OSF), a consortium founded in 1988 by major hardware vendors, including IBM, DEC, and Hewlett-Packard.

The major competitor to OSF/Motif is the Open Look graphical user interface distributed by AT&T and Sun Microsystems.

Graphical User Interfaces

Graphical user interfaces provide an easy-to-use graphical alternative to the cumbersome text-based interfaces that made early computer systems difficult to use. Graphical user interfaces should provide the following facilities:

❑ Extensive use of standard visual control elements such as icons and scroll bars

❑ Direct manipulation of onscreen elements

❑ Consistency across applications and platforms

❑ Simultaneous multiple applications

❑ Attractive, easy-to-use system

No presently available graphical user interfaces actually meet all of these objectives. Popular GUIs include Macintosh Finder and Multifinder, Microsoft Windows (also known as MS-Windows), OS/2 Presentation Manager, Quarterdeck Office System DESQview, and NeXTstep.

CHAPTER

Hello World

*T*raditionally, the first program studied when learning the C programming language is known as Hello World. This simple program calls a C function that prints the character string "Hello, World" on the standard output unit (a terminal, unless some other destination is specified).

```
main()
{
  printf("hello_world\n");
}
```

This chapter presents a similar program written for X Window systems. This program may seem rather complicated for a first program, but that's inevitable: X Window has a lot to do. The X Window programmer must specify in great detail numerous activities that programmers working with C or other high-level languages can safely take for granted. The result is a far different program, one that need not be modified with every change of computer hardware. You may not understand everything the first time around. Don't worry—later chapters cover key points in the program in much greater detail. You should enter this program, compile it, and link it by using a *makefile* such as the one at the end of this chapter. Once you get the program to run, try making simple modifications to see how the pieces fit together.

X Window Program Functions

The Hello World program shown at the end of this chapter includes a minimum number of X Window functions required to generate output on the screen. Of course, useful programs will be considerably more complicated. This program contains Xlib functions exclusively. It does not reference Xt Intrinsics or commercial toolkits such as OSF/Motif. The Hello World program carries out the following activities, some of which require several lines of code:

❑   Identifies the appropriate predefined header files and codes the appropriate declarations for the program.

❑ Establishes a connection to the workstation. This step initiates a link from the application program (client) to the display unit (server).

❑ Creates a window on the display. The Xlib function **XCreateSimpleWindow** uses nine parameters to tell X Window how and where to place the window. This function generates a unique window indentifier that the user must save for future reference within the program.

❑ Notifies the workstation's other current applications about the window that was just created. Remember: X Window can process multiple applications on the same display.

❑ Create a *graphics context (GC)* for the window. A graphics context is a structure that contains information about colors, fonts, and line widths.

❑ Selects the type of input event to process. An *event* is a data structure, sent by the server, that describes an activity that just occurred, which the application may choose to process. Events are a fundamental concept of X Window systems.

❑ Maps the window. *Mapping a window* means making the window visible on the display. This activity is separate from and follows the activity of creating the window.

❑ Executes the main loop. The heart of an X Window program is a loop that reads and processes events, generating output when required. This part of the program does the application's actual work. X Window programs must be ready to process any events (whose type was previously selected) from any client at any time. No wonder X Window programs are complicated.

❑ Terminates the program. Here, the program closes the application and returns resources to the system.

Examining the Hello World Program

This section describes a very minimal version of the Hello World program that was written with Xlib functions. For your convenience, Xlib function calls are printed in boldface characters. The unbroken program listing appears at the end of the chapter.

Including Header Files

The C programming language applies the *#include directive* to access a predefined set of declarations and constants in a named header file. The preprocessor merges the header (#include) into the program source code. X Window uses its own header files, as shown here:

```
#include <X11/Xlib.h>
#include <X11/Xutil.h>
```

Making Declarations

The C programming language applies the *#define directive*, which associates a meaningful programmer-defined name with a C language construct. This directive leads to more easily understood programs. In the following case, the value 1 is defined as TRUE and 0 as FALSE.

```
#define TRUE 1
#define FALSE 0
```

The following declarations reference and initialize three character arrays (strings). The first string contains the output message. The second string identifies a name used for internal purposes. The third string defines the window name that will appear at the top of the output window.

```
char hellow[] = "hello_world";
char theiconname[] = "Helloi";
char thewindowname[] = "hellow";
```

The C programming language requires a single **main** function that indicates the program's first executable function. The parameter *argc* refers to the number of arguments in the command line. The parameter *argv* refers to a pointer to an array of strings that contain the command-line arguments.

```
main(argc, argv)
int argc;
char *argv[];
{
```

The following statements are associated with X Window programs. They declare the display to be opened and the window to appear on the display. The identifier *thedisplay* is a pointer to a data structure that manages the connection to the workstation. The element *thewindow* identifies the window resource, and the element *thegc* identifies the graphics context. The data structures associated with *thewindow* and *thegc* must remain accessible throughout the life of the application. The element *theevent* refers to a complex data structure that contains information associated with each selected input event captured by the server. The element *thekey* identifies the key pressed when a keyboard event occurs. The element *thehint* refers to a data structure by which the current program informs other applications about this window.

```
Display     *thedisplay;
Window      thewindow;
GC          thegc;
XEvent      theevent;
KeySym      thekey;
XSizeHints  thehint;
```

The following statements declare C variables to be used in X Window implementation.

```
int            thescreen;
unsigned long theforeground, thebackground;
char           thebuffer[8];
int            keycount;
int            finished;
```

Establishing a Connection

The first Xlib function to appear in any program is

```
thedisplay = XOpenDisplay("");
```

This function establishes a network connection from the application (client) to the workstation (server) and places information describing this connection in the data structure referenced by the pointer *thedisplay*. The empty argument (" ") directs the system to fetch the display name from an environment variable called *DISPLAY*.

Creating a Window

The line

```
thescreen = DefaultScreen(thedisplay);
```

identifies the default screen for the display unit. X Window may be used with display units that consist of several physical screens: for example, a color screen and a monochrome screen.

```
thebackground = WhitePixel(thedisplay, thescreen);
theforeground = BlackPixel(thedisplay, thescreen);
```

This pair of C macros identifies the pixel values associated with the screen background and foreground. The background need not necessarily be white, and the foreground need not necessarily be black. The data structure pointed to by *thedisplay* contains these pixel values. If you change the workstation display, the program automatically takes the new pixel values into account, maintaining compatibility.

The fields in the data structure variable *thehint* (of the type XSizeHints) contain values describing the window to the window manager as follows:

```
thehint.x = 100;
thehint.y = 150;
thehint.width = 275;
thehint.height = 120;
thehint.flags = PPosition | PSize;
```

The elements *thehint.x* and *thehint.y* indicate the position of the window's upper-left corner: 100 pixels to the right (x value) and 150 pixels down (y value) from the screen's upper-left corner.

Because these two elements are closely related, they may be placed on the same line of the program. The elements *thehint.width* and *the-hint.height* indicate the width and height of the window as measured in pixels. The element *thehint.flags* sets the preferred position and size of this window. The following Xlib function requests the server to create the window.

```
thewindow = XCreateSimpleWindow (thedisplay,
            DefaultRootWindow (thedisplay),
            thehint.x, thehint.y, thehint.width,
            thehint.height, 7, theforeground,
            thebackground);
```

The **XCreateSimpleWindow** function returns the window identifier referred to by the variable *thewindow*. This function contains nine parameters, which must be coded in order: the display identifier, the parent window (in this case, the root window, which covers the entire screen), the window's x and y positions, the window's width and height, the width of the border in pixels, the foreground or border color, and the background color.

 Note All the parameters have been defined prior to the function's being called.

Notifying the Other Applications

The Xlib function

```
XSetStandardProperties (thedisplay, thewindow, thewindowname,
            theiconname, None, argv,
            argc, &thehint);
```

allows an elementary application to inform the window manager of its preferences (*&thehint*), including command-line arguments (*argv* and *argc*). The function references the previously defined window name (*thewindowname*).

Creating a Graphics Context

The Xlib function

```
thegc = XCreateGC (thedisplay, thewindow, 0, 0);
```

creates a graphics context with default values.

The following two functions place the background and foreground values in the graphics context.

```
XSetBackground (thedisplay, thegc, thebackground);
XSetForeground (thedisplay, thegc, theforeground);
```

Selecting the Type of Input Events to Process

The Xlib function

```
XSelectInput (thedisplay, thewindow, (KeyPressMask |
            ExposureMask));
```

instructs the server to inform the application when a key is pressed while the cursor is in its window. In addition, the application receives Expose events, which inform a client when its window has undergone change. For example, if window A is hidden by window B and then window B moves away, an Expose event occurs, and the application program must partially or totally redraw window A, as explained in detail in Chapter 4, "Windows and Windowing Techniques."

Mapping the Windows

The Xlib function

```
XMapRaised (thedisplay, thewindow);
```

displays the window on the screen, on top of other windows. This function sends an Expose event to request that the program redraw a window whenever it is uncovered: for example, when a window covering it moves. The **XSelectInput** function is coded to accept such Expose events.

Executing the Main Loop

The Boolean variable *finished* is initially set to FALSE so that the while loop executes at least once. This loop contains the main processing activities for this program. It solicits an event, displays the string "hello_world" in the window, and accepts keyboard input if the mouse is in the window area and its left button is clicked. The program terminates only if the user enters q from the keyboard. Initially, the variable *finished* is set to FALSE. The next line causes the loop to repeat so long as *finished* equals FALSE. The loop executes at least once.

```
finished = FALSE;
while (finished == FALSE) {
```

The function **XNextEvent** waits until the server detects an event whose type was selected with the **XSelectInput** function.

Note   This and several succeeding lines are indented to show that they depend on the *while* statement.

```
XNextEvent (thedisplay, &theevent);
```

The switch statement routes selected events to the appropriate program section.

```
switch (theevent.type) {
```

Processing Expose Events

Code found within the *case Expose* and *break* lines is executed only for Expose events. Other events are handled by the following case statements. A zero value of the *theevent.xexpose.count* variable corresponds to one of two possibilities: Either only a single Expose event was set, or the last of several associated Expose events was set. The Hello World program ignores all Expose events prior to the last one in a given group.

The **XDrawImageString** function contains seven parameters. The programmer specifies, in order, the display, the window, the graphics context, the horizontal and vertical displacement (measured in pixels) of the text's first character, the identifier of the character string to be drawn, and the length of this character string. This character string is redrawn whenever an Expose event is generated.

```
case Expose:
  if (theevent.xexpose.count == 0)
    XDrawImageString (theevent.xexpose.display,
                      theevent.xexpose.window, thegc,
                      105, 65, hellow, strlen(hellow));
  break;
```

Processing Keyboard Mapping Changes

Although you have not explicitly selected keyboard mapping events, such code should be included in all programs. The following short routine protects the program from unexpected keyboard configuration modification.

```
case MappingNotify:
  XRefreshKeyboardMapping (&theevent);
  break;
```

Processing Keyboard Input

The following code is executed when the user presses any key. The **XLookupString** function converts the keypress into a character string and supplies the string's length, which is often, but not always, equal to 1. If the first character in the string is a lowercase q, the variable *finished* is set to TRUE. The loop then soon terminates, and so does the program.

```
case KeyPress:
  keycount = XLookupString (&theevent, thebuffer, 8,
                            &thekey, 0);
  if ((keycount == 1) && (thebuffer[0] == 'q'))
    finished = TRUE;
  break;
```

Terminating the Program

The two closing braces in the following code segment correspond to the two opening braces found earlier in the program. Note the use of comments enclosed within /* and */. Use comments liberally when writing programs. This practice is particularly important for X Window programming.

```
    } /* switch  (theevent.type) */
} /* while (finished == FALSE) */
```

The three following functions destroy the graphics context area and the window, close the connection between the server and the client, and stop the program.

```
XFreeGC (thedisplay, thegc);
XDestroyWindow (thedisplay, thewindow);
XCloseDisplay (thedisplay);
} /* main */
```

The complete Hello World program appears at the end of this chapter.

Potential Modifications

As long as it may seem, the Hello World program is only the beginning of X Window programming. Now that you know what the program contains, you should consider some of the things that are missing. For starters, the user terminates the program by entering q. But how is the user to know this? The program does not supply any message to that effect. Clearly, what is needed is another window or alternate structure, such as a widget, to display the appropriate message. Displaying a message in a structure may be straightforward, but creating another window is fairly complicated—you will need to describe the relationship between the two windows. There are major differences among creating two side-by-side windows, two overlapping windows, and one window inside another.

The mouse is the major input device in X Window, yet this version of Hello World makes no provision for mouse input. Clearly, you will want to handle mouse input. How will you handle the cursor, for example, when it enters or leaves the window?

The Hello World program does not address what happens when errors occur. For example, what do you do if the **XOpenDisplay** function is unable to establish the network connection? What if the user chooses the same foreground and background colors? This book addresses these and many other questions.

The Hello World Program Source Code

The following is the complete source code of the Hello World program.

```
/* Header Files */
#include <X11/Xlib.h>
#include <X11/Xutil.h>
/* Declarations */

#define TRUE 1
#define FALSE 0
char hellow[] = "hello_world";
char theiconname[] = "Helloi";
char thewindowname[] = "hellow";
main(argc, argv)
int argc;
char *argv[];
{
/* Declarations */
  Display     *thedisplay;
  Window      thewindow;
  GC          thegc;
  XEvent      theevent;
  KeySym      thekey;
  XSizeHints  thehint;
  int         thescreen;
  unsigned long the foreground, thebackground;
  char        thebuffer[8];
  int         keycount;
  int         finished;
/* Establish a connection */
```

```
thedisplay = XOpenDisplay ("");
/* Prepare and create a window */
thescreen = DefaultScreen (thedisplay);
thebackground = WhitePixel (thedisplay, thescreen);
theforeground = BlackPixel (thedisplay, thescreen);
thehint.x = 100;
thehint.y = 150;
thehint.width = 275;
thehint.height = 120;
thehint.flags = PPosition | PSize;
thewindow = XCreateSimpleWindow (thedisplay,
                    DefaultRootWindow (thedisplay),
                    thehint.x, thehint.y,
                    thehint.width, thehint.height,
                    7, theforeground,
                    thebackground);
/* Notify the other applications */
XSetStandardProperties (thedisplay, thewindow, thewindowname,
                        theiconname, None, argv,
                        argc, &thehint);
/* Create a graphics context */
thegc = XCreateGC (thedisplay, thewindow, 0, 0);
XSetBackground (thedisplay, thegc, thebackground);
XSetForeground (thedisplay, thegc, theforeground);
/* Select the type of input events to process */
XSelectInput (thedisplay, thewindow, (KeyPressMask |
            ExposureMask));
/* Map the windows */
XMapRaised (thedisplay, thewindow);
/* Execute the main loop */
finished = FALSE;
while (finished == FALSE) {
  XNextEvent (thedisplay, &theevent);
  switch (theevent.type) {
  /* Process Expose events */
  case Expose:
    if (theevent.xexpose.count == 0)
      XDrawImageString (theevent.xexpose.display,
                        theevent.xexpose.window, thegc,
                        105, 65, hellow, strlen(hellow));
  break;
  /* Process keyboard mapping changes */
```

```
case MappingNotify:
  XRefreshKeyboardMapping (&theevent);
break;
/* Process keyboard input */
case KeyPress:
  keycount = XLookupString (&theevent, thebuffer, 8,
                            &thekey, 0);
  if ((keycount == 1) && (thebuffer[0] == 'q'))
  /* Terminate the program */
    finished = TRUE;
break;
} /* switch  (theevent.type */
} /* while (finished == FALSE) */
XFreeGC (thedisplay, thegc);
XDestroyWindow (thedisplay, thewindow);
XCloseDisplay (thedisplay);
} /* main */
```

The output of this program is shown in Figure 2-1.

UNIX employs the *make* command, which invokes a MAKE file. This file compiles the program source code, links to the necessary libraries,

Output from the Hello World program

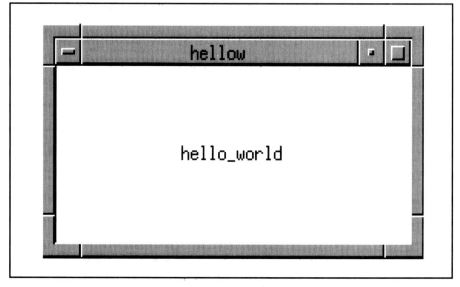

and, finally, creates an executable program. The following listing is the MAKE file for the Hello World program, as run on the SCO ODT X Window system. The MAKE file for other systems will vary. For example, the –lPW library in the fifth line of the following MAKE file is required by SCO but not by other UNIX suppliers.

```
RM = rm -f
CC = cc
CFLAGS = -O
INCLUDES = -I. -I/usr/include -I/usr/include/X11
LIBS = -lXm -lXt -lX11 -lsocket -lmalloc -lPW
.c.o:
$(RM) $@
$(CC) -c $(CFLAGS) $(INCLUDES) $*.c
all:: hellow
hellow: hellow.o
$(RM) $@
$(CC) -o $@ $(CFLAGS) hellow.o $(LIBS)
@echo makefile for hellow - done!
```

Key Points

The First Program

Traditionally, the first program studied when learning the C programming language is known as Hello World. This simple program calls a C function that prints the character string "hello_world" on the standard output unit (a terminal, unless some other destination is specified).

```
main()
{
  printf("hello_world\n");
}
```

continues . . .

X Window Program Functions

The Hello World program includes a minimum number of X Window functions required to generate output on the screen: that is, to perform the following functions:

❏ Identify the appropriate predefined header files and code the appropriate declarations for the program.

❏ Establish a connection to the workstation.

❏ Create a window on the display.

❏ Notify the workstation's other current applications about the window that was just created.

❏ Create a graphics context (GC) for the window. A graphics context is a structure that contains information about colors, fonts, and line widths.

❏ Select the type of input event to process. An event is a data structure sent by the server describing an activity that just occurred, which the application may choose to process.

❏ Map the window. Mapping a window means making the window visible on the display.

❏ Execute the main loop. The heart of an X Window program is a loop that reads and processes events, generating output when required.

❏ Terminate the program.

continues . . .

Key Points
(continued)

Potential Modifications

The Hello World program will function as written, but it would be more useful with a few modifications. The user terminates this program by entering q, but the program does not supply any message to that effect. Clearly, what is needed is another window or alternative structure, such as a widget, and the appropriate display message. This version of Hello World also could provide for mouse input. Finally, the Hello World program neither informs the user when errors occur nor provides any means of error handling. These issues and others are addressed later in this book.

The next step is to gain a deeper understanding of basic X Window terminology, concepts, and windowing techniques. These are the subjects of the following two chapters.

CHAPTER

Basic Concepts and Terminology

Now that you have seen a complete, albeit not very practical, X Window program, you are ready to approach X Window programming in greater detail. This chapter presents the concepts and terminology that will serve as a foundation for programming.

Recall that the actual communication between the server and the client occurs via the X protocol. Protocol messages are classified in four types: requests from the client to the server, replies from the server to the client, errors messages when the request was not successfully completed, and event messages that inform an interested client that an action was taken. Each of these message types has its own particular format.

The Hello World program in Chapter 2, "Hello World," applied several #include files, which supply X Window programs with a wealth of values. X Window Version 11, Release 5, contains 13 #include files that enable programmers to access many useful services: for example, scalable and international fonts. Because there are over 300 Xlib functions, it is imperative that you be familiar with Xlib naming and argument conventions.

Among the objects processed by Xlib functions are resources stored on the X server. These resources include windows, graphics contexts, fonts, cursors, colormaps, and pixmaps. Correct use of resources reduces both the coding effort and the volume of data transferred between the client and the server.

The heart of the X Window system is event processing. At the risk of oversimplification, *events* tell interested clients that something important has happened. The X Window system provides 33 different events, classified into ten categories. This chapter identifies each event and describes it briefly. Later chapters provide full details for relevant events.

X Protocol

X Window systems exchange data between the server (display) and the client (application program) via the X protocol, a two-way asynchronous communications link, as shown in Figure 3-1. The client and server need not run on the same physical computer. Applying the X protocol is similar to machine language programming. End users do not need to concern themselves with the details of the X protocol. Applications programmers rely on Xlib functions, Xt Intrinsics, a proprietary toolkit, or a combination of these facilities to create applications. They do not address the X protocol directly. However, it is important for them to have a basic understanding of what is actually happening in their applications. This understanding can increase the application's efficiency and decrease the likelihood of both design and coding errors.

The standard specification for X protocol is found in *X Window System, Third Edition, X Version 11, Release 5* by Robert W. Scheifler and James Gettys (Burlington, MA: Digital Press, 1992). Scheifler is associated with the Laboratory for Computer Science of the Massachusetts Institute of Technology. Gettys is associated with the Cambridge Research Laboratory of the Digital Equipment Corporation. Schleifer and Gettys are leading figures in the design and realization of the X Window system.

X protocol messages take one of four formats: request format, reply format, error format, or event format.

FIGURE 3-1

Client/server architecture

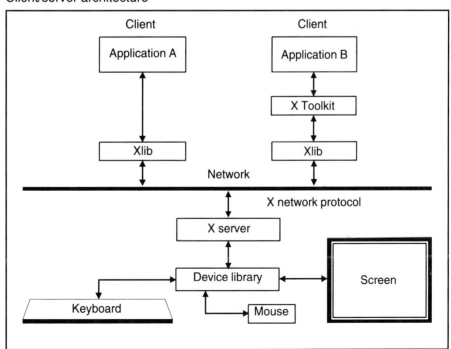

Requests and Request Format

An application informs the server that it requires a service by sending a block of data known as a *request*. Requests contain a one-byte major operation code (identifying the type of service required), a two-byte length field, and at least one data byte. The length field defines the total length of the request, including the operation code and the length field itself. A request's length field equals the minimum length required to contain the request. Additional request major operation codes are reserved for extensions to the X protocol. Unused bytes in the request are not necessarily equal to zero. The system assigns a consecutive sequence number to each request during the life of a given connection. This sequence number identifies the request associated with replies, errors, and events.

Requests are usually *one-way protocol request messages*. Such requests do not require a system reply. For example, when you wish to create a window, you call an Xlib function such as **XCreateSimpleWindow**. Xlib translates this function into a protocol request message containing appropriate information supplied by the application. Xlib then stores the request message in a special memory buffer. Unless the buffer is full, the message is not sent immediately to the workstation. When the buffer is full, Xlib transmits the accumulated request messages to the workstation. Only then is the window created. The application does not do block processing; it continues to compute and to send additional server requests as required. Because the application does not wait for a reply from the server (workstation), the response time is fairly independent of the link's physical transmission speed.

Replies and Reply Format

Sometimes the application program cannot proceed without a specific reply from the server. For example, you may require the specific dimensions of a hardware cursor. The Xlib function **XQueryBestCursor** transmits the buffer contents to the server, blocks additional processing, and transmits the current request to the server. Processing resumes only when the server returns the required information to the application. Such requests are known as *round-trip protocol request messages*. They may involve considerable delay, especially for systems with relatively slow physical transmission speeds. Because round-trip requests "stop the music," you should use them only when necessary.

Replies contain a four-byte length field followed by zero or more bytes containing additional data, as indicated in the length field. Unused bytes in the request are not necessarily equal to zero. Replies contain the least significant 16 bits of the sequence number for the associated request.

Errors and Error Format

As anyone who has done any programming knows, telling the computer what you want it to do is an error-prone process. There is no guarantee that a given request will lead to the desired results. X Window syntax is not easy to use. Even when you get the syntax right, it's possible that the system cannot honor your request for reasons beyond its control: for example, because of the lack of available memory. The **XCreateSimpleWindow** function found in the Hello World program in Chapter 2 can generate four different errors—BadAlloc, BadMatch, BadValue, and BadWindow—among the X errors shown in Table 3-1.

How, then, can the programmer determine the specific error and the function causing the error? The Xlib service function **XSynchronize** enables or disables synchronization, the separate processing of each Xlib function. When *synchronization* is enabled, requests are not buffered. The system accepts a request, blocks processing, transmits the request to the server, and waits for a reply. Synchronization mode makes it easy for the programmer to determine the function that caused the error, but slows down system performance drastically.

X protocol error reports are 32 bytes long. They contain a 1-byte error code, identifying the type of error made. Error messages include the major and minor operation codes of the aborted request and the least significant 16 bits of its sequence number. Remember: A delay may occur between a request's issue time and the time an error report is generated. Some error reports include a reference to the missing object: for example, to the erroneous window identifier. Unused bytes in the error report are not necessarily set to zero. The XErrorEvent data structure is as follows:

```
typedef struct {
  int type;                         /* Event type */
  Display *display;                 /* Display structure */
  unsigned long serial;             /* Number of failed request */
  unsigned char error code;         /* Error code of failed
                                       request */
  unsigned char request_code,       /* Major, minor opcodes of
              minor_code;              failed request */
  XID resourceid;                   /* Resource id */
} XErrorEvent;
```

TABLE 3-1

X Error Codes and Descriptions

X Error Code	Description
BadAccess	One of several access errors
BadAlloc	Requested resource allocation error
BadAtom	Argument not an atom
BadColor	Argument not a colormap
BadCursor	Argument not a cursor
BadDrawable	Argument not a drawable
BadFont	Argument not a font
BadGC	Argument not a graphics context
BadIDChoice	ID already used or out of range
BadImplementation	Deficient server
BadLength	Request length too short or too long
BadMatch	Argument mismatch
BadName	Nonexistent color or font
BadPixmap	Argument not a pixmap
BadRequest	Incorrect request code
BadValue	Argument (integer type) out of range
BadWindow	Argument not a window

Event Format

The Hello World program in Chapter 2 illustrates the importance of events to the X Window system. Essentially, all activities affecting either system input or output generate one or more events. This chapter concludes with a discussion of event types and event processing.

All 33 types of events follow the same event format:

❏ Events are 32 bytes long.

❏ Events contain a 1-byte type code, with the most significant bit set if the event is generated by a SendEvent request associated with another application.

❏ Every event except the KeyMapNotify event generates a message format that contains the least significant 16 bits of the event sequence number. This event sequence number is associated with the last request issued by the client being processed by the server when the event occurred.

❏ Unused bytes within the event message are not necessarily equal to zero.

Header Files

Writing and debugging X Window system applications is an arduous process. Xlib provides numerous standard header files that contain system-specific values. Paying strict attention to the naming and coding conventions reduces the programming effort and makes your programs more portable and easier to maintain.

Standard Header Files

The following files are part of the standard X Window system (some of the following details are specific to Version 11, Release 5).

<X11/Xlib.h>   This is the main header file for Xlib. Placing this file at the top of your program includes the majority of the symbolic constants, data types, and data structure declarations required by Xlib. The <X11/Xlib.h> file for Release 5 also contains the preprocessor symbol XlibSpecificationRelease, whose value is 5. Earlier releases of Xlib did not include this symbol.

Note   The <> that enclose the header filename direct the system to look for this file in the system library before looking for it elsewhere.

<X11/X.h>   This file declares the X protocol types and constants that are to be used by applications. It is included automatically from <X11/Xlib.h>, so application code should never need to reference this file directly.

<X11/Xcms.h>   This file contains symbols for many color management facilities. All functions, types, and symbols with the prefix "Xcms", plus the Color Conversion Contexts macros, are declared in this file. You must include <X11/Xlib.h> before including this file.

<X11/Xutil.h>   This file declares various functions, types, and symbols used for interclient communication and application utility functions. You must include <X11/Xlib.h> before including this file.

<X11/Xresource.h>   This file declares all functions, types, and symbols for resource manager facilities. You must include <X11/Xlib.h> before including this file.

<X11/Xatom.h>   This file declares all predefined atoms, which are symbols with the prefix "XA_".

<X11/cursorfont.h>   This file declares all the cursor symbols for the standard cursor font. All cursor symbols have the prefix "XC_".

<X11/keysymdef.h>   This file declares all standard KeySym values, which are symbols with the prefix "XK_". The KeySyms are arranged in groups, and a preprocessor symbol controls inclusion of each group. The preprocessor symbol must be defined prior to the inclusion of the file to obtain the associated values. The preprocessor symbols are XK_MISCEL-LANY, XK_LATIN1, XK_LATIN2, XK_LATIN3, XK_LATIN4, XK_KATAK-

ANA, XK_ARABIC, XK_CYRILLIC, XK_GREEK, XK_TECHNICAL, XK_SPECIAL, XK_PUBLISHING, XK_APL, and XK_HEBREW.

<X11/keysym.h> This file defines the preprocessor symbols XK_MIS-CELLANY, XK_LATIN1, XK_LATIN2, XK_LATIN3, XK_LATIN4, and XK_GREEK and then includes <X11/keysymdef.h>.

<X11/Xlibint.h> This file declares all the functions, types, and symbols used for extensions to the X Window system standard. This file automatically includes <X11/Xlib.h>.

<X11/Xproto.h> This file declares types and symbols for the basic X protocol for use in implementing extensions. It is included automatically from <X11/Xlibint.h>, so application and extension code should never need to reference this file directly.

<X11/protostr.h> This file declares types and symbols for the basic X protocol for use in implementing extensions. It is included automatically from <X11/Xproto.h>, so application and extension code should never need to reference this file directly.

<X11/X10.h> This file declares all the functions, types, and symbols used for the X10 compatibility functions.

Xlib Naming and Argument Conventions

Approximately 300 Xlib functions interface with the X protocol. Applying Xlib functions is similar to assembly language programming. The following standard conventions make it easier to understand and apply these functions.

❑ Xlib uses mixed case for external symbols (those not defined within an Xlib header file). Variables appear in lowercase letters and user macros in uppercase, according to standard C language programming conventions.

❑ Xlib functions always begin with a capital X.

❏   All function names and symbols start with a capital letter.

❏   All user-visible data structures and objects that users may access via a pointer structure begin with a capital X.

❏   Macros and other symbols do not begin with a capital X. Each letter in a macro is capitalized to distinguish it from user symbols.

❏   All elements or variables in a data structure are written in lowercase. Underscores (_) are used to create compound words reserved for Xlib use. The user may not employ such words except as Xlib specifies.

❏   Any display reference appears as the first argument in the Xlib function.

❏   All resource objects occur immediately after the display argument in the argument list.

❏   When a graphics context occurs with another type of resource (such as a window or a pixmap), the graphics context appears in the argument list after the other resource. Windows and pixmaps, known as *drawables*, are listed before all other resources. These will be discussed later in this chapter.

❏   Source arguments always precede destination arguments in the argument list.

❏   The *x* argument always precedes the *y* argument in the argument list.

❏   The *width* argument always precedes the *height* argument in the argument list.

❏   Where the *x*, *y*, *height*, and *width* arguments are used together, the *x* and *y* arguments precede the *width* and *height* arguments.

❏   Where a group of bits called a *mask* specifies the elements to be selected in an accompanying data structure, the mask always precedes the pointer to the structure in the argument list.

Resources

Resources are objects stored on the X server. They include windows, graphics contexts, fonts, cursors, color maps, and pixmaps. (Chapter 5,

"Toolkit Concepts and Techniques," introduces the related notion of toolkit resources.) Correct use of resources reduces both the coding effort and the volume of data transferred between the client and the server.

Before examining individual resource types, let's consider their common characteristics:

❏ Resources are created via one-way requests from client applications. Xlib selects a resource identifier according to specifications provided by the workstation when the display connection is opened. Xlib subsequently informs the application of the resource identifier.

❏ Resources are controlled by the application but are located in the workstation server. Because resource information is already at the workstation, it need not be transferred prior to each use.

❏ All applications running on a given workstation may share a resource by supplying its reference number. Resource sharing can lead to problems: Any application that has access to a shared resource can modify or delete it. You can protect your private resources by declaring your resource identifiers locally.

❏ Resources may not be shared among workstations. A resource created on workstation A is not accessible to workstation B.

❏ Resources should not be stored on workstations between sessions. However, resources are easy to create and destroy. A typical application uses many windows, graphics contexts, fonts, and other resources.

Windows

Windows generally are rectangular display areas that appear on the display screen. They are the server's most important resource. Whenever an X application draws a graph or displays text, it must specify the output window involved. Furthermore, both mouse and keyboard input enter the system via a window. Literally dozens of Xlib functions control window creation, placement, manipulation, and destruction.

Chapter 2's Hello World program applied the **XCreateSimpleWindow** function. The more powerful Xlib function, **XCreateWindow**, is shown here.

```
Window XCreateWindow(display, parent, x, y, width, height,
                     border_width, depth, class, visual,
                     valuemask, attributes)
    Display *display;              /* Display structure */
    Window parent;                 /* Parent window */
    int x, y;                      /* Coordinates of top-left
                                      corner of created window's
                                      borders */
    unsigned int width, height;    /* Window dimensions */
    unsigned int border_width;     /* Border width in pixels */
    unsigned int depth;            /* Window depth in pixels */
    unsigned int class;            /* InputOutput, InputOnly,
                                      CopyFromParent */
    Visual *visual;                /* Visual type */
    unsigned long valuemask;       /* Mask for window
                                      attributes */
    XSetWindowAttributes
                *attributes;       /* Window attributes */
    Window window;                 /* Returns ID of created
                                      window */
```

Like the **XCreateSimpleWindow** function, the **XCreateWindow** function creates an unmapped window. Chapter 4, "Windowing Techniques," examines windows in detail.

Graphics Contexts

A *graphics context* (abbreviated *GC*) is a data structure that manages graphics features, including line style and width, foreground and background color, and fill patterns. Every request to generate graphical output must reference a graphics context. Unlike other resources, applications should not share graphics contexts.

The **XSetFont** function, for example, sets the current font of a given graphics context. The syntax of **XSetFont** is

```
XSetFont(display, gc, font)
    Display *display;
    GC gc;
    Font font;
```

where *display* is the display structure, *qc* is the graphics context, and *font* is the font.

The **XSetFont** function may generate the following errors:

❏ BadAlloc, in which the server cannot allocate the requested resource

❏ BadFont, in which a value for a font argument does not name a defined font

❏ BadGC, in which a value for a graphics context argument does not name a defined graphics context

Chapter 6, "Text," and Chapter 10, "Color and Graphics," discuss graphics contexts in greater detail.

Fonts

A *font* describes the size and shape of each character within a unified collection of characters. X Window provides a large number of fonts with standard names, such as

Adobe-Courier-Bold-R-Normal-25-180-100-100-M-150

The numbers refer to different aspects of the font size.

X Window supports the use of foreign language fonts. The following Xlib function, **XCreateFontSet** (Release 5), creates an international text drawing font set named XFontSet:

```
XFontSet XCreateFontSet (display, base_font_name_list,
                    display missing_charset_list_return,
                    missing_charset_count_return,
                    def_string_return)
    Display *display;                     /* Display structure */
    char *base_font_name_list;            /* Base font names */
    char **missing_charset_list_return;   /* Missing charsets */
    int *missing_charset_count_return;    /* Count of missing
                                             charsets */
    char **def_string_return;             /* Returns string
                                             drawn for
                                             missing charsets */
```

This bold Courier font is supplied by a company known as Adobe. The font is roman (nonslanting) and of normal width. It is a *monospaced* font: All characters have the same width. Chapter 6, "Text," describes font naming conventions and the use of fonts in creating and modifying text output.

Cursors

The cursor resource describes the size, color, and shape of the onscreen cursor associated with the mouse. When the mouse or other pointing device moves, the cursor moves. One way to create a cursor is by selecting a single character from a special cursor font. The following Xlib function selects the largest cursor size that can appear on the selected display unit.

```
Status XQueryBestCursor (display, d, width, height,
                         width_return, height_return)
   Display *display;               /* Display structure */
   Drawable d;                     /* Drawable, indicates
                                      the screen */
   unsigned int width,             /* Dimensions of requested
             height;                  cursor */
   unsigned int *width_return,     /* Returns dimensions of
             *height_return;          suggested cursor */
```

The **XQueryBestCursor** function generates a round-trip protocol message, and therefore may involve considerable waiting time. Chapter 8, "Mouse and Cursors," discusses the cursor in greater detail, along with the mouse.

Colormaps

Color processing is complicated. Colors that display well on one workstation may look odd on another workstation. The X resource colormap helps programmers manage the hundreds of colors available in X Window systems. A *colormap* is a map associating a pixel value with a color. The following Xlib function, **XInstallColormap**, installs a colormap for a given screen. An installed colormap ensures that all windows on the screen display true colors. Windows on screens that have no installed colormap will not necessarily display true colors.

```
XInstallColormap (display, colormap)
   Display *display;         /* Display structure */
   Colormap colormap;        /* Colormap */
```

Chapter 10, "Color and Graphics," discusses color processing.

Pixmaps

A *pixmap* is a block of memory, associated with the X server, that can be used for drawing. Recall that windows and pixmaps are called drawables. Unlike windows, objects drawn in pixmaps do not appear on the screen. To see them you must copy the pixmap's contents to a visible window. Pixmaps often store special patterns for cursors and window backgrounds. A pixmap whose pixels are each represented by a single bit is known as a *bitmap*.

The **XCreatePixmap** function creates a pixmap. If the function executes successfully, it makes the pixmap's resource ID available to the programmer.

```
Pixmap XCreatePixmap (display, d, width, height, depth)
   Display *display;         /* Display structure */
   Drawable d;               /* Screen on which pixmap
                                created */
   unsigned int width,       /* Pixmap dimensions */
              height;
   unsigned int depth;       /* Pixmap depth */
```

Chapter 9, "Pixmaps, Bitmaps, and Images," discusses pixmaps and bitmaps in greater detail.

Events

Event processing is the central focus of the X Window system. Every activity that affects input or output, and many additional activities as well, generates one or more events. An active application is constantly churning out events, in no particular order. For example, a user may move the mouse across several windows and then double-click the mouse button to select a menu item, causing a popup menu to appear on the screen. This rapid scenario may generate literally dozens of events of different types. The application can choose to select only some event types, but it cannot ignore all events. For example, the application might note when a mouse button is pressed, but not when the button is released. An application that selects no mouse events cannot use the mouse.

Event Types

The X Window system provides 33 distinct event types, which can be classified into distinct categories: keyboard events, pointer events, window-crossing events, input focus events, keymap state notification events, expose events, structure control events, window state notification events, colormap state notification events, and client communication events. In all cases, the events are associated with a data structure defined in the header file <X11/Xlib.h>. Each event category is introduced here. The individual event types are discussed in later chapters.

Keyboard Events

Keyboard events indicate when a key is pressed or when a key is released. The two keyboard events are appropriately named KeyPress and KeyRelease. These two events are associated with the XKeyEvent data structure. This data structure contains 15 fields, including the event type, the serial number of the last request processed, identification of the display and window that registered the event, the time at which the event occurred, the coordinates of the pointer relative to the event window, and a code corresponding to the key associated with the keyboard event. Chapter 7, "Keyboard," discusses keyboard events in greater detail.

Pointer Events

Pointer events are associated with a pointer, typically the mouse pointer. The three types of pointer events are ButtonPress,

ButtonRelease, and MotionNotify. These first two pointer events are associated with the XButtonEvent data structure that contains 15 fields. These data structures can be referred to respectively as the XButtonPressedEvent and the XButtonReleasedEvent. MotionNotify events are associated with the XMotionEvent data structure, which also contains 15 fields, 14 of which are the same as the button events. Among the fields in these data structures are the event type, the serial number of the last request processed, identification of the display and window that registered the event, the time at which the event occurred, and the coordinates of the pointer relative to the event window. The button events also contain a reference to the button pressed or released (numbers 1 to 5). The MotionNotify events also contain a field associated with pointer motion hints. Chapter 8, "Mouse and Cursors," discusses pointer events in greater detail.

Window-Crossing Events

EnterNotify and LeaveNotify events indicate when the mouse pointer enters or leaves the selected window. They are associated with the XCrossingEvent data structure. This structure contains 17 fields, many of which are the same or similar to button and motion notify events. Chapter 8, "Mouse and Cursors," discusses these *window-crossing events* in greater detail.

Input Focus Events

The *keyboard focus*, also called the *input focus*, indicates the window associated with the keyboard. Users change the keyboard focus by moving the mouse into the desired window. (Depending on the specific system, they may have to click the mouse to confirm the selection.) Changing the focus generates FocusIn and FocusOut events, the first to specify the window receiving the input focus, and the second to specify the window relinquishing the input focus. These events are associated with the XFocusChangeEvent data structure that contains seven fields, including the event type, the serial number of the last request processed, and identification of the display and window that registered the event. Chapter 7, "Keyboard," discusses input focus events in greater detail.

Keymap State Notification Event

KeymapNotify is the only type of *keymap state notification event*. This event determines the state of all keys at the time of a FocusIn or EnterNotify event. Recall from the Hello World program in Chapter 2, "Hello World," that this event type should always be selected. The KeymapNotify event is associated with the XKeymapEvent data structure that contains six fields, including the event type, the serial number of the last request processed, and identification of the display and window that registered the event. It also includes a reference to the set of keycodes presently active. Chapter 7, "Keyboard," discusses keymap state notification events in greater detail.

Exposure Events

Exposure events express interference between multiple windows on a single screen. Active screens usually contain more than a single window. X Window systems are not limited to neatly aligned windows. On the contrary, windows may overlap each other. This leads to a problem that must be solved. When window A covers all or part of window B, the relevant contents of window B disappear from the screen. The application must be able to regenerate these contents when window B becomes uncovered, or in more technical terms, is *exposed*. When parts of a window must be redrawn, the server generates an Expose event for every affected area. In general, applications wait for an Expose event before drawing in a given window. Such events signal that the window is ready to receive a drawing.

The other two types of exposure events are GraphicsExpose and NoExpose. A GraphicsExpose event indicates that an attempt to copy from a pixmap to a window was unsuccessful because at least part of the destination window was obscured. A NoExpose event indicates that the copy was completed successfully. The three exposure events are associated with the XExposeEvent data structure that contains nine fields, including the event type, the serial number of the last request processed, the origin and dimensions of the exposed area, and the count of additional exposure events to process. Chapter 9, "Pixmaps, Bitmaps, and Images," discusses exposure events in greater detail.

Structure Control Events

There are four types of *structure control events*: CirculateRequest, ConfigureRequest, MapRequest, and ResizeRequest events. These events are usually handled by the window manager, which is presented in Chapter 4, "Windowing Techniques."

Circulate Request Event   The CirculateRequest event attempts to raise or lower a window. It is associated with the XCirculateRequestEvent data structure, which contains seven fields, including the event type, the serial number of the last request processed, the display connection, identification of the requested window, identification of the requested window's parent, and an indication of whether to raise or lower the window in the stacking order.

ConfigureRequest Event   The ConfigureRequest event attempts to change a window's size, position, border, or stacking order. They are generated when another client issues a ConfigureWindow protocol request on a child window. ConfigureRequest events are associated with the XConfigureRequestEvent data structure, which contains 14 fields, including the event type, the serial number of the last request processed, the display connection, identification of the requested window, identification of the requested window's parent, and the window dimensions.

MapRequest Event   The MapRequest event indicates that a different client desires to map a window. It is associated with the XMapRequestEvent data structure, which contains six fields, including the event type, the serial number of the last request processed, the display connection, identification of the requested window, and identification of the requested window's parent.

ResizeRequest Event   The ResizeRequest event indicates that a different client desires to resize a window. It is associated with the XResizeRequestEvent data structure, which contains seven fields, including the event type, the serial number of the last request processed, the display connection, identification of the requested window, the requested window's width, and the requested window's height.

Window State Notification Events

The server generates *window state notification events* whenever a window moves, changes its size, or changes its place in the stacking order. In alphabetical order, these events are CirculateNotify, ConfigureNotify, CreateNotify, DestroyNotify, GravityNotify, MapNotify, MappingNotify, ReparentNotify, UnmapNotify, and VisibilityNotify. Several of these events are discussed in greater detail in Chapter 4, "Windowing Techniques."

CirculateNotify Event   CirculateNotify events inform interested clients when a window changes its position in the stack. These events are associated with the XCirculateEvent data structure, which contains seven fields, including the event type, the serial number of the last request processed, the display connection, identification of the requested window, and whether to place the window on the top or the bottom of the stacking order.

ConfigureNotify Event   ConfigureNotify events inform interested clients about changes to a window, including its size, position, border, and stacking order. These events are associated with the XConfigureEvent data structure, which contains 13 fields, including the event type, the serial number of the last request processed, the display connection, identification of the affected window, the dimensions of the affected window, and the affected window's border width.

CreateNotify Event   CreateNotify events inform interested clients that a window has been created. These events are associated with the XCreateEvent data structure, which contains 12 fields, including the event type, the serial number of the last request processed, the display connection, identification of the created window and its parent, the dimensions of the created window, and the affected window's border width.

DestroyNotify Event   DestroyNotify events inform interested clients when a window is destroyed. DestroyNotify events are associated with the XDestroyWindowEvent data structure, which contains six fields, including the event type, the serial number of the last request processed, the display connection, and identification of the window destroyed.

GravityNotify Event   GravityNotify events inform interested clients when a window is moved because its parent window changes size. GravityNotify events are associated with the XGravityEvent data structure, which contains eight fields, including the event type, the serial number of the last request processed, the display connection, identification of either the window that was moved or its parent, and the coordinates of the child window with respect to the parent window.

MapNotify Event   MapNotify events inform interested clients when a window's state changes from unmapped to mapped. MapNotify events are associated with the XMapEvent data structure, which contains seven fields, including the event type, the serial number of the last request processed, the display connection, and identification of either the window that was mapped or its parent.

MappingNotify Event   MappingNotify events inform all clients when any client application calls one of the three following Xlib functions: **XSetModifierMapping**, which indicates the key codes to be used as modifiers; **XChangeKeyboardMapping**; and **XSetPointerMapping**. Clients cannot block transmission of MappingNotify events. These events are associated with the XMappingEvent data structure, which contains eight fields, including the event type, the serial number of the last request processed, the display connection, an indication which of the three appropriate Xlib functions was involved, and the number of modified keycodes.

ReparentNotify Event   ReparentNotify events inform interested clients when a window changes its parent. ReparentNotify events are associated with the XReparentEvent data structure, which contains ten fields, including the event type, the serial number of the last request processed, the display connection, identification of the reparented window and its coordinates relative to the new parent window, and identification of the new parent window.

UnmapNotify Event   UnmapNotify events inform interested clients when a window's state changes from mapped to unmapped. UnmapNotify events are associated with the XUnmapEvent data structure, which contains seven fields, including the event type, the serial number of the last request processed, the display connection, and identification of either the window that was mapped or its parent.

VisibilityNotify Event   VisibilityNotify events inform interested clients when a change occurs in the visibility of a specified window. VisibilityNotify events are associated with the XVisibilityEvent data structure, which contains six fields, including the event type, the serial number of the last request processed, the display connection, identification of the window whose visibility changed, and an indication of the visibility change.

Colormap State Notification Event

The only *colormap state notification event* is the ColormapNotify event. This event informs interested clients when the colormap changes, and when a colormap is installed or removed. ColormapNotify events are associated with the XColormapEvent data structure, which contains eight fields, including the event type, the serial number of the last request processed, the display connection, identification of the affected window, the colormap, and whether the colormap was installed or removed.

Client Communication Events

Client communication events permit applications to communicate with each other. Such communication is not direct, but occurs via the workstation. There are five client communication events: ClientMessage, PropertyNotify, SelectionClear, SelectionNotify, and SelectionRequest.

ClientMessage Event   ClientMessage events occur when a client calls the Xlib function **XSendEvent** to send an event to another client. This function should be used judiciously. ClientMessage events are associated with the XClientMessageEvent data structure, which contains eight fields, one of which is the union of three fields. Among the fields in this data structure are the event type, the serial number of the last request processed, the display connection, identification of the receiving window, and the format of the dispatched event.

PropertyNotify Event   A *property* is an arbitrary collection of data used for interclient communication. PropertyNotify events inform interested clients about property changes for a specified window. PropertyNotify events are associated with the XPropertyEvent data structure, which contains eight fields, including the event type, the serial number of the last request processed, the display connection, identification of the affected window, the time that the property changed, and indication of whether the property was modified or deleted.

SelectionClear Event   A *selection* is a special type of buffer used to move data from one application to another. A selection is a way of communicating between clients. Selected data is passed from one application to another and stored in a property. SelectionClear events occur when a client loses ownership of a selection. SelectionClear events are associated with the XSelectionClearEvent data structure, which contains seven fields, including the event type, the serial number of the last request processed, the display connection, identification of the affected window, and the last change time recorded for the selection.

SelectionRequest Event   SelectionRequest events inform the interested owner of a selection that another application has requested conversion of this selection to a different data type. SelectionRequest events are associated with the XSelectionRequestEvent data structure, which contains ten fields, including the event type, the serial number of the last request processed, the display connection, identification of the owner, and identification of selector windows.

SelectionNotify Event   SelectionNotify events are generated by the server in response to a ConvertSelection protocol request when the selection has no owner. SelectionNotify events are associated with the XSelectionEvent data structure, which contains nine fields, including the event type, the serial number of the last request processed, the display connection, and identification of the requester window.

Summary of Event Categories and Types

The following table summarizes the event types associated with each event category.

Event Category	Event Type
Keyboard events	KeyPress, KeyRelease
Pointer events	ButtonPress, ButtonRelease, MotionNotify
Window-crossing events	EnterNotify, LeaveNotify
Input focus events	FocusIn, FocusOut
Keymap state notification events	KeymapNotify
Exposure events	Expose, GraphicsExpose, NoExpose
Structure control events	CirculateRequest, ConfigureRequest, MapRequest, ResizeRequest
Window state notification events	CirculateNotify, ConfigureNotify, CreateNotify, DestroyNotify, GravityNotify, MapNotify, MappingNotify, ReparentNotify, UnmapNotify, VisibilityNotify
Colormap state notification event	ColormapNotify
Client communication events	ClientMessage, PropertyNotify, SelectionClear, SelectionNotify, SelectionRequest

Event Structures

Each of the 33 X Window event types is associated with a data structure declared in the header library <X11/Xlib.h>. The exact components of the event data structure depend on the event in question. For example, some events require the location of the mouse pointer, while others do not. These event structures differ from one event type to another, but all include certain components.

Shared Event Elements

All event structures contain the five fields shown here:

```
typedef struct {
  int type;
  unsigned long serial;    /* # of last request processed by
                              the server */
  Bool send_event;         /* TRUE if event issued by a
                              SendEvent request */
  Display *display;        /* Display the event read on */
  Window window;
}XAnyEvent;
```

The type is a name that uniquely identifies the event, such as Expose. The least significant 16 bits of the serial number generated by the protocol request are expanded to a 32-bit serial value stored in the event data structure. The *send_event* field is set to TRUE if the event was issued by a SendEvent request associated with another application; otherwise, it is set to FALSE. The display field contains a pointer to the display connection that recorded the event. The window field is set to a relevant window, according to the event type.

XEvent Structure

The XEvent data structure is a collection of the individual data structures declared for each event type. You can access individual event data structures through the XEvent data structure shown here:

```
typedef union_XEvent {
  int type;                /* do not change */
  XAnyEvent xany;
  XKeyEvent xkey;
  XButtonEvent xbutton;
  XMotionEvent xmotion;
  XCrossingEvent xcrossing;
  XFocusChangeEvent xfocus;
  XExposeEvent xexpose;
  XGraphicsExposeEvent xgraphicsexpose;
  XNoExposeEvent xnoexpose;
  XVisibilityEvent xvisibility;
  XCreateWindowEvent xcreatewindow;
  XDestroyWindowEvent xdestroywindow;
```

```
XUnmapEvent xunmap;
XMapEvent xmap;
XMapRequestEvent xmaprequest;
XReparentEvent xreparent;
XConfigureEvent xconfigure;
XGravityEvent xgravity;
XResizeRequestEvent xresizerequest;
XConfigureRequestEvent xconfigurerequest;
XCirculateEvent xcirculate;
XCirculateRequestEvent xcirculaterequest;
XPropertyEvent xproperty;
XSelectionClearEvent xselectionclear;
XSelectionRequestEvent xselectionrequest;
XSelectionEvent xselection;
XColormapEvent xcolormap;
XClientMessageEvent xclient;
XMappingEvent xmapping;
XErrorEvent xerror;
XKeymapEvent xkeymap;
long pad [24];
} XEvent;
```

Event Masks

An active X Window server generates vast numbers of events, so that programs would have difficulty dealing with all events generated. Fortunately, many events are irrelevant to a given window or even to a given application. As shown in the Hello World program in Chapter 2, a program selects the event types of interest to it by first setting bits in the *event mask* defined in the standard header library and then invoking the **XSelectInput** function. An event mask is a group of bits whose individual bits refer to the different event types. When the bit equals 1, the associated event type is selected. In general, when the bit equals 0, the associated event type is not selected. Sections describing specific event types indicate any exceptions.

The following table lists the event masks and when you apply them.

Event Mask	Corresponds To
NoEventMask	No events desired
KeyPressMask	Keys pressed
KeyReleaseMask	Keys released
ButtonPressMask	Mouse button pressed
ButtonReleaseMask	Mouse button released
EnterWindowMask	Pointer enters a window
LeaveWindowMask	Pointer leaves a window
PointerMotionMask	Pointer changes location
PointerMotionHintMask	Pointer motion hints wanted
Button1MotionMask	Motion while mouse button 1 is down
Button2MotionMask	Motion while mouse button 2 is down
Button3MotionMask	Motion while mouse button 3 is down
Button4MotionMask	Motion while mouse button 4 is down
Button5MotionMask	Motion while mouse button 5 is down
ButtonMotionMask	Motion while any mouse button is down
KeymapStateMask	Keyboard state at window entry and focus in
ExposureMask	All exposures
VisibilityChangeMask	All changes in visibility
StructureNotifyMask	All changes in window structure
ResizeRedirectMask	Redirect resizing of window
SubstructureNotifyMask	Notify the substructure
SubstructureRedirectMask	Redirect requests related to substructures
FocusChangeMask	All changes in input focus
PropertyChangeMask	All changes in properties
ColormapChangeMask	All changes in colormaps
OwnerGrabButtonMask	Automatic grabs activate when *owner_events* is TRUE

X Protocol

The server and the client communicate via the X protocol. Protocol messages are classified into four types: requests from the client to the server, replies from the server to the client, errors messages when the request was not successfully completed, and event messages that inform an interested client that an action was taken. Each message type has its own particular format.

Requests

An application informs the server that it requires a service by sending a block of data known as a request. Requests are usually one-way protocol request messages. Such requests do not require a system reply.

Replies

Sometimes the application program cannot proceed without a specific reply from the server. For example, the Xlib function **XQueryBestCursor** transmits the buffer contents to the server, blocks additional processing, and transmits the current request to the server. Processing resumes only when the server returns the required information to the application. Such requests are known as round-trip protocol request messages. They may involve considerable delay, especially for systems with relatively slow physical transmission speeds.

continues . . .

Key Points
(continued)

Errors

There is no guarantee that a given request will lead to the desired results—X Window syntax is not easy to use. The Xlib service function **XSynchronize** enables or disables synchronization, the separate processing of each Xlib function. When synchronization is enabled, requests are not buffered. The system accepts a request, blocks processing, transmits the request to the server, and waits for a reply. Synchronization mode makes it easy for the programmer to determine the function that caused the error, but slows down system performance drastically.

Event Format

Essentially all activities affecting either system input or output generate one or more events. All 33 types of events follow the same event format.

Standard Header Files

Standard header files supply information such as X protocol types and constants to be used by applications. The specific header files included depend on the application's needs and the X Window version and release numbers.

continues . . .

Xlib Naming and Argument Conventions

Approximately 300 Xlib functions interface with the X protocol. Applying Xlib functions is similar to assembly language programming. Standard naming and argument conventions make it easier to understand and apply these functions.

Resources

Resources are objects stored on the X server. They include windows, graphics contexts, fonts, cursors, color maps, and pixmaps. Correct use of resources reduces both the coding effort and the volume of data transferred between the client and the server. Resources are created via one-way requests from client applications. Resources are controlled by the application but are located in the workstation server.

Windows

Windows generally are rectangular display areas that appear on the display screen. They are the server's most important resource. Whenever an X application draws a graph or displays text, it must specify the output window involved. Both mouse and keyboard input enter the system via a window.

continues . . .

Graphics Contexts

Graphics contexts (GCs) are data structures that manage graphics features, including line style and width, foreground and background color, and fill patterns. Every request to generate graphical output must reference a graphics context. Unlike other resources, applications should not share graphics contexts.

Fonts

A font describes the size and shape of each character within a unified collection of characters. X provides a large number of fonts with standard names.

Cursors

The cursor resource describes the size, color, and shape of the onscreen cursor associated with the mouse. When the mouse or other pointing device moves, the cursor moves. One way to create a cursor is by selecting a single character from a special cursor font.

Colormaps

Color processing is complicated. Colors that display well on one workstation may look odd on another workstation. The X resource colormap helps programmers manage the hundreds of colors available in X Window systems. A colormap is a map associating a pixel value with a color.

continues . . .

Pixmaps

A pixmap is a block of memory, associated with the X server, that can be used for drawing. Windows and pixmaps are called drawables. Unlike windows, objects drawn in pixmaps do not appear on the screen. To see them, you must copy the pixmap's contents to a visible window. Pixmaps often store special patterns for cursors and window backgrounds. A pixmap whose pixels are each represented by a single bit is known as a bitmap.

Events

Event processing is the central focus of the X Window system. Every activity that affects input or output, and many additional activities as well, generates one or more events. An active application is constantly churning out events, in no particular order.

Event Types

The X Window system provides 33 distinct event types, which can be classified into distinct categories: keyboard events, pointer events, window-crossing events, input focus events, keymap state notification events, exposure events, structure control events, window state notification events, colormap state notification events, and client communication events. In all cases, the events are associated with a data structure defined in the header file <X11/Xlib.h>. All event structures contain five fields denoting the event type, the number of the last request processed by the server, an indication of whether the event was issued by a SendEvent request, and an indication of the display and the window involved.

CHAPTER

Windows and
Windowing Techniques

Chapter 3, "Basic Concepts and Terminology," presented basic X Window concepts and terminology except as related to one important topic: windows themselves. As the product name itself indicates, windows are the essential component in the X Window system. This chapter gets at the heart of windows and their manipulation.

A commonly used analogy compares windows on a display screen to pieces of paper on a desk. This analogy, like any analogy, must be taken with a grain of salt. For example, like pieces of paper, windows can be stacked in any order and shuffled on demand. However, X Window windows are usually rectangular and parallel to the screen.

Another useful analogy compares the interrelationships among windows with individuals on a family tree. X Window talks about parents, children, siblings, ancestors, and descendants. Numerous other technical terms describe a window's geometry, such as its border width; its permanent features, such as whether it is available for both output and input; and its variable aspects, such as its background color and how it reacts when its parent window changes size.

The window life cycle encompasses creating windows, using the window creation functions; setting variable window features; actually making windows visible; and destroying windows when they no longer serve a purpose.

X Window provides numerous functions for manipulating windows. These functions are accompanied by specific event types that the program solicits to know what to do and when to do it. Needless to say, virtually every function can generate one or more errors, either because of a poorly coded request or because the system itself is unable to meet a given request.

Unlike most desktops, X Window display screens are often shared by several users. Rather than let each user access the valuable window real estate, X Window systems rely on a special client application, the window manager, to keep the situation under control. As you will see, hinting to the window manager how you want your windows handled is often the most efficient policy.

Basics

The previous chapter defined six resources: windows, graphics contexts, fonts, cursors, colormaps, and pixmaps. As the software's name itself suggests, windows are X Window's central resource. Usually, a window is a rectangular area on the screen, oriented parallel to the screen borders.

Many other windowing systems place strict requirements on window creation and manipulation. X Window, however, defines windows in the broadest possible terms and lets application developers apply these building blocks as they best see fit. According to the X Window system founders, one of their guiding principles in designing the system was "Provide mechanism rather than policy. In particular, place user interface policy in the clients' hands." In other words, let the client choose the look and feel. This open window concept has profound design implications.

X Window applications are not restricted to a standard look and feel. Systems designers may choose to restrict themselves to *tiled windows,* placed side by side, or they may apply overlapping windows to enable more sophisticated dynamic window interrelationships to better serve end users. Proprietary toolkits, such as OSF/Motif and Open Look, provide applications with a standard look and feel.

Desktop Metaphor

It is common to compare windows in an X Window system to pieces of paper on a desk. First let's consider the similarities:

❑ Like pieces of paper on a desktop, a window is not interesting in and of itself. The window displays current contents and accepts additional data from the user.

❑ A single window, called the root window, corresponds to the physical desktop or the hard cover of your pad of paper. The root window may not be deleted, moved, or otherwise changed.

❏ Windows need not be the same size. Just like tiny scraps of paper are useless, however, it is pointless to create a window that is too small to be legible.

❏ Windows may be transparent, allowing users to see the contents of underlying windows. Most windows, like most pieces of paper, are not transparent.

❏ Windows may overlap each other. A window visible on the screen can fully or partially obscure one or more windows lying below it. The relative window placement may change almost instantly, depending on user needs. Just like users move an urgent message from the bottom to the top of a pile, they can shuffle the order of windows on the screen.

❏ Window contents, like those on scraps of paper, may be stored for future retrieval or discarded.

There are several significant differences between paper on a desktop and windows. These include the following:

❏ Although paper can be in any shape, windows are usually rectangular. Their size can change during the life of the application—unlike paper, their size can grow.

❏ Windows must be oriented parallel to the screen. They may not be slanted.

❏ Any part of the window falling outside the screen cannot be seen.

❏ The relationship among windows is formally defined, unlike the relationship among scraps of paper. The next section introduces terms such as root, parent, child, hierarchy, and stacking order that express the sometimes complex relationships among windows.

❏ Depending on working conditions, a single desk may be shared by several individuals. These individuals may make a conscious attempt not to interfere with each other. For example, they may cordon off part of the desktop for each individual's own papers. No such restrictions exist in X Window. However, just like an office manager coordinates several employees, a window manager coordinates the window-associated activities of several applications.

Basic Terminology

Before examining the specific Xlib functions that govern window manipulation and the ensuing events, it is necessary to define basic windowing terms. These terms are often applied in coding Xlib functions.

The *root window* consists of the entire screen. It may not be moved, resized, or destroyed. It corresponds to the desktop and serves as the base for all windows. Figure 4-1 shows the root window.

The *window hierarchy* expresses vertical relationships among windows. The window hierarchy roughly corresponds to a family tree. Figure 4-2 illustrates a relatively uncluttered screen with three windows: the root window and two smaller windows, A and B. Windows A and B are called *children*, or *subwindows*, of the root window; they are *siblings* of each other. The root window is the *parent* or *parent window* of windows A and B. The root window is the only window that does not itself have a parent. Like human families, a parent may have several children. Unlike human families, each child can have only a single parent.

FIGURE 4-1 Root window

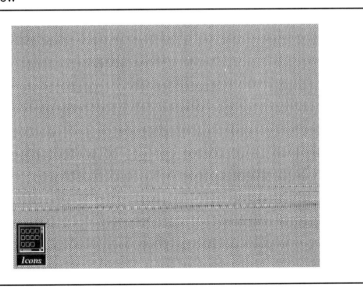

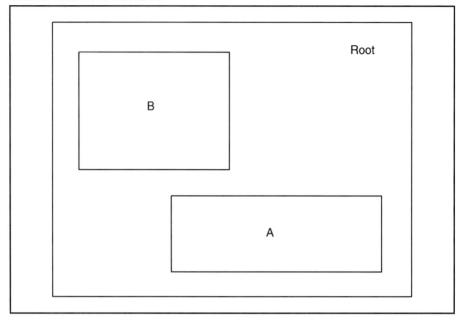

FIGURE 4-2 Screen with three windows

The parent/child window relationship is explicitly defined when creating a child window. Both the **XCreateSimpleWindow** function used in the Hello World program of Chapter 2, "Hello World," and the more general **XCreateWindow** function specify the parent window when creating a child window. Recall that in the Hello World program the **XCreateSimpleWindow** function specified the DefaultRootWindow as the parent window. The **XReparentWindow** function changes a window's parent to another window located on the same screen.

The window hierarchy may span several generations. Figure 4-3 illustrates a three-generation family. Windows A and B are the children of the root window. Window A is the parent of windows A1 and A2. Windows B1, B2, and B3 are the children of window B. A given window's parent, grandparent, and so on are known as its *ancestors*. The root window is the ancestor of all the other windows on the screen. Window A is the ancestor of windows A1 and A2. It is also the ancestor of any children to be created for windows A1 and A2. Note that window A is not the ancestor of windows B1, B2, B3, or any of their eventual children.

Screen with a three-generation family

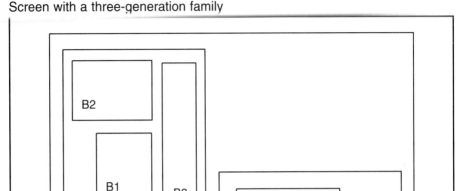

(The reparenting function mentioned earlier could, however, make A the ancestor of window B1.)

The opposite of ancestor is *descendant* or *inferior.* Windows B1, B2, and B3 are descendants of windows B and the root window. One key aspect of the ancestor/descendant relationship is the ability to inherit window features such as background and border.

The child windows shown in Figure 4-2 do not overlap. Each has its own area. Figure 4-3 illustrates a more complex situation without any overlapping windows. Figure 4-4 illustrates a common occurrence in which two siblings overlap. Wherever window A overlaps window B, only window A's contents are visible (unless window A has a transparent background). The *stacking order* describes the relationship among siblings. In this case, window A is higher on the stacking order than window B. This relationship is not permanent. Several Xlib functions change the window stacking order. Figure 4-5 shows both parents and children and one way that they may *obscure* (cover) each other.

FIGURE
4-4

Overlapping siblings

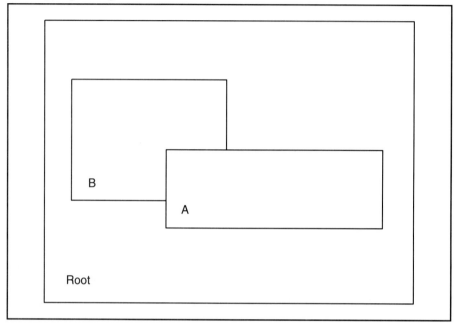

FIGURE
4-5

Obscuring windows

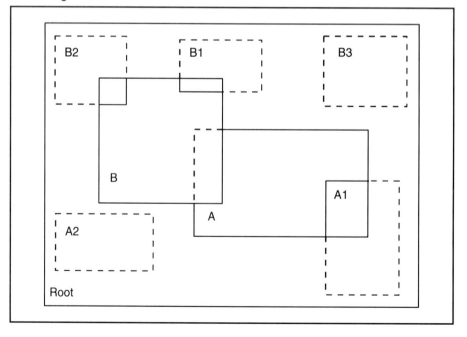

Let's consider an example of restacking windows. In Figure 4-6, the window B2 is partially obscured by its parent window B and another parent window A. The goal is to make window B2 fully visible. This requires two stages. The first stage, illustrated in Figure 4-7, moves window B and its children up. Window B is fully visible and partially obscures window A. However, window B2 is not yet fully visible. The second and final stage, illustrated in Figure 4-8, moves window B2 to the top of the stacking order. Window B2 is now fully visible and partially obscures its parent window B and the other parent window, A.

As windows move or are created, previously visible areas may become covered or obscured. (Window A in Figure 4-6 has become partially obscured by window B in Figure 4-7.) When this happens, it is necessary to address the question of preserving the obscured image. This will be discussed in the "Storage Attributes" section later in this chapter.

Window contents may be *clipped* by their parents—an image does not extend beyond the window's edges. For example, consider an attempt, shown in Figure 4-9, to draw a long line in window A. This line extends to the window's edge. All pixels associated with the line segments outside

Window B2 doubly obscured

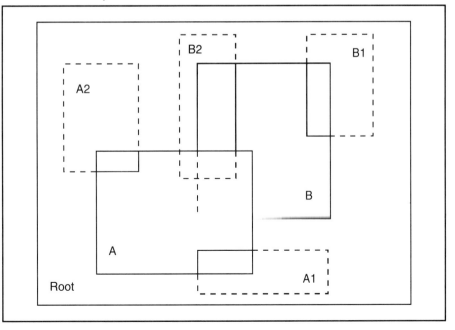

FIGURE
4-7
Window B2 singly obscured

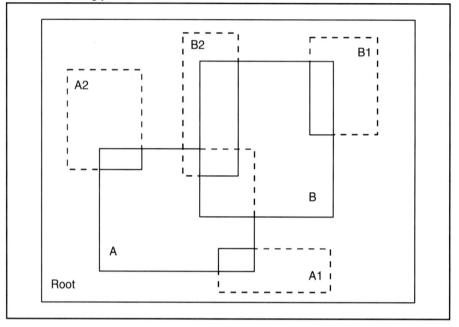

FIGURE
4-8
Window B2 fully visible

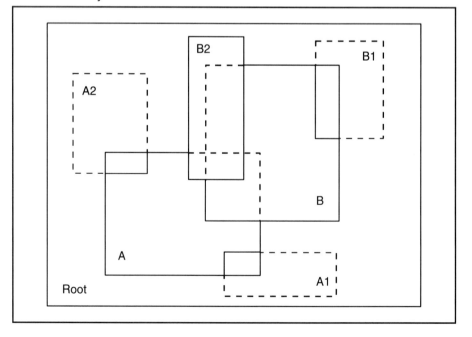

A clipped line

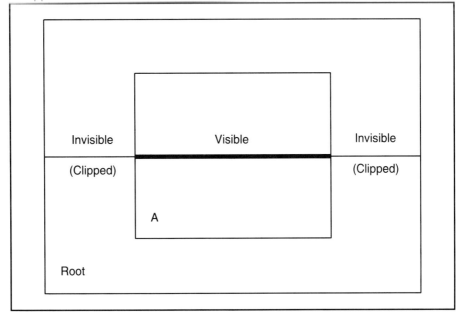

FIGURE 4.9

the window's boundaries are discarded. If window A enlarges, these discarded pixels do not automatically reappear.

The **XCreateSimpleWindow** and **XCreateWindow** functions create windows. However, the act of creating a window does not make the window visible. Before a window can be seen, it must be *mapped*. The Xlib functions **XMapWindow**, **XMapRaised**, and **XMapSubwindows** map windows. While mapping a window is necessary before the window becomes visible, simply mapping the window is not sufficient to make it visible. A window whose ancestors are all mapped is known as *viewable*. Even a viewable window may not be visible—it might be obscured by a sibling. Another possibility is that a window may be completely clipped by an ancestor, which occurs when a window lies completely outside an ancestor's boundaries. In this case, the window remains invisible. (Note that you can create a child window outside the boundaries of the parent window; however, such a child window is not visible.)

In summary, a window is visible only if all the following conditions are met.

❏   It and all its ancestors are mapped.

❏   It is not obscured by a sibling.

❏   It is not completely clipped by an ancestor.

Window Features

Now that you know under what conditions a window may be visible on the screen, it is time to consider the features that give a window its particular look. These features include its geometrical aspects, such as width and height; permanent aspects, such as its depth (number of bits per pixel in its images); and changeable aspects, such as its background and color. Developers apply these features to provide a more user-friendly interface.

Window Geometry

A window's *geometry* is its size, shape, and position within its parent window. Figure 4-10 illustrates the following terms as they apply to window geometry:

origin	The upper-left corner of the window, inside the border
x	The horizontal position of the child window's upper-left corner, relative to the parent window origin
y	The vertical position of the child window's upper-left corner, relative to the parent window origin
width	The window's width measured in pixels, not counting the border
height	The window's height measured in pixels, not counting the border
border_width	The width of the border, measured in pixels

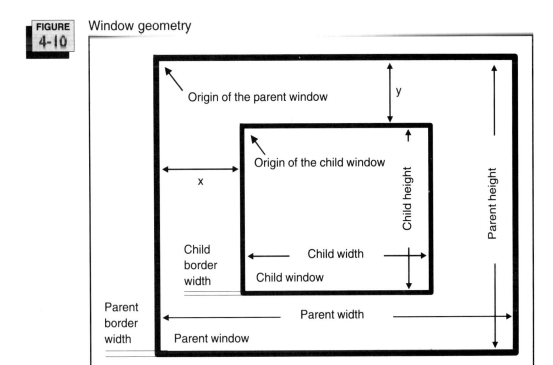

FIGURE 4-10   Window geometry

By definition, the origin is the x, y position 0,0. The x coordinates increase from left to right. The y coordinates increase from top to bottom.

Window Characteristics

A window's permanent features are known as its *characteristics*. Window characteristics are chosen at the time of window creation. The Xlib function **XCreateSimpleWindow** uses default values for window characteristics, whereas **XCreateWindow**, the more powerful Xlib function, enables the coder to select appropriate values.

Class

Two window classes exist: InputOutput and InputOnly. Standard windows belong to the InputOutput class. InputOnly windows are invisible. They are used to manage the screen and help direct mouse and keyboard events. InputOnly windows do not have many of the attributes discussed in the following sections—it doesn't make much sense to talk about an invisible window's border or color. The Xlib function **XCreateSimpleWindow** creates solely InputOutput windows, whereas the Xlib function **XCreateWindow** creates both InputOutput and InputOnly windows.

Depth

A window's *depth* is the number of bits per pixel in its pixel values. InputOnly windows must be set to a depth of 0, or an error occurs. InputOutput windows may assume different depth values, depending on the workstation used. Experienced programmers code a window's depth with the CopyFromParent value so that the application can be transported from one type of workstation to another without recoding. The **XDefaultDepth** function returns the depth of the root window. The **XListDepths** function returns an array of available depths for the given workstation.

Visuals

The way in which a workstation handles display screen output is known as its *visuals*. Elements of visuals include the color and number of pixels per bit. Sophisticated workstations allow the application to select the visuals for each window. This feature provides output tailored to the application but does require careful coding so that applications can be ported to less sophisticated workstations. Visuals are discussed in more detail in Chapter 10, "Color and Graphics."

Window Attributes

A window's features that can be changed are known as its *attributes*. These attributes include the window's background; its border; the disposition of images when the window changes size; the storage mechanism, if any, for preserving the contents of windows covered by other windows; and the way in which the window handles events, colormaps, and cursors. The following sections discuss individual attributes. The section "Changing Window Attributes" presents the procedure for setting and changing window attributes.

Background Attributes

The window background is specified by coding values of the *background_pixmap* or the *background_pixel* attributes. The *background_pixel* attribute generates a solid background. The *background_pixmap* attribute generates a background with a repeating pattern. When *background_pixmap* has a value of None, it generates a transparent background, allowing users to see the contents of underlying windows. A *background_pixmap* attribute of ParentRelative gives a window the same background as its parent. If the child window moves relative to its parent, the child's contents must be redrawn. The size of the background pixmap affects the speed of window drawing. Expect major performance degradation when you use large, irregular pixmaps.

The system generates the selected background pattern when all or part of a window image is erased and whenever a previously obscured window becomes visible. Expose events inform the client if an image needs to be redrawn.

Border Attributes

Specifying border attributes is similar to specifying background attributes. Specify a *border_pixel* value to select a solid border. Specify a *border_pixmap* value to select a border with a repeating pattern. The CopyFromParent attribute sets a child window's border to that of its parent. Setting the *border_width* field to 0 in the **XCreateSimpleWindow** or **XCreateWindow** functions eliminates the border.

Graphics output is always clipped to the inside of the affected window. Such output docs not affect the window border.

Gravity Attributes

Repositioning a child window relative to its parent window is called applying *window gravity*. Repositioning a window image relative to a resized window is known as applying *bit gravity.* In both instances, the affected area is attracted to the window's center, an edge, or a corner. This process is akin to physical gravity, except that objects may "fall" up or to the side, as well as down.

The gravity directions are named for the eight points on a compass. When either the *bit_gravity* or *win_gravity* attribute of a window is set to NorthWestGravity, the image or child window is displaced toward the upper-left corner of the resized parent window. Figure 4-11 shows the eight possible compass gravity settings. The workstation generates Expose events to indicate new areas of a window if its size increases. For example, consider Figure 4-12, for which NorthWestGravity was selected. In this case, the Expose events denote the areas below and to the right of the displaced image.

X Window cannot resize an image to maintain its fraction of the total window. If you choose to redraw the image to maintain its size relative to the window, select the default *bit_gravity* attribute ForgetGravity,

FIGURE 4-11   Eight compass gravity settings

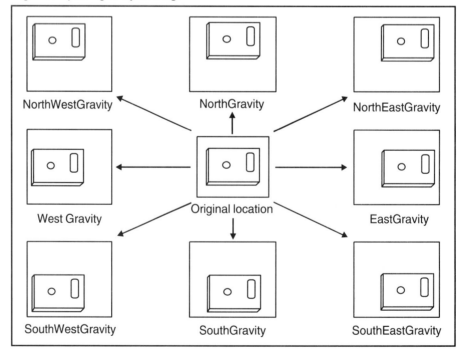

Gravity and Expose events

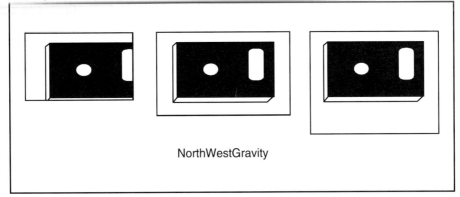

NorthWestGravity

which deletes the image. Expose events let you know that the image should be redrawn.

In addition to the eight compass settings and ForgetGravity, the *bit_gravity* attribute may assume the values CenterGravity, which centers the image in the modified window, and StaticGravity, which fixes the image relative to the root window. The StaticGravity option is used only if the window changes size and position at the same time.

When a parent window changes size, both its *bit_gravity* attribute and its children's *win_gravity* attribute are applied. The children windows generate one or more ConfigureNotify and then GravityNotify events. The *win_gravity* attribute includes the special value UnmapGravity, which causes the relevant child window to disappear from view when its parent window is resized. If you intend to rescale the child window yourself, use this option to avoid displaying a window before changing its size.

Storage Attributes

If the X server itself maintains window contents, the stored pixels are called the *backing store.* Not all X Window implementations include a backing store, and programmers often find that the backing store is physically too small to meet their needs. Reliance on the backing store may reduce an application's portability among workstations. Therefore, it is strongly suggested that programmers take care of saving images themselves.

The backing store has three attribute values: NotUseful (the default), WhenMapped, and Always. The value NotUseful indicates that the backing store serves no purpose for this particular window. The value WhenMapped indicates that the backing store is useful only when the window is mapped. The value Always indicates that the backing store should be maintained even if the window is unmapped. For example, this value might be used when the window is larger than its parent.

Some servers preserve the contents of selected windows under other windows. This process is known as *save-unders*. Save-unders work only if the entire screen image remains the same between the time the image is saved and when it is restored. Save-unders are often used with popup windows.

The *backing_planes* and *backing_pixel* attributes can be used together to reduce the amount of backing store required to save an image. The *backing_planes* attribute denotes those bits in each pixel that must be saved in their entirety. The remaining planes are set to the *backing_pixel* value.

Event Processing Attributes

The event mask, introduced in Chapter 2, "Hello World," and discussed in detail in Chapter 3, "Basic Concepts and Terminology," indicates events of interest for a given window, or in some cases, for the window's inferiors. Events are usually *propagated* from a window to its ancestors. This means that if a given event is not selected for a window, the event is passed to the window's ancestors until it finds a window for which the event has been selected. The *do_not_propagate* mask defines the events to be blocked.

The *override_redirect* attribute is Boolean; it may assume the value TRUE or FALSE (FALSE is the default). When it is TRUE, the window manager may not interfere with your window mapping, configuring, or stacking-order operations. TRUE is the usual selection for popup menus.

Colormap Attribute

The *colormap* attribute specifies the optimum colormap for an InputOutput window. The selected colormap must have the same visual type as the window in question. The CopyFromParent option may be used if the child window has the same visual type as the parent window. Be careful—changes made to the parent colormap after the copy operation do not affect the child colormap.

Cursor Attribute

The cursor attribute specifies the cursor to use when the pointer is in a window. If the cursor is set to None, the parent window's cursor is used. Changing the parent cursor causes a change in the child window's cursor.

Window Life Cycle

The major stages in a window's life are its *creation, mapping,* and *destruction.* Window creation defines the window's relationship to its parent and, implicitly, to its siblings. It sets the window geometry, characteristics, and attributes. Window mapping is required for the window to become visible. Window destruction removes a window and returns its resources to the system. Table 4-1 lists events generated and possible errors for each of the window functions discussed in the text.

Window Creation

X Window provides two Xlib functions for creating windows. The function **XCreateSimpleWindow** creates an InputOutput window that inherits many of its characteristics and attributes from its parent. The function **XCreateWindow** creates a window whose characteristics and attributes must be set.

XCreateSimpleWindow Function

The Xlib function **XCreateSimpleWindow** generates a one-way protocol request and returns the window resource identifier *thewindow* to be used in subsequent references. The function's second parameter is the parent window, in this case the root window for the same screen.

TABLE 4-1   Window Function, Event, and Error Table

Function	Possible Event(s)	Possible Error(s)
XCreateWindow	CreateNotify VisibilityNotify	BadAlloc, BadColor, BadCursor, BadMatch, BadPixmap, BadValue, BadWindow
XCreateSimple-Window	CreateNotify	BadAlloc, BadMatch, BadValue, BadWindow
XDestroyWindow	DestroyNotify Expose	BadWindow
XDestroy-Subwindows	DestroyNotify Expose	BadWindow
XMapWindow	MapRequest MapNotify, Expose	BadWindow
XMapRaised	MapRequest MapNotify, Expose	BadWindow (multiple)
XMapSubwindows	MapRequest MapNotify, Expose	BadWindow
XUnmapWindow	UnmapNotify Expose	BadWindow
XUnmap-Subwindows	UnmapNotify Expose	BadWindow
XConfigureWindow	ConfigureRequest ResizeRequest ConfigureNotify GravityNotify	BadMatch, BadValue, BadWindow
XMoveWindow	Expose ConfigureRequest	BadWindow
XResizeWindow	Expose ConfigureRequest	BadValue, BadWindow
XMoveResizeWindow	Expose ConfigureRequest	BadValue, BadWindow

TABLE
4-1
Cont.

Window Function, Event, and Error Table

Function	Possible Event(s)	Possible Error(s)
XSetWindowBorder-Width		BadWindow
XRaiseWindow	Expose ConfigureRequest	BadWindow
XLowerWindow	Expose ConfigureRequest	BadWindow
XCirculate-Subwindows	CirculateRequest CirculateNotify Expose	BadValue, BadWindow
XCirculate-SubwindowsUp	CirculateRequest CirculateNotify Expose	BadWindow
XCirculate-SubwindowsDown	CirculateRequest CirculateNotify Expose	BadWindow
XRestackWindows	ConfigureRequest Expose	BadMatch, BadWindow
XChangeWindow Attributes		BadAccess, BadColor, BadCursor, BadMatch, BadPixmap, BadValue BadWindow
XSetWindow-Background		BadMatch, BadWindow
XSetWindow BackgroundPixmap		BadMatch, BadPixmap, BadWindow
XSetWindowBorder		BadMatch, BadWindow
XSetWindowBorder Pixmap		BadMatch, BadPixmap, BadWindow
XSetWindow Colormap	ColorMapNotify	BadColor, BadMatch, BadWindow
XDefineCursor		BadCursor, BadWindow
XUndefineCursor		BadWindow

Hints were discussed briefly in Chapter 2, "Hello World," and will be explained in greater detail later in this chapter. The **XCreateSimpleWindow** function looks like this:

```
Window XCreateSimpleWindow(display, parent, x, y, width,
                              height, border_width, border,
                              background)
Display *display;              /* Display structure */
Window parent;                 /* Parent window identifier */
int x, y;                      /* Coordinates of top-left
                                  corner of created window's
                                  borders */
unsigned int width, height;    /* Window dimensions */
unsigned int border_width;     /* Border width in pixels */
unsigned long border;          /* Border pixel value */
unsigned long background;      /* Background pixel value */
```

A sample function call is

```
thewindow = XCreateSimpleWindow(thedisplay,
              DefaultRootWindow(thedisplay), thehint.x,
              thehint.y, thehint.width, thehint.height,
              7, theforeground, thebackground);
```

The **XCreateSimpleWindow** function creates an unmapped child window at the top of the stacking order. Because the window is unmapped, it presently does not obscure any siblings. The parent and newly created child window have a lot in common. They share the same screen. The child window is positioned with respect to the parent (that is, with respect to the x and y coordinates). When the parent moves, the child moves along with it. The child inherits both characteristics and attributes from its parent.

The **XCreateSimpleWindow** function directs the server to generate a CreateNotify event. It can generate BadAlloc, BadMatch, BadValue, and BadWindow errors.

XCreateWindow Function

The **XCreateWindow** function is more general than the **XCreateSimpleWindow** function. The **XCreateWindow** function allows you to specify window characteristics and attributes. Before invoking this function you must declare an XSetWindowAttributes data structure, load it with chosen values, and set selected bits in an associated mask. Be careful—default values may cause surprises, not all of which are pleasant. The **XCreateWindow** function is shown here.

```
Window XCreateWindow(display, parent, x, y, width, height,
                     border_width, depth, class, visual,
                     valuemask, attributes)
Display *display;              /* Display structure */
Window parent;                 /* Parent window */
int x, y;                      /* Coordinates of top-left corner
                                  of created window's borders */
unsigned int width, height;    /* Window dimensions */
unsigned int border_width;     /* Border width in pixels */
unsigned int depth;            /* Window depth in pixels */
unsigned int class;            /* InputOutput, InputOnly,
                                  CopyFromParent */
Visual *visual;                /* Visual type */
unsigned long valuemask;       /* Mask for window attributes */
XSetWindowAttributes
 *attributes;                  /* Window attributes */
```

The **XCreateWindow** function directs the server to generate a CreateNotify event. It can generate BadAlloc, BadColor, BadCursor, BadMatch, BadPixmap, BadValue, and BadWindow errors.

Setting Attributes

To provide a value for a window attribute, apply the OR operand to the appropriate mask bit in the following listing, set the value in the XSetWindowAttributes data structure, and call the **XCreateWindow** function.

The XSetWindowAttributes data structure looks like this:

```
/* Window attribute value mask bits */
#define CWBackPixmap        (1L<<0)
#define CWBackPixel         (1L<<1)
```

```
#define CWBorderPixmap      (1L<<2)
#define CWBorderPixel       (1L<<3)
#define CWBitGravity        (1L<<4)
#define CWWinGravity        (1L<<5)
#define CWBackingStore      (1L<<6)
#define CWBackingPlanes     (1L<<7)
#define CWBackingPixel      (1L<<8)
#define CWOverrideRedirect  (1L<<9)
#define CWSaveUnder         (1L<<10)
#define CWEventMask         (1L<<11)
#define CWDontPropagate     (1L<<12)
#define CWColormap          (1L<<13)
#define CWCursor            (1L<<14)
/* Values */
typedef struct {
Pixmap
   background_pixmap;      /* Background, None, or
                              ParentRelative */
unsigned long
   background_pixel;       /* Background pixel */
Pixmap border_pixmap;      /* Window border or
                              CopyFromParent */
unsigned long
   border_pixel;           /* Border pixel value */
int bit_gravity;           /* Choice of bit gravity values */
int win_gravity;           /* Choice of window
                              gravity values */
int backing_store;         /* NotUseful, WhenMapped, Always */
unsigned long
   backing_planes;         /* Planes to preserve if possible */
unsigned long
   backing_pixel;          /* Pixel value for
                              restoring planes */
Bool save_under;           /* TRUE, save bits for popup menus */
long event_mask;           /* Set of events to be saved */
long
   do_not_propagate_mask;  /* Set of events not to
                              be propagated */
Bool override_redirect;    /* TRUE, override */
Colormap colormap;         /* Colormap associated with window */
Cursor cursor;             /* Cursor to display */
} XSetWindowAttributes;
```

Table 4-2 lists resources and resource default values and indicates whether resources are defined for InputOnly windows.

Note   All the attributes shown in Table 4-2 are defined for InputOutput windows.

Window Mapping

A window and all its ancestors must be mapped before the window can be seen on the screen. As discussed later in this chapter, the window manager can take an active role in mapping a window, relieving the

TABLE 4-2   Resource Attributes

Attribute	Default	InputOnly
background_pixmap	None	No
background_pixel	Undefined	No
border_pixmap	CopyFromParent	No
border_pixel	Undefined	No
bit_gravity	ForgetGravity	No
win_gravity	NorthWestGravity	Yes
backing_store	NotUseful	No
backing_planes	All ones	No
backing_pixel	Zero	No
save_under	FALSE	No
event_mask	Empty set	Yes
do_not_propagate_mask	Empty set	Yes
override_redirect	FALSE	Yes
colormap	CopyFromParent	No
cursor	None	Yes

application program of tasks such as window sizing and placement. Xlib includes three functions to map windows and two functions to unmap them.

Window Mapping Functions

The functions **XMapWindow**, **XMapRaised**, and **XMapSubwindows** are used for window mapping.

The **XMapWindow** function maps the specified window and all of its subwindows that have had map requests. It may generate Expose, MapNotify, or MapRequest events. In general, the window is mapped after the program examines associated Expose events, as shown in the Hello World program in Chapter 2, "Hello World." The **XMapWindow** function, shown here, can generate a BadWindow error:

```
XMapWindow(display, w)
Display *display;              /* Display structure */
Window w;                      /* Window ID */
```

The **XMapRaised** function maps the specified window and all of its subwindows that have had map requests. In addition, it raises the specified window to the top of its stack. The **XMapRaised** function, shown here, can generate multiple BadWindow errors.

```
XMapRaised(display, w)
Display *display;              /* Display structure */
Window w;                      /* Window ID */
```

The **XMapSubwindows** function maps all subwindows for a selected window. The stacking order is top to bottom. The function generates Expose events on each window as the window is displayed. A single **XMapSubwindows** function tends to be more efficient than a group of **XMapWindow** functions, because the **XMapSubwindows** function carries out many operations only once for the group of windows, whereas the **XMapWindow** function must carry out these operations individually for each affected window. The **XMapSubwindows** function, shown here, can generate a BadWindow error.

```
XMapSubwindows(display, w)
Display *display;              /* Display structure */
Window w;                      /* Window ID */
```

Window Unmapping Functions

The functions **XUnmapWindow** and **XUnmapSubwindows** are used for window *unmapping*. Unmapping a window makes it and all its descendants invisible on the screen. An unmapped window does not lose its place in the stacking order.

The **XUnmapWindow** function unmaps a single window. It generates an UnmapNotify event for the window itself and Expose events for windows that were previously obscured by the unmapped window. The **XUnmapWindow** function, shown here, can generate a BadWindow error.

```
XUnmapWindow(display, w)
Display *display;              /* Display structure */
Window w;                      /* Window ID */
```

The **XUnmapSubwindows** function unmaps all subwindows of the specified window, starting at the bottom of the stacking order. A single **XUnmapSubwindows** function executes faster than several **XUnmapWindow** functions. It generates an UnmapNotify event for the window itself and Expose events for windows that were previously obscured by the unmapped window. The **XUnmapSubwindows** function, shown here, can generate a BadWindow error.

```
XUnmapSubwindows(display, w)
Display *display;              /* Display structure */
Window w;                      /* Window ID */
```

Window Destruction

An application can destroy windows implicitly when the display connection closes or explicitly by applying one of the two following Xlib functions. Window destruction starts from the bottom of the hierarchy and proceeds to the top of the hierarchy.

The **XDestroyWindow** function destroys the specified window and all of its subwindows. It generates a DestroyNotify event for each window destroyed. If a window's destruction makes other windows visible, the function generates the appropriate VisibilityNotify and Expose events.

The **XDestroyWindow** function, shown here, can generate a BadWindow error.

```
XDestroyWindow(display, w)
Display *display;              /* Display structure */
Window w;                      /* Window ID */
```

The **XDestroySubwindows** function destroys all of the specified window subwindows, but does not destroy the window itself. It generates a DestroyNotify event for each window destroyed. If a window's destruction renders other windows visible, the function generates the appropriate VisibilityNotify and Expose events. A single **XDestroySubwindows** function executes faster than several **XDestroyWindow** functions. The **XDestroySubwindows** function, shown here, can generate a BadWindow error.

```
XDestroySubwindows(display, w)
Display *display;              /* Display structure */
Window w;                      /* Window ID */
```

Window Configuration Functions

The functions described in the previous section enable users to create, map, unmap, and destroy windows. They do not provide application control. This section describes window configuration functions that move and resize windows and change windows' positions in the stacking order. It then describes functions that modify a window's geometry. The section concludes by presenting a single request that changes both the window's position in the stacking order and its geometry.

Moving and Resizing Windows

Xlib functions allow applications to move and resize windows, either separately or together. These functions are **XMoveWindow**, **XResizeWindow**, and **XMoveResizeWindow**.

The **XMoveWindow** function moves the selected window to a new location specified by the x and y coordinates. These coordinates refer to the top-left pixel of the window border or to the window itself if no border exists. If the window is mapped, its contents may be lost if it is obscured at the new location and there is no backing store or save-unders. In this case, the server generates Expose events to inform the interested application. If windows are no longer obscured after the move, the server generates appropriate Expose events. If the window's *override_redirect* flag is set to FALSE and another client has issued a Substructure-RedirectMask on the parent window, the server generates a Configure-Request event, and the window is not sized. The **XMoveWindow** function, shown here, can generate a BadWindow error.

```
XMoveWindow(display, w, x, y)
Display *display;              /* Display structure */
Window w;                      /* Window ID */
int x, y;                      /* Top-left pixel of window border */
```

The **XResizeWindow** function changes the inside dimensions of the selected window but does not change its borders. Furthermore, this function does not change the window's origin or its position in the stacking order. When the window size changes, its contents may be lost, in which case the function generates Expose events. If decreasing the size of a mapped window uncovers formerly obscured areas on another window, the function generates appropriate Expose events. It is the application's responsibility to distinguish among the various Expose events and take suitable action. If the window's *override_redirect* flag is set to FALSE and another client has issued a SubstructureRedirectMask on the parent window, the server generates a ConfigureRequest event, and the window is not moved. The **XResizeWindow** function, shown here, can generate BadValue and BadWindow errors.

```
XResizeWindow(display, w, width, height)
Display *display;              /* Display structure */
Window w;                      /* Window ID */
unsigned int width,           /* Interior dimensions of
            height;               window */
```

The **XMoveResizeWindow** function changes the inside dimensions and the location of the selected window but does not change its borders or its position in the stacking order. When the window size changes its size, contents may be lost, in which case the function generates Expose events. If decreasing the size of a mapped window uncovers formerly obscured areas on another window, the function generates appropriate Expose events. If the window's *override_redirect* flag is set to FALSE and another client has issued a SubstructureRedirectMask on the parent window, the server generates a ConfigureRequest event, and the window is not moved or resized. The **XResizeWindow** function, shown here, can generate BadValue and BadWindow errors.

```
XMoveResizeWindow(display, w, x, y, width, height)
Display *display;              /* Display structure */
int x, y;                      /* Window position relative to
                                  parent window */
Window w;                      /* Window ID */
unsigned int width,            /* Interior dimensions of
          height;                 window */
```

Setting the Window Border Width

The **XSetWindowBorderWidth** function sets the window's border width. It is one of the relatively few Xlib functions that does not generate any events. The **XSetWindowBorderWidth** function, shown here, changes the width of a window's borders and can generate a BadWindow error.

```
XSetWindowBorderWidth(display, w, width)
Display *display;              /* Display structure */
Window w;                      /* Window ID */
unsigned int width;            /* Width of window border */
```

Changing the Window Stacking Order

Xlib functions allow applications to raise, lower, circulate, or restack windows. These functions are **XRaiseWindow**, **XLowerWindow**, **X-**

CirculateSubwindows   XCirculateSubwindowsUp, XCirculate SubwindowsDown, and **XRestackWindows**.

The **XRaiseWindow** function raises (*pops*) the specified window to the top of the stacking order. If the window is mapped, executing this function may generate Expose events for the given window and for any mapped subwindows that had been obscured. If the window's *override_redirect* flag is set to FALSE and another client has issued a Substructure- RedirectMask on the parent window, the server generates a Configure- Request event, and the window is not raised. The **XRaise- Window** function, shown here, can generate a BadWindow error.

```
XRaiseWindow(display, w)
Display *display;          /* Display structure */
Window w;                  /* Window ID */
```

The **XLowerWindow** function lowers (*pushes*) the specified window to the bottom of the stacking order. If the window is mapped, executing this function generates Expose events for any mapped siblings that had been obscured. If the window's *override_redirect* flag is set to FALSE and another client has issued a SubstructureRedirectMask on the parent window, the server generates a ConfigureRequest event, and the window is not lowered. The **XLowerWindow** function, shown here, can generate a BadWindow error.

```
XLowerWindow(display, w)
Display *display;          /* Display structure */
Window w;                  /* Window ID */
```

Mastering the window circulation functions **XCirculateSubwindows**, **XCirculateSubwindowsUp**, and **XCirculateSubwindowsDown** requires an understanding of the technical term *occlude*. The window I occludes the window J if both windows are mapped, if I is higher in the stacking order than J, and if the rectangle defined by I's outer edges (the window including the border) intersects the rectangle defined by J's outer edges.

 Note Window occlusion is similar to, but not exactly the same as, window obscuring.

The **XCirculateSubwindows** function circulates the specified window's children in the selected direction. The RaiseLowest parameter raises to the top of the stacking order the lowest mapped child occluded by another child. The LowerHighest parameter lowers to the bottom of the stacking order the highest mapped child that occludes another child. In either case, Expose events are generated and processed for formerly obscured windows.

If the window's *override_redirect* flag is set to FALSE and another client has issued a SubstructureRedirectMask on the parent window, the server generates a ConfigureRequest event, and no window circulation takes place. If a child window changes position in the stacking order, the server generates a CirculateNotify event. The **XCirculateSubwindows** function, shown here, can generate BadValue and BadWindow errors.

```
XCirculateSubwindows(display, w, direction)
Display *display;           /* Display structure */
Window w;                   /* Window ID */
int direction;              /* RaiseLowest or
                               LowerHighest */
```

The **XCirculateSubwindowsUp** function is a convenience function equivalent to the **XCirculateSubwindows** function with the *direction* parameter set to RaiseLowest. The **XCirculateSubwindowsUp** function, shown here, can generate a BadWindow error.

```
XCirculateSubwindowsUp(display, w)
Display *display;           /* Display structure */
Window w;                   /* Window ID */
```

The **XCirculateSubwindowsDown** function is a convenience function equivalent to the **XCirculateSubwindows** function with the *direction* parameter set to LowerHighest. The **XCirculateSubwindowsDown** function, shown here, can generate a BadWindow error.

```
XCirculateSubwindowsDown(display, w)
Display *display;           /* Display structure */
Window w;                   /* Window ID */
```

The **XRestackWindows** function restacks windows from top to bottom in the order specified. The first window's stacking order is not affected, but subsequent windows in the array are stacked under the first window, as specified by the array.

If any referenced window's *override_redirect* flag is set to FALSE and another client has issued a SubstructureRedirectMask on the parent window, the server generates a ConfigureRequest event for each window whose flag is FALSE, and no window circulation takes place. The **XRestackWindows** function, shown here, can generate BadMatch and BadWindow errors.

```
XRestackWindows(display, windows, nwindows)
Display *display;              /* Display structure */
Window windows [];             /* Array of windows to be
                                  restacked */
int nwindows;                  /* Number of windows to be
                                  restacked */
```

Changing Window Attributes and Configuration

As previously stated, a window's nonpermanent features are known as its attributes. Among a window's attributes are its background, border, and gravity. X Window provides two ways of changing window attributes: You can use the **XChangeWindowAttributes** function, which lets you change any attribute whose value resides in the associated XSetWindowAttributes data structure and whose bit is set in the associated value mask, or you can use individual functions such as **XSetWindowBackground**.

XChangeWindowAttributes Function

The **XChangeWindowAttributes** function changes one or more window attributes at the same time. Changing window attributes is similar to setting window attributes via the **XCreateWindow** function. To change a value for a window attribute, apply the OR operand to the appropriate mask bit, set the value in the XSetWindowAttributes data structure, and call the **XChangeWindowAttributes** function. The **XChangeWindow Attributes** function, shown here, can generate BadAccess, BadColor, BadCursor, BadMatch, BadPixmap, BadValue, and BadWindow errors.

```
XChangeWindowAttributes(display, w, valuemask, attributes)
Display *display;               /* Display structure */
Window w;                       /* Window ID */
unsigned long valuemask;        /* Mask for window attributes */
XSetWindowAttributes
  *attributes;                  /* Window attributes */
```

Changing Individual Window Attributes

The **XSetWindowBackground** function sets the window background to a given pixel value. This operation does not change the window contents. The **XSetWindowBackground** function, shown here, can generate BadMatch and BadWindow errors.

```
XSetWindowBackground(display, w, background_pixel)
Display *display;               /* Display structure */
Window w;                       /* Window ID */
unsigned long background_pixel; /* Background pixel */
```

The **XSetWindowBackgroundPixmap** function sets the background pixmap of the window to the specified pixmap. This operation does not change the window contents. When the *ParentRelative* parameter is coded, the parent's background pixmap is used. The **XSetWindow-BackgroundPixmap** function, shown here, can generate BadMatch, BadPixmap, and BadWindow errors.

```
XSetWindowBackgroundPixmap(display, w, background_pixmap)
Display *display;               /* Display structure */
Window w;                       /* Window ID */
Pixmap background_pixmap;       /* Background pixmap,
                                   ParentRelative, or None */
```

The **XSetWindowBorder** function sets the window border to the specified pixel value. The **XSetWindowBorder** function, shown here, can generate BadMatch and BadWindow errors.

```
XSetWindowBorder(display, w, border_pixmap)
Display *display;               /* Display structure */
Window w;                       /* Window ID */
unsigned long border_pixel;     /* Colormap entry */
```

The **XSetWindowBorderPixmap** function sets the window border pixmap to the specified pixmap. When the *CopyFromParent* parameter is coded, the parent's border pixmap is used. The **XSetWindow Border-Pixmap** function, shown here, can generate BadMatch, BadPixmap, and BadWindow errors.

```
XSetWindowBorderPixmap(display, w, border_pixel)
Display *display;              /* Display structure */
Window w;                      /* Window ID */
Pixmap border_pixmap;          /* Border pixmap or
                                  CopyFromParent */
```

The **XSetWindowColormap** function sets the specified colormap for the chosen window. The **XSetWindowColormap** function, shown here, can generate BadColor, BadMatch, and BadWindow errors.

```
XSetWindowColormap(display, w, colormap)
Display *display;              /* Display structure */
Window w;                      /* Window ID */
Colormap colormap;             /* Colormap */
```

The **XDefineCursor** function defines which cursor is used in a window. Specifying the parameter *None* is equivalent to executing the **XUndefineCursor** function. The **XDefineCursor** function, shown here, can generate BadCursor and BadWindow errors.

```
XDefineCursor(display, w, cursor)
Display *display;              /* Display structure */
Window w;                      /* Window ID */
Cursor cursor;                 /* Cursor to display or None */
```

The **XUndefineCursor** function rolls back the effect of an **XDefine-Cursor** function for the window in question. If the pointer is in the window, the parent's cursor will be used. If the pointer is in the root window, the default cursor will be restored. The **XUndefineCursor** function, shown here, can generate a BadWindow error.

```
XUndefineCursor(display, w)
Display *display;              /* Display structure */
Window w;                      /* Window ID */
```

XConfigureWindow Function

The **XConfigureWindow** function moves and resizes a window or changes its border width. Changing window configuration is similar to changing window attributes via the **XChangeWindowAttributes** function. To change a value for the window configuration, apply the OR operand to the appropriate mask bit in the following listing, set the value in the XWindowChanges data structure, shown here, and call the **XConfigureWindow** function.

```
/* Configure window value mask bits */
#define CWX              (1<<0)
#define CWY              (1<<1)
#define CWWidth          (1<<2)
#define CWHeight         (1<<3)
#define CWBorderWidth    (1<<4)
#define CWSibling        (1<<5)
#define CWStackMode      (1<<6)
/* Values */
typedef struct {
    int x, y;               /* Upper-left outside corner
                               position */
    int width, height;      /* Inside size of window */
    int border_width;       /* Border width in pixels */
    Window sibling;         /* Sibling window ID for stacking */
    int stack_mode;         /* Above, Below, TopIf,
                               BottomIf, Opposite */
} XWindowChanges;
```

The **XConfigureWindow** function, shown here, applies values stored in the XWindowChanges structure to reconfigure a window's size, position, border, and stacking order.

```
XConfigureWindow(display, w, value_mask, values)
Display *display;            /* Display structure */
Window w;                    /* Window ID */
unsigned int value_mask;     /* Mask for values structure */
XWindowChanges *values       /* XWindowChanges structure */
```

When a sibling is specified, *stack mode* is interpreted as follows:

Above   The window is placed just above the sibling.

Below   The window is placed just below the sibling.

TopIf   If the sibling occludes the window, the window is placed at the top of the stack.

BottomIf   If the window occludes the sibling, the window is placed at the bottom of the stack.

Opposite   If the sibling occludes the window, the window is placed at the top of the stack. If the window occludes the sibling, the window is placed at the bottom of the stack.

When no sibling is specified, *stack_mode* is interpreted as follows:

Above   The window is placed at the top of the stack.

Below   The window is placed at the bottom of the stack.

TopIf   If any sibling occludes the window, the window is placed at the top of the stack.

BottomIf   If the window occludes any sibling, the window is placed at the bottom of the stack.

Opposite   If any sibling occludes the window, the window is placed at the top of the stack. If the window occludes any sibling, the window is placed at the bottom of the stack.

If the *override_redirect* flag of the specified window is FALSE and another client has selected SubStructureMask on the parent window, the server generates a ConfigureRequest event and does not reconfigure the window. In other circumstances the **XConfigureWindow** function generates ConfigureNotify, GravityNotify, and Expose events. The **XConfigureWindow** function can generate BadMatch, BadValue, and BadWindow errors.

Window State Change and Expose Events

Among the 33 event types reported by X Window, ten are associated with a window's change of state. In alphabetical order, these events are

CirculateNotify, ConfigureNotify, CreateNotify, DestroyNotify, GravityNotify, MapNotify, MappingNotify, ReparentNotify, UnmapNotify, and VisibilityNotify. Strictly speaking, Expose events are not window state change events but exposure events. However, because Expose events are closely associated with window state change events, they are discussed at the end of this section.

CirculateNotify Events

CirculateNotify events inform interested clients when a window changes its position in the stacking order. These events are generated by the **XCirculateSubwindows**, **XCirculateSubwindowsUp**, and **XCirculateSubwindowsDown** functions. To receive CirculateNotify events, set StructureNotifyMask to denote the restacked window itself or SubstructureNotifyMask to denote the parent window. Depending on the mask selected, the event window is the restacked window or its parent. The XCirculateEvent structure looks like this:

```
typedef struct {
    int type;                     /* CirculateNotify */
    unsigned long serial;         /* Number of last server
                                     processed request */
    Bool send_event;              /* TRUE if from
                                     SendEvent request */
    Display *display;             /* Display structure */
    Window event;                 /* Event window */
    Window window;                /* Restacked window */
    int place;                    /* PlaceOnTop, PlaceOnBottom */
} XCirculateEvent;
```

ConfigureNotify Events

ConfigureNotify events inform interested clients when a window changes its size, position, border, or position in the stacking order. These events are generated by the **XConfigureWindow**, **XLowerWindow**, **XMapRaised**, **XMoveWindow**, **XMoveResizeWindow**, **XRaiseWindow**, **XResizeWindow**, **XRestackWindows**, and **XSetWindowBorderWidth** functions. To receive ConfigureNotify events, set StructureNotifyMask to denote the reconfigured window itself or SubstructureNotifyMask to denote the parent window. Depending on the mask selected, the event window is the reconfigured window or its parent. Window manager clients usually ignore windows whose *override_redirect* parameter is set to TRUE. The XConfigureEvent structure is shown here.

```
typedef struct {
    int type;                        /* ConfigureNotify */
    unsigned long serial;            /* Number of last server
                                        processed request */

    Bool send_event;                 /* TRUE if from
                                        SendEvent request */

    Display *display;                /* Display structure */
    Window event;                    /* Event window */
    Window window;                   /* Restacked window */
    int x, y;                        /* Window location */
    int width, height;               /* Window size */
    int border_width;                /* Border width */
    Window above;                    /* Sibling window */
    Bool override_redirect;          /* Ignore window if TRUE */
} XConfigureEvent;
```

CreateNotify Events

CreateNotify events inform interested clients when a window is created. These events are generated by the **XCreateWindow** and **XCreateSimpleWindow** functions. To receive CreateNotify events, set the SubstructureNotifyMask associated with the parent of the window to be created. Window manager clients usually ignore windows whose *override_redirect* parameter is set to TRUE. The XCreateWindowEvent structure looks like this.

```
typedef struct {
    int type;                        /* CreateNotify */
    unsigned long serial;            /* Number of last server
                                        processed request */

    Bool send_event;                 /* TRUE if from
                                        SendEvent request */

    Display *display;                /* Display structure */
```

```
    Window parent;              /* Parent window */
    Window window;              /* ID of created window */
    int x, y;                   /* Window location */
    int width, height;          /* Window size */
    int border_width;           /* Border width */
    Bool override_redirect;     /* Ignore window if True */
} XCreateWindowEvent;
```

DestroyNotify Events

DestroyNotify events inform interested clients when a window is destroyed. These events are generated by the **XDestroyWindow** and **XDestroySubwindows** functions. To receive DestroyNotify events, set StructureNotifyMask to denote the destroyed window itself or Substructure NotifyMask to denote the parent window. Depending on the mask selected, the event window is the destroyed window or its parent. Window manager clients usually ignore windows whose *override_redirect* parameter is set to TRUE. The XDestroyWindowEvent structure looks like this:

```
typedef struct {
    int type;                   /* DestroyNotify */
    unsigned long serial;       /* Number of last server
                                   processed request */
    Bool send_event;            /* TRUE if from
                                   SendEvent request */
    Display *display;           /* Display structure */
    Window event;               /* Event window */
    Window window;              /* ID of destroyed window */
} XDestroyWindowEvent;
```

GravityNotify Events

GravityNotify events inform interested clients when a window is moved because its parent changes size. These events are generated by the **XConfigureWindow**, **XMoveResizeWindow**, and **XResizeWindow** functions. To receive GravityNotify events, set StructureNotifyMask to denote the moved window itself or SubstructureNotifyMask to denote the parent window. Depending on the mask selected, the event window is the moved window or its parent. The XGravityEvent structure is shown here.

```
typedef struct {
    int type;                      /* GravityNotify */
    unsigned long serial;          /* Number of last server
                                      processed request */
    Bool send_event;               /* TRUE if from
                                      SendEvent request */
    Display *display;              /* Display structure */
    Window event;                  /* Event window */
    Window window;                 /* ID of destroyed window */
    int x, y;                      /* Window location */
} XGravityEvent;
```

MapNotify Events

MapNotify events inform interested clients when a window is mapped. These events are generated by the **XMapWindow**, **XMapRaised**, **XMapSubwindows**, and **XReparentWindow** functions. To receive MapNotify events, set StructureNotifyMask to denote the mapped window itself or SubstructureNotifyMask to denote the parent window. Depending on the mask selected, the event window is the mapped window or its parent. Window manager clients usually ignore windows whose *override_redirect* parameter is set to TRUE. The XMapEvent structure looks like this:

```
typedef struct {
    int type;                      /* MapNotify */
    unsigned long serial;          /* Number of last server
                                      processed request */
    Bool send_event;               /* TRUE if from
                                      SendEvent request */
    Display *display;              /* Display structure */
    Window event;                  /* Event window */
    Window window;                 /* ID of mapped window */
    Bool override_redirect;        /* Ignore window if True */
} XMapEvent;
```

MappingNotify Events

MappingNotify events inform all clients when any of the functions **XSetModifierMapping**, **XChangeKeyboardMapping**, and **XSetPointer** complete without error. The XMappingEvent structure is shown here.

```
typedef struct {
    int type;                   /* MappingNotify */
    unsigned long serial;       /* Number of last server
                                   processed request */
    Bool send_event;            /* TRUE if from
                                   SendEvent request */
    Display *display;           /* Display structure */
    Window window;              /* Not used */
    int request;                /* MappingModifier,
                                   MappingKeyboard, or
                                   MappingPointer */

    int first_keycode;          /* First keycode */
    int count;                  /* Number of keycodes modified */
} XMappingEvent;
```

ReparentNotify Events

ReparentNotify events inform interested clients when a window changes its parent. These events are generated by the **XReparentWindow** function. To receive ReparentNotify events, set StructureNotifyMask to denote the mapped window itself or SubstructureNotifyMask to denote the old or new parent window. Depending on the mask selected, the event window is the mapped window or its old or new parent. Window manager clients usually ignore windows whose *override_redirect* parameter is set to TRUE. The XReparentEvent structure is shown here.

```
typedef struct {
    int type;                   /* ReparentNotify */
    unsigned long serial;       /* Number of last server
                                   processed request */
    Bool send_event;            /* TRUE if from
```

```
                                SendEvent request */
   Display *display;           /* Display structure */
   Window event;               /* Event window */
   Window window;              /* ID of reparented window */
   Window parent;              /* New parent window */
   int x, y;                   /* Window location */
   Bool override_redirect;     /* Ignore window if TRUE */
} XReparentEvent;
```

UnmapNotify Events

UnmapNotify events inform interested clients when a window ceases
to be mapped. These events are generated by the **XUnmapWindow**, and
XUnmapSubwindows functions. To receive UnmapNotify events, set
StructureNotifyMask to denote the unmapped window itself or Sub-
structureNotifyMask to denote the parent window. The structure
XUnmapEvent looks like this:

```
typedef struct {
   int type;                   /* UnmapNotify */
   unsigned long serial;       /* Number of last server
                                  processed request */
   Bool send_event;            /* TRUE if from
                                  SendEvent request */
   Display *display;           /* Display structure */
   Window event;               /* Event window */
   Window window;              /* ID of unmapped window */
   Bool from_configure;
} XUnmapEvent;
```

Visibility Events

Visibility events inform interested clients when a window changes
visibility. These events are associated with CirculateNotify, ConfigureNotify, GravityNotify, MapNotify, and UnmapNotify events. The
XVisibilityEvent structure is shown here.

```
typedef struct {
  int type;                     /* VisibilityNotify */
  unsigned long serial;         /* Number of last server
                                   processed request */
  Bool send_event;              /* TRUE if from
                                   SendEvent request */
  Display *display;             /* Display structure */
  Window event;                 /* Event window */
  Window window;                /* ID of window whose
                                   visibility changes */
  int state;                    /* VisibilityUnobscured,
                                   VisibilityPartiallyObscured, or
                                   VisibilityFullyObscured */
} XVisibilityEvent;
```

Expose Events

Expose events inform interested clients when full or partial contents of a window are lost. They are associated with a multitude of events, such as the window state change events discussed previously in this chapter. The XExposeEvent structure is shown here.

```
typedef struct {
  int type;                     /* Expose */
  unsigned long serial;         /* Number of last server
                                   processed request */
  Bool send_event;              /* TRUE if from
                                   SendEvent request */
  Display *display;             /* Display structure */
  Window window;                /* ID of exposed window */
  int x, y;                     /* Window location */
  int width, height;            /* Window dimensions */
  int count;                    /* Additional expose events
                                   to come */
} XExposeEvent;
```

Window Managers

You read in Chapter 1, "Introducing the System," that a window manager is a special client responsible for manipulating windows on the screen. Window managers control the screen display; for example, they set window sizes and determine where applications place windows. Some window managers permit only tiled windows; however, most support both tiled and overlapping windows.

Widely used window managers include uwm and twm, supplied by X Window, and the proprietary window manager mwm, part of the OSF/Motif Toolkit. Each window manager has its own visual trademark, perhaps displaying special features, such as title bars and raised buttons.

These decorations do not merely increase the window's eye appeal; they are often quite functional. For example, the window manager may highlight a window's title bar to show that it is ready to receive keyboard input. Depending on the window manager, the user can click a mouse button to cancel actions, such as window resizing.

Applications as well as users communicate with the window manager. They should not explicitly demand that a new or modified window be exactly such-and-such a size, but should instead suggest the window size and let the window manager make the final decision. Application suggestions to the window manager are called *hints*, as shown in the Hello World program in Chapter 2, "Hello World." Common hints relate to window size, window placement, and window decorations. By sending a hint that the window have certain desired characteristics, instead of explicitly requesting these characteristics, the program allows the window manager to do its job: namely, to manage windows. Remember: A single screen may display windows from several different X Window systems simultaneously, and individual applications should not interfere with each other. Don't be a hog—let the window manager make the final decision for sizing and placing your windows. If you really need larger windows, display the message "Please enlarge this window" in the window and let the user communicate with the window manager.

Key Points

Basic Philosophy

Usually, a window is a rectangular area on the screen, oriented parallel to the screen borders. X Window prefers to define windows in the broadest possible terms and let application developers apply these building blocks as they best see fit. A guiding design principle is "Provide mechanism rather than policy."

Basic Windowing Terminology

The root window consists of the entire screen. It may not be moved, resized, or destroyed. The window hierarchy expresses vertical relationships among windows. Windows directly subordinate to another window are its children. Windows that have the same parents are siblings of each other. A given window's parent, parent's parent, and so on are known as its ancestors. The opposite of ancestor is descendant or inferior. The stacking order describes the relationship among siblings.

Window Visibility

As windows move or are created, previously visible areas may become covered or obscured by other windows. Window contents may be clipped by their parents. A window is visible only if all the following conditions are met: It and all its ancestors are mapped, it is not obscured by a sibling, and it is not completely clipped by an ancestor.

continues . . .

Key Points (continued)

Window Geometry Terminology

A window's geometry is its size, shape, and position within its parent window. Terms related to window geometry include origin, x, y, width, height, and border_width.

Window Characteristics and Attributes

A window's permanent features are known as its characteristics. Window characteristics are chosen at the time of window creation. They include window classes InputOutput and InputOnly; depth; and pixel-value format, known as a visual. Window features that can be changed are known as its attributes. They include the window background and border; the disposition of images when the window changes size; any storage mechanism for preserving the contents of windows covered by other windows; and the way in which the window handles events, colormaps, and cursors.

Window Life Cycle

The major stages in a window's life are its creation, mapping, and destruction. Window creation defines the window's relationship to its parent and, implicitly, to its siblings. Creation sets the window's geometry, characteristics, and attributes. Window mapping is required for the window to become visible. Window destruction removes a window and returns its resources to the system. Window configuration functions modify a window's features and geometry. Ten event types are associated with a window's change of state.

continues . . .

*Key Points
(continued)*

Window Managers

A window manager is a special client responsible for manipulating windows on the screen. Window managers control the screen display; for example, they determine where applications place windows and set window sizes. Each window manager has its own visual trademark.

CHAPTER

Toolkit Concepts and Techniques

*T*he previous chapters introduced the fundamentals of the X Window system and low-level X Window programming via Xlib function calls. While it is essential to master Xlib functions, few X Window applications are programmed using only Xlib for the simple reason that easier-to-use tools exist. This chapter introduces the second level of X Window programming, Xt Intrinsics, and the most widely used extension to Xt Intrinsics, the OSF/Motif toolkit.

This chapter begins with basic notions and terminology and then examines the typical Motif application structure. It applies this structure with two versions of the Hello World program written with Xlib functions in Chapter 2, "Hello World." The chapter then discusses in greater detail the concepts and functions required for successful toolkit initialization and effective handling of widgets, resources, and callbacks. It concludes with more sophisticated Motif programs.

Basics

Even at this stage in your exposure to the X Window system, it is fairly clear that Xlib programming requires fastidiousness. The programmer must create, map, coordinate, and destroy dozens of interrelated windows and draw hundreds of lines. Whenever a window moves or otherwise changes visibility, the program must consider saving all or part of its contents. X Window generates events to signal important activities as they occur. The program must be ready at any time to accept relevant events and process them. If this all sounds complicated, it should. Xlib programming is not for the faint at heart or the sloppy minded.

The X Toolkit interface sits between the application programmer and the Xlib function calls, enabling programmers to instruct the computer with a higher-level language than low-level Xlib calls. The X Toolkit replaces windows and events with the more sophisticated entities *widgets* and *callback procedures*. For the time being, you can consider widgets to be graphical user interface building blocks such as menus and dialog boxes. Callback procedures inform an application that the user has referenced a widget, perhaps by making a menu selection.

The X Toolkit consists of two related parts. The Xt Intrinsics defines a basic collection of functions and data structures. These functions and data structures are standard for the X Window system. Proprietary toolkits extend the Xt Intrinsics to provide more flexible, more powerful programming toolkits. Every proprietary toolkit has its own look and feel. Presently, the two most widely used toolkits are the OSF/Motif toolkit associated with such companies as IBM, HP, and DEC, and Open Look, associated with Sun Microsystems and AT&T.

Two categories of programmers access the toolkits in different ways. *Application programmers* employ already existing widgets. To their way of thinking, a widget is a "black box." Application programmers know how to apply selected widgets and what these widgets can do, but they don't necessarily know what's inside the widget. They have enough to worry about without concerning themselves with a widget's internal behavior and composition.

Widget programmers create and sell widgets. They must master the internal details of widget creation and modification. They devise widgets flexible enough to meet varied needs. Widget programmers have a vested interest in keeping internal widget details secret. As the X Window market continues to expand, there are an increasing number of widgets programmers whose products are directed to specific applications. For example, expect to see an increasing number of commercially available widgets of interest to those designing hospital information systems.

Basic Terminology

This chapter and relevant sections of the following chapters depend on a considerable technical vocabulary associated with widgets and the toolkit. Table 5-1 lists key terms in alphabetical order.

Those of you who are familiar with object-oriented programming systems will recognize many of the terms in Table 5.1, such as class, inheritance, and instance. Although the X Window system is not based on an object-oriented programming language such as Smalltalk or C++, it applies principles of object orientation to widgets. Often widget designers need not create a new widget from scratch, but instead modify an existing widget. Correct application of object orientation leads to faster widget development and verification.

TABLE 5-1

Widget and Toolkit Terminology

Term	Definition
Application	A toolkit-based program.
Callback procedure	Also known as a *callback*. An application-dependant function called by a widget that requires information from the application.
Callback list	A series of functions to be performed when a callback procedure is invoked.
Class	An object's type. An object's class defines the legal operations for that object. For example, widget creation is a legal operation, whereas widget addition is not.
Class hierarchy	The formal relationship among classes. Objects such as widgets, lower on the class hierarchy, *inherit* operations from objects higher on the class hierarchy.
Inheritance	The ability to implement specific operations (methods) from the instance's superclass.
Instance	A given occurrence of a particular object, such as a widget.
Intrinsics	The X Window programming layer that defines standard functions and data types applied in creating widgets and in implementing widgets in user applications.
Method	A procedure implementing a given operation supported by the widget class.
Object	A self-contained unit including data and the operations defined for this data. Widgets are the major objects supported by the toolkit.
Resource	A named widget attribute that may be set by the programmer or, perhaps, by the user. Toolkit resources are similar to, but distinct from, Xlib resources defined in Chapter 3, "Basic Concepts and Terminology."

TABLE 5-1 Cont.   Widget and Toolkit Terminology

Term	Definition
Subclass	A class below (within) another class in the class hierarchy. A *subclass* is more specialized than its *superclass*.
Superclass	A class above another class in the class hierarchy. A superclass is less specialized than its subclasses.
Widget	The basic object in a toolkit. Commonly used widgets include scrollbars, popup menus, and dialog boxes.
Widget class	The widget type. The widget class defines all attributes and operations available for a related group of widgets.

Widget Tree

The previous chapter introduced the window hierarchy. The root window sits at the top of the window hierarchy. It is the only window that does not have a parent. The root window may have several children. The child/parent relationship is forged at window creation, but may be changed by the Xlib function **XReparentWindow**. Recall that a child window's contents can never be seen outside the boundaries of its parent window. The widget tree is similar to the window hierarchy.

The widget tree root is known as the *Shell widget*. The toolkit initialization function creates the Shell widget. With the exception of popup menus, the Shell widget is the parent of the other application widgets. The Shell widget interacts with the window manager, sometimes serving as a negotiator between the window manager and its own child widgets. Because the Shell widget is overlaid by the application's main widget, it is invisible.

The middle level of the widget tree consists of the Composite widgets that regroup several child widgets to form the graphical user interface. Composite widgets themselves usually do not display data. Each Composite widget class implements its own physical placement policy for its child widgets. Menu widgets, for example, insist that all children have the same width and line up their children vertically; if the application requests that a menu item become wider, all menu items will become wider. Other Composite widget classes have less strict geometry policies. Box widgets, for example, allow the application to specify the size and location of child widgets. Pane widgets allocate a fixed space to children and let the user divide this space among the children as he or she wishes.

The third, and bottom, level of the widget tree consists of Primitive widgets that have no children. Examples of Primitive widgets include labels, menu items, and pushbuttons.

Intrinsics Widget Classes

Xt Intrinsics defines four basic widget classes that are the superclasses for all other widget classes in the X Window system. These Intrinsics widget classes pass fundamental characteristics to Intrinsics widget subclasses and all the toolkit widget classes. Figure 5-1 illustrates the

FIGURE 5-1   Intrinsics widget classes

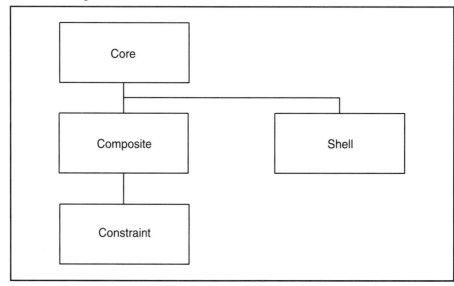

relationship among the Intrinsics widget classes. They are presented starting from the top of the hierarchy.

Core   The *Core widget* class sits at the top of the hierarchy. It plays a role similar to the root window. All widgets inherit resources from the Core. However, no useful widget is a Core widget, unless it belongs to the Shell widget class or to a toolkit widget class. In technical terms, the Core widget class is a *metaclass,* a class for organizing widget classes, not for organizing widgets themselves.

Composite   The Composite widget class is a subclass of the Core class. Widgets belonging to this class are called *Composite widgets.* Proper use of Composite widgets increases an application's consistency and coherence. The Composite widget class is also a metaclass. Composite widgets are discussed in greater detail later in this chapter.

Constraint   The Constraint widget class is a subclass of the Composite class. Widgets belonging to this class are called *Constraint widgets.* Constraint widget classes manage children according to a definite rule, or constraint. For example, the Menu widget class requires that all widgets be placed vertically and have the same width. The Constraint widget class is also a metaclass.

Shell   The Shell widget class is a subclass of the Core widget class that is restricted to a single child. Widgets belonging to the Shell widget class (*Shell widgets*) furnish an interface between the window manager and the other widgets in the application. The Shell widget class is not a metaclass.

Toolkit Widget Classes

Toolkit widget classes are subclasses of Intrinsic widget classes. Actual toolkit widgets are defined in part according to the rules for Xt Intrinsics widget classes. In addition, they have rules and features of their own, composing a major element of the proprietary toolkit. Many proprietary toolkits contain the following toolkit widget classes, presented here in alphabetical order.

Box   A Box widget contains other widgets but does not specify any layout information. The application itself specifies such layout information.

ButtonBox   A ButtonBox widget contains other widgets such as pushbuttons or toggle buttons, packing them tightly to fill the available space.

Command   A Command widget activates a given function when the user selects it by clicking a pointer button, such as a mouse button. The Command widget is synonymous with the PushButton widget.

Confirm   A Confirm widget is a popup widget that requires the user to confirm an action such as deletion of a file. In most cases, the application stops processing pending user confirmation or cancellation.

Label   A Label widget is an onscreen text label that cannot receive user input.

Menu   A Menu widget contains other widgets such as pushbuttons, placing them vertically and setting them to a single width.

MinMax   A MinMax widget is similar to a Box widget, except that the application can specify a minimum and a maximum size.

PushButton   A PushButton widget activates a given function when the user selects it by clicking a pointer button, such as a mouse button. The Pushbutton widget is synonymous with the Command widget.

Scrollbar   A Scrollbar widget enables the user to select the data area visible on the screen.

TextField   A TextField widget receives a text string from the user.

Toggle   A Toggle is a PushButton widget that assumes first one and then the other of two states, similar to the CAPSLOCK key.

VerticalPane   A VerticalPane widget contains children displayed in a vertical column, whose allocated space can be changed by the user.

Interrelationships Among Widget Classes

If you examine the preceding widget classes, you will see that they are not independent. For example, a Toggle widget is a subclass (a particular type) of PushButton widget. It may assume only one of two states and constantly shifts between them. Furthermore, a PushButton widget (and by inference, a Toggle widget) is a particular type of Label widget. Neither of these two widgets can be used to enter text. On the other hand, it should be clear that a TextField widget is not an example of a Label widget—its very name contradicts the notion of a Label widget, which cannot receive user input.

Every operation available to a given widget class is automatically available to the widget class's subclasses. Many key widget operations are defined once for the Core class and apply to all X Window widgets.

When programmers define a new widget class, they do not start from zero. They need only add the specific data declarations and code required to extend the class. The rest is there for the taking.

Widget Naming Conventions

The header filename for a given widget class is the widget class name followed by .h, except that the header filename can be only a maximum of ten characters long. A subdirectory of /usr/include/X11 commonly contains the widget set's header files.

The C language type names for widget instances is composed of the class name followed by the string "Widget": for example, PushButtonWidget and ScrollingWidget. The external reference to the widget class structure is formed by concatenating the class name (this time without a capital letter) to the string "WidgetClass". Thus, the header file contains the names pushbuttonWidgetClass and scrollingWidget Class.

Overview of Widget Resources

Recall from Chapter 3, "Basic Concepts and Terminology," that Xlib defined six categories of resources allocated by the server to a given application: windows, graphics contexts, fonts, cursors, colormaps, and pixmaps. Toolkit resources are different from server resources, even though the two concepts are clearly related. A *toolkit resource* is a named data item required by the widget. In most applications, users will be able to modify toolkit resources in accordance with their own perceived needs. In fact, one of the best ways to ensure an unsuccessful application is to hard-code all widget resources, forcing users to do things your way.

Toolkit resources (referred to as resources in the rest of this chapter) are associated with a specific instance of a widget. For example, a given Pushbutton menu is allotted specific resource values. Such resources are usually, but not always, shared with PushButton menus. The Core widget class is the root of the widget class hierarchy, so all widgets are members of the Core class. All resources associated with Core widgets belong to every widget. The Composite widget class is a subclass of the Core widget class. The Composite widget class is a metaclass, so applications never create Composite widgets as such. However, many application widgets are subclasses of the Composite widget class and inherit its resources.

This chapter now examines the Motif application structure and several functioning Motif programs. Then the chapter discusses resources in greater detail.

Motif Application Structure

To create any Motif application, follow these steps:

1. Include the standard Motif header file <Xm/Xm.h>.
2. Include the public header file for each widget class used. Use the private header file only for writing widgets, not for applying them.
3. Initialize the toolkit using either the **XtAppInitialize** function or the **XtVaAppInitialize** function.
4. Create widgets using the **XtVaCreateManagedWidget** function for each widget.
5. Register callbacks, actions, and event handlers as required.

6. Realize the widgets by a single call of the **XtRealizeWidget** function. This process creates the windows and then maps them on the screen.

7. Call the **XtAppMainLoop** function to initiate loop processing.

Let's examine each of these steps in the light of a familiar application, the Hello World program. Our first example contains only six of the seven steps.

Hello World Program Revisited: Example 1

The first Motif version of the Hello World program is similar to the Xlib version presented in Chapter 2, "Hello World." It follows the general Motif application structure with a single exception—for simplicity, this program skips step 5. It does not register any callbacks, actions, or event handlers.

Step 1: Include the Motif Header File

The Motif header file contains the necessary data definitions required to process Motif applications. To include this file code, enter a single line:

```
#include <Xm/Xm.h>
```

Step 2: Include a Public Header File

X Window supplies a *public header file*, available in a predefined directory. The filename is a maximum of ten characters of the capitalized widget class name: in this case, Label.h. Public header files include the following information:

❏ Directives that prevent the preprocessor from including the public header file more than once.

❏ An include directive for the particular class's superclass.

❏ Definitions for this widget class's names, classes, and resource types, if these definitions are not in the <X11/StringDefs.h> header file.

❏ Data types required for resources associated with this widget.

❏ An external reference to this class's class record pointer that points to the class record declared in the associated private header file.

The private header class is of interest only to widget writers. It is considerably more complicated than the public header class.

This particular program employs a single line of code to specify the one public header file it requires, as shown here:

```
#include <Xm/Label.h>
```

Step 3: Initialize the Program and Toolkit

This step consists of two parts: initializing the program and initializing the toolkit itself.

Initializing the Program

Motif program initialization is a fairly straightforward operation. The following three statements are standard to C language programs. An *application context* is a pointer to a data structure that contains toolkit-designated data for the application. It is mandatory to specify at least one application context for each application. (Few applications specify more than a single application context.) This program declares two widget names, in order of the widget hierarchy.

```
main(argc, argv)
int argc;
char *argv[];
```

```
{
XtAppContext app context;   /* Specifies a connection to
                               the server */
Widget theParent, hellow;   /* Identifies widgets */
```

Initializing the Toolkit

Toolkit initialization is more complicated than program initialization. The **XtVaAppInitialize** function opens a connection to the server and creates a Shell widget, in this case named theParent. The function then reads the resource database to obtain any available command-line arguments that override other resource specifications. Although the **XtVaAppInitialize** function has eight parameters, this program uses only two of them.

```
theParent = XtVaAppInitialize(
   &app_context,          /* Application context */
   "Xexample1",           /* Application class */
   NULL, 0,               /* Command-line option list */
   &argc, argv,           /* Command-line arguments */
   NULL,                  /* Missing app-defaults file */
   NULL);                 /* Terminates varargs list */
```

The first argument of the **XtVaAppInitialize** function passes the address of the application context, accessing a data structure that contains relevant data associated with the application.

The second argument identifies the application's class name. Here, the class name is the same as the application name, except that the first letter of the class name is capitalized. If the first letter is an x, the second letter is also capitalized.

The **XtVaAppInitialize** function returns the name of the Shell widget, the parent of the first widget created by the application. In this example, the Shell widget is called theParent.

Step 4: Create and Manage Widgets

This step involves creating the widgets and informing their parents. It is accomplished with the following code segment.

```
hellow = XtVaCreateManagedWidget(
  "hellow",              /* Widget name */
  xmLabelWidgetClass,    /* Widget class from header file */
  theParent,             /* Parent widget */
  NULL);                 /* Terminates varargs list */
```

The **XtVaCreateManagedWidget** function creates the *hellow* widget, whose widget class is Label (the second argument specifies as much because its value is XmLabelWidgetClass. The third parameter specifies the parent widget, created in the previous step. A *managed widget* is a widget whose geometry is handled by the parent widget. The parent widget allocates space only to its managed children. The *hellow* widget is a managed widget.

Step 5: Register Callbacks, Actions, and Event Handlers

This simple program does not register callbacks, actions, or event handlers. Stay tuned for version 2 following this exercise, which will include step 5.

Step 6: Realize the Widgets

Realizing the widgets means making them and then mapping their windows. It involves a single function:

```
XtRealizeWidget(theParent);
```

This function negotiates with the window manager to place the ensuing windows. It also maps the windows, which, as was the case for Xlib functions, must be done before the windows can become visible.

Step 7: Loop for Events

Both Xlib and Toolkit programs are event driven. However, Xlib programmers are forced to code their own event-handling routines, whereas the toolkit itself takes care of all (or part) of the event handling. This particular example is quite simple because the program does not respond to user events.

```
XtRealizeWidget(theParent);
```

The first version of the OSF/Motif Hello World program is now complete, except that it does not register any callbacks, actions, or event handlers. The next version remedies this situation.

```
/*  Step 1  Motif header file */
#include <Xm/Xm.h>

/*  Step 2  Public header file for widget classes used */
#include <Xm/Label.h>

/*  Step 3  Initialize the Program and the Toolkit */
main(argc, argv)
int argc;
char *argv[];
{
XtAppContext app_context;  /* Specifies a connection to
                                the server */
Widget theParent, hellow;  /* Identifies widgets */

theParent = XtVaAppInitialize(
  &app_context,      /* Application context */
  "XExample1",       /* Application class */
  NULL, 0,           /* Command line option list */
  &argc, argv,       /* Command line arguments */
  NULL,              /* Missing app-defaults file */
  NULL);             /* Terminates varargs list */

/*  Step 4  Create and Manage Widgets */
  hellow = XtVaCreateManagedWidget(
  "hellow",          /* Widget name */
  xmLabelWidgetClass, /* Widget class from header file */
  theParent,         /* Parent widget */
  NULL);             /* Terminates varargs list */

/*  Step 5  Absent from this sample program */
```

```
/*  Step 6  Realize the Widgets */
  XtRealizeWidget(theParent);

/*  Step 7  Event Loop */
  XtAppMainLoop(app_context);
}
```

The results of running this program are shown in Figure 5-2.

This Motif program does not display the character string "hello_world" as in Chapter 2, "Hello World." To display this string, replace the last two lines of the RESOURCE SPECIFICATIONS FOR EXAMPLE 1 with the following:

```
*hellow.labelString: hello_world
```

The following MAKE file was used to process this program in SCO Open Desktop. The MAKE file for other X Window implementations varies.

```
RM = rm - f
CC = cc
CFLAGS = -O
INCLUDES = -I/usr/include -I/usr/include/X11
LIBS = -lXm -lXt -lX11 -lsocket -lmalloc -lPW
.c.o:
$(RM) $@
$(CC) -c $(CFLAGS) $(INCLUDES) $*.c
all:: example1
example1: example1.o
$(RM) $@
$(CC) -o $@ $(CFLAGS) example1.o $(LIBS)
@echo makefile for example1 - done!
```

Hello World Program Revisited: Example 2

The second Motif version of the Hello World program is similar to the version just presented with a single exception: This program registers a single callback. For simplicity, the following discussion refers only to

FIGURE
6-2

Initial Motif program without callbacks

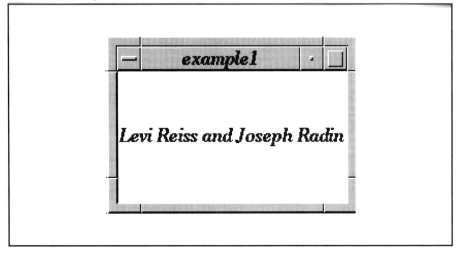

steps that have changed. However, the full listing is supplied for your convenience.

Step 2: Include a Public Header File

Step 2 now consists of two lines; the second public header file is now required because this program incorporates a PushButton widget, associated with the callback function.

```
#include <Xm/Label.h>
#include <Xm/PushB.h>
```

Step 3: Initialize the Program and Toolkit

Step 3 now contains an Exit button callback function. The callback function Exit has a prototype that takes three arguments:

❏ The first argument, *awidget,* is the widget that triggered the callback. The widget is formally specified here and is the first argument in the **XtAddCallback** callback function shown here.

❑   The second argument, *client_data*, is the value passed as the last argument of the **XtAddCallback** callback function.

❑   The third argument, *call_data*, is a data item passed from the widget, depending on the widget class. If a widget does not generate any *call_data*, pass 0 as the third parameter.

   Note   It is standard practice to capitalize the first letter of a callback function to distinguish it from the associated widget.

The rest of the code in Step 3 is unchanged and does not appear here.

```
void Exit(awidget, client_data, call_data)
Widget awidget;
XtPointer client_data, call_data;
```

Step 5: Register Callbacks, Actions, and Event Handlers

This program now registers a single callback function that registers Exit as the Pushbutton widget's callback. The first argument, *hellow*, is the widget that triggers the callback. The second argument, *XmNactivateCallback*, is a symbolic constant that identifies which callback resources are set. The third argument is the function that the widget will call. The fourth argument is the data to be passed to that function, which in this case is none.

```
XtAddCallBack(hellow, XmNactivateCallback, Exit, 0);
```

The remainder of the program is exactly the same as the previous program. The major difference between the two programs is the addition of a callback function, which generates additional code in several places in the program.

```
/*  Step 1  Motif header file as before */
#include <Xm/Xm.h>

/*  Step 2  Public header file for widget classes used */
/*          Additional include file for PushButton widget */
#include <Xm/Label.h>
```

```
#include <Xm/PushB.h>

/*  Step 3  Initialize the Program and the Toolkit */
/*          Additional Quit button callback function */
void Exit(awidget, client_data, call_data)
Widget awidget;
XtPointer client_data, call_data;
{
  exit(0);
}


main(argc, argv)
int argc;
char *argN[];
{
XtAppContext app_context;  /* Specifies a connection to
                              the server */
Widget theParent, hellow;  /* Identifies widgets */
theParent = XtVaAppInitialize(
  &app_context,    /* Application context */
  "XExample2",     /* Application class */
  NULL, 0,         /* Command line option list */
  &argc, argv,     /* Command line arguments */
  NULL,            /* Missing app-defaults file */
  NULL);           /* Terminates varargs list */

/*  Step 4  Create and Manage Widgets */
/*          Widget is now of Pushbutton class */
hellow = XtVaCreateManagedWidget(
  "ghellow",             /* Widget name */
  xmPushButtonClass,     /* Widget class from header file */
  theParent,             /* Parent widget */
  NULL);                 /* Terminates varargs list */

/*  Step 5  Callback Function now Present */
  XtAddCallback(hellow, XmNactivateCallback, Exit, 0);
                         /* client_data */
/*  Step 6  Realize the Widgets */
  XtRealizeWidget(theParent);

/*  Step 7  Event Loop */
  XtAppMainLoop(app_context);
}
```

The results of running this program are shown in Figure 5-3.

To modify the output of this program, change the RESOURCE SPEC-IFICATIONS FOR EXAMPLE 2 as explained for Example 1.

The following MAKE file was used to process this program in SCO Open Desktop. The MAKE file for other X Window implementations varies.

```
RM = rm - f
CC = cc
CFLAGS = -O
INCLUDES = -I/usr/include -I/usr/include/X11
LIBS  = -lXm -lXt -lX11 -lsocket -lmalloc -lPW
.c.o:
$(RM) $@
$(CC) -c $(CFLAGS) $(INCLUDES) $*.c
all:: example2
example2: example2.o
$(RM) $@
$(CC) -o $@ $(CFLAGS) example2.o $(LIBS)
@echo makefile for example2 - done!
```

FIGURE 5-3   Initial Motif screen with callbacks

Toolkit Initialization and Related Functions

Now that you have seen two toolkit versions of the Hello World program in action, it is time to explore in greater depth many of the concepts and functions introduced in these programs. You will see alternative, more sophisticated functions that enable you to build more powerful toolkit-based programs.

Default Initialization

The two Hello World programs used the Intrinsics function **XtVaApp-Initialize**. This function and the related Intrinsics function **XtAppInitialize** call four Intrinsics functions in the following order: **XtToolkitInitialize**, **XtCreateApplicationContext**, **XtOpenDisplay**, and **XtAppCreateShell**. The **XtVaAppInitialize** and **XtAppInitialize** functions differ in the way that they specify parameters. Both functions call the **XtOpenDisplay** function with parameters *display_string* and *application_string* set to NULL. In addition, they both call the **XtAppCreateShell** function with the *application_name* parameter set to NULL and the widget class set to applicationShellWidgetClass. The function **XtAppInitialize** follows.

```
Widget XtAppInitialize(app_context_return,
                       application_class, options,
                       num_options, argc_in_out,
                       argv_in_out, fallback_resources,
                       args, num_args)
   XtAppContext *app_context_return;
                              /* Returns application context
                                 if not NULL */
   String application_class;  /* Specifies class name of the
                                 application */
   XrmOptionDescList options; /* Specifies command line
                                 options table */
   Cardinal num_options;      /* Number of entries in
                                 options table */
```

```
Cardinal *argc_in_out;        /* Pointer to number of
                                 command line arguments */
String *argv_in_out;          /* Pointer to command line
                                 arguments */
String *fallback_resources;   /* Resource values to use if
                                 application class resource
                                 file unavailable */
ArgList args;                 /* Argument list for created
                                 shell widget resources */
Cardinal num_args;            /* Number of entries in
                                 argument list */
```

The function **XtVaAppInitialize** is shown here.

```
Widget XtVaAppInitialize(app_context_return,
                    application_class, options,
                    num_options, argc_in_out,
                    argv_in_out,
                    fallback_resources,...)
    XtAppContext *app_context_return;
                              /* Returns application context
                                 if not NULL */
    String application_class;  /* Specifies class name of the
                                 application */
    XrmOptionDescRec options[];  /* Specifies command line
                                 options table */
    Cardinal num_options;      /* Number of entries in
                                 options table */
    Cardinal *argc_in_out;     /* Pointer to number of
                                 command line arguments */
    String *argv_in_out;       /* Pointer to command line
                                 arguments */
    String *fallback_resources; /* Resource values to use if
                                 application class resource
                                 file unavailable */
    ...                        /* Variable argument list to
                                 override other resource
                                 specifications for shell */
```

The **XtVaAppInitialize** and **XtAppInitialize** functions are similar.

Initializing Toolkit Internals

The **XtToolkitInitialize** function initializes the Intrinsics. It creates application contexts, opens displays, and creates Shell widgets. It is certainly easier for programmers to code a single initialization command than to code several initialization functions, as required by Xlib.

The **XtToolkitInitialize** function is automatically invoked by the **XtVaAppInitialize** and **XtAppInitialize** functions. It should not be called more than once in any X Window program.

Handling Application Contexts

The application context **XtAppContext** is *opaque*—clients cannot read it. Recall that an application context, in essence, specifies a connection to the server. You create an application context by calling the **XtCreateApplicationContext** function (which returns the application context) as follows:

XtAppContext XtCreateApplicationContext()

This function is automatically invoked by the **XtVaAppInitialize** and **XtAppInitialize** functions.

The **XtWidgetToApplicationContext** function determines the application context associated with a given widget. It is coded as follows:

```
XtAppContext XtWidgetToApplicationContext(w)
   Widget (w);                  /* Specifies the widget whose
                                   application context is
                                   requested */
```

Note The requested widget must be of the Object class or a subclass of the Object class.

The **XtDestroyApplicationContext**, shown next, removes the selected application context, but not before completing the callback procedure or other action that called the function.

```
void XtDestroyApplicationContext(app_context)
   XtAppContext app_context;   /* Specifies the application
                                  context */
```

Handling Displays

The **XtOpenDisplay** function opens the display, initializes it, and adds it to the specified application context by invoking the **XtDisplayInitialize** function. The **XtOpenDisplay** function, shown here, is itself automatically invoked by the **XtVaAppInitialize** and **XtAppInitialize** functions.

```
Display *XtOpenDisplay(app_context, display_string,
                       application_name,
                       application_class, options,
                       num_options, argc, argv)
   XtAppContext app_context;    /* Specifies the application
                                   context */
   String display_string;       /* Display string or NULL */
   String application_name;     /* Name of application
                                   instance usually NULL */
   String application_class;    /* Application class */
   XrmOptionDescRec options;    /* Specifies command line
                                   parsing for resources */
   Cardinal num_options;        /* Number of entries in
                                   options list */
   Cardinal *argc;              /* Pointer to number of
                                   command line arguments */
   String *argv;                /* Command line parameters */
```

The specific display string is system dependent. UNIX systems use the format *hostname:display-number:screen-number*. Default values include the current host and the screen specified by the server.

The **XtOpenDisplay** function determines the application name by checking for the following conditions, in order:

❏ The application name follows the *-name* entry in a command line specified by the parameter *argv*, if any command is specified.

❏ The application name is found in the *application_name* parameter, provided that this parameter is not NULL.

❏ The application name is the value of the environment variable RESOURCE_NAME if this variable is not.

❏ The application name is derived from the name used to invoke the program found in *argv*[0] if this value is not NULL. All directory and file type components must be removed.

❏ If none of the preceding conditions are met, the application name is "main".

The **XtDisplayInitialize** function actually places display information in the application context. This function must be called implicitly or explicitly before any widgets can be created for the given display. The **XtDisplayInitialize** function is usually invoked by the **XtOpenDisplay** function. The only difference between these two functions is that the **XtDisplayInitialize** function, shown here, uses the *display* parameter, whereas the **XtOpenDisplay** function uses the *display_string* parameter.

```
Display *XtDisplayInitialize(app_context, display_string,
                             application_name,
                             application_class, options,
                             num_options, argc, argv)
  XtAppContext app_context;     /* Specifies the application
                                    context */
  Display *display_string       /* Display to initialize */
  String application_name;      /* Name of application
                                    instance usually NULL */
  String application_class;     /* Application class */
  XrmOptionDescRec options;     /* Specifies command line
                                    parsing for resources */
  Cardinal num_options;         /* Number of entries in
                                    options list */
  Cardinal *argc;               /* Pointer to number of
                                    command line arguments */
  String *argv;                 /* Command line parameters */
```

Creating the Initial Shell Widget

The **XtAppCreateShell** function creates a Shell widget, one of whose classes is applicationShellWidgetClass, the class of the root widget found at the top of every widget tree. All widget applications must have a Shell widget and thus must call this function explicitly or implicitly. They may create the applicationShell widget by calling either the **XtVaAppInitialize** or **XtAppInitialize** function. **XtAppCreateShell** takes the following form:

```
Widget XtAppCreateShell(application_name, application_class,
                 widget_class, display, args,
                 num_args);
    String application_name;      /* Name of application
                                     instance usually NULL */
    String application_class;     /* Application class */
    WidgetClass widget_class;     /* Widget class of top-level
                                     widget */
    Display *display;             /* Display furnishing
                                     resources */
    ArgList args;                 /* Argument list for created
                                     shell widget resources */
    Cardinal num_args;            /* Number of entries in
                                     argument list */
```

Note The *application_name* and *application_class* parameters of the **XtDisplayInitialize** function must be the same as the corresponding parameters of the **XtAppCreateShell** function. The easiest way to ensure this correspondance is to use the **XtVaAppInitialize** or **XtAppInitialize** function to initialize the application.

Exiting Applications

There are several ways to exit X Window programs. The simplest way is via an operating system procedure, such as the UNIX **exit** procedure. This procedure frees the client's resources associated with the application and undoes the X server connection. The server releases all its resources associated with the application, including the windows.

Sometimes a program must continue processing after closing its displays. In this case, use either the **XtDestroyApplicationContext** or **XtCloseDisplay** function.

```
void XtDestroyApplicationContext(app context)
  XtAppContext app_context;   /* Specifies application
                                 context to destroy */
```

The function **XtDestroyApplicationContext** can be called from anywhere within the application. It closes all displays in the application
context and ensures that all buffered requests are sent to the server
before breaking the link to the server. The application context is destroyed
only when all relevant events have been processed.

The function **XtCloseDisplay** closes a display but does not destroy
the application context. It also ensures that all buffered requests are sent
to the server before breaking the link to the server.

```
void XtCloseDisplay(display)
  Display *display;        /* Specifies display to close */
```

 Note   Before using either the function **XtCloseDisplay** or **XtDestroy-
ApplicationContext**, be sure to call the function **XtDestroyWidget** to
destroy the top-level Shell widget associated with the display. Otherwise, the widget data structure remains in the application program
but serves no useful purpose.

The function **XtDestroyWidget**, shown here, destroys the specified
widget and all its children.

```
void XtDestroyWidget(w)
  Widget w;                /* Specifes widget to destroy */
```

This function also destroys the widget's window. The actual widget destruction process involves two steps but is transparent to application writers.

Widgets

Widgets are at the heart of the Intrinsics and Motif toolkits. Now that
you have seen widgets in action in Motif programs, it is time to explore

widgets in greater depth. First, this section introduces the widget life cycle; then it examines a particular type of widget, Shell widgets. The next section, "Resources," looks at Core widgets and Composite widgets and their resources.

Widget Life Cycle

Recall from Chapter 4, "Windows and Windowing Techniques," that the window life cycle included window creation, window mapping and unmapping, and window destruction. The widget life cycle is similar to the window life cycle, including widget creation, widget realization, widget mapping and unmapping, and widget destruction. The complete widget creation process consists of the following activities:

❏ The widgets are allocated and provided with resources. These widgets may or may not be added to their parent's managed widgets. This step invokes the **XtCreateWidget** function and may invoke the **XtManageChild** function.

❏ Composite widgets are notified of managed children. This process begins at the bottom of the widget tree and moves up the tree. Depending on the space available, a parent widget may change some or all of its children's sizes and positions. It may also negotiate with its own parent to obtain more space on the screen.

❏ The **XtRealizeWidget** function creates and maps the windows, from the top of the widget tree down. It then maps all managed widgets.

Widget Creation

The **XtCreateWidget** function creates a widget instance. Among its activities are the following:

❏ Determining whether the widget class and its superclasses have been initialized and initializing them if necessary

❏ Allocating memory for the widget instance

❏ Allocating memory for the parent's constraints, if any

❏ Initializing the resource fields

❏ Initializing the widget

❏ Placing the widget in the list of its parent's children, if the parent is a Composite widget

❏ Initializing the parent's constraints, if the parent is a Constraint widget

These activities are transparent to the application writer.

XtCreateWidget looks like this:

```
Widget XtCreateWidget(name, object_class, parent, args,
                      num_args)
  String name;                /* Specifies resource instance
                                 name for created widget */
  WidgetClass object_class;  /* Widget class pointer for
                                 created object */
  Widget parent;              /* Parent widget */
  ArgList args;               /* Argument list overriding
                                 all other resource
                                 specifications */
  Cardinal num_args;          /* Number of entries in argument
                                 list */
```

Several restrictions govern **XtCreateWidget** arguments. The *name* argument must be different from the resource instance names of all of its siblings. The *object_class* parameter must be of the class objectClass or one of its subclasses. The *parent* argument must be of the class Object or one of its subclasses.

The **XtVaCreateWidget** function is similar to the **XtCreateWidget** function, with the *args* and *num_args* parameters replaced by a *varargs* list.

The **XtCreateManagedWidget** function, shown here, creates managed widgets. It is a convenience function that calls the **XtCreateWidget** function and then the **XtManageChild** function.

```
Widget XtCreateManagedWidget(name, widget_class, parent,
                             args, num_args)
  String name;                /* Specifies resource instance
                                 name for created widget */
```

```
WidgetClass widget_class;  /* Widget class pointer for
                              created object */
Widget parent;             /* Parent widget */
ArgList args;              /* Argument list overriding
                              all other resource
                              specifications */
Cardinal num_args;         /* Number of entries in argument
                              list */
```

Several restrictions govern **XtCreateManagedWidget** arguments. The *widget_class* parameter must be of the class rectObjClass or one of its subclasses. The *parent* argument must be of the class Composite or one of its subclasses.

The **XtVaCreateManagedWidget** function is similar to the **XtCreateManagedWidget** function, with the *args* and *num_args* parameters replaced by a varags list.

Widget Realization

The **XtRealizeWidget** function realizes (creates and maps a window for) a widget instance. Among its activities are the following:

❑ Calling a procedure to handle any managed children for each composite widget within the widget tree from the bottom up.

❑ Creating an XSetWindowAttributes data structure and populating it with information derived from the Core widget fields.

❑ Adding widget related information to the XSetWindowAttributes data structure, realizing the widget, and creating the window.

❑ Realizing managed children of composite widgets, mapping their windows if the Boolean parameter *mapped_when_managed* is TRUE.

XtRealizeWidget looks like this:

```
void XtRealizeWidget(w)
  Widget w;                /* Specifies the widget */
```

The specified widget must be of the Core class or any subset of that class. The activities in the preceding list are transparent to the application writer.

The **XtIsRealize** function, shown next, verifies whether a given widget has been realized. The specified widget must be of the Core class or any subset of that class.

```
Boolean XtIsRealize(w)
   Widget w;              /* Specifies the widget */
```

Widget Unrealization

The **XtUnrealizeWidget** function *unrealizes* a widget instance. It destroys windows for a specified widget and its descendants but does not destroy popup windows. Among its activities are the following:

❑ Unmanaging a managed widget.

❑ Executing any procedures named **XtUnrealizeCallback**.

❑ Destroying the widget's window and any subwindows by invoking the **XDestroyWindow** function.

XtUnrealizeWidget is shown here.

```
void XtUnrealizeWidget(w)
   Widget w;              /* Specifies the widget */
```

The specified widget must be of the Core class or any subset of that class. The activities in the preceding list are transparent to the application writer.

Widget Destruction

The **XtDestroyWidget** function destroys a widget instance. Widget destruction requires two steps to prevent any reference to destroyed widgets.

In the first step, **XtDestroyWidget** prepares widgets for destruction, but does not actually destroy them, by doing the following:

❏ The function verifies the widget's *being_destroyed* field. If this Boolean field has the value TRUE, the procedure returns without further processing. If the widget's *being_destroyed* field is FALSE, the procedure sets the field to TRUE for the widget and all its descendants, including popup children.

❏ The function adds the widget to a widget destroy list. Descendants may not occur after their parents on the destroy list.

The second step of widget destruction occurs only after all procedures associated with the current event have been called. In the second phase, **XtDestroyWidget** does the following:

❏ The function calls destroy callback procedures for the widget and its descendants, including popups, starting from the children.

❏ The function calls the **XtUnmanageChild** function where required and then calls the widget parent's *delete_child* procedure. These calls are not performed for popup children.

❏ The function calls destroy procedures for the widget and its descendants.

❏ The function calls the **XDestroyWindow** function for widgets that have windows (realized widgets).

❏ The function descends the widget tree and destroys windows for all realized popup windows, deallocates callback lists, and deallocates children of composite widgets.

The preceding activities are transparent to the application writer. Consult your system manual for more detailed information on widget destruction.

Shell Widgets

A Shell widget is an interface between the window manager and the application. The root of every widget tree contains exactly one shell widget, which itself contains a single child widget. The child widget completely fills the shell. The Shell widget insulates its unique child from the outside world much as an eggshell surrounds and insulates the egg from the outside world.

Xt Intrinsics defines four classes of shells available to users: OverrideShell, TransientShell, TopLevelShell, and ApplicationShell. Other shell classes are for internal use and do not appear in this book.

The OverrideShell contains very transient widgets whose windows are not handled by the window manager. OverrideShells often contain popup menus.

The TransientShell holds transient widgets that are children of a main widget. Their windows are handled by the window manager. TransientShells may contain popup dialog boxes.

The TopLevelShell holds relatively permanent widgets associated with the top-level windows in an application.

The ApplicationShell holds the application's main widget. Usually each application has one, and only one, application shell.

Resources

Resources are named data elements whose value may change. The most common resources are associated with widgets, but any data structure can contain modifiable resources. Resources allow both technical personnel and end users to customize applications with a minimum of errors. If the application programmer (or widget writer) has judiciously employed default resource values, most users can meet their information needs without having to specify resource values. However, power users can customize resources as they see fit. To do so, they must be familiar with the order in which X Window looks for resource specifications and with resource naming conventions.

Resource Specification Order

At the time of widget creation, the toolkit determines resource specification as follows:

1. First the toolkit looks for the resource specification in the argument list or the *varargs* parameter of the widget creation function.

2. Then the toolkit looks for the resource specification in the display's resource database.

3. Finally, if the toolkit cannot find the resource specification either in the widget creation function or the display's resource database, the toolkit assigns the widget the default resource value for its particular widget class. This value may be inherited from any of the widget's superclasses.

 Note   It is very important to spell resource names correctly. A mis-spelled name will not generate an error message. Instead, it generates the wrong resource. Such errors can be quite difficult to detect.

Resource Naming Conventions

To reduce the frequency of resource naming errors, employ the following resource naming conventions:

❏ Start the resource name with a lowercase letter and capitalize individual words. The resource name should reference field names that contain only lowercase letters and underscores. Its *symbolic name* is the resource name preceded by the string "XtN". The compiler can detect spelling errors in the symbolic name.

❏ Start symbolic names for resource classes with the string "XtC". *Resource classes* are groups of related resources that can be assigned a common value. For example, all border widths may be assigned a value of 2.

❏ Use the resource representation types, whose names start with the string "XtR" followed by an uppercase letter, that are defined in the header file <X11/StringDefs.h>.

Table 5-2 lists in alphabetical order resource types appearing in the <X11/StringDefs.h> header file, their type, and where they are defined.

Wildcards in Resource Specifications

The *resource specification* indicates the resource value for one or a related group of widgets. A given widget's explicit resource specification

Resource Representation Types

Resource Type	Field	Where Defined
XtRAcceleratorTable	XtAccelerators	Intrinsics
XtRAtom	Atom	Xlib
XtRBitmap	Pixmap	Xlib
XtRBoolean	Boolean	Intrinsics
XtRBool	Bool	Xlib
XtRCallback	XtCallbackList	Intrinsics
XtRCardinal	Cardinal	Intrinsics
XtRColor	XColor	Xlib
XtRColormap	Colormap	Xlib
XtRCursor	Cursor	Xlib
XtRDimension	Dimension	Intrinsics
XtRDisplay	Display *	Xlib
XtREnum	XtEnum	Intrinsics
XtRFile	FILE *	<stdio.h>
XtRFloat	float	C language
XtRFont	XFontStruct *	Xlib
XtRFunction	(*)( )	C language
XtRGeometry	String	Intrinsics
XtRInitialState	int	ICCCM
XtRInt	int	C language
XtRLongBoolean	long	C language
XtRObject	Object	Intrinsics
XtRPixel	Pixel	Xlib
XtRPixmap	Pixmap	Xlib

TABLE
5-2
Cont.

Resource Representation Types

Resource Type	Field	Where Defined
XtRPointer	XtPointer	Intrinsics
XtRPosition	Position	Intrinsics
XtRScreen	Screen *	Xlib
XtRShort	short	C language
XtRString	String	Intrinsics
XtRStringArray	String *	Intrinsics
XtRStringTable	String *	Intrinsics
XtRTranslationTable	XtTranslations	Intrinsics
XtRUnsignedChar	unsigned char	C language
XtRVisual	Visual *	Xlib
XtRWidget	Widget	Intrinsics
XtRWidgetClass	WidgetClass	Intrinsics
XtRWidgetList	WidgetList	Intrinsics
XtRWindow	Window	Xlib

Notes: Asterisks (*) represent wildcards.
ICCCM stands for *Inter-Client Communications Convention Manual.*

lists the names of all its ancestors, starting with the Shell widget. It also includes the program name and the name and selected value of the specified resource.

For example, in the first version of this chapter's Hello World program, you can set the *hellow* widget's border color to gray with the following resource specification:

```
example1.XHellow.hellow.borderColor : gray
```

The value example1 refers to the program name. The value XHellow refers to the Shell widget name, which is also the application class. The value hellow refers to the widget name, returned by the **XtVaCreateManaged-Widget** function. The resource borderColor is set to gray.

Coding explicit resource specifications can be tedious. Proper use of the wildcard (*) simplifies the coding burden when, as is often the case, similar resources assume the same value. For example, to assign a gray border color to all child widgets of the XHellow Shell widget, code the following resource specification:

```
example1.XHellow*borderColor : gray
```

The asterisk denotes that for the program example1, all widgets descending from the XHellow widget (the Shell widget) have a gray border color.

The wildcard symbol is quite powerful. To assign a gray border color to all widgets, code the following resource specification:

```
*borderColor : gray
```

These resource specifications can be placed within the resource database by using Xlib functions such as **XrmPutResource**. Most applications do not create or modify the resource database. However, they may specify desired resources that override the database resource specifications.

All widgets of the resource class XtCBorderColor can be set to gray with the following specification:

```
*BorderColor : gray
```

Resource Files

Users can specify desired resources in the command line as shown in Table 5-3.

Several examples show how to specify window resources through the command line.

The following command executes the *prog* application, generating a window whose width is 200 pixels and whose height is 150 pixels on the

TABLE
5-3

Command-Line Resource Specifications

Option	Resource Name	Resource Value
–background	*background	Next argument
–bg	*background	Next argument
–bordercolor	*borderColor	Next argument
–bd	*borderColor	Next argument
–borderwidth	.borderWidth	Next argument
–bw	.borderWidth	Next argument
–display	.display	Next argument
–foreground	*foreground	Next argument
–fg	*foreground	Next argument
–font	*font	Next argument
–fn	*font	Next argument
–geometry	.geometry	Next argument
–iconic	.iconic	"on"
–name	.name	Next argument
–reverse	.reverseVideo	"on"
–rv	.reverseVideo	"on"
+rv	.reverseVideo	"off"
–selectionTimeout	.selectionTimeout	Next argument
–synchonous	.synchronous	"on"
+synchonous	.synchronous	"off"
–title	.title	Next argument
–xnllanguage	.xnlLanguage	Next argument
–xrm	next argument	Next argument
Note: Asterisks (*) represent wildcards.		

screen. The window's right edge is 20 pixels inside the right edge of the screen and 25 pixels below the top of the screen.

```
prog -geometry 200x150-20+25
```

The following command places a window whose width is 200 pixels and whose height is 150 pixels on the screen. The window's left edge is 20 pixels inside the left edge of the screen and 25 pixels below the top of the screen.

```
prog -geometry 200x150+20+25
```

The following command sets the window background color to light gray and the foreground color to yellow. Beware of eyestrain when using such commands.

```
prog -bg lightgray -fg yellow
```

Core Widget Resources

Table 5-4 lists core widget resources. A typical core resource name is XtNborderColor. This resource belongs to the class XtCBorderColor. Usually, to generate the class name from the resource name, replace the third letter (N) with a C and capitalize the next letter. The following description indicates the class name when the name transformation rule does not apply. Motif replaces the second letter (t) in the resource name and resource class by an m; for example, Motif defines a resource name XmNborderColor and an associated resource class name XmCBorder Color. Watch your spelling—errors are easy to make and can be hard to locate.

The XtNdestroyCallback resource is a list of callback procedures invoked when the widget is destroyed. Its class name is XtCCallback. This resource is infrequently used by applications.

The XtNx, XtNy, XtNwidth, XtNheight, and XtNborderWidth resources determine the widget's window geometry. XtNx and XtNy resources have the class name XtCPosition. Always use these resources to move and resize widgets; if you use the corresponding Xlib function calls, Xt

TABLE 5-4

Core Widget Resources

Name	Type	Default Value
XtNdestroyCallback	XtCallbackList	NULL
XtNx	Position	0
XtNy	Position	0
XtNwidth	Dimension	0
XtNheight	Dimension	0
XtNsensitive	Boolean	TRUE
XtNancestorsensitive	Boolean	TRUE
XtNscreen	Screen pointer	(Description follows)
XtNdepth	Cardinal	(Description follows)
XtNcolormap	Colormap pointer	(Description follows)
XtNbackground	Pixel	(Description follows)
XtNbackgroundPixmap	Pixmap	(Description follows)
XtNborderWidth	Dimension	1
XtNborderColor	Pixel	(Description follows)
XtNborderPixmap	Pixmap	(Description follows)
XtNmappedWhenManaged	Boolean	TRUE
XtNtranslations	XtTranslations	(Description follows)
XtNaccelerators	XtAccelerators	None

Intrinsics will have incorrect information about the widget's window geometry.

The XtNsensitive and XtNancestorsensitive resources both have the class name XtCSensitive. They indicate whether a widget reacts to user input and, consequently, invokes the appropriate callback functions. Sensitivity propagates downward from parent to child. To turn off a pushbutton widget, set its XtNsensitive resource to FALSE by using the **XtSetSensitive** function. The XtNancestorsensitive resource indicates whether a widget's parent (or previous ancestor) reacts to user input. Applications may not modify this resource.

The XtNscreen, XtNdepth, and XtNcolormap resources contain pointers to the display screen, the screen's depth (number of bits per pixel), and colormap. The XtNscreen resource is specified only for shell widgets; other widgets are displayed on the same screen as their parent. The XtNdepth resource may be specified only at widget creation time. Top-level Shell widgets obtain default values for these resources from the root window's default values; other widgets obtain default values from their parents.

The XtNbackground, XtNbackgroundPixmap, XtNborderWidth, XtNborderColor, and XtNborderPixmap resources determine the widget's background and border attributes. Both the resource XtNbackgroundPixmap and the resource XtNborderPixmap have the class name XtCPixmap. You can set either the background color or the background pixmap, but not both. The resource set last takes precedence. The same rules apply to the border color and border pixmap. The default value of the XtNbackground resource is XtDefaultBackground, usually the WhitePixel value. The default value of the XtNbackgroundPixmap resource is XtUnspecifiedPixmap, which sets the background to XtNbackground. The default value of the XtNborderColor resource is XtDefaultForeground, usually the BlackPixel value. The default value of the XtNborderPixmap resource is XtUnspecifiedPixmap.

The XtNmappedWhenManaged resource indicates whether the widget appears on the screen when its parent allocates it space and manages its geometry.

The XtNtranslations resource defines a translation table that converts server-generated input events into widget and application functions. The widget programmer defines a default value for all widgets belonging to a given class. The XtNaccelerators resource defines an extended translation table associating an event for one widget and its impact on other widgets.

Composite Widget Resources

The Composite widget class is a superclass for other classes. Applications do not create widgets belonging to the Composite widget class. Applications rarely use any of the following resources:

Name	Type	Default
XtNinsertPosition	XtOrderProc	InsertAtEnd
XtNchildren	Widget pointer	(Description follows)
XtNnumChildren	Cardinal	(Description follows)

The XtNinsertPosition resource of type XtOrderProc specifies a procedure that returns the new child's position in the list of children.

The associated XtNchildren and XtNnumchildren resources (both of class XtCReadOnly) supply the list and number of children.

A composite widget is responsible for managing its children, in particular for the following:

❏ Handling *widget geometry*—the widget's size, border width, position on the screen, and stacking order—for the widget's children

❏ Mapping and unmapping the widget's children

❏ Deciding which child has the keyboard input focus—in other words, which child receives the keyboard input—at any given time

❏ Returning memory to the system when it is destroyed, which, in the case of a Composite widget's memory, is only after all its children have been destroyed

Callbacks

An essential aspect of toolkit programming is the use of callback functions, which inform an application that a user has referenced a widget. Rare is the toolkit program that does not contain at least one callback function. Usually, toolkit applications do not directly solicit user input, but involve a toolkit input handling procedure that itself solicits user input and invokes the appropriate callback routines.

Widget designers determine the specific callback procedure or procedures for their widgets. For example, a Scrollbar widget could have different callbacks for moving the slider and scrolling up or down by a page or a single unit. On the other hand, the widget designer can create a more sophisticated widget with a single callback procedure. In this case, the widget itself makes the necessary calculations. The application becomes simpler, but the widget becomes more complicated.

Coding Callback Procedures

Callback procedures are of the type XtCallbackProc. They assume the following form:

```
typedef void (*XtCallbackProc)(w, XtPointer, XtPointer);
    Widget w;                   /* Specifies widget for which the
                                   callback is registered */
    XtPointer client_data;  /* Data object defined by the
                                   application */
    XtPointer call_data;     /* Data object defined by the
                                   widget class */
```

Simple widgets, such as Pushbutton, usually set the *call_data* parameter to NULL. A single callback procedure may be used for more than one widget. In this case, the callback tests the *call_data* parameter to determine the appropriate widget. The Intrinsics pass the *client_data* to the application without any interpretation.

Adding and Removing Callbacks

Five Xt Intrinsics functions add and remove callbacks: **XtAddCallback**, **XtAddCallbacks**, **XtRemoveCallback**, and **XtRemoveCallbacks**. **XtRemoveAllCallbacks** removes all callbacks from a given callback list. **XtHasCallbacks** checks the status of a callback list.

The **XtAddCallback** function, shown here, adds the specifed callback procedure to the named callback list for the widget.

```
void XtAddCallback(w, callback_name, callback, client_data)
Widget w;                    /* Specifies widget to add the
                                callback procedure to */
String callback_name;        /* Specifies callback list to
                                add callback procedure to */
XtCallbackProc callback;     /* Specifies callback procedure */
XtPointer client_data;       /* Specifies value passed to
                                callback procedure or NULL */
```

Next, the **XtAddCallbacks** function adds the list of callback procedures, terminated by a NULL string, to the named callback list for the widget.

```
void XtAddCallbacks(w, callback_name, callbacks)
Widget w;                    /* Specifies widget to add the
                                callback procedures to */
String callback_name;        /* Specifies callback list to
                                add callback procedures to */
XtCallbackList callbacks;    /* Specifies list of callback
                                procedures and
                                associated client data */
```

The **XtRemoveCallback** function, shown next, removes the specifed callback procedure from the named callback list for the widget.

```
void XtRemoveCallback(w, callback_name, callback, client_data)
Widget w;                      /* Specifies widget to remove the
                                  callback procedure from */
String callback_name;          /* Specifies callback list to
                                  remove callback procedure
                                  from */
XtCallbackProc callback;       /* Specifies callback procedure
                                  to remove from list */
XtPointer client_data;         /* Specifies client data to match
                                  to remove the procedure */
```

The client data and the procedure must match for the **XtRemove-Callback** to remove the procedure.

Next, the **XtRemoveCallbacks** function removes all specifed callback procedures from the named callback list for the widget.

```
void XtRemoveCallbacks(w, callback_name, callbacks)
Widget w;                  /* Specifies widget to remove the
                              callback procedure from */
String callback_name;      /* Specifies callback list to
                              remove callback procedure
                              from */
XtCallbackList callbacks;  /* Specifies list of callback
                              procedures and associated
                              client data */
```

The client data and the procedure must match for the **XtRemove-Callbacks** to remove the procedure.

The **XtRemoveAllCallbacks** function, shown next, removes all callback procedures from a specified callback list.

```
void XtRemoveAllCallbacks(w, callback_name)
Widget w;                  /* Specifies widget to remove all
                              callback procedures from */
String callback_name;      /* Specifies callback list to
                              be removed */
```

The **XtHasCallbacks** function, shown here, checks a callback list's status.

```
typedef enum {
            XtCallbackNoList,
            XtCallbackHasNone,
            XtCallbackHasSome
          } XtCallbackStatus;
XtCallbackStatus XtHasCallbacks (w, callback_name)
Widget w;                  /* Specifies widget to check */
String callback_name;      /* Specifies callback list to
                              check */
```

If the widget does not have the specified callback list, **XtHasCallbacks** returns the value XtCallbackNoList. If the callback list exists but is empty, **XtHasCallbacks** returns the value XtCallbackHasNone. If the callback list exists and has at least one callback procedure, **XtHasCallbacks** returns the value XtCallbackHasSome.

RowColumn Widget Program: Example 3

The next example applies a composite RowColumn widget to create three buttons: the fbutton, which contains the character string "Levi Reiss"; the sbutton, which contains the character string "Joseph Radin"; and the tbutton, which contains the character string "To Exit Click Here Once !!!".

The following callback routine includes the **exit** function, which terminates the program when it is invoked, thus doing exactly what it says.

```
void tbutton_func (w, client_data, call_data)
Widget w;
XtPointer client_data;
XtPointer call_data;
{
  printf("tbutton was selected and program terminated\n");
  exit(0);
}
```

The **XtVaCreateManagedWidget** function is invoked several times to create all widgets except for the top-level widget. Each of these function calls takes four arguments: the widget name in quotation marks, the widget class, the parent widget, and NULL to terminate the *varargs* list. The "rc" widget belongs to the xmRowColumnWidgetClass, and its three child widgets belong to the xmPushButtonWidgetClass. For example,

```
rc = XtVaCreateManagedWidget("rc",
                    xmRowColumnWidgetClass,
                    theParent, NULL);
```

and

```
fbutton = XtVaCreateManagedWidget("fbutton",
                    xmPushButtonWidgetClass,
                    rc, NULL);
```

The three button widget creation functions are interspersed with the **XtAddCallback** function which includes four parameters in this case, the widget that triggers the callback; the callback resource list; the callback procedure defined at the top of the program; and 0, because no data is passed to the callback procedure. A typical function is

```
XtAddCallback(fbutton, XmNactivateCallback,
            fbutton_func, 0);
```

The complete listing for Example 3 is shown here.

```
/*  Step 1  Motif header file */
#include <Xm/Xm.h>

/*  Step 2  Public header files for widget classes used */
#include <Xm/RowColumn.h>
#include <Xm/PushB.h>

/*  Callback for first button defined */
void fbutton_func (w, client_data, call_data)
Widget w;
XtPointer client_data;
XtPointer call_data;

/* Print if above callback executed */
{
  printf("fbutton was selected and responded here ... \n");
}

/*  Callback for second button defined */
void sbutton_func (w, client_data, call_data)
Widget w;
XtPointer client_data;
XtPointer call_data;
{  printf("sbutton was selected and responded here ... \n");
}

/*  Callback for third button defined */
void tbutton_func (w, client_data, call_data)
Widget w;
XtPointer client_data;
XtPointer call_data;
```

```
{
  printf("tbutton was selected and program terminated\n");
  exit(0);
}

/* Step 3  Initialize the Program and the Toolkit */
main(argc, argv)
int    argc;
char   *argv[];
{
/* Declares variables of the Window type data structure */
Window theParent, rc, fbutton, sbutton, tbutton;
XtAppContext app_context;

  theParent = XtVaAppInitialize(&app_context, "XExample3", NULL,
                                0, &argc, argv, NULL, NULL);

/* Step 4  Create and Manage Widgets */
  rc = XtVaCreateManagedWidget("rc",
                                xmRowColumnWidgetClass,
                                theParent, NULL);

  fbutton = XtVaCreateManagedWidget("fbutton",
                                    xmPushButtonWidgetClass,
                                    rc, NULL);

/* Step 5  Add a callback function */
  XtAddCallback(fbutton, XmNactivateCallback,
                fbutton_func, 0);

  sbutton = XtVaCreateManagedWidget("sbutton",
                                    xmPushButtonWidgetClass,
                                    rc, NULL);

  XtAddCallback(sbutton, XmNactivateCallback,
                sbutton_func, 0);

  tbutton = XtVaCreateManagedWidget("tbutton",
                                    xmPushButtonWidgetClass,
                                    rc, NULL);

  XtAddCallback(tbutton, XmNactivateCallback,
```

```
                           tbutton_func, 0);

/*  Step 6   Realize the Widget */
   XtRealizeWidget(theParent);

/*  Step 7   Event Loop */
   XtAppMainLoop(app_context);

}
```

The results of running this program are shown in Figure 5-4.

The following MAKE file was used to process this program in SCO Open Desktop. The MAKE file for other X Window implementations varies.

```
RM = rm - f
CC = cc
CFLAGS = -O
INCLUDES = -I/usr/include -I/usr/include/X11
LIBS = -lXm -lXt -lX11 -lsocket -lmalloc -lPW
.c.o.
$(RM) $@
$(CC) -c $(CFLAGS) $(INCLUDES) $*.c
all:: example3
example3: example3.o
$(RM) $@
$(CC) -o $@ $(CFLAGS) example3.o $(LIBS)
@echo makefile for example3 - done!
```

Several Widgets Program: Example 4

The following program demonstates the creation of several widgets of different types. It generates a MainWindow widget that manages the gcometry of its work area with a scrollbar, and a Frame widget, which is an empty area that looks three dimensional. Pressing a pushbutton produces another pushbutton that allows the user to quit the program.

The more complicated nature of this application requires the use of seven include files. The standard Motif include file is <Xm/Xm.h>. The file <Xm/MainW.h> is required to create a MainWindow widget. The file

FIGURE
5-4

Highlighting right window of a RowColumn widget

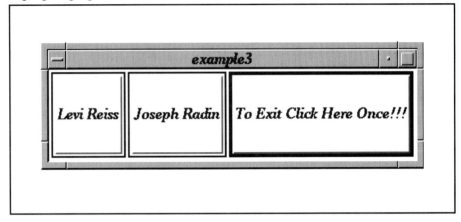

<Xm/RowColumn.h> is required for RowColumn widgets and was used in the previous example. The file <Xm/Frame.h> refers to Frame widgets. The file <Xm/PushB.h> is used for PushButton widgets as in the previous example. The file <Xm/CascadeB.h> is used for Cascade buttons that you click to pull down a menu, and the file <Xm/MessageB.h> is used for help message boxes.

The **XmCreateMenuBar** function creates a special RowColumn widget known as a menu bar. Because it only creates the menu bar but does not manage it, this function is followed by the **XtManageChild** function. After creating the Frame widget, the program calls the **XmMainWindow-SetAreas** function that defines the widgets for the main window. Although MainWindow is a subclass of ScrolledWindow, it is a good idea to define the main window scrollbars to promote maximum flexibility. The **XmCreatePulldownMenu** function creates the pulldown menu. The **XtVaSetValues** function sets resources for the pushbutton widget.

The complete program listing for Example 4 is shown here.

```
#include <Xm/Xm.h>
#include <Xm/MainW.h>
#include <Xm/RowColumn.h>
#include <Xm/Frame.h>
#include <Xm/PushB.h>
#include <Xm/CascadeB.h>
#include <Xm/MessageB.h>
```

```
/*  Callback for quit button definition */
void quitbutton_func (w, client_data, call_data)
Widget w;
XtPointer client_data;
XtPointer call_data;

/* Print if quit callback executed */
{
 printf("Quit button was selected and program terminated\n");
 exit(0);
}

main(argc, argv)
int    argc;
char  *argv[];
{
Window theParent, thewindow, thebar, theframe, thebutton,
        themenu, quitbutton;
XtAppContext app_context;

   theParent = XtVaAppInitialize(&app_context, "XExample4",
                              NULL, 0, &argc, argv,
                              NULL, NULL);

   thewindow = XtVaCreateManagedWidget("thewindow",
                                    xmMainWindowWidgetClass,
                                    theParent, NULL);

   thebar = XmCreateMenuBar(thewindow, "thebar", NULL, 0);

   XtManageChild(thebar);

   theframe = XtVaCreateManagedWidget("theframe",
                                    xmFrameWidgetClass,
                                    thewindow, NULL);

   XmMainWindowSetAreas(thewindow, thebar, NULL, NULL, NULL,
                    theframe);

   thebutton = XtVaCreateManagedWidget("thebutton",
                                  xmCascadeButtonWidgetClass,
```

```
                               thebar, NULL);

     themenu = XmCreatePulldownMenu(thebar, "themenu", NULL, 0);

     quitbutton = XtVaCreateManagedWidget("quitbutton",
                                  xmPushButtonWidgetClass,
                                  themenu, NULL);

     XtVaSetValues(thebutton, XmNsubMenuId, themenu, NULL);
     XtAddCallback(quitbutton, XmNactivateCallback,
                    quitbutton_func, 0);

         XtRealizeWidget(theParent);

         XtAppMainLoop(app_context);

}
```

The results of running this program are shown in Figure 5-5.

The following MAKE file was used to process this program in SCO Open Desktop. The MAKE file for other X Window implementations varies.

PushButton widgets — after pushing

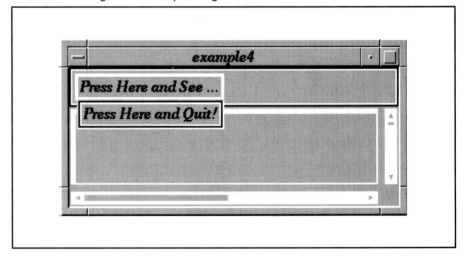

```
RM = rm - f
UU = cc
CFLAGS = -O
INCLUDES = -I/usr/include -I/usr/include/X11
LIBS = -lXm -lXt -lX11 -lsocket -lmalloc -lPW
.c.o:
$(RM) $@
$(CC) -c $(CFLAGS) $(INCLUDES) $*.c
all:: example4
example4: example4.o
$(RM) $@
$(CC) -o $@ $(CFLAGS) example4.o $(LIBS)
@echo makefile for example4 - done!
```

Popups

Popups are transient widgets; they appear on the screen for a short time. Most popup widgets are either menus or dialog boxes. A *dialog box* is an onscreen box that requests user input or displays a message, or both. For example, a dialog box may request that a user confirm file deletion. Dialog boxes appear on the screen only for the time of the dialog. For example, a box pops up when the user attempts to delete a file and disappears when the user confirms or cancels file deletion. Clicking a Cascade button pops up a menu. The menu disappears when the user selects an item.

Motif offers several functions for creating popups. The **XmCreate-PopupMenu** function creates a popup menu that can be invoked by pressing a button in the selected window or in the main application window. The menu usually pops up at the pointer location. The **XmCreatePulldownMenu** function creates a pulldown menu that is positioned just below the button that in essence created it. In spite of its name, a pulldown menu is a type of popup.

There are five steps in creating a pulldown menu:

1. Create a menu bar.

2. Create a xmCascadeButtonWidgetClass button that is a child of the menu bar.

3. Create an empty menu using the XmCreatePulldownMenu as a child of the menu bar.

4. Create pushbuttons (widgets of the xmPushButtonWidgetClass) as children of the pushbutton menu.

5. Pop up the pulldown (Cascade) menu.

These steps are illustrated in the program in Example 5.

Popup Help Menu Program: Example 5

The final example in this chapter creates a popup help menu. It includes a few items worthy of particular note. The following lines assign the *client_data* parameter to a local variable of type Widget and call the **XtManageChild** function to place the dialog widget on the screen.

```
{
Widget keep_data;

  keep_data = client_data;
  printf("Help button was selected ...\n");
  XtManageChild(keep_data);
}
```

The following lines create the widget associated with the Help box.

```
thehelp = XtVaCreateManagedWidget("thehelp",
                xmCascadeButtonWidgetClass,
                thebar, NULL);

XtVaSetValues(thebar, XmNmenuHelpWidget, thehelp, NULL);

thehelpbox = XmCreateMessageDialog(thehelp, "thehelpbox",
                                   NULL, 0);
```

The standard box contains a Cancel button and a HELP button. The following lines remove these two buttons.

```
dummy = XmMessageBoxGetChild(thehelpbox,
                XmDIALOG_CANCEL_BUTTON);
```

```
XtUnmanageChild (dummy),

   dummy = XmMessageBoxGetChild(thehelpbox,
                                 XmDIALOG_HELP_BUTTON);
```

The complete program listing for Example 5 is shown here.

```c
#include <Xm/Xm.h>
#include <Xm/MainW.h>
#include <Xm/RowColumn.h>
#include <Xm/Frame.h>
#include <Xm/PushB.h>
#include <Xm/CascadeB.h>
#include <Xm/MessageB.h>

void help_func (w, client_data, call_data)
Widget w;
XtPointer client_data;
XtPointer call_data;
{
Widget keep_data;

  keep_data = client_data;
  printf("Help button was selected ...\n");
  XtManageChild(keep_data);
}

void quitbutton_func (w, client_data, call_data)
Widget w;
XtPointer client_data;
XtPointer call_data;

{
 printf("Quit button was selected and program terminated\n");
 exit(0);
}

main(argc, argv)
int    argc;
char   *argv[];
{
```

```
Window theParent, thewindow, thebar, theframe, thebutton,
        themenu, quitbutton;
Window thehelp, thehelpbox, dummy;
XtAppContext app_context;

  theParent = XtVaAppInitialize(&app_context, "XExample5",
                                NULL, 0, &argc, argv,
                                NULL, NULL);

  thewindow = XtVaCreateManagedWidget("thewindow",
                                xmMainWindowWidgetClass,
                                theParent, NULL);

  thebar = XmCreateMenuBar(thewindow, "thebar", NULL, 0);

  XtManageChild(thebar);

  theframe = XtVaCreateManagedWidget("theframe",
                                      xmFrameWidgetClass,
                                      thewindow, NULL);

  XmMainWindowSetAreas(thewindow, thebar, NULL, NULL,
                    NULL, theframe);

  thebutton = XtVaCreateManagedWidget("thebutton",
                                      xmCascadeButtonWidgetClass,
                                      thebar, NULL);

  themenu = XmCreatePulldownMenu(thebar, "themenu", NULL, 0);

  quitbutton = XtVaCreateManagedWidget("quitbutton",
                                      xmPushButtonWidgetClass,
                                      themenu, NULL);

  XtVaSetValues(thebutton, XmNsubMenuId, themenu, NULL);

  XtAddCallback(quitbutton, XmNactivateCallback,
                quitbutton_func, 0);

  thehelp = XtVaCreateManagedWidget("thehelp",
                        xmCascadeButtonWidgetClass,
                        thebar, NULL);
```

```
XtVaSetValues(thebar, XmNmenuHelpWidget, thehelp, NULL);

thehelpbox = XmCreateMessageDialog(thehelp, "thehelpbox",
                                   NULL, 0);

dummy = XmMessageBoxGetChild(thehelpbox,
                            XmDIALOG_CANCEL_BUTTON);

XtUnmanageChild(dummy);

dummy = XmMessageBoxGetChild(thehelpbox,
                            XmDIALOG_HELP_BUTTON);

XtUnmanageChild(dummy);

XtAddCallback(thehelp, XmNactivateCallback,
              help_func, thehelpbox);

XtRealizeWidget(theParent);

XtAppMainLoop(app_context);

}
```

The results of running this program are shown in Figures 5-6 and 5-7.

The following MAKE file was used to process this program in SCO Open Desktop. The MAKE file for other X Window implementations varies.

```
RM = rm - f
CC = cc
CFLAGS = -O
INCLUDES = -I/usr/include -I/usr/include/X11
LIBS = -lXm -lXt -lX11 -lsocket -lmalloc -lPW
.c.o:
$(RM) $@
$(CC) -c $(CFLAGS) $(INCLUDES) $*.c
all:: example5
example5: example5.o
$(RM) $@
$(CC) -o $@ $(CFLAGS) example5.o $(LIBS)
@echo makefile for example5 - done!
```

**FIGURE
5-6**

Initial state of a popup menu

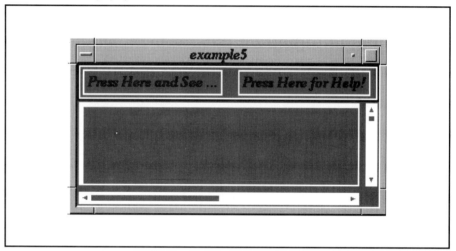

**FIGURE
5-7**

Help function of a popup menu

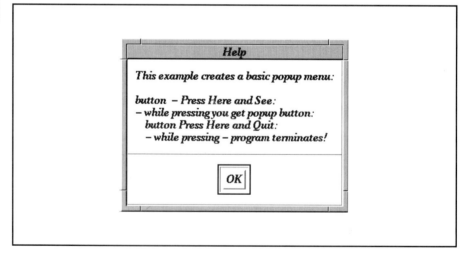

Resource Specifications for All Examples

The following resource specifications are associated with all the examples or with specific examples. For example, the resource specification

```
*borderWidth:2
```

indicates that all border widths are two pixels wide, unless otherwise specified. The resource specification

```
*hellow.foreground:black
```

associated with Example 1 indicates that the foreground of the *hellow* widget is black. Other resource specifications will be discussed later. For example, Chapter 6, "Text," discusses font resource specifications.

```
*fontList:*times-bold*180*iso8859-1
*borderWidth:2
*XmRowColumn.XmPushButton.background: lightgray
*XmRowColumn.XmPushButton.foreground: white
*XmRowColumn.XmPushButton.borderColor: black
#   BEGINNING OF RESOURCE SPECIFICATIONS FOR EXAMPLE1
*hellow.width:445
*hellow.height:50
*hellow.alignment:XmALIGNMENT_END
*helow.background: lightgray
*hellow.foreground:black
*hellow.labelString: Levi Reiss and Joseph Radin
 - X Window Inside and Out!
#   END OF RESOURCE SPECIFICATIONS FOR EXAMPLE1
#
#
#   BEGINNING OF RESOURCE SPECIFICATIONS FOR EXAMPLE2
*ghellow.width:445
*ghellow.height:100
*ghellow.alignment:XmALIGNMENT_END
*ghellow.background: gray
```

```
*ghellow.foreground: black
*ghellow.labelString: Levi Reiss and Joseph Radin
 - To Exit Click Here Once!
#   END OF RESOURCE SPECIFICATIONS FOR EXAMPLE2
#
#
#   BEGINNING OF RESOURCE SPECIFICATIONS FOR EXAMPLE3
#*rc.packing: XmPACK_TIGHT
*rc.background: gray
*rc.foreground: white
*rc.borderColor: black
*rc.orientation: XmHORIZONTAL
*fbutton.labelString: Levi Reiss
*sbutton.labelString: Joseph Radin
*tbutton.labelString: To Exit Click Here Once!!!
#   END OF RESOURCE SPECIFICATIONS FOR EXAMPLE3
#
#
#   BEGINNING OF RESOURCE SPECIFICATIONS FOR EXAMPLE4
*thewindow.width: 500
*thewindow.scrollingPolicy: XmAUTOMATIC
*thewindow.background: gray
*thewindow.foreground: lightgray
*thebar.background: gray
*thebar.foreground: black
*theframe.width: 700
*theframe.height: 700
*theframe.background: lightgray
*theframe.foreground: gray
*theframe.borderColor: white
*themenu.background: white
*themenu.foreground: gray
*thebutton.background: gray
*thebutton.foreground: black
*thebutton.borderColor: white
*thebutton.labelString: Press Here and See ...
*quitbutton.labelString: Press Here and Quit!
*quitbutton.background: gray
*quitbutton.foreground: black
*quitbutton.borderColor: white
#   END OF RESOURCE SPECIFICATIONS FOR EXAMPLE4
#
#
```

```
#  BEGINNING OF RESOURCE SPECIFICATIONS FOR EXAMPLE5
*thehelp.width: 200
*thehelp.scrollingPolicy: XmAUTOMATIC
*thehelp.background: lightgray
*thehelp.foreground: black
*thehelp.borderColor: white
*thehelp.labelString: Press Here for Help!
*thehelpbox.background: gray
*thehelpbox.foreground: black
*thehelpbox.width: 300
*thehelpbox.height: 400
*thehelpbox.messageString:This example creates a
 basic popup menu:\n\n\
button  - Press Here and See:\n\
- while pressing you get popup button:\n\
    button Press Here and Quit:\n\
    - while pressing - program terminates!
*thehelpbox.dialogTitle: Help
#  END OF RESOURCE SPECIFICATIONS FOR EXAMPLE5
#
#
```

Key Points

The Role of Toolkit

The X Toolkit interface sits between the applications programmer and the Xlib function calls, enabling programmers to instruct the computer with a higher-level language than the low-level Xlib calls. It replaces windows and events with the more sophisticated entities, widgets and callback procedures. The X Toolkit consists of two related parts: Xt Intrinsics and a proprietary toolkit. Xt Intrinsics defines a standard basic collection of functions and data structures. Proprietary toolkits are more flexible, powerful programming toolkits, each with its own look and feel.

continues . . .

Key Points

Toolkit Programmers

Two categories of programmers access the toolkits in different ways. Application programmers employ already existing widgets. To their way of thinking, a widget is a "black box," to be used but not necessarily completely understood. Widget programmers create and sell widgets. They must master the internal details of widget creation and modification.

Widget Tree

The widget tree is similar to the window hierarchy. The widget tree root is the Shell widget, associated with a child of the root window. The middle level consists of Composite widgets that regroup several child widgets to form the graphical user interface. The bottom level consists of Primitive widgets that have no children, such as labels, menu items, and pushbuttons.

Widget Classes

Xt Intrinsics defines four basic widget classes that pass fundamental characteristics to Intrinsics widget subclasses and all the toolkit widget classes. They are the Core, Composite, Constraint, and Shell widget classes. Toolkit widget classes are defined according to the rules for Intrinsics widget subclasses, plus they have rules and features of their own.

continues . . .

Key Points
(continued)

Motif Applications

You can create Motif applications with the following steps: Include the standard Motif header file; include the public header file for each widget class used; initialize the toolkit; create widgets; register callbacks, actions, and event handlers as required; realize the widgets; and initiate loop processing.

Widget Life Cycle

The widget life cycle is similar to the window life cycle. It includes widget creation, widget realization, widget mapping and unmapping, and widget destruction.

Resources

Resources are named data elements whose value may change. They allow both technical personnel and end users to customize applications. The toolkit recognizes resource specifications in the following order: First, it recognizes the argument list or *varargs* parameter of the widget creation function; if no value is specified here, it recognizes the resource specification in the display's resource database; finally, if none of these values is specified, it recognizes the default resource value of the widget class or superclass.

continues . . .

Key Points
(continued)

Callbacks

An essential aspect of toolkit programming is the use of callback functions. Usually, toolkit applications do not directly solicit user input, but invoke the appropriate callback routines.

Popups

Popups are transient widgets; they appear on the screen for a short time. Most popup widgets are either menus or dialog boxes. A dialog box is an onscreen box that requests user input or displays a message, or both.

CHAPTER

Text

*T*he previous chapter presented the two upper layers of X Window programming: Xt Intrinsics and the OSF/Motif proprietary toolkit. It introduced and applied basic toolkit components including widgets, toolkit resources, and callbacks. It developed several programs illustrating the Motif applications structure. These programs used toolkit resources to generate text, communicating with the user.

This chapter examines text generation in greater detail. It returns to the first level of X Window programming: Xlib functions. When correctly applied, these functions provide programmers with the power and flexibility required for the most sophisticated text processing, including foreign language character sets.

Fonts are a fundamental server resource. X Window offers a wide range of fonts to help the programmer convey messages to the user. Applying fonts to generate the text you want means mastering three interrelated aspects of X Window systems: font naming conventions; the font data structures; and programming, including the Xlib function calls. The chapter concludes with a series of graduated exercises that apply the fundamental aspects of text processing.

Font Names and Data Structures

Fonts are an associated group of bits that describe the size and shape of characters. Each font has a unique descriptive name. When you display text, you explicitly or implicitly apply one or more fonts.

Font Names

A font name uniquely denotes a given font. The maximum name length is 255 characters. The name is computer legible and conveys information to people. The font name contains 14 fields, as follows:

❏ The FOUNDRY field denotes the font supplier. A sample value for this field is Bitstream.

❏ The FAMILY_NAME field identifies a group of related fonts. A sample value for this field is Charter.

- ❏ The WEIGHT_NAME field denotes the font's blackness, as defined by FOUNDRY. A sample value for this field is Bold.

- ❏ The SLANT field identifies a font's inclination or slant. A sample value for this field is I, denoting italic.

- ❏ The SETWIDTH_NAME field denotes the FOUNDRY's estimate of the font's width. A sample value for this field is Normal.

- ❏ The ADD_STYLE_NAME field identifies additional typographical information describing the font. A sample value for this field is Serif. This field is not always present in the font name.

- ❏ The PIXEL_SIZE field denotes the font's body size for a given POINT_SIZE and RESOLUTION_Y. A sample value for this field is 12.

- ❏ The POINT_SIZE field identifies the body size for which the font was designed. A sample value for this field is 120.

- ❏ The RESOLUTION_X field denotes the horizontal resolution for which the font was designed. This value is measured in dots per inch. A sample value for this field is 75.

- ❏ The RESOLUTION_Y field denotes the vertical resolution for which the font was designed. This value is measured in dots per inch. A sample value for this field is 75.

- ❏ The SPACING field identifies how individual characters are assigned a width. The value P denotes a *proportional font,* in which character widths vary. The value M denotes a *monospaced font,* in which character widths are the same, independent of the character used. The body of this text is set in proportional fonts. Computer listings in this text are set in a monospaced font.

- ❏ The AVERAGE_WIDTH field denotes the average width of characters within the font, measured in tenths of pixels. A sample value for this field is 75.

- ❏ The CHARSET_REGISTRY field identifies the registration authority that owns the specific encoding. A sample value for this field is ISO8859.

- ❏ The CHARSET_ENCODING field identifies the coded character set. A sample value for this field is 1.

A sample font name is

Bitstream-Charter-Bold-I-Normal-12-120-75-75-P-75-ISO8859-1

Data Structures

The XFontStruct data structure contains extensive data describing each font. It is defined in the <X11/Xlib.h> header library as follows:

```
typedef struct {
    XExtData *ext_data;         /* Pointer to font
                                   extension data */
    Font fid;                   /* Font id */
    unsigned direction;         /* Hint about font
                                   drawing direction */
    unsigned min_char_or_byte2; /* First character in font */
    unsigned max_char_or_byte2; /* Last character in font */
    unsigned min_byte1;         /* First existing row */
    unsigned max_byte1;         /* Last existing row */
    Bool all_chars_exist;       /* Flag if all characters non
                                   zero size */
    unsigned default_char;      /* Print this for
                                   undefined character */
    int n_properties;           /* Number of properties */
    XFontProp *properties;      /* Pointer to array containing
                                   additional properties */
    XCharStruct min_bounds;     /* Minimum bounds over all
                                   existing characters */
    XCharStruct max_bounds;     /* Maximum bounds over all
                                   existing characters */
    XCharStruct *per_char;      /* First_char to last_char
                                   information */
    int ascent;                 /* Logical extent
                                   above baseline */
    int descent;                /* Logical extent
                                   below baseline */
} XFontStruct;
```

Several elements in the XFontStruct data structure are themselves composite objects, defined with the XCharStruct data structure, which describes aspects of the characters in a given font. XFontStruct is defined as follows:

```
typedef struct {
  short lbearing;              /* Distance from origin
                                  to raster's left edge */
  short rbearing;              /* Distance from origin
                                  to raster's right edge */
  short width;                 /* Advance to origin of
                                  next character */
  short ascent;                /* Baseline to raster's
                                  top edge */
  short descent;               /* Baseline to raster's
                                  bottom edge */
  unsigned short attributes;   /* Flags for each character */
} XCharStruct;
```

Figure 6-1 illustrates field names used in the XCharStruct data structure, and Table 6-1 defines them. These names are often used when
discussing fonts.

FIGURE 6-1

XCharStruct components

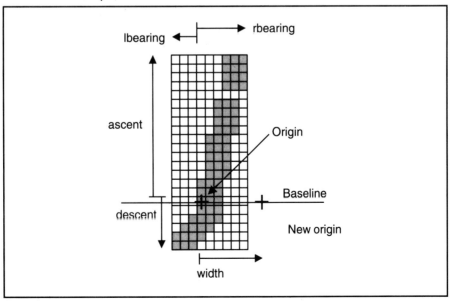

TABLE 6-1	Field Names in XCharStruct Data Structure

Field Name	Meaning
lbearing	Distance in pixels from origin to left edge of bounding rectangle
rbearing	Distance in pixels from origin to right edge of bounding rectangle
width	Character string width in pixels
ascent	Distance in pixels from origin to top edge of bounding rectangle
descent	Distance in pixels from origin to bottom edge of bounding rectangle
attributes	Reserved for extensions to X Window

Loading and Unloading Fonts

A font must reside in the X server's memory before any program can use it. Because the server memory is limited, a font is often loaded just prior to use. The **XLoadFont** function, shown here, loads the designated font and returns the font ID. It can generate BadAlloc and BadName errors.

```
Font XLoadFont(display, name)
   Display *display;              /* Specifies connection to
                                     the X server */
   Char *name;                    /* Font name */
```

The font name is a NULL-terminated string. The **XLoadFont** returns the font name but no other information.

A program requiring additional information such as the font size may invoke the Xlib **XQueryFont** function, shown next, which returns a pointer to the XFontStruct data structure. The program then extracts required information from the data structure.

```
XFontStruct *XQueryFont(display, font_ID)
    Display *display;              /* Specified connection to
                                      the X server */
    XID font_ID;                   /* Font ID or the GContextID */
```

The **XLoadQueryFont** function, shown next, combines the font load and query operations in a single function. It loads the designated font and returns a pointer to the XFontStruct data structure. It can generate a BadAlloc error.

```
Font XLoadQueryFont(display, name)
    Display *display;              /* Specifies connection to
                                      the X server */
    Char *name;                    /* Font name */
```

The font name is a NULL-terminated string.

When you know that you will no longer need a font, you should inform the server, which recovers the memory once the font is no longer referenced by any application.

The **XUnloadFont** function unloads a font previously loaded by the **XLoadFont** function. It removes the link between the font resource ID and the font. The font is freed only when there is no further reference to it. Do not reference either the data structure or the font after executing the **XUnloadFont** function. This function can generate a BadFont error. **XUnloadFont** looks like this:

```
XUnloadFont(display, font)
    Display *display;              /* Specifies connection to
                                      the X server */
    Font font;                     /* Font to be unloaded */
```

The **XFreeFont** function unloads a font previously loaded by the **XLoadQueryFont** function. It frees the XFontStruct data structure and removes the link between the font resource ID and the font. The font is freed only when there is no further reference to it. Do not reference either the data structure or the font after executing the **XFreeFont** function. This function can generate a BadFont error. **XFreeFont** looks like this:

```
XFreeFont(display, font_struct)
    Display *display;              /* Specifies connection to
```

```
                                    the X server */
   XFontStruct;                   /* Storage area associated
                                    with the font */
```

Listing Fonts

A dynamic text processing application might load and unload fonts continuously. It is often important to determine the active fonts at any given time. Xlib provides several functions to do so. The **XListFonts** function, shown here, returns an array of available font names.

```
char **XListFonts(display, pattern, maxnames,
                actual_count_return)
   Display *display;            /* Specifies connection to
                                   the X server */
   char* pattern;               /* Null-terminated
                                   character string */
   int maxnames;                /* Maximum number of names
                                   to be returned */
   int actual_count_return;     /* Returns number of
                                   font names */
```

The pattern string uses the asterisk (*) and question mark (?) wildcards. The asterisk can replace any number of characters, and the question mark can replace a single character.

The **XListFontsWithInfo** function, shown next, generates the names and information about available fonts that match the supplied pattern.

```
char **XListFontsWithInfo(display, pattern, maxnames,
                    count_return, info_return)
   Display *display;            /* Specifies connection to
                                   the X server */
   char* pattern;               /* Null-terminated
                                   character string */
   int maxnames;                /* Maximum number of names
                                   to be returned */
   int *count_return;           /* Returns number of matched
                                   font names */
   XFontStruct **info_return;  /* Returns font information */
```

The **XListFontsWithInfo** function employs the asterisk and question mark wildcards, like the **XListFonts** function.

The array containing the font information should be freed when it is no longer needed. The **XFreeFontNames** function, shown here, frees the font names array and the strings returned by the **XListFonts** and **XListFontsWithInfo** functions.

```
XFreeFontNames(list)
    char *list[];                  /* Specifies the array of strings
                                      to be freed */
```

The **XFreeFontInfo** function, shown here, frees the font information array.

```
XFreeFontInfo(names, free_info, actual_count)
    char **names;                  /* Specifies list of font names
                                      returned by
                                      XListFontsWithInfo */
    XFontStruct *free_info;        /* Font information returned
                                      by XListFontsWithInfo */
    int actual_count;              /* Actual number of matched font
                                      names returned by
                                      XListFontsWithInfo */
```

Obtaining Information About Fonts

Applications must not apply fonts blindly, or the application may generate hard-to-read output. Several Xlib functions provide information about font properties and the size of character strings for a given font.

Font Properties

Font properties are descriptions of a font's characteristics. They often take the form of suggested values to maintain a font's visual appeal. For example, one font property denotes the maximum suggested space to leave between words. Although programmers are free to ignore the font designer's suggestions, most programmers are happy to apply the font properties and focus their efforts on the application itself.

An *atom* is a unique 32-bit identifier that replaces a string name. Proper use of atoms reduces the volume of data transmitted between the server and the workstation. Atom names start with the characters XA_.

The Boolean function **XGetFontProperty** accesses font properties for specified atoms. The header library <X11/Xatom.h> contains a list of predefined font atoms. Table 6-2 lists standard font properties and briefly describes their meaning.

```
Bool XGetFontProperty (font_struct, atom, value_return)
   XFontStruct *font_struct;        /* Font data structure */
   Atom atom;                       /* Atom for requested
                                       property name */
   unsigned long value_return;      /* Returns font
                                       property value */
```

XGetFontProperty returns the value TRUE if the specified property is defined, and FALSE if the specified property is not defined.

The **XInternAtom** function returns the atom identifier associated with the specified *atom_name* string.

```
Atom XInternAtom(display, atom_name, only_if_exists)
   Display *display;                /* Specifies connection
                                       to the server */
   char *atom_name;                 /* Name associated with
                                       atom to be returned */
   Bool only_if_exists;             /* If FALSE, function creates
                                       the atom */
```

The *atom_name* string is case dependent. The atom continues to be defined after the client server connection is closed. It becomes undefined when the last client application terminates. The **XInternAtom** function can generate BadAlloc and BadValue errors.

The **XGetAtomName** function returns a name for the specified atom identifier.

```
char *XGetAtomName(display, atom)
   Display *display;                /* Specifies connection
```

```
                                           to the server */
 Atom atom;               /* Atom for the property name
                                           to be returned */
 Bool only_if_exists;      /* If FALSE, function creates
                                           the atom */
```

The **XGetAtomName** function can generate a BadAtom error.

Calculating the Size of Character Strings

Font sizes vary greatly. A given character string might easily fit inside a window when displayed in one font and overflow the same window when displayed in another. In this case, the image is clipped, generating erroneous output. Xlib provides several functions that calculate the size of a given character string. Other Xlib functions calculate the maximum distance below the baseline and the maximum distance above the baseline for a given character string, depending on the font.

The **XTextWidth** function calculates the width of an 8-bit character string. Use this function or its 16-bit equivalent, **XTextWidth16**, to avoid generating a text string that exceeds the maximum display width for the associated window. **XTextWidth** is shown here.

```
int XTextWidth(font_struct, string, count)
  XFontStruct *font_struct;  /* Specifies font for which
                                     width calculated */
  char *string;              /* Character string */
  int count;                 /* Character count in
                                     the string */
```

The **XTextWidth16** function, shown next, calculates the width of a 16-bit (2-byte) character string.

```
int XTextWidth16(font_struct, string, count)
  XFontStruct *font_struct;  /* Specifies font for which
                                     width calculated */
  char *string;              /* Character string */
  int count;                 /* Character count in
                                     the string */
```

TABLE 6-2 Font Atoms and Properties

Atom Name	Property
XA_MIN_SPACE	Minimum interword spacing in pixels
XA_NORM_SPACE	Normal interword spacing in pixels
XA_MAX_SPACE	Maximum interword spacing in pixels
XA_END_SPACE	Spacing in pixels at end of sentence
XA_SUPERSCRIPT_X	Horizontal offset from origin for superscript
XA_SUPERSCRIPT_Y	Vertical offset from origin for superscript
XA_SUBSCRIPT_X	Horizontal offset from origin for subscript
XA_SUBSCRIPT_Y	Vertical offset from origin for subscript
XA_UNDERLINE_POSITION	Vertical offset from origin to top of underline
XA_UNDERLINE_THICKNESS	Height of underline in pixels
XA_STRIKEOUT_ASCENT	Vertical offset in pixels to top of strikeout box
XA_STRIKEOUT_DESCENT	Vertical offset in pixels to bottom of strikeout box
XA_ITALIC_ANGLE	Angle of italics
XA_X_HEIGHT	Nominal height in pixels of lowercase letters
XA_QUAD_WIDTH	Nominal quad (em) spacing
XA_WEIGHT	Font boldness (0 to 1000)
XA_POINT_SIZE	Size of font, in printer's points
XA_RESOLUTION	Font resolution, measured in 1/100 pixels per point
XA_CAP_HEIGHT	Vertical offset of tallest capital letters, in pixels

The **XTextExtents** function, shown next, computes the dimensions of the rectangle containing a given 8-bit character string. This function and its 16-bit equivalent, **XTextExtents16**, can set hints, such as height and width, for the string's display window.

```
XTextExtents(font_struct, string, nchars, direction_return,
            font_ascent_return, font_descent_return,
            overall_return)
  XFontStruct *font_struct;   /* Specifies font for which
                                 extent calculated */
  char *string;               /* Character string */
  int nchars;                 /* Character count in
                                 the string */
  int *direction_return;      /* Returns direction
                                 hint value */
  int font_ascent_return,     /* Returns font ascent
      font_descent_return;      returns font descent */
  XCharStruct *overall_return;
                              /* Returns overall size in
                                 specified XCharStruct
                                 data structure */
```

The **XTextExtents16** function computes the dimensions of the rectangle containing a given 16-bit (2-byte) character string. **XTextExtents16** looks like this:

```
XTextExtents16(font_struct, string, nchars, direction_return,
            font_ascent_return, font_descent_return,
            overall_return)
  XFontStruct *font_struct;   /* Specifies font for which
                                 extent calculated */
  char *string;               /* Character string */
  int nchars;                 /* Character count in
                                 the string */
  int *direction_return;      /* Returns direction
                                 hint value */
  int font_ascent_return,     /* Returns font ascent
      font_descent_return;      returns font descent */
  XCharStruct *overall_return;
                              /* Returns overall size in
                                 specified XCharStruct
                                 data structure */
```

Both the **XTextExtents** function and the similar **XTextExtents16** function calculate string sizes locally without generating a round-trip protocol message, in contrast to the **XQueryTextExtents** function and the **XQueryTextExtents16** functions that follow. All four functions calculate parameters according to these rules: The *direction_return* parameter has the value FontLeftToRight for languages such as English and French and the value FontRighttoLeft for languages such as Arabic and Hebrew. The *ascent_return* parameter is the maximum value of all the character ascents within the designated string. The *descent_return* parameter is the maximum of all the character descents within the designated string.

The **XQueryTextExtents** function requests that the server compute the dimensions of the rectangle containing a given 8-bit character string. Because it communicates with the server, it requires more time and resources than does the associated **XTextExtents** function. **XQueryTextExtents** is shown here.

```
XQueryTextExtents(display, font_ID, string, nchars,
               direction_return, font_ascent_return,
               font_descent_return, overall_return)
   Display *display;          /* Specifies connection to
                                 the X server */
   XID font_ID;               /* Font ID or GContextID that
                                 contains the font */
   char *string;              /* Character string */
   int nchars;                /* Character count in
                                 the string */
   int *direction_return;     /* Returns direction
                                 hint value */
   int *font_ascent_return,   /* Returns font ascent
      *font_descent_return;      returns font descent */
   XCharStruct *overall_return;
                              /* Returns overall size in
                                 specified XCharStruct
                                 data structure */
```

The **XQueryTextExtents16** function requests that the server compute the dimensions of the rectangle containing a given 16-bit (2-byte) character string. **XQueryTextExtents16** looks like this:

```
XQueryTextExtents16(display, font_ID, string, nchars,
                    direction_return, font_ascent_return,
                    font_descent_return, overall_return)
    Display *display;           /* Specifies connection to
                                   the X server */
    XID font_ID;                /* Font ID or GContextID that
                                   contains the font */
    XChar2b *string;            /* Character string */
    int nchars;                 /* Character count in
                                   the string */
    int *direction_return;      /* Returns direction
                                   hint value */
    int *font_ascent_return,    /* Returns font ascent
        *font_descent_return;    returns font descent */
    XCharStruct *overall_return;
                                /* Returns overall size in
                                   specified XCharStruct
                                   data structure */
```

XQueryTextExtents, **XQueryTextExtents16**, **XTextExtents**, and **XTextExtents16** all calculate size parameters according to these rules: The *direction* hint has the value FontLeftToRight for languages such as English and French and the value FontRighttoLeft for languages such as Arabic and Hebrew. The *ascent_return* parameter is the maximum value of all the character ascents within the designated string. The *descent_return* parameter is the maximum of all the character descents within the designated string.

Graphics Contexts

The graphics context is one of the fundamental server resources. It contains extensive information describing graphics output. Both graphics and text functions reference the graphics context. The parameters that the graphics context controls are shown here in the XGCValues data structure.

```
/* GC attribute value mask bits */
#define GCFunction          (1L<<0)
```

```
#define GCPlaneMask           (1L<<1)
#define GCForeground          (1L<<2)
#define GCBackground          (1L<<3)
#define GCLineWidth           (1L<<4)
#define GCLineStyle           (1L<<5)
#define GCCapStyle            (1L<<6)
#define GCJoinStyle           (1L<<7)
#define GCFillStyle           (1L<<8)
#define GCFillRule            (1L<<9)
#define GCTile                (1L<<10)
#define GCStipple             (1L<<11)
#define GCTileStipXOrigin     (1L<<12)
#define GCTileStipYOrigin     (1L<<13)
#define GCFont                (1L<<14)
#define GCSubwindowMode       (1L<<15)
#define GCGraphicsExposures   (1L<<16)
#define GCClipXOrigin         (1L<<17)
#define GCClipYOrigin         (1L<<18)
#define GCClipMask            (1L<<19)
#define GCDashOffset          (1L<<20)
#define GCDashList            (1L<<21)
#define GCArcMode             (1L<<22)
/* Values */
typedef struct {
  int function;                 /* Logical operation */
  unsigned long plane_mask;     /* Plane mask */
  unsigned long foreground;     /* Foreground pixel */
  unsigned long background;     /* Background pixel */
  int line_width;               /* Line width in pixels */
  int line_style;               /* LineSolid, LineOnOffDash,
                                   LineDoubleDash */
  int cap_style;                /* CapNotLast, CapButt
                                   CapRound, CapProjecting */
  int join_style;               /* JoinMiter, JoinRound,
                                   JoinBevel */
  int fill_style;               /* FillSolid, FillTiled,
                                   FillStippled,
                                   FillOpaqueStippled */
  int fill_rule;                /* EvenOddRule, WindingRule */
  int arc_mode;                 /* ArcChord, ArcPieSlice */
  Pixmap tile;                  /* Pixmap for tiling */
```

```
    Pixmap stipple;              /* Pixmap for stippling */
    int ts_x_origin;             /* Offset for tiling
    int ts_y_origin;                or stippling */
    Font font;                   /* Default text font */
    int subwindow_mode;          /* ClipByChildren,
                                    Include Interiors */

    Bool graphics_exposures;     /* Generate graphics
                                    exposures or not */
    int clip_x_origin;           /* Origin for clipping */
    int clip_y_origin;
    Pixmap clip_mask;            /* Bitmap clipping */
    int dash_offset;             /* Information for patterned
                                    and dashed lines */
    char dashes;
} XGCValues;
```

The **XSetFont** function, shown here, sets the current font of a given graphics context.

```
XSetFont(display, gc, font)
    Display *display;            /* Specifies connection to
                                    the X server */
    GC gc;                       /* Specifies graphics context */
    Font font;                   /* Specifies the font */
```

When the application does not invoke **XSetFont**, the graphics context's default font will be used, perhaps sacrificing application portability.

Drawing Text

Xlib provides several functions for drawing text characters. The **XDrawText** function draws text referenced in the XTextItem data structure. The **XDrawString** function draws the foreground bits of 8-bit text characters. The **XDrawImageString** function draws both the foreground and background bits of 8-bit text characters. These functions may reference the graphics context. Similar functions manipulate 16-bit characters, which are often used with non-Latin fonts such as Japanese.

DrawText Functions

The **XDrawText** and **XDrawText16** functions draw text referenced in the XTextItem and XTextItem16 data structures. XTextItem is shown here.

```
typedef struct {
  char *chars;              /* Specifies pointer to
                               string to draw */
  int nchars;               /* Number of characters to draw */
  int delta;                /* Gap between strings */
  Font font;                /* Font to use for string */
} XTextItem;
```

XTextItem16 is shown here.

```
typedef struct {
  XChar2b *chars;           /* Specifies pointer to
                               two-byte character string
                               to draw */
  int nchars;               /* Number of characters to draw */
  int delta;                /* Gap between strings */
  Font font;                /* Font to use for string */
} XTextItem16;
```

Specify a *font* parameter of None to apply the font presently stored in the graphics context. When you specify a *font* parameter other than None, the designated font is printed and stored in the graphics context for future use.

The **XDrawText** function, shown next, applies the graphics context to draw complex 8-bit characters.

```
XDrawText(display, d, gc, x, y, items, nitems)
  Display *display;         /* Specifies connection
                               to the server */
  Drawable d;               /* Window or pixmap */
  GC gc;                    /* Graphics context */
  int x, y;                 /* Coordinates defining origin
                               of first character relative
                               to window or pixmap origin */
  XTextItem *items;         /* Array of text items */
```

```
    int nitems;                    /* Number of text items
                                      in above array */
```

The **XDrawText16** function applies the graphics context to draw complex 16-bit images.

```
XDrawText16(display, d, gc, x, y, items, nitems)
   Display *display;               /* Specifies connection
                                      to the server */
   Drawable d;                     /* Window or pixmap */
   GC gc;                          /* Graphics context */
   int x, y;                       /* Coordinates defining origin
                                      of first character relative
                                      to window or pixmap origin */
   XTextItem16 *items;             /* Array of text items */
   int nitems;                     /* Number of text items
                                      in above array */
```

XDrawText and **XDrawText16** access text components in the graphics context. These components, in order of their declaration in the XGCValues data structure, are *plane_mask*, *foreground*, *background*, *fill_style*, *tile*, *stipple*, *ts_x_origin*, *ts_y_origin*, *font*, *subwindow_mode*, *clip_x_origin*, *clip_y_origin*, and *clip_mask*. **XDrawText** and **XDraw-Text16** can generate BadDrawable, BadFont, BadGC, and BadMatch errors.

DrawString Functions

The **XDrawString** function, shown next, draws the foreground bits of 8-bit text characters. It makes extensive use of the graphics context.

```
XDrawString(display, d, gc, x, y, string, length)
   Display *display;               /* Specifies connection
                                      to the server */
   Drawable d;                     /* Window or pixmap */
   GC gc;                          /* Graphics context */
   int x, y;                       /* Coordinates defining origin
                                      of first character relative
                                      to window or pixmap origin */
   char *string;                   /* Character string to draw */
```

```
int length;                    /* Number of characters in the
                                  string to draw */
```

The **XDrawString16** function draws the foreground bits of 16-bit (2-byte) text characters. It also makes extensive use of the graphics context.

```
XDrawString16(display, d, gc, x, y, string, length)
  Display *display;            /* Specifies connection
                                  to the server */
  Drawable d;                  /* Window or pixmap */
  GC gc;                       /* Graphics context */
  int x, y;                    /* Coordinates defining origin
                                  of first character relative
                                  to window or pixmap origin */
  XChar2b *string;             /* Character string to draw */
  int length;                  /* Number of characters in the
                                  string to draw */
```

XDrawString and **XDrawString16** access text components in the graphics context. These components, in order of their declaration in the **XGCValues** data structure, are *plane_mask*, *foreground*, *background*, *fill_style*, *tile*, *stipple*, *ts_x_origin*, *ts_y_origin*, *font*, *subwindow_mode*, *clip_x_origin*, *clip_y_origin*, and *clip_mask*. This list is the same as the data items associated with **XDrawText** and **XDrawText16**. **XDrawString** and **XDrawString16** can generate BadDrawable, BadGC, and BadMatch errors.

DrawImageString Functions

Use the **XDrawImageString** function, shown here, to draw both the foreground and background bits for 8-bit text characters. Drawing both the foreground and background bits tends to reduce flicker.

```
XDrawImageString(display, d, gc, x, y, string, length)
  Display *display;            /* Specifies connection
                                  to the server */
  Drawable d;                  /* Window or pixmap */
  GC gc;                       /* Graphics context */
```

```
    int x, y;                   /* Coordinates defining origin
                                   of first character relative
                                   to window or pixmap origin */
    char *string;               /* Character string to draw */
    int length;                 /* Number of characters in the
                                   string to draw */
```

The **XDrawImageString16** function draws both the foreground and background bits for 16-bit (2-byte) text characters. Drawing both the foreground and background bits tends to reduce flicker.

```
XDrawImageString16(display, d, gc, x, y, string, length)
    Display *display;           /* Specifies connection
                                   to the server */
    Drawable d;                 /* Window or pixmap */
    GC gc;                      /* Graphics context */
    int x, y;                   /* Coordinates defining origin
                                   of first character relative
                                   to window or pixmap origin */
    char *string;               /* Character string to draw */
    int length;                 /* Number of characters in the
                                   string to draw */
```

XDrawImageString and **XDrawImageString16** employ the following components of the graphics context, in order of their declaration in the **XGCValues** data structure: *plane_mask, foreground, background, font, subwindow_mode, clip_x_origin, clip_y_origin,* and *clip_mask*. **XDrawImageString** and **XDrawImageString16** can generate BadDrawable, BadGC, and BadMatch errors.

Exercise 6-1: Applying the XDrawText Function

The following Xlib program applies the XFontStruct data structure and the Xlib functions **XLoadQueryFont** and **XDrawText** to draw three windows with text in different fonts. If you are unsure of Xlib functions such as **XSelectInput** and **XMapRaised**, review Chapter 2, "Hello World."

The program declares an array of three commonly used fonts as follows:

```
char *font[] = {
                "*helvetica-bold-r*140*",
                "*helvetica-medium-o*140*",
                "*courier-bold-r*140*",
        };
```

The program defines pointers to an array of data font structures. Because the constant MAX_ELEMENTS has been set to 3, this array has three elements.

```
XFontStruct *font_struct[MAX_ELEMENTS];
```

Each item declared with the data type XTextItem has four elements: a character string, the length of the character string, the space between succeeding character strings, and the font to be used. The declaration follows immediately. Specific values are assigned after the font is selected.

```
XTextItem   line[MAX_ELEMENTS];
```

The program calls five C language functions in order: **init**, **load_fonts_and_strings**, **set_hints**, **create_window_set_properties**, and **cleanup**. The function **init** initializes the environment. The function **load_fonts_and_strings** loads the fonts and the text. It terminates the program if a requested font cannot be found. The function **set_hints** informs the window manager of requested values for the windows to be created. The function **create_window_set_properties** creates a window using the hints to the window manager, creates the graphics context, and sets standard properties for the window. The function **cleanup** unloads the fonts, destroys the window, and disconnects from the server.

The C language function **init**, shown here, takes the program name from the command line, opens the display unit, returns the screen identifier, and gets the colors of the screen's background and foreground.

```
void init(argv);
char *argv[];
```

```
{
  p name = argv[0];
  thedisplay = XOpenDisplay("");
  thescreen = DefaultScreen(thedisplay);
  background = WhitePixel(thedisplay, thescreen);
  foreground = BlackPixel(thedisplay, thescreen);
}
```

The C language function **load_fonts_and_strings** applies the Xlib function **XLoadQueryFont** to load the specified fonts into the associated font structures. The function returns an error flag if a desired font is not available. A more robust program would define the actions to take when the desired font is not available. The following code segment appears three times, once for each selected font.

```
font_struct[index] = XLoadQueryFont(thedisplay, font[index]);
if (font_struct[index] == 0)
  return(ERROR);
else
  printf("\n font %s loaded\n",font[index]);
```

After loading the specified font, the function assigns values to the array element *line[index]* associated with the XTextItem data structure. The variable *line[index].chars* refers to the character string associated with the text line. The C function **strlen** calculates the length of the character string. Consider the following:

font_struct[index]->max_bounds.width

The font structure font_struct includes an element *max_bounds* that is itself a data structure (of type XCharStruct). The element *max_bounds* contains the parameter *width*, which refers to the distance between the same point in succeeding characters. Half this distance is the separation between the end of one character and the beginning of the next character.

The final element of the XTextItem data structure is the font to use.

```
line[index].chars = "Joseph Radin";
line[index].nchars = strlen("Joseph Radin");
line[index].delta = font_struct[index]->max_bounds.width/2;
line[index].font = font_struct[index]->fid;
```

If the function **load_fonts_and_strings** succeeds in loading all the requested fonts, it returns the value OK; otherwise, it returns the value ERROR. The return value is tested when the function is invoked, as follows:

```
if ((result = load_fonts_and_strings()) == ERROR)
{
    printf("\n ERROR: Cannot load fonts. Exiting ...\n");
    exit(0);
}
```

The C language function **create_window_set_properties** invokes three Xlib functions: **XCreateSimpleWindow**, which creates the display window; **XCreateGC**, which creates the graphics context; and **XSetStandardProperties**, which informs the window manager of the application's preferences, including size hints.

When the count of Expose events is 0, it is time to draw the text. First the **XClearWindow** function clears the window in preparation for drawing. Then the **XDrawText** function actually draws the text array in the window. This function includes seven parameters denoting the connection to the X server: the drawable (in this case, a window), the graphics context, the x and y coordinates relative to the origin of the drawable, the array of text items, and the number of items in the array.

```
XClearWindow(thedisplay, thewindow);
XDrawText(thedisplay, thewindow, thegc, 40, 30,
          line, MAX_ELEMENTS);
```

 Note This single **XDrawText** function draws the entire text array, not only one text string.

Clicking the mouse button invokes the C language function **cleanup**, shutting down the application in an orderly fashion. This function invokes three Xlib functions: **XUnloadFont**, which releases all fonts and font structures; **XDestroyWindow**, which destroys the window; and **XCloseDisplay**, which breaks the connection to the server.

The following listing shows the complete source code of Exercise 6-1.

```
/* Exercise 6-1 */
/* Applying the XDrawText Function */
```

```
#include <X11/Xlib.h>
#include <X11/Xutil.h>
#define BORDER_WIDTH 2
#define MAX_ELEMENTS 3
#define FALSE 0
#define TRUE 1
#define ERROR -1
#define OK 0
Display        *thedisplay;
Window         *thewindow;
int            thescreen;
char *font[] = {
                "*helvetica-bold-r*140*",
                "*helvetica-medium-o*140*",
                "*courier-bold-r*140*",
               };
char           *p_name;
XFontStruct    *font_struct[MAX_ELEMENTS];
XTextItem      line[MAX_ELEMENTS];
unsigned long foreground;
unsigned long background;
XSizeHints     thehints;
GC             thegc;

void init();
int load_fonts_and_strings();
void set_hints();
void create_window_set_properties();
void cleanup();

main(argc, argv)
int            argc;
char           *argv[];
{
XEvent         event;
int            done = FALSE;
int            result;

   init(argv);
   if ((result = load_fonts_and_strings()) == ERROR)
   {
     printf("\n ERROR: Cannot load fonts. Exiting ...\n");
```

```
      exit(0);
  }

  set_hints();

  create_window_set_properties(argc,argv);

  XSelectInput(thedisplay, thewindow, ButtonPressMask
            | KeyPressMask | ExposureMask);

  XMapRaised(thedisplay, thewindow);

  while (!done)
  {
    XNextEvent(thedisplay, &event);
    switch(event.type)
      {
        case Expose:
          if (event.xexpose.count == 0)
            {
              XClearWindow(thedisplay, thewindow);
              XDrawText(thedisplay, thewindow, thegc, 40, 30,
                      line, MAX_ELEMENTS);
            }
          break;

        case ButtonPress:
          done = TRUE;
          cleanup();
          printf("\n Ready to exit ...\n");
          break;
    }/* End switch */
  }  /*  End while  */
}  /*  End main  */

void init(argv)
char *argv[];
{
  p_name = argv[0];
  thedisplay = XOpenDisplay("");
  thescreen = DefaultScreen(thedisplay);
  background = WhitePixel(thedisplay, thescreen);
```

```
    foreground = BlackPixel(thedisplay, thescreen);
}


int load_fonts_and_strings()
{
int index = 0;

    font_struct[index] = XLoadQueryFont(thedisplay,
                                         font[index]);
    if (font_struct[index] == 0)
      return(ERROR);
    else
    {
      printf("\n font %s loaded\n",font[index]);
      line[index].chars = "Joseph Radin";
      line[index].nchars = strlen("Joseph Radin");
      line[index].delta = font_struct[index]->
                          max_bounds.width/2;
      line[index].font = font_struct[index]->fid;
      printf("\n string # %d initiated \n", index + 1);
    }
++index;
    font_struct[index] = XLoadQueryFont(thedisplay,
                                         font[index]);
    if (font_struct[index] == 0)
      return(ERROR);
    else
    {
      printf("\n font %s loaded\n",font[index]);
      line[index].chars = "Levi Reiss";
      line[index].nchars = strlen("Levi Reiss");
      line[index].delta = font_struct[index]->
                          max_bounds.width/2;
      line[index].font = font_struct[index]->fid;
      printf("\n string # %d initiated \n", index + 1);
    }
++index;
    font_struct[index] = XLoadQueryFont(thedisplay,
                                         font[index]);
    if (font_struct[index] == 0)
      return(ERROR);
    else
```

```
    {
      printf("\n font %s loaded\n",font[index]);
      line[index].chars = "Inside and Out";
      line[index].nchars = strlen("Inside and Out");
      line[index].delta = font_struct[index]->
                            max_bounds.width/2;
      line[index].font = font_struct[index]->fid;
      printf("\n string # %d initiated \n", index + 1);
    }
    return (OK);
}

void set_hints()
{
  thehints.flags = PPosition | PSize;
  thehints.height = 50;
  thehints.width = 400;
  thehints.x = 100;
  thehints.y = 50;
}

void create_window_set_properties(argc, argv)
int argc;
char *argv[];
{
  thewindow = XCreateSimpleWindow(thedisplay,
                DefaultRootWindow(thedisplay), thehints.x,
                thehints.y, thehints.width, thehints.height,
                BORDER_WIDTH, foreground, background);

  thegc = XCreateGC(thedisplay, thewindow, 0, 0);

  XSetStandardProperties(thedisplay, thewindow, p_name,
                          p_name, None,
                          argv, argc, &thehints);

}

void cleanup()
{
  int index = 0:
  for (index = 0; index < MAX_ELEMENTS; index++)
```

```
{
    ████ ██████ (██████████, ███ ██ ████ [██████] = ██████;
}
printf("\n Remove fonts - done\n");

XDestroyWindow(thedisplay, thewindow);
printf("\n Destroy window - done\n");

XCloseDisplay(thedisplay);
printf("\n Disconnect from server - done\n");
}
```

Results of executing this program are shown in Figure 6-2.

The following listing is the MAKE file for Exercise 6-1 as run on the X Window system using the Santa Cruz Operation Open Desktop software. The MAKE file for other X Window implementations varies.

```
RM = rm - f
CC = cc
CFLAGS = -O
INCLUDES = -I/usr/include -I/usr/include/X11
LIBS = -lXm -lXt -lX11 -lsocket -lmalloc -lPW
.c.o:
$(RM) $@
$(CC) -c $(CFLAGS) $(INCLUDES) $*.c
all:: exercise6-1
exercise6-1: exercise6-1.o
$(RM) $@
$(CC) -o $@ $(CFLAGS) exercise6-1.o $(LIBS)
@echo makefile for exercise6-1 - done!
```

To generate MAKE files for the remaining exercises, change all lines that refer to Exercise 6-1.

Exercise 6-2: Applying the XDrawString Function

This program applies the **XDrawString** function to draw three text strings. Only changes from the previous program are discussed.

FIGURE 6-2   Text generated by the **XDrawText** function

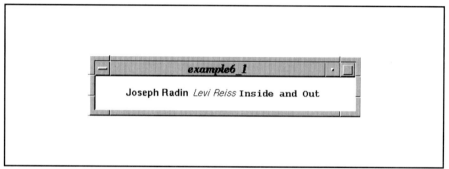

The constant SHIFT denotes the distance separating the origin (*x* variable) of each succeeding character string. Unlike the previous program, which declared a single graphics context, this program declares an array of three graphics contexts. It also declares an integer array *width* denoting the width of the character string, an integer variable *element* for accessing the array elements, and an integer variable *position* denoting the value of the *x* variable, initially set to 10 for the first string.

```
#define SHIFT 200

GC          thegc[MAX_ELEMENTS];
int         width[MAX_ELEMENTS];
int         element;
int         position = 10;
```

The previous program invoked a single **XDrawText** function and a single graphics context to draw an array of strings. This program invokes the **XDrawString** function three times, each time with a different graphics context.

```
XDrawString(thedisplay, thewindow,
            thegc[element], position, 30,
            line[element].chars,
            line[element].nchars);
```

The following listing shows the complete source code of Exercise 6-2.

```
/* Exercise 6-2 */
/* Applying the XDrawString Function */
#include <X11/Xlib.h>
#include <X11/Xutil.h>
#define BORDER_WIDTH 2
#define SHIFT 200
#define MAX_ELEMENTS 3
#define FALSE 0
#define TRUE 1
#define ERROR -1
#define OK 0
Display        *thedisplay;
Window         *thewindow;
int            thescreen;
char *font[] = {
                "*helvetica-bold-r*140*",
                "*helvetica-medium-o*140*",
                "*courier-bold-r*140*",
               };
char           *p_name;
XFontStruct    *font_struct[MAX_ELEMENTS];
XTextItem      line[MAX_ELEMENTS];
unsigned long foreground;
unsigned long background;
XSizeHints     thehints;
GC             thegc[MAX_ELEMENTS];

void init();
int load_fonts_and_strings();
void set_hints();
void create_window_set_properties();
void cleanup();

main(argc, argv)
int            argc;
char           *argv[];
{
XEvent         event;
int            done = FALSE;
int            result;
```

```
int             width[MAX_ELEMENTS];
int             element;
int             position = 10

  init(argv);
  set_hints();
  create_window_set_properties(argc,argv);
  XSelectInput(thedisplay, thewindow, ButtonPressMask
               | KeyPressMask | ExposureMask);

  XMapRaised(thedisplay, thewindow);

  if ((result = load_fonts_and_strings()) == ERROR)
  {
    printf("\n ERROR: Cannot load fonts. Exiting ...\n");
    exit(0);
  }
  while (!done)
  {
    XNextEvent(thedisplay, &event);
    switch(event.type)
      {
        case Expose:
          if (event.xexpose.count == 0)
            {
              XClearWindow(thedisplay, thewindow);
              for (element = 0; element < MAX_ELEMENTS;
                   position+=SHIFT, element++)
              {
                XDrawString(thedisplay, thewindow,
                            thegc[element], position, 30,
                            line[element].chars,
                            line[element].nchars);
              }
            }
        break;

        case ButtonPress:
          done = TRUE;
          cleanup();
          printf("\n Ready to exit ...\n");
        break;
```

```
    }/* End switch */
  }  /*  End while  */
}  /*  End main  */

void init(argv)
char *argv[];
{
  p_name = argv[0];
  thedisplay = XOpenDisplay("");
  thescreen = DefaultScreen(thedisplay);
  background = WhitePixel(thedisplay, thescreen);
  foreground = BlackPixel(thedisplay, thescreen);
}

int load_fonts_and_strings()
{
int index;

for (index = 0; index < MAX_ELEMENTS; index++)
  {
    thegc[index] = XCreateGC(thedisplay, thewindow, 0, 0);
  }
  index = 0;
  font_struct[index] = XLoadQueryFont(thedisplay,
                                      font[index]);
  if (font_struct[index] == 0)
    return(ERROR);
  else
  {
    printf("\n font %s loaded\n",font[index]);
    line[index].chars = "Joseph Radin";
    line[index].nchars = strlen("Joseph Radin");
    line[index].delta = font_struct[index]->
                        max_bounds.width/2;
    line[index].font = font_struct[index]->fid;
    printf("\n string # %d initiated \n", index + 1);
  }
  ++index;
  font_struct[index] = XLoadQueryFont(thedisplay,
                                      font[index]);
  if (font_struct[index] == 0)
    return(ERROR);
```

```
    else
    {
      printf("\n font %s loaded\n",font[index]);
      line[index].chars = "Levi Reiss";
      line[index].nchars = strlen("Levi Reiss");
      line[index].delta = font_struct[index]->
                          max_bounds.width/2;
      line[index].font = font_struct[index]->fid;
      printf("\n string # %d initiated \n", index + 1);
    }
    ++index;
    font_struct[index] = XLoadQueryFont(thedisplay,
                                        font[index]);
    if (font_struct[index] == 0)
      return(ERROR);
    else
    {
      printf("\n font %s loaded\n",font[index]);
      line[index].chars = "Inside and Out";
      line[index].nchars = strlen("Inside and Out");
      line[index].delta = font_struct[index]->
                          max_bounds.width/2;
      line[index].font = font_struct[index]->fid;
      printf("\n string # %d initiated \n", index + 1);
    }
    return (OK);
}
void set_hints()
{
  thehints.flags = PPosition | PSize;
  thehints.height = 50;
  thehints.width = 400;
  thehints.x = 100;
  thehints.y = 50;
}

void_create_window_set_properties(argc, argv)
int argc;
char *argv[];
```

```
{
   thewindow = XCreateSimpleWindow(thedisplay,
               DefaultRootWindow(thedisplay), thehints.x,
               thehints.y, thehints.width, thehints.height,
               BORDER_WIDTH, foreground, background);

   XSetStandardProperties(thedisplay, thewindow, p_name,
                    p_name, None, argv, argc, &thehints);

}
void cleanup()
{
   int index = 0:

   for (index = 0; index < MAX_ELEMENTS; index++)
   {
      XUnloadFont(thedisplay, font_struct[index]->fid);
   }
   printf("\n Remove fonts - done\n");

   XDestroyWindow(thedisplay, thewindow);
   printf("\n Destroy window - done\n");

   XCloseDisplay(thedisplay);
   printf("\n Disconnect from server - done\n");
}
```

Results of executing this program are shown in Figure 6-3.

Exercise 6-3: Applying the XDrawImageString Function

The only difference between this program and the previous example is the Xlib function used to draw the text. The previous example employed the **XDrawString** function; this program employs the **XDrawImage-String** function.

FIGURE
6-3

Text generated by the **XDrawString** function

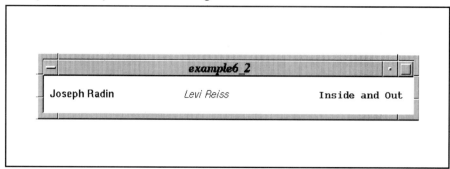

```
XDrawImageString(thedisplay, thewindow,
                thegc[element], position, 30,
                line[element].chars
                line[element].nchars);
```

The **XDrawImageString** function draws both the foreground and background pixels, providing a clearer image, especially when the screen has a tendency to flicker.

Because the only change between these two examples is the replacement of the **XDrawString** function with the **XDrawImageString** function, the program listing is not shown. Results of executing this program are shown in Figure 6-4.

FIGURE
6-4

Text generated by the XDraw ImageString function

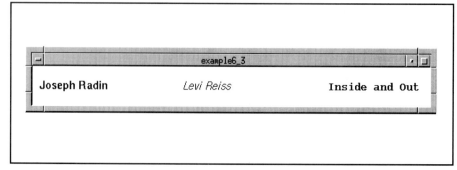

Exercise 6-4: Applying the XDrawString and XFillRectangle Functions

This example is more complicated than the previous examples. It generates text that is underlined for effect. This program requires the header library <X11/Xatom.h>, which declares all predefined atoms. Recall that an atom is a unique 32-bit identifier that replaces a string name. Proper use of atoms reduces the amount of data transmitted between the server and the workstation. Atom names start with the characters XA_. This program uses the atoms XA_UNDERLINE_POSITION and XA_UNDERLINE_THICKNESS.

The following lines declare variables for the location, width, and thickness of the underlines.

```
int place[MAX_ELEMENTS];
unsigned int thickness[MAX_ELEMENTS];
int width[MAX_ELEMENTS];
```

The **XGetFontProperty** function accesses the font data structure to determine font properties such as the position and thickness of the underline. The first such function assigns the distance of the underline from the font baseline to a variable called *place[index]*. In the event that no value is available from the data structure, this variable is set to the value 3. The second **XGetFontProperty** function similarly assigns a value to the *thickness[index]* variable. The **XSetFont** function sets the font for the specified graphics context.

```
if (!XGetFontProperty(font_struct[index],
                XA_UNDERLINE_POSITION, &place[index]))
    place[index] = 3;
if (!XGetFontProperty(font_struct[index],
            XA_UNDERLINE_THICKNESS, &thickness[index]))
    thickness[index] = 3;
XSetFont(thedisplay, thegc[index],
        font_struct[index]->fid);
```

The **XTextWidth** function calculates the width of a text string. This width is required to draw the underline with the **XFillRectangle** function. The **XFillRectangle** function, described in detail in Chapter 10, "Color and Graphics," fills a rectangular area in a drawable. Its parameters are the display, the drawable, the graphics context, the x and y coordinates of the rectangle with respect to the drawable, the rectangle's height, and its width.

```
width[element] = XTextWidth(font_struct[element],
                    line[element].chars,
                    line[element].nchars);
XDrawString(thedisplay, thewindow,
            thegc[element], position, 30,
            line[element].chars,
            line[element].nchars);
XFillRectangle(thedisplay, thewindow,
                thegc[element], position,
                30+place[element],
                width[element],
                thickness[element]);
```

The following listing shows the complete source code of Exercise 6-4.

```
/* Exercise 6-4 */
/* Applying the XDrawString and XFillRectangle Functions */
#include <X11/Xlib.h>
#include <X11/Xatom.h>
#include <X11/Xutil.h>
#define BORDER_WIDTH 2
#define SHIFT 200
#define MAX_ELEMENTS 3
#define FALSE 0
#define TRUE 1
#define ERROR -1
#define OK 0
Display     *thedisplay;
Window      *thewindow;
int         thescreen;
char *font[] = {
            "*helvetica-bold-r*140*",
            "*helvetica-medium-o*140*",
            "*courier-bold-r*140*",
            };
char        *p_name;
XFontStruct *font_struct[MAX_ELEMENTS];
XTextItem   line[MAX_ELEMENTS];
```

```
unsigned long  foreground;
unsigned long  background;
XSizeHints     thehints;
GC             thegc[MAX_ELEMENTS];
int            place[MAX_ELEMENTS];
unsigned int   thickness[MAX_ELEMENTS];

void init();
int load_fonts_and_strings();
void set_hints();
void create_window_set_properties();
void cleanup();

main(argc, argv)
int            argc;
char           *argv[];
{
XEvent         event;
int            done = FALSE;
int            result;
int            width[MAX_ELEMENTS];
int            element;
int            position = 10;

  init(argv);
  set_hints();
  create_window_set_properties(argc,argv);
  XSelectInput(thedisplay, thewindow, ButtonPressMask
               | KeyPressMask | ExposureMask);

  XMapRaised(thedisplay, thewindow);

  if ((result = load_fonts_and_strings()) == ERROR)
  {
    printf("\n ERROR: Cannot load fonts. Exiting ...\n");
    exit(0);
  }
  while (!done)
  {
    XNextEvent(thedisplay, &event);
    switch(event.type)
      {
```

```
              case Expose:
                if (event.xexpose.count == 0)
                  {
                    XClearWindow(thedisplay, thewindow);
                    for (element = 0; element < MAX_ELEMENTS;
                         position+=SHIFT, element++)
                      {
                        width[element] =
                             XTextWidth(font_struct[element],
                                       line[element].chars
                                       line[element].nchars);
                        XDrawString(thedisplay, thewindow,
                                    thegc[element], position, 30,
                                    line[element].chars,
                                    line[element].nchars);
                        XFillRectangle(thedisplay, thewindow,
                                       thegc[element], position,
                                       30+place[element],
                                       width[element],
                                       thickness[element]);
                      }
                  }
                break;
            case ButtonPress:
                done = TRUE;
                cleanup();
                printf("\n Ready to exit ...\n");
                break;
        }/* End switch */
    }  /*  End while  */
}  /*  End main  */

void init(argv)
char *argv[];
{
  p_name = argv[0];
  thedisplay = XOpenDisplay("");
  thescreen = DefaultScreen(thedisplay);
  background = WhitePixel(thedisplay, thescreen);
  foreground = BlackPixel(thedisplay, thescreen);
}
```

```
int load_fonts_and_strings()
{
int index;

for (index = 0; index < MAX_ELEMENTS; index++)
  {
    thegc[index] = XCreateGC(thedisplay, thewindow, 0, 0);
  }
  index = 0;
  font_struct[index] = XLoadQueryFont(thedisplay,
                                      font[index]);
  if (font_struct[index] == 0)
    return(ERROR);
  else
  {
    printf("\n font %s loaded\n",font[index]);
    line[index].chars = "Joseph Radin";
    line[index].nchars = strlen("Joseph Radin");
    line[index].delta = font_struct[index]->
                        max_bounds.width/2;
    line[index].font = font_struct[index]->fid;
    if (!XGetFontProperty(font_struct[index],
                          XA_UNDERLINE_POSITION,
                          &place[index]))
      place[index] = 3;
    if (!XGetFontProperty(font_struct[index],
                          XA_UNDERLINE_THICKNESS,
                          &thickness[index]))
      thickness[index] = 3;
    XSetFont(thedisplay, thegc[index],
             font_struct[index]->fid);
    printf("\n string # %d initiated \n", index + 1);
  }
  ++index;
  font_struct[index] = XLoadQueryFont(thedisplay,
                                      font[index]);
  if (font_struct[index] == 0)
    return(ERROR);
  else
  {
    printf("\n font %s loaded\n",font[index]);
    line[index].chars = "Levi Reiss";
```

```
      line[index].nchars = strlen("Levi Reiss");
      line[index].delta = font_struct[index]->
                          max_bounds.width/2;
      line[index].font = font_struct[index]->fid;
      if (!XGetFontProperty(font_struct[index],
                          XA_UNDERLINE_POSITION,
                          &place[index]))
         place[index] = 3;
      if (!XGetFontProperty(font_struct[index],
                          XA_UNDERLINE_THICKNESS,
                          &thickness[index]))
         thickness[index] = 3;
    XSetFont(thedisplay, thegc[index],
             font_struct[index]->fid);
    printf("\n string # %d initiated \n", index + 1);
  }
  ++index;
  font_struct[index] = XLoadQueryFont(thedisplay,
                                      font[index]);
  if (font_struct[index] == 0)
    return(ERROR);
  else
  {
    printf("\n font %s loaded\n",font[index]);
    line[index].chars = "Inside and Out";
    line[index].nchars = strlen("Inside and Out");
    line[index].delta = font_struct[index]->
                        max_bounds.width/2;
    line[index].font = font_struct[index]->fid;
    if (!XGetFontProperty(font_struct[index],
                        XA_UNDERLINE_POSITION,
                        &place[index]))
       place[index] = 3;
    if (!XGetFontProperty(font_struct[index],
                        XA_UNDERLINE_THICKNESS,
                        &thickness[index]))
       thickness[index] = 3;
    XSetFont(thedisplay, thegc[index],
             font_struct[index]->fid);
    printf("\n string # %d initiated \n", index + 1);
  }
  return (OK);
```

```
}

void set_hints()
{
  thehints.flags = PPosition | PSize;
  thehints.height = 50;
  thehints.width = 550;
  thehints.x = 100;
  thehints.y = 50;
}

void create_window_set_properties(argc, argv)
int argc;
char *argv[];
{
  thewindow = XCreateSimpleWindow(thedisplay,
                 DefaultRootWindow(thedisplay), thehints.x,
                 thehints.y, thehints.width, thehints.height,
                 BORDER_WIDTH, foreground, background);

  XSetStandardProperties(thedisplay, thewindow, p_name,
                         p_name, None, argv, argc, &thehints);

}
void cleanup()
{
  int index = 0;

  for (index = 0; index < MAX_ELEMENTS; index++)
  {
    XUnloadFont(thedisplay, font_struct[index]->fid);
  }
  printf("\n Remove fonts - done\n");

  XDestroyWindow(thedisplay, thewindow);
  printf("\n Destroy window - done\n");

  XCloseDisplay(thedisplay);
  printf("\n Disconnect from server - done\n");
}
```

Results of executing this program are shown in Figure 6-5.

Text generated by the **XDrawString** and **XFillRectangle** functions

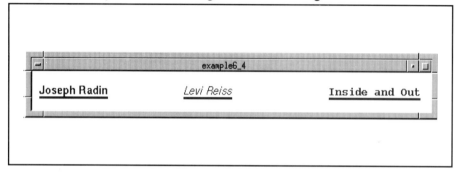

Exercise 6-5: Generating Clipped Text

The following program shows what happens if a window width were set too small. Except for the C language function **set_hints**, shown here, this program is identical to Exercise 6-1.

```
void set_hints()
{
  thehints.flags = PPosition | PSize;
  thehints.height = 50;
  thehints.width = 200;
  printf("\n Wrong window width ... This width should be
          corrected \n");
  thehints.x = 100;
  thehints.y = 50;
}
```

Results of executing this program are shown in Figure 6-6.

Exercise 6-6: Applying the XTextWidth Function

The preceding program used an erroneous value of the *thehints.width* parameter. This program applies the **XTextWidth** function to generate

FIGURE 6-6

Clipped text

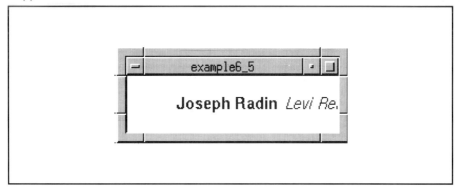

a correct value. This program differs from Exercise 6-1 in two respects. It includes a constant GAP, whose value is 8, to indicate the spacing between strings, as follows:

```
#define GAP 8
```

This statement defines a constant used in the following **set_hints** function. The GAP is shown in Figure 6-7, which shows the results of executing this program.

The expanded version of the **set_hints** function follows.

FIGURE 6-7

Text generated by the **XTextWidth** function

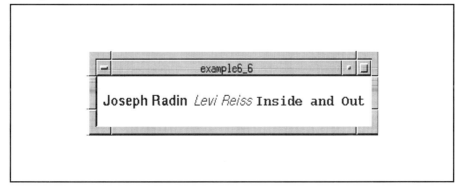

```
void set_hints()
{
int width[MAX_ELEMENTS];
int index;

  thehints.flags = PPosition | PSize;
  thehints.width = 0;
  for (index = 0; index < MAX_ELEMENTS;
       thehints.width+=width[index],index++)
  {
     width[index] = XTextWidth(font_struct[index],
                              line[index].chars,
                              line[index].nchars) + GAP;
  }
  printf("\n Corrected ... Calculated window width is %d\n",
         thehints.width);
  thehints.height = 50;
  thehints.x = 100;
  thehints.y = 50;
}
```

Key Points

Font Naming Conventions

Each font has a unique descriptive name. The font name contains 14 fields: FOUNDRY field, denoting the font supplier; FAMILY_NAME field, identifying a group of related fonts; WEIGHT_NAME field, denoting the font's blackness; SLANT field, identifying a font's inclination; SETWIDTH_NAME field, denoting the font's width; the optional ADD_STYLE_NAME field, identifying additional typographical information describing the font; PIXEL_SIZE field, denoting the font's body size for a given POINT_SIZE and RESOLUTION_Y;

continues . . .

POINT_SIZE field, identifying the body size for which the font was designed; RESOLUTION_X field, denoting the horizontal resolution for which the font was designed; RESOLUTION_Y field, denoting the vertical resolution for which the font was designed; SPACING field, identifying how individual characters are assigned a width; AVERAGE_WIDTH field, denoting the average width of characters; CHARSET_REGISTRY field, identifying the registration authority that owns the specific encoding; and CHARSET_ ENCODING field, identifying the coded character set. A sample font name is

Bitstream-Charter-Bold-I-Normal-12-120-75-75-P-75-ISO8859-1

Font Data Structures

The XFontStruct data structure contains extensive data describing each font. It is defined in the <X11/Xlib.h> header library. Several elements in the XFontStruct data structure are themselves composite objects, defined with the XCharStruct data structure.

Loading and Unloading Fonts

A font must reside in the X server's memory before any program can use it. Because the server memory is limited, a font is often loaded just prior to use. The **XLoadFont** function loads the designated font and returns the font ID. The **XQueryFont** function returns a pointer to the XFontStruct data structure for the program to use. The **XLoadQueryFont** function combines the font load and query operations in a single function.

The **XUnloadFont** function frees fonts loaded by the **XLoadFont** function. The **XFreeFont** function frees fonts loaded by the **XLoadQueryFont** function.

continues . . .

Listing Fonts

The **XListFonts** function returns an array of available font names, using the familiar asterisk (*) and question mark (?) wildcards. The **XListFontsWithInfo** function generates the names and information about available fonts that match the supplied pattern.

The **XFreeFontNames** function frees the font names array and the strings returned by the **XListFonts** and the **XListFontsWithInfo** functions. The **XFreeFontInfo** function frees the font information array.

Font Properties

Font properties are descriptions of a font's characteristics. They often take the form of suggested values to maintain a font's visual appeal. An atom is a unique 32-bit identifier that replaces a string name. Proper use of atoms reduces the volume of data transmitted between the server and the workstation. Atom names start with the characters XA_. The Boolean function **XGetFontProperty** accesses font properties for specified atoms.

Calculating the Size of Character Strings

Font sizes vary greatly. The **XTextWidth** function calculates the width of an 8-bit character string. Use this function or its 16-bit equivalent to avoid generating a text string that exceeds the maximum display width for the associated window. The **XTextExtents** function computes the dimensions of the rectangle containing a given 8-bit character string. This function and its 16-bit equivalent can set hints for the string's display window.

continues . . .

The **XQueryTextExtents** function requests that the server compute the dimensions of the rectangle containing a given 8-bit character string. Because it communicates with the server, it requires more time and resources than the associated **XTextExtents** function.

Graphics Contexts

The graphics context is one of the fundamental server resources. It contains extensive information describing graphics output. Both graphics and text functions reference the graphics context. The **XSetFont** function sets the current font of a given graphics context.

Drawing Text

Xlib provides several functions for drawing text characters. The **XDrawText** function draws text referenced in the XTextItem data structure. The **XDrawString** function draws the foreground bits of 8-bit text characters. The **XDrawImageString** function draws both the foreground and the background bits of 8-bit text characters. These functions may reference the graphics context. Similar functions manipulate 16-bit characters, often used with non-Latin fonts, such as Japanese.

CHAPTER

Keyboard

X Window systems supply a large variety of fonts to help generate effective output. The previous chapter described these fonts, their names, and their data structures; presented numerous Xlib functions for text generation; and concluded with several exercises displaying textual output.

Computer input is the antipodal twin of computer output. The keyboard is one of the fundamental devices for entering data and commands into the X Window system. Pay particular attention to keyboard manipulation. A mistake can freeze the keyboard, making it necessary to reboot the system. On occasion, keyboard errors can even destroy part of the operating system, requiring painstaking system reinitialization.

This chapter begins by presenting keyboard events and their associated data structures and explaining how they are processed. At any one time, the keyboard is assigned to a single window, called the keyboard focus. Xlib functions set and get the keyboard *focus*. Changing the focus generates events. Window managers and clients may attempt to reserve the keyboard for their own use, effectively shutting out other applications.

X Window enables system developers to transport applications from one workstation to another without time-consuming, expensive recoding. This portability is partially the result of the indirect manner with which the system handles keys on the keyboard. When the keyboard changes, compatability is maintained by changing the keyboard mapping, instead of recoding the application. The chapter concludes with exercises illustrating fundamental aspects of the keyboard.

Keyboard Events

Events inform the application that something of interest has happened. The aptly named keyboard events KeyPress and KeyRelease indicate when a key is pressed or released. Not all workstations can determine when users release keys. Therefore, to maintain maximum compatibility, your programs should not rely on KeyRelease events.

KeyPress and KeyRelease Events

The following event structure, XKeyEvent, describes both KeyPress events and KeyRelease events. Similar event structures are associated with mouse and pointer events discussed in Chapter 8, "Mouse."

```
typedef struct {
    int type;                    /* KeyPress or KeyRelease */
    unsigned long serial;        /* # of last server
                                    processed request */
    Bool send_event;             /* True if from SendEvent
                                    request */
    Display *display;            /* Display from where
                                    event came */
    Window window;               /* Window for which event
                                    reported */
    Window root;                 /* Root window for which event
                                    occurred */
    Window subwindow;            /* Child window */
    Time time;                   /* Time in milliseconds */
    int x, y;                    /* Event window coordinates */
    int x_root, y_root;          /* Coordinates relative to
                                    root window */
    unsigned int state;          /* Key or button mask */
    unsigned int keycode;        /* Detail */
    Bool same_screen;            /* Same screen or not */
} XKeyEvent;
typedef XKeyEvent XKeyPressedEvent;
typedef XKeyEvent XKeyReleasedEvent;
```

The XKeyEvent data structure contains three variables of the *Window* type. The *source window* is the viewable window containing the pointer. The source window itself does not appear in the XKeyEvent data structure. However, its ultimate ancestor, the root window, does appear in this data structure. The *window* variable reports the event. The X server determines this variable by ascending the window hierarchy until it either finds an interested (event mask on) window or encounters the *do_not_propagate* flag. The Boolean variable *same_screen* has the value TRUE if the root window and the event window are on the same physical screen. The Boolean variable *same_screen* has the value FALSE if the root window and the event window are on different physical screens.

The X server sets the *subwindow* variable as follows: If the source window is an inferior (descendant) of the event window, the *subwindow* variable is set to the event window child that is either the source window or an ancestor of the source window. If the source window is not an inferior of the event window, the server sets this variable to None.

Processing Keyboard Events

The Hello World program in Chapter 2, "Hello World," illustrated the steps involved in processing keyboard events. First, the **XSelectInput** function indicates events of interest to the application. Then, in the main processing loop, the **XNextEvent** function reads the registered event. Inside the main processing loop, a *case* statement contains the necessary code for KeyPress events, including the **XLookupString** function to translate the keyboard event for further use.

The **XSelectInput** function asks that the X server report selected events for a given window. Events are selected by setting to ON the appropriate bits in the event mask. A window that is not interested in a given event may propagate the event to its parent or another ancestor. The event is propagated up the window hierarchy until one of two things happens:

❑ An ancestor interested in the event type is found, and the event is processed

❑ The *do_not_propagate* flag is encountered, and the event is discarded.

The structure of **XSelectInput** is as follows:

```
XSelectInput(display, w, event_mask)
   Display *display;          /* Specifies connection
                                 to server */
   Window w;                  /* Window associated with
                                 events of interest */
   long event_mask;           /* Event mask */
```

The following **XSelectInput** function example selects KeyPress and Exposure events but does not select KeyRelease events.

```
XSelectInput(thedisplay, thewindow, (KeyPressMask
            | ExposureMask))
```

The **XNextEvent** function, shown next, copies the first event from the event queue into the specified XEvent data structure. It is used for general event types, not only Keyboard events.

```
XNextEvent(display, event_return)
   Display *display;              /* Specifies connection
                                     to the X server */
   XEvent *event_return;          /* Returns the next event
                                     in the event queue */
```

The following **XNextEvent** function example processes the first event in the event queue.

```
XNextEvent(thedisplay, &theevent)
```

The following pair of C language instructions directs the program to the code associated with KeyPress events. Other *case* statements handle different event types already specified by the **XSelectInput** function.

```
switch(theevent.type)
Case KeyPress;
```

KeyPress events execute the code situated between the *Case KeyPress* statement and the *break* statement. The **XLookUpString** function, shown here, translates a keyboard event to a character string and a *keysym*, an encoding of a symbol engraved on the physical key.

```
int XLookupString(event_struct, buffer_return, bytes_buffer,
                  keysym_return, status_in_out)
   XKeyEvent *event_struct;    /* XKeyPressedEvent or
                                  XKeyReleasedEvent */
   char *buffer_return;        /* Returns translated
                                  characters */
   int bytes_buffer;           /* Length of the buffer */
   KeySym *keysym_return;      /* Returns event's KeySym if
                                  not NULL */
   XComposeStatus *status_in_out;
```

```
                                /* Specifies or returns
                                   XComposeStatus structure
                                   or NULL */
```

XLookupString may return several characters for a single KeyPress or KeyRelease event.

The following code within the Hello World program determines whether a lowercase q was pressed.

```
keycount = XLookupString (&theevent, thebuffer, 8,
                          &thekey, 0);
if ((keycount == 1) && (thebuffer[0] == 'q'))
   finished = TRUE;
```

Associated Events

KeymapNotify events determine the state of all keys at the time of a FocusIn or EnterNotify event. The data structure for KeymapNotify events is as follows:

```
typedef struct {
   int type;                    /* KeymapNotify */
   unsigned long serial;        /* # of last server
                                   processed request */
   Bool send_event;             /* TRUE if from SendEvent
                                   request */
   Display *display;            /* Display from where
                                   event came */
   Window window;               /* Window for which event
                                   reported */
   char key_vector[32];
} XKeymapEvent;
```

MappingNotify events inform all clients when any client application calls one of the following Xlib functions: **XSetModifierMapping**, **XChangeKeyboardMapping**, and **XSetPointerMapping**. Only the first two of these Xlib functions are associated with the keyboard. The data structure for MappingNotify events is as follows:

```
typedef struct {
  int type;                         /* MappingNotify */
  unsigned long serial;             /* # of last server
                                       processed request */
  Bool send_event;                  /* TRUE if from SendEvent
                                       request */
  Display *display;                 /* Display from where
                                       event came */
  Window window;                    /* Unused */
  int request;                      /* MappingModifier,
                                       MappingKeyBoard, or
                                       MappingPointer */
  int first_keycode;                /* First keycode */
  int count;                        /* Defines range of change
                                       with first_keycode */
} XMappingEvent;
```

The *first_keycode* and *count* variables are defined only when the *request* variable is set to MappingKeyboard. The value of the *first_keycode* indicates the first keycode in the altered mapping, and the *count* indicates the number of keycodes altered.

KeyboardFocus

The keyboard focus assigns the keyboard to a particular window. It is set with the **XSetInputFocus** function and read with the **XGetInput-Focus** function. Changing this focus generates events that enable the application to keep track of the window associated with KeyPress and KeyRelease events.

Setting and Getting the Focus

The **XSetInputFocus** function, shown here, assigns the keyboard focus to a specified window. It causes the X server to generate FocusIn and FocusOut events.

```
XSetInputFocus(display, focus, revert_to, time)
  Display *display;          /* Specifies connection
                                to server */
  Window focus;              /* Window, PointerRoot,
                                or None */
  int revert_to;             /* Where input focus reverts to
                                if window not viewable */
  Time time;                 /* Timestamp or CurrentTime */
```

If the *focus* parameter is set to a window identifier, the specified window obtains the keyboard focus. If the *focus* parameter is set to PointerRoot, the root window obtains the keyboard focus. If the workstation has more than one screen, the root window of the screen containing the pointer obtains the keyboard focus. In this case, the *revert_to* parameter is ignored. If the *focus* parameter is set to None, keyboard events are ignored, and the *revert_to* parameter is ignored.

If the focus window is not viewable when the **XSetInputFocus** function is called, a BadMatch error occurs. If the focus window becomes unviewable (it may be unmapped, destroyed, or totally occluded by other windows), the *revert_to* parameter determines the new focus window.

When the *revert_to* parameter has the value RevertToParent, the parent window (or its first viewable ancestor) becomes the focus window. The *revert_to* parameter then assumes the value RevertToNone.

When the *revert_to* parameter has the value RevertToPointerRoot, the root window for the screen containing the pointer becomes the focus window. The X server generates FocusIn and FocusOut events.

When the *revert_to* parameter has the value RevertToNone, the focus does not revert, and no FocusIn or FocusOut events are generated.

The **XGetInputFocus** function returns the focus window and the focus state: RevertToParent, RevertToPointerRoot, or RevertToNone.

```
XGetInputFocus(display, focus_return, revert_to_return)
  Display *display;          /* Specifies connection
                                to server */
  Window focus_return;       /* Focus window, PointerRoot,
                                or None */
  int revert_to_return;      /* Returns current focus state */
```

FocusIn and FocusOut Events

Setting the FocusChangeMask bit in the *event_mask* parameter of the function **XSelectInput** solicits FocusIn events when the specified window gains the keyboard focus and solicits FocusOut events when the specified window loses the keyboard focus. The program may apply focus change events to highlight the focus window, smoothing the user interface.

The XFocusChangeEvent data structure, shown here, contains seven parameters, five of which are found in all event data structures.

```
typedef struct {
    int type;                  /* FocusIn or FocusOut */
    unsigned long serial;  /* # of last server
                              processed request */
    Bool send_event;       /* TRUE if from SendEvent request */
    Display *display;      /* Display from where event came */
    Window window;         /* Window for which event reported */
    int mode;              /* NotifyNormal, NotifyGrab,
                              NotifyUngrab, NotifyWhileGrabbed */
    int detail;            /* NotifyAncestor, NotifyVirtual,
                              NotifyInferior, NotifyNonlinear,
                              NotifyNonlinearVirtual,
                              NotifyPointer, NotifyPointerRoot,
                              NotifyDetailNone */
} XFocusChangeEvent;
    typedef XFocusChangeEvent XFocusInEvent;
    typedef XFocusChangeEvent XFocusOutEvent;
```

XFocusChangeEvent has two special parameters. The first, *mode*, indicates whether the focus change was a normal focus change or a focus change associated with a *keyboard grab*, also called an *active keyboard grab*, an application's attempt to obtain exclusive control of the keyboard. The second, *detail*, returns a value describing the relationship between the previous and the present focus windows.

Changing the Focus

When the focus changes, the workstation informs all its applications by generating first FocusOut events and then FocusIn events. Applications solicit these events by setting the previously described Focus-ChangeMask before calling the **XSelectInput** function.

Losing the Focus

Four categories of windows receive FocusOut events when they lose the input focus. Recall that the **XSetInputFocus** function includes a *focus* parameter that assumes one of the following values: Window, PointerRoot, or None. When the *focus* parameter assumes the value Window, it is necessary to distinguish among three categories of windows: the inferiors (descendants) of the window that lost the focus (but only if they contain the pointer), the window that lost the focus, and the ancestors of the window that lost the focus. The fourth category of window occurs when the *focus* parameter assumes the value PointerRoot or None. For simplicity, call these window categories A, B, C, and D. The workstation generates FocusOut events by working its way up the window hierarchy, starting with windows in category A and ending with windows in category D.

A: Inferiors of the Window That Lost the Focus All windows situated in the window hierarchy between the window containing the pointer and the window losing the focus receive a FocusOut event. The windows can no longer expect to receive keyboard events. Event windows in group A are identified by one of two values of the *detail* parameter in the XFocusChangeEvent data structure.

NotifyPointer   An ancestor of the event window lost the focus.
NotifyPointerRoot   The focus was PointerRoot.

B: The Window That Itself Lost the Focus This group contains one window, unless the *focus* was set to None or PointerRoot. Event windows in group B are identified by one of three values of the *detail* parameter in the XFocusChangeEvent data structure.

NotifyAncestor   The event window lost the focus to an ancestor.
NotifyInferior   The event window lost the focus to an inferior window.

NotifyNonlinear

The event window lost the focus to a window that is neither an ancestor nor an inferior window, or the *focus* parameter of the **XSetInputFocus** function became either PointerRoot or None.

C: Ancestors of the Window That Lost the Focus   Event windows in group C are identified by one of two values of the *detail* parameter in the XFocusChangeEvent data structure.

NotifyVirtual

An inferior of the event window lost the focus to an ancestor of the event window.

NotifyNonlinear

An inferior of the event window lost the focus to a window that is neither its ancestor nor its inferior window, or the *focus* parameter of the **XSetInput-Focus** function became either PointerRoot or None.

D: The focus Parameter Has the Value PointerRoot or None   The event window must be a root window. Event windows in group D are identified by one of two values of the *detail* parameter in the XFocusChangeEvent data structure.

NotifyPointerRoot

The value of the *detail* parameter was PointerRoot.

NotifyDetailNone

The value of the *detail* parameter was None.

Note   The value of the *detail* parameter in the XFocusChangeEvent data structure indicates the group for the event window. If this parameter equals NotifyPointerRoot, you must examine the contents of the *detail* parameter as well.

Gaining the Focus

Four categories of windows receive FocusIn events when they gain the input focus. These categories are similar to the four categories of windows that receive FocusOut events when they lose the input focus. However, the order of windows receiving FocusIn events is the opposite of the order of windows receiving FocusOut events. For simplicity, call the four window categories E, F, G, and H. Category E is similar to category D.

Category F is similar to category C. Category G is similar to category B. Category H is similar to category A. The workstation generates FocusOut events by working its way down the window hierarchy, starting with windows in category E and ending with windows in category H.

E: The focus Parameter Has the Value PointerRoot or None   The event window must be a root window. Event windows in group E are identified by one of two values of the *detail* parameter in the XFocusChangeEvent data structure.

NotifyPointerRoot   The value of the *detail* parameter was PointerRoot.

NotifyDetailNone   The value of the *detail* parameter was None.

F: Ancestors of the Window That Gained the Focus   Event windows in group F are identified by one of two values of the *detail* parameter in the XFocusChangeEvent data structure.

NotifyVirtual   An inferior of the event window gained the focus from an ancestor of the event window.

NotifyNonlinear   An inferior of the event window gained the focus from a window that is neither its ancestor nor its inferior window, or the *focus* parameter of the **XSetInputFocus** function was either PointerRoot or None.

G: The Window That Itself Gained the Focus   This group contains one window, unless the *focus* was set to None or PointerRoot. Event windows in group G are identified by one of three values of the *detail* parameter in the XFocusChangeEvent data structure.

NotifyAncestor   The event window gained the focus from an ancestor.

NotifyInferior   The event window gained the focus from an inferior window.

NotifyNonlinear   The event window gained the focus from a window that is neither an ancestor nor an inferior window, or the *focus* parameter of the **XSetInputFocus** function was either PointerRoot or None.

H: Inferiors of the Window That Gained the Focus All windows situated in the window hierarchy between the window containing the pointer and the window gaining the focus receive a FocusIn event. Event windows in group H are identified by one of two values of the *detail* parameter in the XFocusChangeEvent data structure.

NotifyPointer   An ancestor of the event window gained the focus.

NotifyPointerRoot   The new focus is PointerRoot.

 Note The value of the *detail* parameter in the XFocusChangeEvent data structure indicates the group for the event window. If this parameter equals NotifyPointerRoot, you must examine the contents of the *detail* parameter as well.

Grabbing the Keyboard

An application may demand the exclusive right to keyboard events by issuing the round-trip **XGrabKeyboard** function. If the server grants this request, all keyboard events are delivered to a window specified by the application. Usually keyboard grabs are requested by window managers rather than client applications.

```
int XGrabKeyboard(display, grab_window, owner_events,
                pointer_mode, keyboard_mode, time)
  Display *display;              /* Specifies connection
                                    to server */
  Window grab_window;           /* Window associated with
                                    events of interest */
  Bool owner_events;            /* If TRUE, report
                                    keyboard events as usual
                                    If FALSE, report
                                    keyboard events via
                                    grab window */
  int pointer_mode;             /* Further pointer event
                                    processing
                                    GrabModeAsync, GrabModeSync */
  int keyboard_mode;            /* Further keyboard event
                                    processing
                                    GrabModeAsync, GrabModeSync */
  int time;                     /* Timestamp or Current Time */
```

XGrabKeyboard generates FocusIn and FocusOut events as described in the preceding sections. The *grab_window* must be viewable when the function is issued. If the *grab_window* becomes unviewable or the application terminates, the grab is automatically released. The usual setting for the *pointer-mode* parameter is GrabModeAsync, in which case keyboard event processing occurs normally. The setting GrabModeAsync effectively freezes the keyboard and the mouse until the grab is released or an **XAllowEvents** function is issued. The *time* parameter does not establish request priority; it helps keep track of this round-trip request.

The following is an example of an **XGrabKeyboard** function call:

```
status = XGrabKeyboard (display, grab_window, owner_events,
                        pointer_mode, keyboard_mode, time);
```

The *status* variable returns a value indicating a successful keyboard grab or one of several errors:

❑ GrabSuccess indicates that the keyboard grab was completed without error.

❑ AlreadyGrabbed indicates that another client has already grabbed the keyboard.

❑ GrabInvalidTime may indicate that another client attempted to grab the keyboard relying on the same event. It may also indicate that the *time* parameter was specified incorrectly.

❑ GrabFrozen indicates that the keyboard is frozen (because of a *keyboard_mode* parameter set to GrabModeSync).

❑ GrabNotViewable indicates that the *grab_window* is not viewable.

In addition to unsuccessful attempts to grab the keyboard, the **XGrab-Keyboard** function can generate BadValue and BadWindow errors.

Grabbing a Single Key

An application may want to enable users to enter special keystroke combinations that perform desired activities, such as printing the screen. The **XGrabKey** function establishes a *passive keyboard grab*. A passive keyboard grab alerts the system to look for the following conditions:

❏   The user presses a specified combination of keyboard modifier
    keys such as SHIFT or CONTROL.

❏   The user presses a grabbed key.

❏   The KeyPress event generated when the user pressed the
    grabbed key belongs to the specified window or an inferior of that
    window. This situation occurs when the specified window or an
    ancestor of that window contains the input focus.

When these three conditions all occur, the passive grab issues an
active keyboard grab. The **XGrabKey** function is shown here.

```
XGrabKey(display, keycode, modifiers, grab_window,
        owner_events, pointer_mode, keyboard_mode, time)
Display *display;           /* Specifies connection
                               to server */
int keycode;                /* Keycode or AnyKey */
unsigned int modifiers;     /* Set of keymasks
                               or AnyModifier */
Window grab_window;         /* Grab window */
Bool owner_events;          /* If TRUE, report
                               keyboard events as usual
                               If FALSE, report
                               keyboard events via
                               grab window */
int pointer_mode;           /* Further pointer event
                               processing
                               GrabModeAsync, GrabModeSync */
int keyboard_mode;          /* Further keyboard event
                               processing
                               GrabModeAsync, GrabModeSync */
int time;                   /* Timestamp or Current Time */
```

XGrabKey can generate BadAccess, BadValue, and BadWindow errors.

Ungrabbing the Keyboard

The **XUngrabKeyboard** function, shown next, releases the keyboard
for active grabs issued directly by the **XGrabKeyboard** function or
indirectly by the **XGrabKey** function.

```
XUngrabKeyboard(display, time)
  Display *display;            /* Specifies connection
                                  to server */
  int time;                    /* Timestamp or Current Time */
```

The **XUngrabKeyboard** function generates FocusIn and FocusOut events. It is automatically generated if the event window associated with an active key grab becomes unviewable.

Keycodes, Keymaps, and Keysyms

A major feature of X Window is the ability to transport applications from one workstation to another without time-consuming, expensive recoding. This flexibility is ensured in part by assigning integers between 8 and 255, inclusive, called *keycodes*, to a workstation's physical keys. The set of keycodes depends on the specific workstation model. Keycodes can be assigned individually or in groups using a *keymap*, an array of bytes containing 1 bit per keycode. *Keysyms* are standard mnemonic codes for keycap symbols. For example, the keysym *XK_F1* refers to the function key F1 no matter where this key is located on the keyboard—provided, of course, that the keyboard has function keys.

Most physical keys have at least two states: one without the SHIFT key pressed and one with the SHIFT key pressed. To deal with this complication, X Window assigns two indexes to each keysym. The keysym with index zero is the unshifted key, and the keysym with index 1 is the shifted key. The header file <X11/keysym.h> defines the keysym values. Xlib includes several functions processing keycodes, keymaps, and keysyms.

Keyboard Mapping Functions

Xlib includes several functions associated with keyboard mapping. These functions notify the application when the keyboard mapping has changed, get the keyboard mapping, or change the mapping. The following discussion also presents the **XDisplayKeycodes** function, which furnishes required information to some of the keyboard mapping functions.

RefreshKeyboardMapping

The **XRefreshKeyboardMapping** function updates Xlib's knowledge of the keyboard by refreshing the stored modifier and keyboard information.

```
XRefreshKeyboardMapping(event_map)
  XMappingEvent *event_map;  /* Mapping event to be used */
```

The **XRefreshKeyboardMapping** function processes MappingNotify events. All applications should call this function to prevent unpleasant surprises should the keyboard mapping change.

XDisplayKeycodes

The **XDisplayKeycodes** function, shown next, obtains the legal keycodes for a given display. The number of keycodes returned is between 8 and 255, inclusive. This function returns the minimum and maximum number of keycodes required by functions that get or change the keycodes.

```
XDisplayKeycodes(display, min_keycodes_return,
              max_keycodes_return)
  Display *display;          /* Specifies connection
                                to server */
  min_keycodes_return;       /* Returns minimum number
                                of keycodes */
  max_keycodes_return;       /* Returns maximum number
                                of keycodes */
```

XGetKeyboardMapping

The **XGetKeyboardMapping** function, shown next, obtains the keysyms for one or more keycodes.

```
KeySym *XGetKeyboardMapping(display, first_keycode,
                          keycode_count,
                          keysyms_per_keycode_return)
  Display *display;          /* Specifies connection
                                to server */
```

```
KeyCode first_keycode;      /* First keycode
                               to be returned */
int keycode_count;          /* Number of keycodes
                               to be returned */
int *key_syms_per_keycode_return;
                            /* Returns number of keysyms
                               per keycode */
```

The **XGetKeyboardMapping** function can generate a BadValue error if the *first_keycode* is less than the minimum keycode given by the *min_keycode* parameter of the **XDisplayKeycodes** function discussed previously. It can generate a BadValue error if the following expression is TRUE:

first_keycode + *keycode_count* – 1 > *max_keycode*

where *max_keycode* is generated by the **XDisplayKeycodes** function.

The X server determines the value of the *key_syms_per_keycode_return* parameter to encompass the keycode with the most keysyms. This parameter is used in two common calculations:

The number of elements in the keysyms list is

keycode_count x *key_syms_per_keycode_return*

The index for keysym number *N* for keycode *K* is

(*K* – *first_code*) x *key_syms_per_keycode_return* + *N*

XChangeKeyboardMapping

The **XChangeKeyboardMapping** function, shown here, modifies the keysyms for one or more keycodes.

```
XChangeKeyboardMapping(display, first_keycode,
              keysyms_per_keycode, keysyms, num_codes)
  Display *display;         /* Specifies connection
                               to server */
  int first_keycode;        /* First keycode
                               to be changed */
  int key_syms_per_keycode; /* Number of keysyms
```

```
                                    per keycode */
KeySym *keysyms;                /* Array of keysyms
int num_codes;                  /* Number of keycodes
                                   to be changed */
```

The **XChangeKeyboardMapping** function parameters resemble those for the **XGetKeyboardMapping** function. The client specifies the value of the *key_syms_per_keycode* to encompass the keycode with the most keysyms. **XChangeKeyboardMapping** can generate BadAlloc and BadValue errors.

XQueryKeymap

The **XQueryKeymap** function, shown here, obtains a bit vector 32 bytes long, in which each bit set to 1 represents a pressed key on the keyboard.

```
XQueryKeymap(display, keys_return)
  Display *display;             /* Specifies connection
                                   to server */
  char keys_return[32];         /* Identifies which keys are
                                   pressed */
```

Keysym and Keycode Conversion Functions

Xlib provides several functions that convert between different keysym and keycode representations.

The **XLookupKeysym** function obtains the keysym for the keycode of an event.

```
KeySym XLookupKeysym(key_event, index)
  XKeyEvent *key_event;         /* Specifies KeyPress
                                   or KeyRelease event */
  int index;                    /* Index to keysyms list
                                   for event's keycode */
```

When a keycode for an event does not have a corresponding keysym, the function generates the return value NoSymbol.

The **XKeycodeToKeysym** function returns a keysym for a given keycode.

```
KeySym XKeycodeToKeysym(display, keycode, index)
    Display *display;           /* Specifies connection
                                    to server */
    KeyCode keycode;            /* Keycode */
    int index;                  /* Element of keycode vector */
```

If no keysym is defined for the given keycode, the function generates the return value NoSymbol.

The **XKeysymToKeycode** function returns a keycode for a given keysym.

```
KeyCode XKeysymToKeycode(display, keysym)
    Display *display;           /* Specifies connection
                                    to server */
    KeySym keysym;              /* Keysym to be searched for */
```

If the specified keysym is not defined for a given keycode, the function returns zero.

The standard keysym name is obtained by removing the XF_ prefix from the name found in the <X11/keysymdef.h> header file. The **XStringToKeysym** function, shown next, converts the name of the keysym to the keysym code.

```
KeySym XStringToKeysym(string)
    char *string;               /* Specifies name of keysym
                                    to be converted */
```

If the specified string does not match any valid keysym, the function returns the value NoSymbol.

The **XKeysymToString** function converts a keysym code to the name of the keysym.

```
char *XKeysymToString(keysym)
    KeySym keysym;              /* Specifies keysym
                                    to be converted */
```

If the specified keysym is undefined, the function returns the value NULL.

Keysym Classification Macros

Xlib offers several macros that enable you to test the type of keysym: for example, whether a given keysym is a cursor key.

The macro **IsCursorKey** returns the value TRUE if the specified keysym is a cursor key.

```
IsCursorKey(keysym)
  keysym                    /* Specifies keysym to be tested */
```

The macro **IsFunctionKey** returns the value TRUE if the specified keysym is a function key.

```
IsFunctionKey(keysym)
  keysym                    /* Specifies keysym to be tested */
```

The macro **IsKeypadKey** returns the value TRUE if the specified keysym is a keypad key.

```
IsKeypadKey(keysym)
  keysym                    /* Specifies keysym to be tested */
```

The macro **IsMiscFunctionKey** returns the value TRUE if the specified keysym is a miscellaneous function key.

```
IsMiscFunctionKey(keysym)
  keysym                    /* Specifies keysym to be tested */
```

The macro **IsModifierKey** returns the value TRUE if the specified keysym is a modifier key.

```
IsModifierKey(keysym)
  keysym                    /* Specifies keysym to be tested */
```

The macro **IsPFKey** returns the value TRUE if the specified keysym is a PF (programmable function) key.

```
IsPFKey(keysym)
  keysym                    /* Specifies keysym to be tested */
```

Additional Keyboard Functions

Xlib offers additional functions that extend the use of the keyboard. These functions include the **XRebindKeysym** function, which assigns long strings to a given keysym, and the **XChangeKeyboardControl** function, which enables the application to set keyboard values such as a bell and the autorepeat mode.

The **XRebindKeysym** function, shown here, assigns long strings to a given keysym. The client must supply correctly encoded strings.

```
XRebindKeysym(display, keysym, list, mod_count,
          string, num_bytes)
  Display *display;          /* Specifies connection
                                to server */
  KeySym keysym;             /* KeySym to be rebound */
  KeySym list[];             /* Keysyms to be used as
                                modifiers */
  int mod_count;             /* Number of modifiers in list */
  unsigned char *string;     /* String that is copied
                                and to be returned by
                                XLookupString */
  int num_bytes;             /* Number of bytes in
                                string argument */
```

The **XChangeKeyboardControl** function, shown next, controls keyboard characteristics as defined by the XKeyboardControl data structure.

```
XChangeKeyboardControl(display, value_mask, values)
  Display *display;          /* Specifies connection
                                to server */
  unsigned long value_mask;  /* The controls to change */
  XKeyboardControl *values;  /* Value for each bit set to 1
                                in mask */
```

XChangeKeyboardControl can generate BadMatch and BadValue errors.

The following illustrates the mask bits and data structure associated with keyboard control.

```
/* Mask bits for ChangeKeyboardControl */
#define KBKeyClickPercent     (1L<<0)
#define KBBellPercent         (1L<<1)
#define KBBellPitch           (1L<<2)
#define KBBellDuration        (1L<<3)
#define KBLed                 (1L<<4)
#define KBLedMode             (1L<<5)
#define KBKey                 (1L<<6)
#define KBAutoRepeatMode      (1L<<7)
/* Values */
typedef struct {
  int key_click_percent;
  int bell_percent;
  int bell_pitch;
  int bell_duration;
  int led;
  int led_mode;                 /* LedModeOn, LedModeOff */
  int key;
  int auto_repeat_mode;         /* AutoRepeatModeOff,
                                   AutoRepeatModeOff,
                                   AutoRepeatModeDefault */
} XKeyboardControl;
```

The **XGetKeyboardControl** function, shown here, places current control values of the keyboard into the XKeyboardState data structure.

```
XGetKeyboardControl(display, values_return)
  Display *display;             /* Specifies connection
                                   to server */
  XKeyboardState *values_return;
                                /* Returns current keyboard
                                   controls in specified
                                   data structure */
```

The following is the XKeyboardState data structure:

```
typedef struct {
  int key_click_percent;
  int bell_percent;
  unsigned int bell_pitch;
  unsigned int bell_duration;
  unsigned long led_mask;
```

```
        int global_auto_repeat;
        char auto_repeats[32];
    } XKeyboardState;
```

The **XAutoRepeatOn** function, shown next, turns on the keyboard autorepeat.

```
XAutoRepeatOn(display)
    Display *display;           /* Specifies connection
                                   to server */
```

The **XAutoRepeatOff** function, shown next, turns off the keyboard autorepeat.

```
XAutoRepeatOff(display)
    Display *display;           /* Specifies connection
                                   to server */
```

The **XBell** function, shown next, rings the bell on the keyboard for the specified display.

```
XBell(display, percent)
    Display *display;           /* Specifies connection
                                   to server */
    int percent;                /* Bell volume, -100 to 100 */
```

XBell can generate a BadValue error.

Applying Fundamental Keyboard Functions: Example 1

The following Xlib program applies fundamental keyboard functions **XlookupString** and **XKeysymToString**. It requires four header librairies, including <X11/Xos.h>, which contains UNIX system files and <X11/keysym.h>, which contains information about the keysyms.

The macro max obtains the maximum of two values.

```
#define max(val1,val2) ((val1) > (val2) ? (val1) : (val2))
```

The variable *thehints* is of the data type XSizeHints, discussed in Chapter 2, "Hello World," and the variable *attributes* is of the data type XSetWindowAttributes, discussed in Chapter 4, "Windows and Windowing Techniques."

```
XSizeHints      thehints;
XSetWindowAttributes attributes;
```

The **XSetStandardProperties** function sets properties for a window, including size hints. The version used here extracts the window name and the icon name from the command line.

```
XSetStandardProperties (thedisplay, thewindow, prog_name,
                        prog_name, 0, argv, argc,
                        &thehints);
```

The *switch* statement processes 12 different event types. The associated event masks are included as well. Many of these event types, such as ButtonPress and ButtonRelease, are not presently implemented. The associated C language functions, such as **Button_Func**, are empty. When these event types are implemented, the associated functions will be completed.

```
        case ButtonPress:
        case ButtonRelease:
          Button_Func (&event);
        break;
...
attributes.event_mask = ...ButtonPressMask
                            | ButtonReleaseMask |...;
...
Button_Func (eventp)
  XEvent *eventp;
  {
    return;
  }
```

The **XParseGeometry** function generates the window size hints. The code itself is fairly complicated and is not discussed further here.

The **Key_Func** C language function is executed when either a KeyPress or a KeyRelease event is detected. The **XLookupString** function translates a keyboard event to a keysym (in the parameter *&keysym*), the translated characters (in the parameter *string*), and the number of characters returned (in the parameter *n*). The program performs extensive error checking: for example, looking for nonexistent keysyms, keysyms without names, and incorrect number of characters returned.

```
n = XLookupString (event, string, 256, &keysym, NULL);
if (keysym == NULL)
  keysymname = "NoSymbol";
else
if (!(keysymname == XKeysymToString (keysym)))
  keysymname = "(no name)";
if (n < 0)
  n = 0;
if (n > MAX_CHARS)
  n = MAX_CHARS;
string[n] = '\0';
printf ("\n XLookupString: pressed %d
        character(s) -> \"%s\"\n", n, string);
```

The program terminates when **ℚ** (keysym of XK_Q) or **q** (keysym of XK_q) is entered.

```
if ((keysym == XK_Q) || (keysym == XK_q))
{
  printf("\n Exiting from program ... \n");
  exit(0);
}
return;
```

The complete listing for Example 7-1 is shown here.

```
/* Example 7-1 */
#include <X11/Xos.h>
#include <X11/Xlib.h>
#include <X11/Xutil.h>
#include <X11/keysym.h>

#define WINDOW_WIDTH 50
#define WINDOW_HEIGHT 50
#define WINDOW_BORDER 4
#define WINDOW_X 10
```

```
#define WINDOW_Y 10
#define WINDOW_MIN_WIDTH (WINDOW_WIDTH + \
        2 * (WINDOW_BORDER + WINDOW_X))
#define WINDOW_MIN_HEIGHT (WINDOW_HEIGHT + \
        2 * (WINDOW_BORDER + WINDOW_Y))
#define WINDOW_DEF_WIDTH (WINDOW_MIN_WIDTH + 100)
#define WINDOW_DEF_HEIGHT (WINDOW_MIN_HEIGHT + 100)
#define WINDOW_DEF_X 100
#define WINDOW_DEF_Y 100
#define TRUE 1
#define FALSE 0
#define BAD -1
#define MAX_CHARS 256
#define max(val1,val2) ((val1) > (val2) ? (val1) : (val2))

char          *prog_name;
Display       *thedisplay;
int           thescreen;
XSizeHints    thehints;
XSetWindowAttributes attributes;
unsigned long mask = 0L;
char          *thegeometry;

void init_app();

main (argc, argv)
  int argc;
  char **argv;
{
  int borderwidth = 2;
  Window thewindow;
  XEvent event;
  int done = FALSE;

  init_app(argv);

  thewindow = XCreateWindow (thedisplay,
                    RootWindow (thedisplay, thescreen),
                    thehints.x, thehints.y,
                    thehints.width, thehints.height,
                    borderwidth, 0, InputOutput,
                    (Visual *)CopyFromParent, mask,
```

```
                                  &attributes);

XSetStandardProperties (thedisplay, thewindow, prog_name,
                        prog_name, 0, argv, argc,
                        &thehints);

XMapWindow (thedisplay, thewindow);

printf("\n Main loop (point into created window,");
printf(" to quit press Q or q) ... \n");
while(!done)
{

  XNextEvent (thedisplay, &event);

  switch (event.type)
  {
    case KeyPress:
    case KeyRelease:
      Key_Func (&event);
    break;
    case ButtonPress:
    case ButtonRelease:
      Button_Func (&event);
    break;
    case MotionNotify:
      MotionNotify_Func (&event);
    break;
    case EnterNotify:
    case LeaveNotify:
      Notify_Func (&event);
    break;
    case FocusIn:
    case FocusOut:
      Focus_Func (&event);
    break;
    case KeymapNotify:
      KeymapNotify_Func (&event);
    break;
    case Expose:
      Expose_Func (&event);
    break;
```

```
      case NoExpose:
        NoExpose Func (&event);
      break;
      default:
      break;
    }
  }

  XCloseDisplay (thedisplay);
  exit (0);
}

void init_app(argv)
char **argv;
{

  prog_name = argv[0];

  thedisplay = XOpenDisplay ("");
  if (!thedisplay)
  {
    exit (1);
  }

  set_sizehints (&thehints, WINDOW_MIN_WIDTH,
                 WINDOW_MIN_HEIGHT,
                 WINDOW_DEF_WIDTH, WINDOW_DEF_HEIGHT,
                 WINDOW_DEF_X, WINDOW_DEF_Y, thegeometry);

  thescreen = DefaultScreen (thedisplay);

  attributes.background_pixel =
            BlackPixel (thedisplay, thescreen);
  attributes.border_pixel =
            WhitePixel (thedisplay, thescreen);
/* select for all events */
  attributes.event_mask = KeyPressMask | KeyReleaseMask
                    | ButtonPressMask | ButtonReleaseMask
                    | EnterWindowMask | LeaveWindowMask
                    | PointerMotionMask
                    | PointerMotionHintMask | ExposureMask
                    | ButtonMotionMask | KeymapStateMask
```

```
                          | FocusChangeMask | PropertyChangeMask;

   mask |= (CWBackPixel | CWBorderPixel | CWEventMask);
}


   set_sizehints (hintptr, min_width, min_height,
                   defwidth, defheight, defx, defy, geometry)
   XSizeHints *hintptr;
   int min_width, min_height, defwidth, defheight, defx, defy;
   char *geometry;
   {
     int result;

/* set the size hints according to xlib */

   hintptr->width = min_width;
   hintptr->min_width = min_width;
   hintptr->height = min_height;
   hintptr->min_height = min_height;
   hintptr->flags = PMinSize;
   hintptr->x = 0;
   hintptr->y = 0;
   result = BAD;

   if (geometry != NULL)
   {
     result = XParseGeometry (geometry, &hintptr->x,
                     &hintptr->y,
                     (unsigned int *)&hintptr->width,
                     (unsigned int *)&hintptr->height);
     if ((result & WidthValue) && (result & HeightValue))
     {
       hintptr->width =
               max (hintptr->width, hintptr->min_width);
       hintptr->height =
               max (hintptr->height, hintptr->min_height);
       hintptr->flags |= USSize;
     }
     if ((result & XValue) && (result & YValue))
     {
       hintptr->flags += USPosition;
     }
```

```
    }
    if (!(hintptr->flags & USSize))
    {
      hintptr->width = defwidth;
      hintptr->height = defheight;
      hintptr->flags |= PSize;
    }
    if (result & XNegative)
    {
      hintptr->x = DisplayWidth (thedisplay,
                          DefaultScreen (thedisplay))
                          + hintptr->x - hintptr->width;
    }
    if (result & YNegative)
    {
      hintptr->y = DisplayHeight (thedisplay,
                          DefaultScreen (thedisplay))
                          + hintptr->y - hintptr->height;
    }
    return;
}

Key_Func (eventp)
  XEvent *eventp;
{
  XKeyEvent *event = (XKeyEvent *) eventp;
  KeySym keysym;
  char *keysymname;
  int n;
  char string[MAX_CHARS+1];

  n = XLookupString (event, string, 256, &keysym, NULL);
  if (keysym == NULL)
    keysymname = "NoSymbol";
  else
  if (!(keysymname == XKeysymToString (keysym)))
    keysymname = "(no name)";
  if (n < 0)
    n = 0;
  if (n > MAX_CHARS)
    n = MAX_CHARS;
  string[n] = '\0';
```

```
    printf ("\n XLookupString: pressed %d
            character(s) -> \"%s\"\n", n, string);
    if ((keysym == XK_Q) || (keysym == XK_q))
    {
      printf("\n Exiting from program ... \n");
      exit(0);
    }
    return;
}

Button_Func (eventp)
  XEvent *eventp;
  {
    return;
  }

MotionNotify_Func (eventp)
  XEvent *eventp;
  {
    return;
  }

Notify_Func (eventp)
  XEvent *eventp;
  {
    return;
  }

Focus_Func (eventp)
  XEvent *eventp;
  {
    return;
  }

KeymapNotify_Func (eventp)
  XEvent *eventp;
  {
    return;
  }

Expose_Func (eventp)
  XEvent *eventp;
```

```
{
   return;
}


NoExpose_Func (eventp)
  XEvent *eventp;
  {
    return;
  }
```

Results of executing this program are shown in Figure 7-1.

The following listing is the MAKE file for Exercise 7-1 as run on the X Window system using the Santa Cruz Open Desktop software. The MAKE file for other X Window implementations varies.

```
RM = rm - f
CC = cc
CFLAGS = -0
INCLUDES = -I. -I/usr/include -I/usr/include/X11
LIBS = -1Xm -1Xt -1X11 -1socket -1malloc -1PW
.c.o:
$(RM) $@
$(CC) -c $(CFLAGS) $(INCLUDES) $*.c
all:: exercise7-1
exercise7-1: exercise 7-1.o
$(RM) $@
$(CC) -o $@ $(CFLAGS) exercise7-1.o $(LIBS)
@echo makefile for exercise 7-1 - done!
```

Rebinding the Keyboard: Example 2

This example is fairly similar to the previous exercise. It *rebinds* several keys—in other words, it associates predefined character strings with selected keys. The only changes to the program are in the **Key_Func** function.

The function **XBell** rings the bell when the user enters any key. The variable *keysym[2]* indicates a *dyadic key*, a key with two keysyms. The function **XRebindKeysym** provides an easy way for long strings to be

Result of applying the **XLookupString** and **XKeysymToString** functions

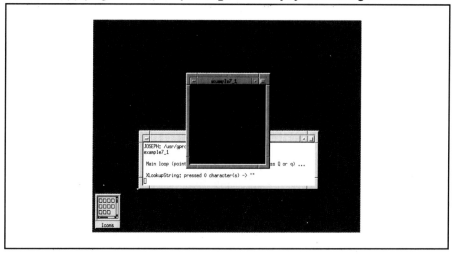

associated with keys. The following code binds the string "string1" to the function key F1, and the string "Help Message" to the keystroke combination CTRL-F1. This program assumes the existence of the CTRL-F1 and CTRL-F2 combination keystrokes. If these keystrokes are unavailable, the program must be modified slightly to use existing keystroke combinations.

```
XRebindKeysym(thedisplay, XK_F1, NULL, 0,
             "string1", strlen("string1"));
keysym[1] = XK_Control_L;
XRebindKeysym(thedisplay, XK_F1, keysym, 1,
             "Help Message", strlen("Help Message"));
```

The complete modifed C language function **Key_Func** is shown here.

```
Key_Func (eventp)
  XEvent *eventp;
{
```

```
XKeyEvent *event = (XKeyEvent *) eventp;
Keysym keysym[2];
char *keysymname;
int n;
char string[MAX_CHARS+1];

XBell(thdisplay, 0);
XRebindKeysym(thedisplay, XK_F1, NULL, 0,
              "string1", strlen("string1"));
keysym[1] = XK_Control_L;
XRebindKeysym(thedisplay, XK_F1, keysym, 1,
              "Help Message", strlen("Help Message"));
XRebindKeysym(thedisplay, XK_F2, NULL, 0,
              "string2", strlen("string2"));
keysym[1] = XK_Control_L;
XRebindKeysym(thedisplay, XK_F2 keysym, 1,
              "Warning Message", strlen("Warning Message"));
n = XLookupString (event, string, 256, keysym, NULL);
if (keysym == NULL)
  keysymname = "NoSymbol";
else
if (!(keysymname == XKeysymToString (keysym)))
  keysymname = "(no name)";
if (n < 0)
  n = 0;
if (n > MAX_CHARS)
  n = MAX_CHARS;
string[n] = '\0';
printf ("\n XLookupString: pressed %d
        character(s) -> \"%s\"\n", n, string);
if ((keysym == XK_Q) || (keysym == XK_q))
{
  printf("\n Exiting from program ... \n");
  exit(0);
}
return;
```

Results of executing this program are shown in Figure 7-2.

FIGURE 7-2

Result of rebinding the keyboard

Key Points

Summary of Keyboard Events

The aptly named keyboard events KeyPress and KeyRelease indicate when a key is pressed or released. To maintain maximum compatibility, your programs should not rely on KeyRelease events, since not all keyboards report key releases. Both events are associated with the XKeyEvent data structure.

Processing Keyboard Events

The **XSelectInput** function indicates events of interest to the application. Then, in the main processing loop, the **XNextEvent** function reads the registered event. The **XLookUpString** function translates a keyboard event to a character string and a keysym, an encoding of a symbol engraved on the physical key.

continues . . .

KeyboardFocus

The keyboard focus assigns the keyboard to a particular window. The **XSetInputFocus** function assigns the keyboard focus to a specified window. The **XGetInputFocus** function returns the focus window. When the focus changes, the workstation informs all its applications by generating first FocusOut events and then FocusIn events. Four categories of windows receive FocusOut events when they lose the input focus. Four similar categories of windows receive FocusIn events when they gain the input focus.

Grabbing the Keyboard

An application may demand the exclusive right to keyboard events by issuing the round-trip **XGrabKeyboard** function. Usually keyboard grabs are requested by window managers rather than client applications. An application can issue the **XGrabKey** function to enable users to enter special keystroke combinations that perform desired activities such as printing the screen. The **XUngrabKeyboard** function releases the keyboard after a grab.

Keycodes, Keymaps, and Keysyms

A major aspect of X Window is the ability to transport applications from one workstation to another without time-consuming, expensive recoding. This flexibility is ensured in part by assigning integers between 8 and 255, called keycodes, to a workstation's physical keys. The set of keycodes depends on the specific workstation model.

continues . . .

Keycodes can be assigned individually or in groups using a keymap, an array of bytes containing 1 bit per keycode. Keysyms are standard mnemonic codes for keycap symbols. Xlib includes several functions associated with the keyboard mapping.

Xlib provides several functions that convert between different keysym and keycode representations. Xlib offers several macros that enable you to test the type of keysym: for example, whether a given keysym is a cursor key. Xlib offers additional functions that extend use of the keyboard. These functions include the **XRebindKeysym** function that assigns long strings to a given keysym and the **XChangeKeyboardControl** function that enables the application to set keyboard values such as a bell.

CHAPTER

Mouse

*T*he previous chapter described the keyboard, one of the fundamental devices for entering data and commands into the X Window system. It discussed the keyboard events, their associated data structures, and how they are processed. It presented functions that grab the keyboard for an application's own use, effectively shutting out other applications.

This chapter discusses the other major input device: the mouse. It presents strategies for processing the mouse, mouse events, and their associated data structures. It describes functions that manipulate the mouse pointer: for example, resetting the mouse's sensitivity to meet specific user needs.

The *cursor* points to a specific screen location. The X Window server contains six resources, one of which is the cursor resource. This chapter examines several functions that generate and manipulate the cursor: for example, generating over 70 distinctive cursors.

Just as applications or the window manager can grab the keyboard, they may also grab the mouse pointer or a single button for their exclusive use. This chapter defines two types of grabs—active grabs and passive grabs—and illustrates their interrelationship. After examining additional pointer functions, the chapter concludes with a series of programs that illustrate fundamental concepts and functions.

Controlling the Pointer

For X Window systems, the most common pointer-control device is the mouse. X Window defines five mouse buttons, conveniently designated Button1 to Button5. However, the most common model includes three buttons, and consequently, most X Window software assumes a three-button mouse. On a two-button mouse, such as the Microsoft mouse, the third button can be simulated by clicking the two buttons simultaneously (in practice, within a predetermined time period). On a one-button mouse, such as that associated with the Macintosh computer, the second and third buttons can be simulated by clicking the mouse button and pressing predefined keys.

Mouse Strategies

The application designer must determine how to respond to the mouse, deciding which events to solicit and which to ignore. The decision depends on the nature of the application. The following choices are available:

❏ The application responds only when the user presses a mouse button. It solicits ButtonPress events.

❏ The application responds when the user moves the cursor into or out of a window. It solicits EnterNotify and LeaveNotify events.

❏ The application responds when the user holds a mouse button and moves the mouse. It solicits MotionNotify events. It may also solicit ButtonPress and ButtonRelease events.

❏ The application responds when the user moves the mouse pointer. It solicits MotionNotify events. In some cases, this option is impractical because of the large number of events generated.

❏ The application queries the workstation to determine the mouse location. This option generates no events.

❏ The application does not respond to the mouse.

Mouse-Associated Events

X Window includes several types of events for processing information related to the mouse. Button events announce when the user has pressed or released a specified button. MotionNotify events indicate when the pointer has moved. WindowCrossing events indicate when the pointer has entered or left a specified window.

Button Events

Button events indicate when a given button is pressed or released. XButtonPressedEvent and XButtonReleasedEvent are similar to the XKeyPressed and XKeyReleased events discussed in Chapter 7,

"Keyboard." The XButtonEvent data structure, serving both XButtonPressedEvent and XButtonReleasedEvent, is shown here.

```
typedef struct {
  int type;                    /* ButtonPress
                                  or ButtonRelease */

  unsigned long serial;        /* Number of last server-
                                  processed request */
  Bool send_event;             /* TRUE if from SendEvent
                                  request */
  Display *display;            /* Display from where
                                  event came */
  Window window;               /* Window for which event
                                  reported */
  Window root;                 /* Root window for which event
                                  occurred */
  Window subwindow;            /* Child window */
  Time time;                   /* Time in milliseconds */
  int x, y;                    /* Event window coordinates */
  int x_root, y_root;          /* Coordinates relative to
                                  root window */
  unsigned int state;          /* Key or button mask */
  unsigned int button;         /* Detail */
  Bool same_screen;            /* Same screen or not */
} XButtonEvent;
typedef XButtonEvent XButtonPressedEvent;
typedef XButtonEvent XButtonReleasedEvent;
```

The XButtonEvent data structure contains three *Window* type variables. The *source window* is the viewable window containing the pointer. The source window itself does not appear in the XButtonEvent data structure. However, its ultimate ancestor, the root window, does appear in this data structure. The *window* variable reports the event. The X server determines this variable by ascending the window hierarchy until it either finds an interested (event mask on) window or encounters the do_not_propagate flag. The Boolean variable *same_screen* has the value TRUE if the root window and the event window are on the same physical screen. The Boolean variable *same_screen* has the value FALSE if the root window and the event window are on different physical screens.

The X server sets the *subwindow* variable as follows: If the source window is an inferior of the event window, the *subwindow* variable is set to the event window child that is either the source window or an ancestor of the source window. If the source window is not an inferior of the event window, the server sets this variable to None.

The *button* variable represents the pointer button whose state has changed. This variable can have one of the following values: Button1, Button2, Button3, Button4, or Button5.

MotionNotify Events

MotionNotify events indicate when the pointer has moved. The MotionNotify event data structure is similiar to that of the preceding XButtonEvent events and the XKeyEvent events discussed in Chapter 7, "Keyboard."

```
typedef struct {
    int type;                    /* MotionNotify */
    unsigned long serial;        /* # of last server
                                    processed request */
    Bool send_event;             /* TRUE if from SendEvent
                                    request */
    Display *display;            /* Display from where
                                    event came */
    Window window;               /* Window for which event
                                    reported */
    Window root;                 /* Root window for which event
                                    occurred */
    Window subwindow;            /* Child window */
    Time time;                   /* Time in milliseconds */
    int x, y;                    /* Event window coordinates */
    int x_root, y_root;          /* Coordinates relative to
                                    root window */
    unsigned int state;          /* Key or button mask */
    char is_hint;                /* Detail */
    Bool same_screen;            /* Same screen or not */
} XMotionEvent;
typedef XMotionEvent XPointerMovedEvent;
```

The XPointerMovedEvent event includes the *is_hint* variable, which can have the value NotifyNormal or NotifyHint. The XButtonEvent data structure handles windows, as does the XKeyEvent data structure.

Window-Crossing Events

The X Window server generates EnterNotify and LeaveNotify *window-crossing events* when the pointer changes windows, either because of pointer motion or because of window hierarchy changes. Window hierarchy changes are expressed by CirculateNotify, ConfigureNotify, GravityNotify, MapNotify, and UnmapNotify events, which occur prior to the window-crossing events. EnterNotify and LeaveNotify events may also be generated by the functions **XGrabPointer** and **XUngrabPointer**, described later in this chapter. The data structure for window-crossing events follows.

```
typedef struct {
    int type;                    /* EnterNotify or LeaveNotify */
    unsigned long serial;        /* Number of last server
                                    processed request */
    Bool send_event;             /* TRUE if from SendEvent
                                    request */
    Display *display;            /* Display from where
                                    event came */
    Window window;               /* Window for which event
                                    reported */
    Window root;                 /* Root window for which event
                                    occurred */
    Window subwindow;            /* Child window */
    Time time;                   /* Time in milliseconds */
    int x, y;                    /* Event window coordinates */
    int x_root, y_root;          /* Coordinates relative to
                                    root window */
    int mode;                    /* NotifyNormal, NotifyGrab,
                                    NotifyUngrab */
    int detail;                  /* NotifyAncestor, NotifyVirtual,
                                    NotifyInferior, NotifyNonlinear,
                                    NotifyNonlinearVirtual */
    Bool same_screen;            /* Same screen or not */
    Bool focus;                  /* Boolean focus */
    unsigned int state;          /* Key or button mask */
} XCrossingEvent;
typedef XCrossingEvent XEnterWindowEvent;
typedef XCrossingEvent XLeaveWindowEvent;
```

In general, variables associated with the XCrossingEvent data structure have the same meaning as those associated with the XMotionEvent, XButtonEvent, and XKeyEvent data structures, with the following differences: For LeaveNotify events, the *subwindow* variable is set to a child window if the child of the event window contains the initial pointer position. Otherwise, it is set to None. For EnterNotify events, the *subwindow* variable is set to a child window if the child of the event window contains the final pointer position. Otherwise, it is set to None.

The *focus* variable did not appear in the XMotionEvent, XButtonEvent, and XKeyEvent data structures. The server sets this Boolean variable in the XCrossingEvent data structure. A TRUE value for the *focus* variable indicates that the event window is either the focus window or an inferior of the focus window. A FALSE value for the *focus* variable indicates that the event window is neither the focus window nor an inferior of the focus window. The *state* variable indicates the state of the pointer buttons and modifier keys immediately prior to the event. The server sets the *state* variable to the bitwise OR of one or more of the following masks: Button1Mask, Button2Mask, Button3Mask, Button4Mask, Button5Mask, ShiftMask, LockMask, ControlMask, Mod1Mask, Mod2Mask, Mod3Mask, Mod4Mask, and Mod5Mask.

Pointer-Manipulation Functions

X Window furnishes several functions that manipulate the pointer. The **XQueryPointer** function determines the pointer's absolute and relative coordinates. The Boolean function **XTranslateCoordinates** asks the server to translate coordinates from one window to another. The **XChangePointerControl** function changes the pointer's sensitivity. The **XGetPointerControl** function retrieves the pointer's sensitivity. The **XWarpPointer** function moves the pointer under program control.

XQueryPointer

The **XQueryPointer** function, shown here, determines the absolute and relative (to a specified window) pointer coordinates. Because it is a two-way request, frequent function calls degrade system performance.

```
Bool XQueryPointer(display, w, root_return, child_return,
                   root_x_return, root_y_return,
                   win_x_return, win_y_return, mask_return)
   Display *display;         /* Specifies connection
                                to the server */
   Window w;                 /* Specifies the window */
   Window *root_return;      /* Returns root window
                                containing the pointer */
   Window *child_return;     /* Returns child window
                                containing the pointer */
   int *root_x_return, *root_y_return;
                             /* Returns pointer coordinates
                                relative to origin of root */
   int *wint_x_return, *win_y_return;
                             /* Returns pointer coordinates
                                relative to specified window */
   unsigned int *mask_return;
                             /* Returns current state of modifier
                                keys and pointer buttons */
```

The Boolean function **XQueryPointer** returns the value TRUE if the pointer and the specified window are on the same physical screen. In this case, the pointer coordinates *win_x_return* and *win_y_return* are relative to the specified window's origin. The function also sets the *child_return* parameter to the window containing the pointer or the value None.

XQueryPointer returns the value FALSE if the pointer and the specified window are not on the same physical screen. In this case, the pointer coordinates *win_x_return* and *win_y_return* are set to zero, and the *child_return* parameter is set to the value None. If device event processing is frozen because of an application's pointer or button grab (such as **XGrabPointer** and **XGrabButton**), the device may seem to lag. **XQueryPointer** can generate a BadWindow error.

XTranslateCoordinates

The Boolean function **XTranslateCoordinates**, shown here, asks the server to translate coordinates from one window to another. Excessive use of **XTranslateCoordinates** can degrade system performance.

```
Bool XTranslateCoordinates(display, src_w, dest_w, src_x,
                           src_y, dest_x_return,
                           dest_y_return, child_return)
   Display *display;            /* Specifies connection
                                   to the server */
   Window src_w;                /* Source window */
   Window dest_w;               /* Destination window */
   int src_x, src_y;            /* x and y coordinates within
                                   source window */
   int *dest_x_return, *dest_y_return;
                                /* Returns x and y coordinates
                                   within destination window */
   Window *child_return;        /* Returns child window
                                   or None */
```

XTranslateCoordinates returns the value TRUE when the source and destination windows are on the same physical screen. In this case, the function accepts the source-window coordinates in the parameters *src_x* and *src_y* and returns the transformed destination-window coordinates in the parameters *dest_x_return* and *dest_y_return*.

XTranslateCoordinates returns the value FALSE when the source and destination windows are on different physical screens. In this case, the function returns the value zero in the parameters *dest_x_return* and *dest_y_return*. If the transformed coordinates are contained in a mapped child of the destination window, the *child_return* parameter returns the child window identifier. Otherwise, this parameter returns the value None. **XTranslateCoordinates** can generate a BadWindow error.

XChangePointerControl

The **XChangePointerControl** function, shown here, changes the pointer's sensitivity. Increasing the acceleration makes the pointer move faster once the number of pixels in the *threshold* parameter have been crossed.

```
XChangePointerControl(display, do_accel, do_threshold,
                      accel_numerator, accel_denominator,
                      threshold)
```

```
Display *display;            /* Specifies connection
                                to the server */
Bool do_accel,               /* Value controlling use of
                                accel_numerator or
                                accel_denominator */
     do_threshold;           /* Controls whether threshold
                                value is used */
int accel_numerator;         /* Numerator for
                                acceleration multiplier */
int accel_denominator;       /* Denominator for
                                acceleration multiplier */
int threshold;               /* Acceleration threshold */
```

A TRUE value of the *do_accel* parameter invokes the value in the *accel_numerator* parameter, increasing the acceleration for a value greater than 1. A FALSE value of the *do_accel* parameter invokes the value in the *accel_denominator* parameter, decreasing the acceleration for a value greater than 1. Setting the *threshold* parameter to –1 reinstates the default acceleration, as does a FALSE value of the *do_accel* parameter. **XChangePointerControl** can generate a BadValue error.

XGetPointerControl

The **XGetPointerControl** function, shown here, retrieves the parameters describing the pointer's sensitivity set by the **XChange PointerControl** function.

```
XGetPointerControl(display, accel_numerator_return,
                            accel_denominator_return,
                            threshold_return)
  Display *display;                /* Specifies connection
                                      to the server */
  int *accel_numerator_return;     /* Returns numerator for
                                      acceleration multiplier */
  int *accel_denominator_return; /* Returns denominator for
                                      acceleration multiplier */
  int threshold_return;            /* Returns acceleration
                                      threshold */
```

XWarpPointer

The **XWarpPointer** function, shown next, moves the pointer under program control. Under normal circumstances, the user moves the pointer.

```
XWarpPointer(display, src_w, dest_w, src_x, src_y,
          src_width, src_height, dest_x, dest_y)
  Display *display;            /* Specifies connection
                                  to the server */
  Window src_w;                /* Source window */
  Window dest_w;               /* Destination window */
  int src_x, src_y;            /* x and y coordinates within
                                  source window */
  unsigned int src_width;      /* Source window
                                  rectangle width */
  unsigned int src_height;     /* Source window
                                  rectangle height */
  int dest_x, dest_y;          /* x and y coordinates within
                                  destination window */
```

XWarpPointer moves the pointer to the location specified by the parameters *dest_x* and *dest_y*. These parameters are measured relative to the origin of the destination window (*dest_w*), if specified, or to the current pointer position, if the parameter *dest_w* is set to None. If the parameter *src_w* is a window, the pointer will move only if it is contained in the source window rectangle defined by the parameters *src_width* and *src_height*. When the parameter *src_width* is equal to zero, the source rectangle width is set to the current width of window *src_w* minus the parameter *src_x*. When the parameter *src_height* is equal to zero, the source rectangle height is set to the current height of window *src_w* minus the parameter *src_y*. The **XWarpPointer** function cannot move the pointer beyond limits set by the **XGrabPointer** function. **XWarpPointer** can generate a BadWindow error.

Cursor Functions

The cursor points to a selected area on the screen. The cursor resource describes the size, color, and shape of the onscreen cursor associated with the mouse. The cursor source is a bitmap, and perhaps a cursor mask bitmap. Bitmaps are discussed in Chapter 9, "Pixmaps, Bitmaps, and Images." X Window provides several functions that create and process cursors. These functions include the **XCreateFontCursor** function, which creates a cursor from a standard cursor font; the **XQueryBestCursor** function, which determines the largest cursor size that can be displayed on a given screen; the **XCreatePixmapCursor** function, which creates a cursor from two bitmaps; the **XRecolorCursor** function, which changes the color of the specified cursor; the **XFreeCursor** function, which destroys the specified cursor; and the **XCreateGlyphCursor**, which creates a cursor from fonts.

XCreateFontCursor

The **XCreateFontCursor** function, shown here, creates a cursor from a standard cursor font supplied by the system in the <X11/cursorfont.h> library. Before invoking this function, include the header library <X11/cursorfont.h>.

```
Cursor XCreateFontCursor(display, shape)
    Display *display;          /* Specifies connection
                                  to the server */
    unsigned int shape;        /* Cursor shape */
```

XCreateFontCursor can generate BadAlloc and BadValue errors.

XQueryBestCursor

The **XQueryBestCursor** function, shown next, determines the largest cursor size that can be displayed on a given screen.

```
Status XQueryBestCursor(display, d, width, height,
                    width_return, height_return)
    Display *display;          /* Specifies connection
                                  to the server */
    Drawable d;                /* Drawable */
    unsigned int width, height; /* Width and height of cursor
                                  to be queried */
    unsigned int *width_return,
```

```
                    *height_return;
                                      /* Returns best width and
                                         height of cursor */
```

XQueryBestCursor can generate a BadDrawable error.

XCreatePixmapCursor

The **XCreatePixmapCursor** function, shown next, creates a cursor from two bitmaps and returns the cursor ID.

```
Cursor XCreatePixmapCursor(display, source, mask,
                           foreground_color,
                           background_color, x, y)
  Display *display;            /* Specifies connection
                                  to the server */
  Pixmap source;               /* Shape of source cursor */
  Pixmap mask;                 /* Cursor's source bits to
                                  display or None */
  XColor foreground_color;     /* RGB values for
                                  source foreground */
  XColor background_color;     /* RGB values for
                                  source background */
  unsigned int x, y;           /* Coordinates of hotspot
                                  relative to source's origin */
```

The *foreground_color* parameter is associated with pixels whose *source* arguments are set to 1. The *background_color* parameter is associated with pixels whose *source* arguments are set to zero. The *mask* parameter defines the cursor shape. The *source* and *mask* arguments must have a depth of 1, if they are specified. Furthermore, they must be the same size. The *hotspot* is the location that the cursor points to. **XCreatePixmap-Cursor** can generate BadAlloc, BadMatch, and BadPixmap errors.

XRecolorCursor

The **XRecolorCursor** function, shown next, changes the color of the specified cursor.

```
XRecolorCursor(display, cursor, foreground_color,
               background_color)
    Display *display;             /* Specifies connection
                                     to the server */
    Cursor cursor;                /* Cursor to change color */
    XColor foreground_color;      /* RGB values for
                                     source foreground */
    XColor background_color;      /* RGB values for
                                     source background */
```

XRecolorCursor can generate a BadCursor error.

XFreeCursor

The **XFreeCursor** function, shown next, destroys a specified cursor.

```
XFreeCursor(display, cursor)
    Display *display;             /* Specifies connection
                                     to the server */
    Cursor cursor;                /* Cursor to be freed */
```

XFreeCursor deletes the association between the specified cursor and the cursor resource ID. The cursor is freed only when no other resource refers to it. You should not refer to the cursor after freeing it. **XFreeCursor** can generate a BadCursor error.

XCreateGlyphCursor

The **XCreateGlyphCursor** function, shown here, creates a cursor from font *glyphs*, identified abstract graphical symbols independent of any actual images.

```
Cursor XCreateGlyphCursor(display, source_font, mask_font,
                          source_char, mask_char,
                          foreground_color, background_color)
    Display *display;               /* Specifies connection
                                       to the server */
    Font source_font;               /* Font for source glyph */
    Font mask_font;                 /* Font for mask glyph
                                       or None */
```

```
unsigned int source_char;   /* Character glyph for source */
unsigned int mask_char;     /* Character glyph for mask */
XColor foreground_color;    /* RGB values for
                               source foreground */
XColor background_color;    /* RGB values for
                               source background */
```

XCreateGlyphCursor is similar to the **XCreatePixmapCursor** function. **XCreateGlyphCursor** can generate BadAlloc, BadFont, and BadValue errors.

Pointer and Button Grabbing Functions

The previous chapter introduced the **XGrabKeyboard** function, which accords an application the exclusive right to keyboard events. Similar functions accord an application the exclusive right to mouse events. It is important not to abuse grabs, especially when several applications are active simultaneously.

The **XGrabPointer** function grabs the pointer for the application's exclusive use. The **XUngrabPointer** function releases the pointer grab. The **XChangeActivePointerGrab** function changes specified parameters for a pointer grab. The **XGrabButton** function grabs a button for the application's exclusive use. The **XUngrabButton** function releases the button grab.

XGrabPointer

The **XGrabPointer** function, shown here, grabs the pointer for the application's exclusive use. Its effect is called an *active grab*, in contrast to the passive grab by the **XGrabButton** function. After a successful pointer grab, pointer events are reported exclusively to the application that invoked the function.

```
int XGrabPointer(display, grab_window, owner_events,
            event_mask, pointer_mode, keyboard_mode,
            confine_to, cursor, time)
  Display *display;           /* Specifies connection
                                 to server */
```

```
Window grab_window;          /* Window associated with
                                events of interest */
Bool owner_events;           /* If TRUE, report
                                keyboard events as usual
                                If FALSE, report
                                keyboard events via
                                grab window */
unsigned int event_mask;     /* Specifies pointer events to
                                report to client */
int pointer_mode;            /* Further pointer event
                                processing
                                GrabModeAsync, GrabModeSync */
int keyboard_mode;           /* Further keyboard event
                                processing
                                GrabModeAsync, GrabModeSync */
Window confine_to;           /* Window to confine pointer to
                                or None */
Cursor cursor;               /* Cursor to display during
                                grab or None */
int time;                    /* Timestamp or Current Time */
```

XGrabPointer is similar to the **XGrabKeyboard** function presented in Chapter 7, "Keyboard." If the Boolean parameter *owner_events* is TRUE, a pointer event normally reported to a given client is reported as usual. Other pointer events are reported with respect to the *grab_window*, if selected by an *event_mask*. If the Boolean parameter *owner_events* is FALSE, all pointer events are reported with respect to the *grab_window*, if selected by an *event_mask*.

The usual setting for the *pointer_mode* parameter is GrabModeAsync; in this case, pointer-event processing occurs normally. If the pointer is frozen by the client, pointer-event processing is resumed. Setting the *pointer_mode* parameter to GrabModeAsync effectively freezes the pointer until the grab is released or an **XAllowEvents** function is issued. When the *keyboard_mode* parameter is set to GrabModeAsync, the grab does not affect keyboard processing. Setting the *keyboard_mode* parameter to GrabModeSync effectively freezes the pointer until the grab is released or an **XAllowEvents** function is issued.

The specified cursor is displayed independently of the window containing the cursor. The value None for the *cursor* parameter displays the normal cursor for a window if the pointer is in a grab window or a child of a grab window. Otherwise, the system displays the cursor for the grab window. The window specified by the *confine_to* parameter need not be the grab window. The *time* parameter does not establish request priority; it helps keep track of this round-trip request.

The **XGrabPointer** function generates EnterNotify and LeaveNotify events. It returns GrabSuccess for a grab that occurs without error, GrabNotViewable if either the grab window or the confine window is not viewable or is a confine window completely outside the root window, AlreadyGrabbed if the pointer is grabbed by another client, and GrabFrozen if the pointer is frozen by another client. The function can generate BadCursor, BadValue, and BadWindow errors.

XUngrabPointer

The **XUngrabPointer** function, shown next, releases the pointer that was grabbed by **XGrabPointer** or **XGrabButton**.

```
XUngrabPointer(display, time)
    Display *display;           /* Specifies connection
                                   to server */
    int time;                   /* Timestamp or Current Time */
```

XUngrabPointer is automatically generated by the server if either the event window or the confine window becomes unviewable, or if the confine window is reconfigured to lie completely outside the root window. **XUngrabPointer** generates EnterNotify and LeaveNotify events.

XChangeActivePointerGrab

The **XChangeActivePointerGrab** function, shown next, changes specified parameters for an active pointer grab generated by **XGrab-Pointer**.

```
XChangeActivePointerGrab(display, event_mask, cursor, time)
    Display *display;           /* Specifies connection
                                   to server */
    unsigned int event_mask;    /* Specifies pointer events to
                                   report to client */
    Cursor cursor;              /* Cursor to display during
```

```
                                    grab or None */
   int time;                     /* Timestamp or Current Time */
```

XChangeActivePointerGrab can generate BadCursor and BadValue errors.

XGrabButton

The **XGrabButton** function, shown next, grabs a pointer button for the application's exclusive use. This grab is known as a *passive grab*, in contrast to the active grab established by **XGrabPointer**.

```
XGrabButton(display, button, modifiers, grab_window,
            owner_events, event_mask, pointer_mode,
            keyboard_mode, confine_to, cursor)
   Display *display;            /* Specifies connection
                                    to server */
   unsigned int button;         /* Pointer button to be grabbed
                                    or None */
   unsigned int modifiers;      /* Set of keymasks
                                    or AnyModifier */
   Window grab_window;          /* Window associated with
                                    events of interest */
   Bool owner_events;           /* If TRUE, report
                                    keyboard events as usual
                                    If FALSE, report
                                    keyboard events via
                                    grab window */
   unsigned int event_mask;     /* Specifies pointer events to
                                    report to client */
   int pointer_mode;            /* Further pointer event
                                    processing
                                    GrabModeAsync, GrabModeSync */
   int keyboard_mode;           /* Further keyboard event
                                    processing
                                    GrabModeAsync, GrabModeSync */
   Window confine_to;           /* Window to confine pointer to
                                    or None */
   Cursor cursor;               /* Cursor to display during
                                    grab or None */
```

The passive grab generated by the **XGrabButton** function is transformed into an active grab such as that generated by the **XGrabPointer** function if all the following conditions are met:

❏ The pointer is not grabbed, and the button specified is pressed when the specified modifiers are pressed, but no other modifiers or buttons are pressed.

❏ The grab window contains the pointer.

❏ The confine window (if specified) is viewable.

❏ No passive grab exists on the same button and modifier combination for any ancestor of the grab window.

XGrabButton can generate BadAccess, BadCursor, BadValue, and BadWindow errors.

XUngrabButton

The **XUngrabButton** function, shown next, releases the passive grab generated by the **XGrabButton** function.

```
XUngrabButton(display, button, modifiers, grab_window)
  Display *display;           /* Specifies connection
                                 to server */
  unsigned int button;        /* Pointer button to be
                                 released or AnyButton */
  unsigned int modifiers;     /* Set of keymasks
                                 or AnyModifier */
  Window grab_window;         /* Window associated with
                                 events of interest */
```

XUngrabButton has no effect on an active grab, whether generated by **XGrabPointer** or **XGrabButton**. **XUngrabButton** can generate BadValue and BadWindow errors.

Other Pointer Functions

Other pointer functions supplied by X Window systems include the **XGetMotionEvents** function that returns all motion events, the

XSetPointerMapping function that sets the pointer mapping, and the **XGetPointerMapping** function that returns the current pointer mapping.

XGetMotionEvents

The **XGetMotionEvents** function, shown here, returns in the motion-history buffer all motion events located in the specified window that occur between specified start and stop times. This function can generate extensive data and can be useful when generating graphics. This function is not available on all workstations (such as the one used here).

```
XTimeCoord *XGetMotionEvents(display, w, start, stop,
                            nevents_return)
   Display *display;            /* Specifies connection
                                   to the server */
   Window w;                    /* Window */
   Time start, stop;            /* Time interval during which
                                   events returned from motion
                                   history buffer */
   int *nevents_return;         /* Returns number of events
                                   from motion history buffer */
```

XGetMotionEvents returns the value NULL if the server does not support motion history, the start time is in the future, or the start time is later than the stop time. Specifying a future stop time is equivalent to specifying CurrentTime.

The XTimeCoord data structure returned by **XGetMotionEvents** is shown here.

```
typedef struct {
  Time time;
  short x, y;
} XTimeCoord;
```

In this data structure, the *time* field is defined in milliseconds. The *x* and *y* fields assume the pointer coordinates relative to the specified window. **XGetMotionEvents** can generate a BadWindow error.

XDisplayMotionBufferSize

The **XDisplayMotionBufferSize** function, shown next, determines the approximate maximum number of elements in the motion-history buffer.

```
unsigned long XDisplayMotionBufferSize(display)
  Display *display;          /* Specifies connection
                                to the server */
```

XSetPointerMapping

The **XSetPointerMapping** function sets the pointer mapping.

```
int XSetPointerMapping(display, map, nmap)
  Display *display;          /* Specifies connection
                                to the server */
  unsigned char map[];       /* Mapping list */
  int nmap;                  /* Number of items
                                in mapping list */
```

If **XSetPointerMapping** is successful, it returns the value MappingSuccess and generates a MappingNotify event. The array element *map[i]* is associated with physical button *i+1*. For example, *map[0]* is associated with button 1. If any buttons to be remapped are pressed, the function returns the value MappingBusy, and the mapping is not changed. No two elements of the *map* array can have the same value, except for the value zero. **XSetPointerMapping** can generate a BadValue error.

XGetPointerMapping

The **XGetPointerMapping** function, shown next, returns the pointer's current mapping.

```
int XGetPointerMapping(display, map return, nmap)
  Display *display;          /* Specifies connection
                                to the server */
  unsigned char map_return[]; /* Returns mapping list */
  int nmap;                  /* Number of items
                                in mapping list */
```

Generating All Font Cursors: Example 1

The following exercise generates all 77 cursors available in the <X11/cursorfont.h> header library. This version of the program does not provide any method for exiting, should the user prefer not to view all available cursors.

The following data structure is an array of cursor types that can be used with the **XCreateFontCursor** function. For brevity, only a single cursor name is shown.

```
int cursor_type[NUM_CURSORS] =
 {
  XC_X_cursor,
...
 };
```

 Note   All font cursor names begin with the characters XC_.

The **XSelectInput** function processes four types of events: ButtonPress, Exposure, ButtonRelease, and OwnerGrabButton. The Expose event indicates when to draw the initial text. The Button events display the font cursors.

The C language function **load_strings** applies the Xlib functions **XCreateGC**, **XSetForeground**, **XDrawString**, and **XFreeGC** to display text in the window that solicits pointer input.

```
thegc = XCreateGC(thedisplay, thewindow, 0, 0);
XSetForeground(thedisplay, thegc,
              BlackPixel(thedisplay, thescreen));
XDrawString(thedisplay, thewindow, thegc, 30, 30,
            "You will see now 77 cursors ...",
            strlen("You will see now 77 cursors ..."));
XDrawString(thedisplay, thewindow, thegc, 30, 50,
            "Point to created window.",
            strlen("Point to created window."));
XDrawString(thedisplay, thewindow, thegc, 30, 70,
            "To see cursor press right button,",
            strlen("To see cursor press right button,"));
XDrawString(thedisplay, thewindow, thegc, 30, 90,
```

```
            "for next cursor, press left button.",
            strlen("for next cursor, press left button."));
  XFreeGC(thedisplay, thegc);
```

Usually, the left button is associated with the Button1 event. If this button is pressed, the program does several things. First, it calls the **XUndefineCursor** function to remove any present cursor. Then it tests the cursor counter (in the variable *entry*) to determine the message to display. Possibilities include a message prompting the user to press the right button to see the cursor and to press the left button to access the next cursor. The exit takes place only when all cursors have been referenced, as shown in the following program fragment.

```
case Button1:
  XUndefineCursor(thedisplay, thewindow);
  printf("\nLeft button pressed ...\n");
  if (entry < NUM_CURSORS)
  {
    printf("To see cursor #%d press right button, ",
            entry+1);
    if (entry < NUM_CURSORS-1)
    {
      printf("\nFor next cursor, press
            left button ...\n");
    }
  }
  if (entry == NUM_CURSORS)
  {
    printf("\nReady to exit ...\n");
    done = TRUE;
    cleanup();
  }
  else
    entry++;
break;
```

The right button is associated with the Button3 event. If this button is pressed, the program does several things. If the cursor counter (in the variable *entry*) is less than the number of available cursors, the program calls the Xlib functions **XCreateFontCursor** and **XDefineCursor** to create the font cursor and associate it with the active window. Appropriate messages prompt the user to press the left button and announce that the program is ready to exit, as shown here.

```
case Button3:
  printf("\nRight button pressed ...\n");
  if (entry < NUM_CURSORS)
  {
    printf("This is cursor #%d\n", entry);
    thecursor = XCreateFontCursor(thedisplay,
                      cursor_type[entry]);
    XDefineCursor(thedisplay, thewindow, thecursor);
    printf("Still You can see %d cursor(s)\n",
           NUM_CURSORS-entry);
    if (entry < NUM_CURSORS-1)
    {
      printf("For next cursor, press left
              button ...\n");
    }
  }
  if (entry == NUM_CURSORS)
  {
    printf("This is cursor#%d\n", entry);
    printf("\nReady to exit ...\n");
    done = TRUE;
    cleanup();
  }
break;
```

Here is the complete program listing.

```
/*  example 8_1 */
#include <X11/Xlib.h>
#include <X11/Xutil.h>
#include <X11/cursorfont.h>

#define BORDER_WIDTH 2
#define NUM_CURSORS 77
#define FALSE 0
#define TRUE 1

Display         *thedisplay;
Window          thewindow;
```

```
int          thescreen;
Cursor       thecursor;

int cursor_type[NUM_CURSORS] =
 {
  XC_X_cursor,
  XC_arrow,
  XC_based_arrow_down,
  XC_based_arrow_up,
  XC_boat,
  XC_bogosity,
  XC_bottom_left_corner,
  XC_bottom_right_corner,
  XC_bottom_side,
  XC_bottom_tee,
  XC_box_spiral,
  XC_center_ptr,
  XC_circle,
  XC_clock,
  XC_coffee_mug,
  XC_cross,
  XC_cross_reverse,
  XC_crosshair,
  XC_diamond_cross,
  XC_dot,
  XC_dotbox,
  XC_double_arrow,
  XC_draft_large,
  XC_draft_small,
  XC_draped_box,
  XC_exchange,
  XC_fleur,
  XC_gobbler,
  XC_gumby,
  XC_hand1,
  XC_hand2,
  XC_heart,
  XC_icon,
  XC_iron_cross,
  XC_left_ptr,
  XC_left_side,
  XC_left_tee,
```

```
        XC_leftbutton,
        XC_ll_angle,
        XC_lr_angle,
        XC_man,
        XC_middlebutton,
        XC_mouse,
        XC_pencil,
        XC_pirate,
        XC_plus,
        XC_question_arrow,
        XC_right_ptr,
        XC_right_side,
        XC_right_tee,
        XC_rightbutton,
        XC_rtl_logo,
        XC_sailboat,
        XC_sb_down_arrow,
        XC_sb_h_double_arrow,
        XC_sb_left_arrow,
        XC_sb_right_arrow,
        XC_sb_up_arrow,
        XC_sb_v_double_arrow,
        XC_shuttle,
        XC_sizing,
        XC_spider,
        XC_spraycan,
        XC_star,
        XC_target,
        XC_tcross,
        XC_top_left_arrow,
        XC_top_left_corner,
        XC_top_right_corner,
        XC_top_side,
        XC_top_tee,
        XC_trek,
        XC_ul_angle,
        XC_umbrella,
        XC_ur_angle,
        XC_watch,
        XC_xterm
    };
```

```
char           *p_name;
unsigned long foreground;
unsigned long background;
XSizeHints     thehints;
GC             thegc;
XColor         frgr_color, bcgr_color;
int            entry = 0;

void init();
void load_strings();
void set_hints();
void create_window_set_properties();
void cleanup();

main(argc, argv)
int argc;
char *argv[];
{
XEvent theevent;
int done = FALSE;

  init(argv);

  set_hints();

  create_window_set_properties(argc,argv);

  XSelectInput(thedisplay, thewindow, ButtonPressMask
               | ExposureMask | ButtonReleaseMask
               | OwnerGrabButtonMask);

  XMapWindow(thedisplay, thewindow);

  while (!done)
  {
    XNextEvent(thedisplay, &theevent);
    switch(theevent.type)
    {
      case Expose:
        if (theevent.xexpose.count == 0)
        {
        /*  Draw the text in the window  */
```

```
        load_strings();
      }
    break;

    case ButtonPress:
      switch(theevent.xbutton.button)
      {
        case Button1:
          XUndefineCursor(thedisplay, thewindow);
          printf("\nLeft button pressed ...\n");
          if (entry < NUM_CURSORS)
          {
            printf("To see cursor #%d press right button, ",
                    entry+1);
            if (entry < NUM_CURSORS-1)
            {
              printf("\nFor next cursor, press
                      left button ...\n");
            }
          }
          if (entry == NUM_CURSORS)
          {
            printf("\nReady to exit ...\n");
            done = TRUE;
            cleanup();
          }
          else
            entry++;
        break;

        case Button3:
          printf("\nRight button pressed ...\n");
          if (entry < NUM_CURSORS)
          {
            printf("This is cursor #%d\n", entry);
            thecursor = XCreateFontCursor(thedisplay,
                                  cursor_type[entry]);
            XDefineCursor(thedisplay, thewindow, thecursor);
            printf("Still You can see %d cursor(s)\n",
                    NUM_CURSORS-entry);
            if (entry < NUM_CURSORS-1)
```

```
                    {
                      printf("For next cursor, press left
                              button ...\n");
                    }
                 }
                 if (entry == NUM_CURSORS)
                 {
                   printf("This is cursor#%d\n", entry);
                   printf("\nReady to exit ...\n");
                   done = TRUE;
                   cleanup();
                 }
             break;
          }/* End switch */
       break;
    }/* End switch */
  }  /*  End while  */
} /*  End main  */

void init(argv)
char         *argv[];
{

  p_name = argv[0];
  thedisplay = XOpenDisplay("");
  thescreen = DefaultScreen(thedisplay);

  background = WhitePixel(thedisplay, thescreen);
  foreground = BlackPixel(thedisplay, thescreen);
}

void load_strings()
{
  thegc = XCreateGC(thedisplay, thewindow, 0, 0);
  XSetForeground(thedisplay, thegc,
              BlackPixel(thedisplay, thescreen));
  XDrawString(thedisplay, thewindow, thegc, 30, 30,
              "You will see now 77 cursors ...",
              strlen("You will see now 77 cursors ..."));
  XDrawString(thedisplay, thewindow, thegc, 30, 50,
              "Point to created window.",
              strlen("Point to created window."));
```

```
   XDrawString(thedisplay, thewindow, thegc, 30, 70,
               "To see cursor press right button,",
               strlen("To see cursor press right button,"));
   XDrawString(thedisplay, thewindow, thegc, 30, 90,
               "for next cursor, press left button.",
               strlen("for next cursor, press left button."));
   XFreeGC(thedisplay, thegc);
}

void set_hints()
{
int height;
int width;

  width = DisplayWidth(thedisplay, thescreen);
  height = DisplayHeight(thedisplay, thescreen);
  thehints.flags = PPosition | PSize | PMinSize;
  thehints.height = height/4;
  thehints.width = 300;
  thehints.x =  width/3;
  thehints.y =  height/3;
  thehints.min_height = 110;
  thehints.min_width = 300;
}

void create_window_set_properties(argc, argv)
int          argc;
char         *argv[];
{

  thewindow = XCreateSimpleWindow(thedisplay,
                      DefaultRootWindow(thedisplay),
                      thehints.x, thehints.y,
                      thehints.width, thehints.height,
                      BORDER_WIDTH, foreground,
                      background);

  XSetStandardProperties(thedisplay, thewindow, p_name,
                      p_name, None, argv, argc, &thehints);
}

void cleanup()
```

```
{

  XUndefineCursor(thedisplay, thewindow);
  printf("\n Undefine cursor - done\n");

  XDestroyWindow(thedisplay, thewindow);
  printf("\n Destroy window  - done\n");

  XCloseDisplay(thedisplay);
  printf("\n Disconnect from server - done\n");
}
```

Sample output of this program is shown in Figure 8-1.

The following MAKE file was used to process this program using SCO Open Desktop. The MAKE file for other X Window implementations varies.

```
RM = rm - f
CC = cc
CFLAGS = -O
INCLUDES = -I/usr/include -I/usr/include/X11
LIBS = -lXm -lXt -lX11 -lsocket -lmalloc -lPW
.c.o:
$(RM) $@
$(CC) -c $(CFLAGS) $(INCLUDES) $*.c
all:: exercise8-1
exercise8-1: exercise8-1.o
$(RM) $@
$(CC) -o $@ $(CFLAGS) exercise8-1.o $(LIBS)
@echo makefile for exercise8-1 - done!
```

Generating Some Font Cursors: Example 2

The following exercise generates some or all of the 77 cursors available in the <X11/cursorfont.h> header library. The user can exit the program by pressing the left button twice, as indicated by an onscreen prompt. Only lines that differ from the first version of the program are discussed.

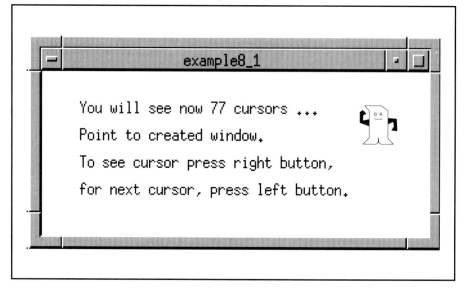

FIGURE
8-1

Sample results of cursor display program

The program includes four variables that determine whether the mouse button was double-clicked, indicating that the user wishes to exit before displaying all font cursors.

❑ The *is_button_pressed* variable indicates the first click of the left button. This variable is initially set to FALSE and then set to TRUE in the statement following the *case Button1* statement.

❑ The *clicked* variable indicates the second click of the left button. This variable is initially set to FALSE and then set to TRUE in the *case ButtonRelease* statement.

❑ The *click_time* variable and the *c_t* variable determine whether the two clicks took place within a predetermined period of time: namely, 300 milliseconds. When the first click event is registered, the variable *c_t* is set to the event time. When the second click event is registered, the program tests whether the event time difference is less than the predetermined period of time. If it is, the variable *done* is set to TRUE, and the program terminates. The new program declarations are as follows:

```
int is_button_pressed = FALSE;
int clicked = FALSE;
Time click_time = 300;
int   c_t;
```

Pressing button 1 sets the *is_button_pressed* variable to TRUE, registering the first click.

```
case Button1:
  is_button_pressed = TRUE;
```

The rest of this *case* statement is the same as in example 1.

The *case ButtonRelease* statement, shown here, tests for the second button click, as described previously.

```
case ButtonRelease:
  if (clicked)
  {
    is_button_pressed = FALSE;
    clicked = FALSE;
    if ((theevent.xbutton.time - c_t) <= click_time)
      done = TRUE;
  }
  if (is_button_pressed)
  {
    c_t = theevent.xbutton.time;
    clicked = TRUE;
    is_button_pressed = FALSE;
  }
break;
```

The C language function **load_strings** invokes the following **XDrawString** function to tell the user how to exit the program without processing all 77 font cursors.

```
XDrawString(thedisplay, thewindow, thegc, 30, 110,
            "To exit, press left button twice!",
            strlen("To exit, press left button twice!"));
```

The only other change to the program is increasing the value of the variable *thehints.min_height* to 130, from 110 in the previous program.

Figure 8-2 shows sample output.

Tracking the Cursor Position: Example 3

The following exercise applies the **XGetMotionEvents**, **XDrawPoint**, **XFree**, and **XQueryPointer** functions and the associated data structures to track the cursor position. Only changes to the previous example are discussed.

The program requires several additional variables. The Boolean variable *is_history* indicates whether a motion-history buffer is available. This variable is initially set to TRUE. The Xlib function **XGet-MotionEvents** requires a motion-history buffer. This function places results in the xtc data structure whose type is XTimeCoord.

The integer variable *num_events* indicates the number of motion events recorded during the specified time period. The **XQueryPointer**

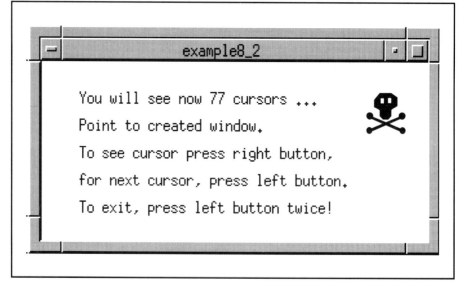

FIGURE 8-2   Sample results of second cursor display program

example8_2

You will see now 77 cursors ...

Point to created window.

To see cursor press right button,

for next cursor, press left button.

To exit, press left button twice!

function returns the *r_w* variable, which identifies the root window containing the pointer, and the *c_w* variable, which identifies the child window containing the pointer. The function returns the *x_r* and *y_r* variables, which refer to the pointer coordinates in the root window, and the *x_w* and *y_w* variables, which refer to the pointer coordinates in the specified window.

The *button_mask* variable is also used by the **XQueryPointer** function. The integer variable *index* is a counter associated with the motion events.

The declarations follow.

```
int is_history = TRUE;
XTimeCoord *xtc;
int num_events;
Window r_w, c_w;
int x_r, y_r;
int x_w, y_w;
int button_mask;
int index;
```

The **XSelectInput** function now includes a reference to the ButtonMotionMask, as shown here.

```
XSelectInput(thedisplay, thewindow, ButtonPressMask
              | ExposureMask | ButtonReleaseMask
              | OwnerGrabButtonMask
              | PointerMotionHintMask
              | ButtonMotionMask);
```

The program verifies if the motion-history buffer is available with the following code.

```
if (XDisplayMotionBufferSize(thedisplay) == FALSE)
{
  printf("\n No motion history buffer \n");
  is_history = FALSE;
}
```

The "No motion history buffer" message is displayed, as the motion-history buffer is not available on this system. Therefore, the *is_history* flag is set to FALSE.

The program reacts to MotionNotify events. It tests the *is_history* variable initialized to TRUE and perhaps set to FALSE in the preceding code. If the history buffer is available, the program applies the **XGetMotionEvents** function to accept motion events for the period from the event time to the current time. It then applies the **XDrawPoint** function to draw a single point for each event and finally applies the **XFree** function to release the event motion-history data structure. If the history buffer variable is unavailable, the program applies the **XQueryPointer** function to determine root and child window data and then prints this data.

The program segment processing MotionNotify events follows.

```
  case MotionNotify:
if (is_history)
{
  xtc = XGetMotionEvents(thedisplay, thewindow,
                         theevent.xmotion.time,
                         CurrentTime, &num_events);
  for (index = 0; index < num_events; index++)
  {
    XDrawPoint(thedisplay, thewindow, thegc,
               xtc[index].x, xtc[index].y);
  }
  XFree(xtc);
}
else
{
  XQueryPointer(thedisplay, theevent.xmotion.window,
                &r_w, &c_w, &x_r, &y_r, &x_w, &y_w,
                &button_mask);
  printf("\nRoot_X=%d, Root_Y=%d, Window_X=%d,
         Window_Y=%d\n", x_r, y_r, x_w, y_w);
}
break;
```

Figure 8-3 shows the results of running this program.

FIGURE
8-3

Sample results of cursor position program

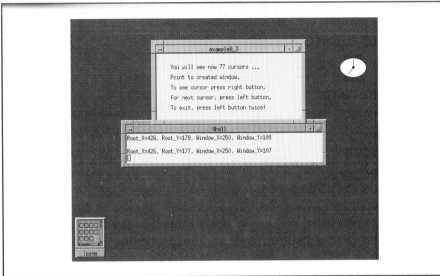

Key Points

Mouse-Associated Events

X Window includes several types of events for processing information related to the mouse. Button events announce when the user has pressed or released a specified button; they process data contained in the XButtonEvent data structure. MotionNotify events indicate when the pointer has moved; they process data contained in the XMotionEvent data structure. WindowCrossing events indicate when the pointer has entered or left a specified window; they process data contained in the XCrossingEvent data structure.

continues . . .

Pointer Manipulation

X Window furnishes several functions that manipulate the pointer. **XQueryPointer** determines the pointer's absolute and relative coordinates. The Boolean function **XTranslateCoordinates** asks the server to translate coordinates from one window to another. **XChangePointerControl** changes the pointer's sensitivity. **XGetPointerControl** retrieves the pointer's sensitivity. **XWarpPointer** moves the pointer under program control.

Cursor Processing

X Window provides several functions that create and process cursors. These functions include the **XCreateFontCursor** function, which creates a cursor from a standard cursor font; **XQueryBestCursor**, which determines the largest cursor size that can be displayed on a given screen; **XCreatePixmapCursor**, which creates a cursor from two bitmaps; **XRecolorCursor**, which changes the color of the specified cursor; **XFreeCursor**, which destroys the specified cursor; and **XCreateGlyphCursor**, which creates a cursor from fonts.

CHAPTER

Pixmaps, Bitmaps, and Images

*T*he previous chapter discussed a major input device, the mouse. It presented strategies for processing the mouse, mouse events, and their associated data structures. It described functions that manipulate the mouse pointer. It examined several functions that generate and manipulate a fundamental server resource, the cursor. It explored how applications or the window manager grab the mouse pointer or a single button for their exclusive use. The chapter concluded with a series of programs that illustrate fundamental concepts and functions.

This chapter describes how to create and modify groups of pixels by applying three fundamental X Window structures: pixmaps, server resources that draw off-screen pictures; bitmaps, pixmaps whose depth is one; and images, data structures that represent visual data in memory and provide basic operations on this data. The chapter concludes by presenting two programs that apply pixmaps and bitmaps.

Pixmaps

As first defined in Chapter 3, "Basic Concepts and Terminology," a pixmap is a block of memory associated with the X server that can be used for drawing. Pixmaps are one of the six fundamental categories of server resources. They are closely related to windows. Consider the following similarities and differences relating to pixmaps and windows.

Similarities Between Pixmaps and Windows

The following features characterize both pixmaps and windows:

❑ Pixmaps and windows are both created with a fixed, positive height and width.

❑ Pixmaps and windows employ the same coordinate system in which *x* measures the number of pixels from the drawable's left edge, and *y* measures the number of pixels from the drawable's top edge.

❑ Pixmaps and windows both are defined with a depth that indicates the number of bits per pixel.

❑ Pixmap and window contents are both clipped to the drawable's boundaries.

Differences Between Pixmaps and Windows

The following features differentiate pixmaps and windows:

❑ Unlike windows, pixmaps do not have background attributes, borders, visual types, or colormap attributes.

❑ Pixmaps are not mapped and do not form a hierarchy. They are never obscured.

❑ Pixmaps appear on the screen only when they are copied to a viewable window.

Pixmaps are associated with two types of events: GraphicsExpose and NoExpose events. To solicit these events, set the *graphics_exposure* field in the graphics context.

Pixmap Functions

The **XCreatePixmap** function creates a pixmap. The **XGetGeometry** function is a round-trip request that determines the basic geometrical values for pixmaps and windows. The **XFreePixmap** function releases the storage area associated with a given pixmap.

XCreatePixmap

The **XCreatePixmap** function, shown here, creates a pixmap without initializing it. (The pixmap can be initialized with the **XFillRectangle** function discussed in Chapter 10, "Color and Graphics.")

```
Pixmap XCreatePixmap(display, d, width, height, depth)
   Display *display;              /* Specifies the connection
                                     to the server */
   Drawable d;                    /* Screen on which
```

```
                                      pixmap is created */
unsigned int width, height;  /* Pixmap dimensions */
unsigned int depth;          /* Pixmap depth */
```

XCreatePixmap returns the pixmap identifier after creating the pixmap. The *drawable* parameter contains the X Window resource identifier of a previously existing window or pixmap.

Multiple-screen workstations reference this parameter to identify the screen associated with the new pixmap. X Window will not copy a pixmap from one screen to another. The value of the *depth* argument must be supported by the workstation screen.

XCreatePixmap may fail to create a pixmap for several reasons, including a lack of available memory. You should test whether the pixmap was properly created before attempting to use it. You can use the **XGetGeometry** function for this purpose. **XCreatePixmap** can generate BadAlloc, BadDrawable, and BadValue errors.

XGetGeometry

The **XGetGeometry** function, shown next, is a round-trip request that determines the root window and the location, size, border width, and depth of any window or pixmap.

```
Status XGetGeometry(display, d, root_return, x_return,
                y_return, width_return, height_return,
                border_width_return, depth_return)
   Display *display;              /* Specifies the connection
                                     to the server */
   Drawable d;                    /* Window or pixmap */
   Window *root_return;           /* Returns root window */
   int *x_return, *y_return;      /* Returns drawable
                                     coordinates */
   unsigned int *width_return;    /* Returns drawable width */
   unsigned int *height_return;   /* Returns drawable height */
   unsigned int *border_width_return;
                                  /* Returns border width
                                     in pixels */
   unsigned int *depth_return;    /* Returns depth
                                     in bits per pixel */
```

If the drawable is a pixmap, the parameters *x_return* and *y_return* both return 0, as does the parameter *border_width_return*. The *Status* value equals 1 if the function executes without error, and the *Status* value equals 0 if an error occurs. **XGetGeometry** can generate a BadDrawable error.

XFreePixmap

The **XFreePixmap** function, shown next, releases the storage area associated with a given pixmap.

```
XFreePixmap(display, pixmap)
  Display *display;            /* Specifies the connection
                                  to the server */
  Pixmap pixmap;               /* Pixmap */
```

XFreePixmap deletes the association between the specified pixmap and the pixmap resource ID. The pixmap is freed only when no other resource refers to it. You should not refer to the pixmap after freeing it. **XFreePixmap** can generate a BadPixmap error.

Bitmaps

As introduced in Chapter 3, a bitmap resource is a pixmap with a depth of 1. A *bitmap file* is a text file that can be loaded into a bitmap resource. The #include directive makes bitmap files available to C language programs.

Reading and Writing Bitmap Files

Bitmap files are read by the **XReadBitmapFile** function. They are written by the **XWriteBitmapFile** function or by the bitmap utility program supplied with the X Window system.

XReadBitmapFile

The **XReadBitmapFile** function, shown here, reads a bitmap from a specified file.

```
int XReadBitmapFile(display, d, filename, width_return,
                    height_return, bitmap_return,
                    x_hot_return, y_hot_return)
    Display *display;              /* Specifies the connection
                                      to the server */
    Drawable d;                    /* Drawable indicating screen */
    char *filename;                /* Operating-system-
                                      dependent filename */
    unsigned int *width_return;    /* Returns bitmap file width */
    unsigned int *height_return;   /* Returns bitmap file height */
    Pixmap *bitmap_return;         /* Returns created bitmap */
    int *x_hot_return;             /* Returns hotspot */
    int *y_hot_return;                coordinates */
```

XReadBitmapFile reads the file containing the bitmap. The format of the filename depends on the operating system. This read operation generates one of the following return values: BitmapOpenFailed, BitmapFileInvalid, BitmapNoMemory, or BitmapSuccess.

If the file is successfully opened, the function creates a pixmap whose size is determined by the *width_return* and *height_return* parameters, reads the bitmap data into the pixmap, and associates this pixmap with the variable *bitmap_return*. If the bitmap does not specify a hotspot, the function sets the parameters *x_hot_return* and *y_hot_return* to −1. **XReadBitmapFile** can generate BadAlloc and BadDrawable errors.

XWriteBitmapFile

The **XWriteBitmapFile** function, shown next, writes a bitmap to a specified file using the X Window Version 11 bitmap file format.

```
int XWriteBitmapFile(display, filename, bitmap, width,
                     height, x_hot, y_hot)
    Display *display;              /* Specifies the connection
                                      to the server */
    char *filename;                /* Full filename including
                                      path specification */
    Pixmap bitmap;                 /* Bitmap */
    unsigned int width, height;    /* Dimensions */
    int x_hot, y_hot;              /* Hotspot coordinates */
```

XWriteBitmapFile returns one of the following values: BitmapOpen-Failed, BitmapNoMemory, or BitmapSuccess. BitmapOpenFailed occurs because the specified directory does not exist or the application has not been granted permission to create a bitmap file. **XWriteBitmapFile** can generate BadDrawable and BadMatch errors.

Creating Bitmaps from Data

Xlib provides several functions that process bitmap data. The **XCreateBitmapFromData** function applies a bitmap file previously written by the **XWriteBitmapFile** function. The **XCreatePixmapFromBitmapData** function creates a pixmap and then stores bitmap data in it.

XCreateBitmapFromBitmapData

The **XCreateBitmapFromData** function, shown here, enables the program to access bitmap files written by the **XWrite BitmapFile** function by using the C language directive #include instead of specifically reading these files at program run time.

```
Pixmap XCreateBitmapFromData(display, d, data, width, height)
  Display *display;             /* Specifies the connection
                                   to the server */
  Drawable d;                   /* Screen on which
                                   pixmap is created */
  char *data;                   /* Location of bitmap data */
  unsigned int width, height;   /* Pixmap dimensions */
```

The following example shows how **XCreateBitmapFromData** can be used to create a red bitmap.

```
#include "red_bitmap"
...
Pixmap pixmap;
pixmap = XCreateBitmapFromData(thedisplay, thewindow,
                   red_bitmap_bits, red_bitmap_width,
                   red_bitmap_height)
```

XCreateBitmapFromData can generate a BadAlloc error.

XCreatePixmapFromData

The **XCreatePixmapFromBitmapData** function, shown next, creates a pixmap and then stores bitmap data in it.

```
Pixmap XCreatePixmapFromBitmapData(display, d, data, width,
                                    height, fg, bg, depth)
    Display *display;              /* Specifies the connection
                                      to the server */
    Drawable d;                    /* Screen on which
                                      pixmap is created */
    char *data;                    /* Data in bitmap format */
    unsigned int width, height;    /* Pixmap dimensions */
    unsigned long fg, bg;          /* Foreground and background
                                      pixel values */
    unsigned int depth;            /* Depth of pixmap */
```

XCreatePixmapFromBitmapData can generate BadAlloc and BadMatch errors.

Images

Images are data structures that represent visual data in memory and provide basic operations on this data. These operations include image creation, image destruction, pixel retrieval, pixel setting, subimage extraction, and addition of a constant to the image. Correct use of the image data structure and image operations simplifies drawing pictures for a wide range of workstations and reduces the volume of data transmitted between the server and the workstation.

XImage Data Structure

The XImage data structure, shown here, describes an image found in the workstation memory. It contains fields that define the specific image format, which can vary from one workstation to another.

```
typedef struct_XImage {
    int width, height;              /* Image size */
    int xoffset;                    /* X offset
                                       in number of pixels */
    int format;                     /* XYBitmap, XYPixmap,
                                       or ZPixmap */
    char *data;                     /* Pointer to image data */
    int byte_order;                 /* LSBFirst, MSBFirst */
    int bitmap_unit;                /* Scan line quantum
                                       8, 16, 32 */
    int bitmap_bit_order;           /* LSBFirst, MSBFirst */
    int bitmap_pad;                 /* 8, 16, 32 XYPixmap
                                       or ZPixmap */
    int depth;                      /* Image depth */
    int bytes_per_line;             /* Bytes per scan line */
    int bits_per_pixel;             /* Bits per pixel (ZPixmap) */
    unsigned long red_mask;         /* Bits in z arrangement */
    unsigned long green_mask;
    unsigned long blue_mask;
    XPointer obdata;                /* Hook for object routines */
    struct funcs {                  /* Image manipulation routines */
      struct_XImage *(*create_image)();
      int (*destroy_image)();
      unsigned long(*get_pixel)();
      int(*put_pixel)();
      struct_XImage *(*sub_image)();
      int(*add_pixel)();
      }f;
} XImage;
```

A row of pixels across the display screen is known as a *scan line.* The image *width* indicates the number of pixels in each scan line. The image *height* indicates the number of scan lines in the image. The *xoffset* indicates the number of pixels to ignore at the beginning of each scan line; its value is always 0 for ZPixmap format images. The *format* element in the data structure assumes one of three options:

❑ XYBitmap denotes a bitmap image composed of a single bit per pixel (*depth* of 1).

❑ XYPixmap denotes a pixmap image whose *depth* is given by the drawable that displays the image. This value can be greater than 1.

❏ ZPixmap also denotes a pixmap image whose *depth* is given by the drawable that displays the image. ZPixmap images are arrays of pixel values in memory.

The *data* parameter is a pointer to the pixel-value data for the image. The *byte_order* indicates whether the bytes of each *bitmap_unit* (described next) are stored in image memory least-significant byte first or most-significant byte first. The *bitmap_unit* indicates the number of bits in each scan line unit, known as a *quantum*. The *bitmap_bit_order* indicates whether the bytes of each *bitmap_unit* are displayed in the image least-significant byte first or most-significant byte first. The *bitmap_bit_order* field does not apply to images whose format is ZPixmap. For XYPixmap and ZPixmap images, the end of scan lines may be padded so that the next scan line begins on a byte boundary (*bitmap_pad* = 8), on a short integer boundary (*bitmap_pad* = 16), or on a long integer boundary (*bitmap_pad* = 32).

The *depth* indicates the image's number of bits per pixel. The *bytes_per_line* field indicates the number of bytes between the initial pixels of two consecutive scan lines. It includes the values of *xoffset* and *bitmap_pad*. The *bits_per_pixel* is defined for ZPixmap format fields and can have the value 1, 4, 8, 16, 24, or 32.

The *red_mask* is copied from the *red_mask* field of the Visual data structure. It specifies the bits of each pixel used for the *red* subfield and is meaningful for DirectColor and TrueColor images only. The *green_mask* and *blue_mask* parameters are similarly defined. Color is discussed in greater detail in Chapter 10, "Color and Graphics." The XImage data structure terminates with a structure that contains the addresses of the image manipulation functions.

Image Manipulation Functions

The **XCreateImage** function allocates memory for an XImage structure for the specified display. The **XSubImage** function creates a rectangular subimage by copying part of an existing image. The **XPutPixel** function sets a pixel value in a specified image. The **XGetPixel** function returns the pixel value from the specified image. The **XAddPixel** function adds a constant value to every pixel in the specified image. The **XPut-Image** function draws a memory-resident image into a window or a pixmap. The **XGetImage** and **XGetSubImage** functions retrieve from the workstation rectangular pixel arrays. The **XDestroyImage** function releases the memory allocated to an image.

XCreateImage

The **XCreateImage** function, shown here, allocates memory for an XImage structure for the specified display but does not allocate space for the image itself. The application must access the memory containing the actual image, which may have been created by a software package other than Xlib.

```
XImage *XCreateImage(display, visual, depth, format, offset,
                data, width, height, bitmap_pad,
                bytes_per_line)
   Display *display;             /* Specifies the connection
                                    to the server */
   Visual *visual;               /* Visual structure */
   unsigned int depth;           /* Depth of pixmap */
   int format;                   /* XYBitmap, XYPixmap,
                                    or ZPixmap */
   int offset;                   /* Pixels to ignore at start
                                    of scan line */
   char *data;                   /* Image data */
   unsigned int width;           /* Image width in pixels */
   unsigned int height;          /* Image height in pixels */
   int bitmap_pad;               /* Scan line offset */
   int bytes_per_line;           /* Bytes per scan line */
```

If the *format* is ZPixmap, the red, blue, and green mask values are obtained from the data structure referenced by the *visual* parameter. If the *format* is XYBitmap or XYPixmap, these mask values are not defined. A 0 value for the *bytes_per_line* parameter implies that the scan lines are contiguous in memory, and the server calculates the number of bytes per line. If **XCreateImage** does not successfully create an image data structure, it returns a NULL pointer.

XSubImage

XSubImage, shown next, creates a rectangular subimage by copying part of an existing image. It allocates the memory for the new XImage data structure and returns a pointer to this structure.

```
XImage *XSubImage(ximage, x, y, subimage_width, subimage_height)
   XImage *ximage;                 /* Specifies the image */
   int x, y;                       /* Image coordinates */
   unsigned int subimage_width;    /* Width of new subimage
                                      in pixels */
   unsigned int subimage_height;   /* Height of new subimage
                                      in pixels */
```

XSubImage is defined in the <X11/Xutil.h> header file.

XPutPixel

XPutPixel, shown next, sets a pixel value in a specified image.

```
XPutPixel(ximage, x, y, pixel)
   XImage *ximage;           /* Specifies the image */
   int x, y;                 /* Image coordinates */
   unsigned long pixel;      /* New pixel value */
```

XPutPixel is defined in the <X11/Xutil.h> header file. The image must contain the x and y coordinates.

XGetPixel

XGetPixel, shown next, returns the pixel value from the specified image.

```
unsigned long XGetPixel(ximage, x, y)
   XImage *ximage;           /* Specifies the image */
   int x, y;                 /* Image coordinates */
```

XGetPixel is defined in the <X11/Xutil.h> header file. The image must contain the x and y coordinates.

XAddPixel

XAddPixel, shown next, adds a constant value to every pixel in the specified image.

```
XAddPixel(ximage, value)
   XImage *ximage;            /* Specifies the image */
   long value;                /* Constant to be added */
```

XAddPixel is defined in the <X11/Xutil.h> header file.

XPutImage

The **XPutImage** function, shown next, copies (draws) an image in memory (or any rectangular portion) in a drawable (a window or a pixmap).

```
XPutImage(display, d, gc, image, src_x, src_y,
         dest_x, dest_y, width, height)
   Display *display;           /* Specifies the connection
                                  to the server */
   Drawable d;                 /* Drawable */
   GC gc;                      /* Graphics context */
   XImage *image;              /* Image to combine
                                  with rectangle */
   int src_x, src_y;           /* Offset with respect to
                                  XImage structure */
   int dest_x, dest_y;         /* Coordinates of subimage */
   unsigned int width, height; /* Dimensions of rectangle */
```

XPutImage accesses the graphics context and the image data structure to obtain image data. The *foreground* pixel value attribute of the graphics context is applied to all pixels with value 1 in the image. The *background* pixel value attribute of the graphics context is applied to all pixels with value 0 in the image. Other graphics contexts elements applied by **XPutImage** include the *function, plane_mask, subwindow_ mode, clip_x_origin, clip_y_origin,* and *clip_mask.*

If the image format is XYBitmap, the depth must be 1. If the image format is XYPixmap or ZPixmap, the image depth must equal the drawable depth. **XPutImage** can generate BadDrawable, BadGC, BadMatch, and BadValue errors.

XGetImage

The **XGetImage** function, shown next, creates an XImage data structure for the retrieved pixels. The function can be used for an elementary screen dump.

```
XImage *XGetImage(display, d, x, y, width, height
                  plane_mask, format)
  Display *display;              /* Specifies the connection
                                    to the server */
  Drawable d;                    /* Drawable */
  int x, y;                      /* Upper-left corner
                                    of rectangle */
  unsigned int width, height;    /* Dimensions of rectangle */
  unsigned long plane_mask;      /* Plane mask */
  int format;                    /* XYPixmap or ZPixmap */
```

XGetImage returns a pointer to the newly created XImage data structure. If the format is XYPixmap, the image includes only the bit planes specified in the *plane_mask* parameter. If the format is ZPixmap, the bits in all bit planes not specified in the *plane_mask* parameter are set to 0. If the drawable is a pixmap, the rectangle specified by the *width* and *height* parameters must be entirely within the pixmap.

If the drawable is a window, this rectangle must be fully visible on the screen and entirely within the window, without taking into consideration the window's inferior. The contents of obscured windows are given by the backing store, if any. **XGetImage** can generate BadDrawable, BadMatch, and BadValue errors.

XGetSubImage

The **XGetSubImage** function, shown next, copies the contents of a displayed rectangle to an area within an image data structure that has already been defined.

```
XImage *XGetSubImage(display, d, x, y, width, height,
                  plane_mask, format, dest_image,
                  dest_x, dest_y)
   Display *display;              /* Specifies the connection
                                     to the server */
   Drawable d;                    /* Drawable */
   int x, y;                      /* Upper-left corner
                                     of rectangle */
   unsigned int width, height;    /* Dimensions of rectangle */
   unsigned long plane_mask;      /* Plane mask */
   int format;                    /* XYPixmap or ZPixmap */
   XImage *dest_image;            /* Destination image */
   int dest_x, dest_y;            /* Subimage location with
                                     respect to the
                                     destination image */
```

XGetSubImage returns a pointer to the existing XImage data structure. Parameter restrictions for the **XGetSubImage** function are similar to those for the **XGetImage** function previously described. The **XGetSubImage** function can generate BadDrawable, BadGC, BadMatch, and BadValue errors.

XDestroyImage

The **XDestroyImage** function, shown next, releases the memory allocated to an image by **XCreateImage**, **XGetImage**, or **XSubImage**.

```
XDestroyImage(ximage)
   XImage *ximage;                /* Specifies the image
                                     to be destroyed */
```

Defining a Pixmap and Creating an Icon: Example 1

The following example defines a pixmap and uses it to place an icon on the screen.

UNIX systems contain a collection of bitmap files in the directory /usr/include/X11/bitmaps. The sorceress bitmap file resides on this directory and should be available before running the program.

Some of the statements that set the pixmap dimensions and load the pixmap with values are shown here.

```
#define sorceress_width 75
#define sorceress_height 75
static char sorceress_bits[] = {
  0xfc, 0x7e, 0x40, 0x20, 0x90, 0x00, 0x07, 0x80,
...
  0x41, 0xf0, 0xff, 0xff, 0xff, 0x07};
```

The C language function **create_window_set_properties**, shown here, creates a simple window, generates a bitmap from the pixmap previously defined, and sets the window's standard properties.

```
void create_window_set_properties(argc, argv)
int argc;
char *argv[];
{

  thewindow = XCreateSimpleWindow(thedisplay,
                       RootWindow(thedisplay, thescreen),
                       thehints.x, thehints.y,
                       thehints.width, thehints.height,
                       BORDER_WIDTH,
                       foreground, background);
  pixmap = XCreateBitmapFromData(thedisplay,
                       RootWindow(thedisplay, thescreen),
                       sorceress_bits, sorceress_width,
                       sorceress_height);
  XSetStandardProperties(thedisplay, thewindow, w_name,
                  i_name, pixmap, argv, argc, &thehints);
}
```

This program processes two event types, Expose events and ButtonPress events, both shown here. Expose events invoke the C language **load_strings** function. ButtonPress events prepare program exiting.

```
    case Expose:
      if (theevent.xexpose.count == 0)
      {
        load_strings();
      }
    break;

    case ButtonPress:
      done = TRUE;
      cleanup();
      printf("\n Ready to exit ...\n");
    break;
```

The C language **load_strings** function, shown next, creates the graphics context, sets the foreground and background pixels, and draws text on the screen.

```
void load_strings()
{

  thegc = XCreateGC(thedisplay, thewindow, 0, 0);
  XSetForeground(thedisplay, thegc,
               BlackPixel(thedisplay, thescreen));
  XSetBackground(thedisplay, thegc,
               WhitePixel(thedisplay, thescreen));
  XDrawString(thedisplay, thewindow, thegc, 30, 30,
             "You will see icon ...",
             strlen("You will see icon ..."));
  XDrawString(thedisplay, thewindow, thegc, 30, 60,
             "Point to created window.",
             strlen("Point to created window."));
  XDrawString(thedisplay, thewindow, thegc, 30, 90,
             "Press on mouse button to exit.",
             strlen("Press on mouse button to exit."));
}
```

The complete program listing follows.

```
/* example9_1 */
#include <X11/Xlib.h>
#include <X11/Xutil.h>
```

```
#define sorceress_width 75
#define sorceress_height 75
static char sorceress_bits[] = {
  0xfc, 0x7e, 0x40, 0x20, 0x90, 0x00, 0x07, 0x80,
  0x23, 0x00, 0x00, 0xc6, 0xc1, 0x41, 0x98, 0xb8,
  0x01, 0x07, 0x66, 0x00, 0x15, 0x9f, 0x03, 0x47,
  0x8c, 0xc6, 0xdc, 0x7b, 0xcc, 0x00, 0xb0, 0x71,
  0x0e, 0x4d, 0x06, 0x66, 0x73, 0x8e, 0x8f, 0x01,
  0x18, 0xc4, 0x39, 0x4b, 0x02, 0x23, 0x0c, 0x04,
  0x1e, 0x03, 0x0c, 0x08, 0xc7, 0xef, 0x08, 0x30,
  0x06, 0x07, 0x1c, 0x02, 0x06, 0x30, 0x18, 0xae,
  0xc8, 0x98, 0x3f, 0x78, 0x20, 0x06, 0x02, 0x20,
  0x60, 0xa0, 0xc4, 0x1d, 0xc0, 0xff, 0x41, 0x04,
  0xfa, 0x63, 0x80, 0xa1, 0xa4, 0x3d, 0x00, 0x84,
  0xbf, 0x04, 0x0f, 0x06, 0xfc, 0xa1, 0x34, 0x6b,
  0x01, 0x1c, 0xc9, 0x05, 0x06, 0xc7, 0x06, 0xbe,
  0x11, 0x1e, 0x43, 0x30, 0x91, 0x05, 0xc3, 0x61,
  0x02, 0x30, 0x1b, 0x30, 0xcc, 0x20, 0x11, 0x00,
  0xc1, 0x3c, 0x03, 0x20, 0x0a, 0x00, 0xe8, 0x60,
  0x21, 0x00, 0x61, 0x1b, 0xc1, 0x63, 0x08, 0xf0,
  0xc6, 0xc7, 0x21, 0x03, 0xf8, 0x08, 0xe1, 0xcf,
  0x0a, 0xfc, 0x4d, 0x99, 0x43, 0x07, 0x3c, 0x0c,
  0xf1, 0x9f, 0x0b, 0xfc, 0x5b, 0x81, 0x47, 0x02,
  0x16, 0x04, 0x31, 0x1c, 0x0b, 0x1f, 0x17, 0x89,
  0x4d, 0x06, 0x1a, 0x04, 0x31, 0x38, 0x02, 0x07,
  0x56, 0x89, 0x49, 0x04, 0x0b, 0x04, 0xb1, 0x72,
  0x82, 0xa1, 0x54, 0x9a, 0x49, 0x04, 0x1d, 0x66,
  0x50, 0xe7, 0xc2, 0xf0, 0x54, 0x9a, 0x58, 0x04,
  0x0d, 0x62, 0xc1, 0x1f, 0x44, 0xfc, 0x51, 0x90,
  0x90, 0x04, 0x86, 0x63, 0xe0, 0x74, 0x04, 0xef,
  0x31, 0x1a, 0x91, 0x00, 0x02, 0xe2, 0xc1, 0xfd,
  0x84, 0xf9, 0x30, 0x0a, 0x91, 0x00, 0x82, 0xa9,
  0xc0, 0xb9, 0x84, 0xf9, 0x31, 0x16, 0x81, 0x00,
  0x42, 0xa9, 0xdb, 0x7f, 0x0c, 0xff, 0x1c, 0x16,
  0x11, 0x00, 0x02, 0x28, 0x0b, 0x07, 0x08, 0x60,
  0x1c, 0x02, 0x91, 0x00, 0x46, 0x29, 0x0e, 0x00,
  0x00, 0x00, 0x10, 0x16, 0x11, 0x02, 0x06, 0x29,
  0x04, 0x00, 0x00, 0x00, 0x10, 0x16, 0x91, 0x06,
  0xa6, 0x2a, 0x04, 0x00, 0x00, 0x00, 0x18, 0x24,
  0x91, 0x04, 0x86, 0x2a, 0x04, 0x00, 0x00, 0x00,
  0x18, 0x27, 0x93, 0x04, 0x96, 0x4a, 0x04, 0x00,
  0x00, 0x00, 0x04, 0x02, 0x91, 0x04, 0x86, 0x4a,
```

```
0x0c, 0x00, 0x00, 0x00, 0x1e, 0x23, 0x93, 0x04,
0x56, 0x88, 0x08, 0x00, 0x00, 0x00, 0x90, 0x21,
0x93, 0x04, 0x52, 0x0a, 0x09, 0x80, 0x01, 0x00,
0xd0, 0x21, 0x95, 0x04, 0x57, 0x0a, 0x0f, 0x80,
0x27, 0x00, 0xd8, 0x20, 0x9d, 0x04, 0x5d, 0x08,
0x1c, 0x80, 0x67, 0x00, 0xe4, 0x01, 0x85, 0x04,
0x79, 0x8a, 0x3f, 0x00, 0x00, 0x00, 0xf4, 0x11,
0x85, 0x06, 0x39, 0x08, 0x7d, 0x00, 0x00, 0x18,
0xb7, 0x10, 0x81, 0x03, 0x29, 0x12, 0xcb, 0x00,
0x7e, 0x30, 0x28, 0x00, 0x85, 0x03, 0x29, 0x10,
0xbe, 0x81, 0xff, 0x27, 0x0c, 0x10, 0x85, 0x03,
0x29, 0x32, 0xfa, 0xc1, 0xff, 0x27, 0x94, 0x11,
0x85, 0x03, 0x28, 0x20, 0x6c, 0xe1, 0xff, 0x07,
0x0c, 0x01, 0x85, 0x01, 0x28, 0x62, 0x5c, 0xe3,
0x8f, 0x03, 0x4e, 0x91, 0x80, 0x05, 0x39, 0x40,
0xf4, 0xc2, 0xff, 0x00, 0x9f, 0x91, 0x84, 0x05,
0x31, 0xc6, 0xe8, 0x07, 0x7f, 0x80, 0xcd, 0x00,
0xc4, 0x04, 0x31, 0x06, 0xc9, 0x0e, 0x00, 0xc0,
0x48, 0x88, 0xe0, 0x04, 0x79, 0x04, 0xdb, 0x12,
0x00, 0x30, 0x0c, 0xc8, 0xe4, 0x04, 0x6d, 0x06,
0xb6, 0x23, 0x00, 0x18, 0x1c, 0xc0, 0x84, 0x04,
0x25, 0x0c, 0xff, 0xc2, 0x00, 0x4e, 0x06, 0xb0,
0x80, 0x04, 0x3f, 0x8a, 0xb3, 0x83, 0xff, 0xc3,
0x03, 0x91, 0x84, 0x04, 0x2e, 0xd8, 0x0f, 0x3f,
0x00, 0x00, 0x5f, 0x83, 0x84, 0x04, 0x2a, 0x70,
0xfd, 0x7f, 0x00, 0x00, 0xc8, 0xc0, 0x84, 0x04,
0x4b, 0xe2, 0x2f, 0x01, 0x00, 0x08, 0x58, 0x60,
0x80, 0x04, 0x5b, 0x82, 0xff, 0x01, 0x00, 0x08,
0xd0, 0xa0, 0x84, 0x04, 0x72, 0x80, 0xe5, 0x00,
0x00, 0x08, 0xd2, 0x20, 0x44, 0x04, 0xca, 0x02,
0xff, 0x00, 0x00, 0x08, 0xde, 0xa0, 0x44, 0x04,
0x82, 0x02, 0x6d, 0x00, 0x00, 0x08, 0xf6, 0xb0,
0x40, 0x02, 0x82, 0x07, 0x3f, 0x00, 0x00, 0x08,
0x44, 0x58, 0x44, 0x02, 0x93, 0x3f, 0x1f, 0x00,
0x00, 0x30, 0x88, 0x4f, 0x44, 0x03, 0x83, 0x23,
0x3e, 0x00, 0x00, 0x00, 0x18, 0x60, 0xe0, 0x07,
0xc3, 0x0f, 0xfc, 0x00, 0x00, 0x00, 0x70, 0x70,
0xe4, 0x07, 0xc7, 0x1b, 0xfe, 0x01, 0x00, 0x00,
0xe0, 0x3c, 0xe4, 0x07, 0xc7, 0xe3, 0xfe, 0x1f,
0x00, 0x00, 0xff, 0x1f, 0xfc, 0x07, 0xc7, 0x03,
0xf8, 0x33, 0x00, 0xc0, 0xf0, 0x07, 0xff, 0x07,
0x87, 0x02, 0xfc, 0x43, 0x00, 0x60, 0xf0, 0xff,
```

```
    0xff, 0x07, 0x8f, 0x06, 0xbe, 0x87, 0x00, 0x30,
    0xf8, 0xff, 0xff, 0x07, 0x8f, 0x14, 0x9c, 0x8f,
    0x00, 0x00, 0xfc, 0xff, 0xff, 0x07, 0x9f, 0x8d,
    0x8a, 0x0f, 0x00, 0x00, 0xfe, 0xff, 0xff, 0x07,
    0xbf, 0x0b, 0x80, 0x1f, 0x00, 0x00, 0xff, 0xff,
    0xff, 0x07, 0x7f, 0x3a, 0x80, 0x3f, 0x00, 0x80,
    0xff, 0xff, 0xff, 0x07, 0xff, 0x20, 0xc0, 0x3f,
    0x00, 0x80, 0xff, 0xff, 0xff, 0x07, 0xff, 0x01,
    0xe0, 0x7f, 0x00, 0xc0, 0xff, 0xff, 0xff, 0x07,
    0xff, 0x0f, 0xf8, 0xff, 0x40, 0xe0, 0xff, 0xff,
    0xff, 0x07, 0xff, 0xff, 0xff, 0xff, 0x40, 0xf0,
    0xff, 0xff, 0xff, 0x07, 0xff, 0xff, 0xff, 0xff,
    0x41, 0xf0, 0xff, 0xff, 0xff, 0x07};

#define BITMAPDEPTH 1
#define BORDER_WIDTH 2
#define FALSE 0
#define TRUE 1

Display        *thedisplay;
Window         thewindow;
int            thescreen;
Pixmap         pixmap;
char           *w_name;
char           *i_name =  "woman";
unsigned long foreground;
unsigned long background;
XSizeHints     thehints;
GC             thegc;

void init();
void load_strings();
void set_hints();
void create_window_set_properties();
void cleanup();

main(argc, argv)
int argc;
char *argv[];
{
XEvent theevent;
```

```
int done = FALSE;
int result;

  init(argv);

  set_hints();

  create_window_set_properties(argc,argv);

  XMapRaised(thedisplay, thewindow);

  XSelectInput(thedisplay, thewindow,
              ButtonPressMask | ExposureMask);
  while (!done)
  {
    XNextEvent(thedisplay, &theevent);

    switch(theevent.type)
    {
      case Expose:
        if (theevent.xexpose.count == 0)
        {
          load_strings();
        }
      break;

      case ButtonPress:
        done = TRUE;
        cleanup();
        printf("\n Ready to exit ...\n");
      break;
    }
  } /*  End while  */
} /*  End main  */

void init(argv)
char *argv[];
{

  w_name = argv[0];
  thedisplay = XOpenDisplay("");
  thescreen = DefaultScreen(thedisplay);
```

```
   background = WhitePixel(thedisplay, thescreen);
   foreground = BlackPixel(thedisplay, thescreen);
}


void load_strings()
{

   thegc = XCreateGC(thedisplay, thewindow, 0, 0);
   XSetForeground(thedisplay, thegc,
                  BlackPixel(thedisplay, thescreen));
   XSetBackground(thedisplay, thegc,
                  WhitePixel(thedisplay, thescreen));
   XDrawString(thedisplay, thewindow, thegc, 30, 30,
               "You will see icon ...",
               strlen("You will see icon ..."));
   XDrawString(thedisplay, thewindow, thegc, 30, 60,
               "Point to created window.",
               strlen("Point to created window."));
   XDrawString(thedisplay, thewindow, thegc, 30, 90,
               "Press on mouse button to exit.",
               strlen("Press on mouse button to exit."));
}


void create_window_set_properties(argc, argv)
int argc;
char *argv[];
{

   thewindow = XCreateSimpleWindow(thedisplay,
                        RootWindow(thedisplay, thescreen),
                        thehints.x, thehints.y,
                        thehints.width, thehints.height,
                        BORDER_WIDTH,
                        foreground, background);
   pixmap = XCreateBitmapFromData(thedisplay,
                        RootWindow(thedisplay, thescreen),
                        sorceress_bits, sorceress_width,
                        sorceress_height);
```

```
    XSetStandardProperties(thedisplay, thewindow, w_name,
              i_name, pixmap, argv, argc, &thehints);
}


void cleanup()
{
  XFreePixmap(thedisplay, pixmap);
  printf("\n Free pixmap  - done\n");

  XFreeGC(thedisplay, thegc);
  printf("\n Free gc  - done\n");

  XDestroyWindow(thedisplay, thewindow);
  printf("\n Destroy window  - done\n");

  XCloseDisplay(thedisplay);
  printf("\n Disconnect from server - done\n");
}


void set_hints()
{
int height;
int width;

  width = DisplayWidth(thedisplay, thescreen);
  height = DisplayHeight(thedisplay, thescreen);
  thehints.flags = PPosition | PSize | PMinSize;
  thehints.height = height/4;
  thehints.width = 250;
  thehints.x =  width/3;
  thehints.y =  height/3;
  thehints.min_height = 90;
  thehints.min_width = 250;
}
```

The results of running this program are shown in Figure 9-1.

The following MAKE file was used to process this program using SCO Open Desktop. The MAKE file for other X Window implementations varies.

Generating an icon from a pixmap

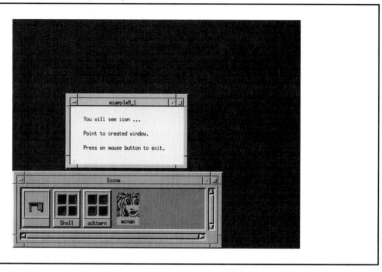

```
RM = rm - f
CC = cc
CFLAGS = -O
INCLUDES = -I. -I/usr/include -I/usr/include/X11
LIBS = -lXm -lXt -lX11 -lsocket -lmalloc -lPW
.c.o:
$(RM) $@
$(CC) -c $(CFFLAGS) $(INCLUDES) $*.c
all:: example9_1
example9_1: example9_1.o
$(RM) $@
$(CC) -o $@ $(CFLAGS) example9_1.o $(LIBS)
@echo makefile for example9_1
```

Defining Two Pixmaps and Displaying Two Icons: Example 2

The following exercise defines two pixmaps and uses them to place two icons on the screen.

Some of the statements that set the pixmap dimensions and load the pixmap with values are shown here. The mensetmanus bitmap file referenced in this program is available in the /usr/include/X11/bitmaps directory.

The X Window software comes with a utility program called *bitmap* that enables the user to edit these bitmap files or create new ones. A command to create a bitmap file named ex9_2, whose width and height are both 32, appears here.

bitmap ex9_2 32x32

You should create the bitmap file before running the program. This file must be included in the program either with an explicit #include declaration (#include "ex9_2") or by copying the file contents into the program. Because you don't have this bitmap file on your system, the program explicitly shows the file contents.

```
#define mensetmanus_width 161
#define mensetmanus_height 145

static char mensetmanus_bits[] = {
   0x00, 0x00, 0x00, 0x00, 0x00, 0x00, 0x00, 0x00,
. . .
   0x00, 0x00, 0x00, 0x00, 0x00 };
```

Some of the statements that set the ex9_2 pixmap dimensions and load the pixmap with values are shown here.

```
#define ex9_2_width 32
#define ex9_2_height 32
static char ex9_2_bits[] =
{
   0x00, 0xf8, 0x0f, 0x00, 0x00, 0xf8, 0x0f, 0x00,
. . .
   0x00, 0x01, 0x00, 0x0c, 0x00, 0x00, 0x00, 0x00
};
```

The C language function **create_window_set_properties** creates two simple windows, generates two bitmaps from the previously defined pixmaps, and sets the windows' standard properties.

The program processes two event types: Expose events and ButtonPress events. Expose events invoke the C language **load_strings_and_icons** function. ButtonPress events prepare to exit the program.

The C language **load_strings_and_icons** function creates the graphics context, sets the foreground and background pixels, clears the window, draws text on the screen, and copies a bit plane of the drawable using the **XCopyPlane** function discussed in Chapter 10, "Color and Graphics."

```c
void load_strings_and_icons()
{
int index = 0;

    thegc = XCreateGC(thedisplay, thewindow, 0, 0);
    XSetForeground(thedisplay, thegc,
                BlackPixel(thedisplay, thescreen));
    XSetBackground(thedisplay, thegc,
                WhitePixel(thedisplay, thescreen));
    XClearWindow(thedisplay, thewindow);
    XDrawString(thedisplay, thewindow, thegc, 210, 50,
                "Point to created window.",
                strlen("Point to created window."));
    XDrawString(thedisplay, thewindow, thegc, 210, 80,
                "Press on mouse button to exit.",
                strlen("Press on mouse button to exit."));
    XCopyPlane(thedisplay, pixmap[index], thewindow,
                thegc, 0, 0,
                mensetmanus_width,
                mensetmanus_height,
                0, 0, BITMAPDEPTH);
    index++;
    XCopyPlane(thedisplay, pixmap[index], thewindow,
                thegc, 0, 0,
                ex9_2_width,
                ex9_2_height,
                thehints.min_width/2-ex9_2_width/2,
                thehints.min_height-ex9_2_height,
                BITMAPDEPTH);
}
```

The complete program listing follows.

```
/* example9_2 */
#include <X11/Xlib.h>
#include <X11/Xutil.h>

#define mensetmanus_width 161
#define mensetmanus_height 145

static char mensetmanus_bits[] = {
  0x00, 0x00, 0x00, 0x00, 0x00, 0x00, 0x00, 0x00,
  0x00, 0x00, 0x00, 0x00, 0x00, 0x00, 0x00, 0x00,
  0x00, 0x00, 0x00, 0x00, 0x00, 0x00, 0x00, 0x00,
  0x00, 0xc0, 0x7f, 0x00, 0x00, 0x00, 0x00, 0x00,
  0x00, 0x00, 0x00, 0x00, 0x00, 0x00, 0x00, 0x00,
  0x00, 0x00, 0x00, 0x00, 0x00, 0x00, 0xf8, 0xff,
  0x01, 0x00, 0x00, 0x00, 0x00, 0xfc, 0xff, 0xff,
  0x7f, 0x00, 0x00, 0x00, 0x00, 0x00, 0x00, 0x00,
  0x00, 0x00, 0x00, 0xff, 0xff, 0x07, 0x00, 0x00,
  0x00, 0x00, 0xff, 0xff, 0xff, 0xff, 0x00, 0x00,
  0x00, 0x00, 0x00, 0x00, 0x00, 0x00, 0x00, 0x00,
  0x3f, 0xdb, 0x0f, 0x00, 0x00, 0x00, 0x80, 0x07,
  0x00, 0x00, 0xe0, 0x01, 0x00, 0x00, 0x00, 0x00,
  0x00, 0x00, 0x00, 0x00, 0x00, 0xf7, 0xff, 0x0f,
  0x00, 0x00, 0x00, 0x80, 0x61, 0x00, 0x00, 0xc6,
  0x01, 0x00, 0x00, 0x00, 0x00, 0x00, 0x00, 0x00,
  0x00, 0x80, 0xc3, 0xff, 0x1f, 0x00, 0x00, 0x00,
  0xc0, 0xe1, 0xff, 0xff, 0x87, 0x01, 0x00, 0x00,
  0x00, 0x00, 0x00, 0x00, 0x00, 0x00, 0x80, 0xc3,
  0xf6, 0x1f, 0x00, 0x00, 0x00, 0xc0, 0xc0, 0xff,
  0xff, 0x87, 0x01, 0x00, 0x00, 0x00, 0x00, 0x00,
  0x00, 0x00, 0x00, 0x80, 0x9f, 0x65, 0x1f, 0x00,
  0x00, 0x00, 0xc0, 0x00, 0x07, 0x80, 0x87, 0x01,
  0x00, 0x00, 0x00, 0x00, 0x00, 0x00, 0x00, 0x00,
  0x80, 0x9f, 0x6d, 0x1f, 0x00, 0x00, 0x00, 0xc0,
  0x00, 0xff, 0xff, 0xc7, 0x01, 0x00, 0x00, 0x00,
  0x00, 0x00, 0x00, 0x00, 0x00, 0x80, 0x89, 0x6d,
  0x1b, 0x00, 0x00, 0x00, 0xc0, 0xe0, 0xff, 0xff,
  0xff, 0x00, 0x00, 0x00, 0x00, 0x00, 0x00, 0x00,
  0x00, 0x00, 0xc0, 0x81, 0x6d, 0x1b, 0x00, 0x00,
  0x00, 0xc0, 0xe1, 0x5b, 0xdb, 0x7f, 0x00, 0x00,
  0x00, 0x00, 0x00, 0x00, 0x00, 0x00, 0x00, 0xc0,
  0x81, 0x6d, 0x1b, 0x00, 0x00, 0x00, 0x80, 0x83,
  0x5b, 0xdb, 0x1c, 0x00, 0x00, 0x00, 0x00, 0x00,
```

```
0x00, 0x00, 0x00, 0x00, 0xc0, 0x81, 0x6d, 0x1b,
0x00, 0x00, 0x00, 0x00, 0xcf, 0x5b, 0x1b, 0x0c,
0x00, 0x00, 0x00, 0x00, 0x00, 0x00, 0x00, 0x00,
0x00, 0xc0, 0x80, 0x6d, 0x1b, 0x00, 0x00, 0x00,
0x00, 0xfe, 0x5b, 0x1b, 0x0c, 0x00, 0x00, 0x00,
0x00, 0x00, 0x00, 0x00, 0x00, 0x00, 0xe0, 0x80,
0x6d, 0x1b, 0x00, 0x00, 0x00, 0x00, 0xf8, 0x5b,
0x0b, 0x0c, 0x00, 0x00, 0x00, 0x00, 0x00, 0x00,
0x00, 0x00, 0x00, 0xe0, 0x83, 0x6d, 0x19, 0x00,
0x00, 0x00, 0x00, 0x80, 0x5b, 0x0b, 0x0e, 0x00,
0x00, 0x00, 0x00, 0x00, 0x00, 0x00, 0x00, 0x00,
0xe0, 0x83, 0x6d, 0x1b, 0x00, 0x00, 0x00, 0x00,
0x80, 0x5b, 0x0f, 0x0e, 0x00, 0x00, 0x00, 0x00,
0x00, 0x00, 0x00, 0x00, 0x00, 0x00, 0x83, 0x6d,
0x1b, 0x00, 0x00, 0x00, 0x00, 0x80, 0x4b, 0x0f,
0x07, 0x00, 0x00, 0x00, 0x00, 0x00, 0x00, 0x00,
0x00, 0x00, 0x00, 0x83, 0x79, 0x1b, 0x00, 0x00,
0x00, 0x00, 0x80, 0x6b, 0xbf, 0x07, 0x00, 0x00,
0x00, 0x00, 0x00, 0x00, 0x00, 0x00, 0x00, 0x00,
0x03, 0xfb, 0x3b, 0x00, 0x00, 0x00, 0x00, 0x80,
0x6d, 0xb7, 0x07, 0x00, 0x00, 0x00, 0x00, 0x00,
0x00, 0x00, 0x00, 0x00, 0x00, 0x03, 0xff, 0x3f,
0x00, 0x00, 0x00, 0x00, 0xc0, 0xed, 0xf7, 0x07,
0x00, 0x00, 0x00, 0x00, 0x00, 0x00, 0x00, 0x00,
0x00, 0x80, 0x07, 0xfe, 0x7f, 0x00, 0x00, 0x00,
0x00, 0xc0, 0xed, 0xd7, 0x07, 0x00, 0x00, 0x00,
0x00, 0x00, 0x00, 0x00, 0x00, 0x00, 0xfc, 0x7f,
0xf8, 0xff, 0x07, 0x00, 0x00, 0x00, 0xe0, 0xfe,
0xd7, 0xfe, 0x00, 0x00, 0x00, 0x00, 0x00, 0x00,
0x00, 0x00, 0x80, 0xff, 0x7f, 0xe0, 0xff, 0x3f,
0x00, 0x00, 0x00, 0xf0, 0xff, 0xd6, 0xfe, 0x07,
0x00, 0x00, 0x00, 0x00, 0x00, 0x00, 0x00, 0xc0,
0xbf, 0x73, 0x80, 0x3b, 0x7c, 0x00, 0x00, 0x00,
0xf8, 0xe7, 0xd6, 0xef, 0x1f, 0x00, 0x00, 0x00,
0x00, 0x00, 0x00, 0x00, 0xf0, 0xb9, 0x73, 0xc0,
0x3b, 0xf0, 0x01, 0x00, 0x00, 0xff, 0xc3, 0xbf,
0xe7, 0x3f, 0x00, 0x00, 0x00, 0x00, 0x00, 0x00,
0x00, 0x78, 0xb8, 0x7f, 0xe0, 0x3b, 0xc0, 0x03,
0x00, 0xc0, 0xbf, 0xc7, 0xbf, 0xe7, 0x7e, 0x00,
0x00, 0x00, 0x00, 0x00, 0x00, 0x00, 0x1c, 0xb8,
0xff, 0xf8, 0x3b, 0x80, 0x07, 0x00, 0xe0, 0x61,
0x87, 0xfd, 0xe7, 0xe6, 0x00, 0x00, 0x00, 0x00,
```

```
0x00, 0x00, 0x00, 0x0e, 0xb8, 0xf3, 0xff, 0x3b,
0x00, 0x0f, 0x00, 0x78, 0x60, 0x8e, 0xf1, 0x67,
0xc7, 0x01, 0x00, 0x00, 0x00, 0x00, 0x00, 0x00,
0x07, 0xb8, 0xc3, 0x8f, 0x7b, 0x00, 0x0e, 0x00,
0x38, 0xe0, 0x8c, 0x03, 0x66, 0x87, 0x03, 0x00,
0x00, 0x00, 0x00, 0x00, 0x80, 0x07, 0xb8, 0x03,
0x83, 0x7b, 0x00, 0x1e, 0x00, 0x1c, 0xe0, 0x1d,
0x03, 0x76, 0x07, 0x07, 0x00, 0x00, 0x00, 0x00,
0x00, 0xc0, 0x07, 0xb8, 0xe3, 0x8f, 0xbb, 0x01,
0x39, 0x00, 0x1e, 0xe0, 0x3b, 0x03, 0xf6, 0x87,
0x0f, 0x00, 0x00, 0x00, 0x00, 0x00, 0xc0, 0x0f,
0xb8, 0xe3, 0x8f, 0x3b, 0xc6, 0x38, 0x00, 0x17,
0xe0, 0x73, 0x07, 0xfe, 0xff, 0xff, 0x7f, 0x00,
0x00, 0x00, 0x00, 0xe0, 0x0b, 0xb8, 0xe7, 0x8e,
0x3b, 0x38, 0x78, 0x00, 0x13, 0xe0, 0x77, 0x06,
0xfe, 0xff, 0xff, 0xff, 0x0f, 0x00, 0x00, 0x00,
0xe0, 0x12, 0x3c, 0xff, 0xce, 0x3b, 0x00, 0x78,
0x80, 0x13, 0x60, 0xef, 0x0e, 0xfe, 0x00, 0x00,
0x60, 0x08, 0x00, 0x00, 0x00, 0x70, 0x22, 0x3e,
0xfc, 0xfe, 0x39, 0x00, 0xe8, 0x80, 0x61, 0x60,
0xce, 0x0f, 0xfe, 0x00, 0x00, 0x60, 0xf8, 0x00,
0x00, 0x00, 0x70, 0xc2, 0x39, 0xf8, 0x7e, 0x38,
0x00, 0xc8, 0xc0, 0x81, 0x71, 0xde, 0x0f, 0xfe,
0x00, 0x00, 0x60, 0x88, 0x00, 0x00, 0x00, 0x70,
0x04, 0x38, 0xe0, 0x0e, 0x38, 0x00, 0xc4, 0xc0,
0x01, 0x7e, 0xbc, 0x1f, 0xfe, 0x00, 0x00, 0x60,
0x88, 0x00, 0x00, 0x00, 0x78, 0x04, 0x38, 0xe0,
0x0e, 0x38, 0x00, 0xc4, 0xc1, 0x01, 0x60, 0x3c,
0x1f, 0xfe, 0x00, 0x00, 0x60, 0x84, 0x0f, 0x00,
0x00, 0x78, 0x08, 0x38, 0xe0, 0x0f, 0x38, 0x00,
0x82, 0xe1, 0x01, 0x60, 0x74, 0x3e, 0xfe, 0x00,
0x00, 0x60, 0x44, 0x08, 0x00, 0x00, 0xb8, 0x10,
0x38, 0xe0, 0x0f, 0x38, 0x00, 0x81, 0xe1, 0x00,
0x60, 0xe4, 0x3e, 0xfe, 0x00, 0x00, 0x60, 0x44,
0x08, 0x00, 0x00, 0x98, 0x20, 0x38, 0xf8, 0x3f,
0x38, 0x80, 0x80, 0xc1, 0x01, 0x60, 0xc4, 0x3c,
0xfe, 0x00, 0x00, 0x60, 0x24, 0x0c, 0x00, 0x00,
0x1c, 0xc1, 0x39, 0x3c, 0x78, 0x38, 0x40, 0x80,
0x61, 0x01, 0x60, 0xc4, 0x79, 0xfe, 0x00, 0x00,
0x60, 0x22, 0x32, 0x00, 0x00, 0x1c, 0x01, 0x3e,
0x1c, 0xf0, 0x38, 0xf0, 0x9f, 0x61, 0x01, 0x60,
0x84, 0x7b, 0xee, 0x00, 0x00, 0x60, 0x12, 0x21,
```

```
0x00, 0x00, 0x1c, 0x02, 0x38, 0x0e, 0xe7, 0xf8,
0x3f, 0xe0, 0x61, 0x00, 0x60, 0x04, 0xf7, 0xce,
0x00, 0x00, 0x60, 0x92, 0x10, 0x00, 0x00, 0x1c,
0x04, 0x38, 0x06, 0xff, 0x38, 0x40, 0x80, 0x61,
0x02, 0x60, 0x04, 0xe7, 0xcf, 0x00, 0x00, 0x60,
0x8a, 0x18, 0x00, 0x00, 0x1c, 0x18, 0x38, 0x07,
0xf0, 0x38, 0x00, 0x81, 0x61, 0x02, 0x60, 0x04,
0xee, 0xcf, 0xff, 0x03, 0x60, 0x49, 0xe4, 0x00,
0x00, 0x1c, 0x70, 0x38, 0x07, 0xe7, 0x38, 0x00,
0x82, 0x61, 0x04, 0x60, 0x04, 0xdc, 0xcf, 0x01,
0x04, 0x60, 0x25, 0x42, 0x00, 0x00, 0x1c, 0xfe,
0x3f, 0x03, 0xff, 0x38, 0x00, 0x84, 0x61, 0x08,
0x60, 0x04, 0xfc, 0xcf, 0xf8, 0xff, 0x60, 0x95,
0x31, 0x00, 0x00, 0xfc, 0x01, 0xff, 0x03, 0xf0,
0xf8, 0x1f, 0x88, 0x61, 0x10, 0xe0, 0xff, 0xff,
0xff, 0x00, 0x00, 0xe1, 0x53, 0x0c, 0x00, 0x00,
0x38, 0xf0, 0xff, 0x03, 0xef, 0xf8, 0x7f, 0x90,
0x61, 0x40, 0xe0, 0xff, 0xff, 0xff, 0x00, 0xff,
0xe3, 0x2b, 0xfe, 0x00, 0x00, 0x18, 0xf8, 0xff,
0x03, 0xff, 0x7c, 0xf0, 0x90, 0x61, 0x00, 0x3e,
0x36, 0xe3, 0xe1, 0x00, 0x00, 0xe3, 0x9f, 0x60,
0x00, 0x00, 0x38, 0x3c, 0x00, 0x03, 0xf0, 0x1f,
0xe0, 0xa0, 0xe1, 0x00, 0x30, 0x22, 0xe2, 0xc0,
0x00, 0xff, 0xe3, 0x7f, 0x18, 0x00, 0x00, 0x38,
0x0e, 0x00, 0x07, 0xe7, 0x07, 0xc0, 0xe1, 0xc1,
0x00, 0x18, 0x22, 0xe2, 0xc0, 0x00, 0x00, 0xe1,
0x1f, 0x07, 0x00, 0x00, 0x38, 0x06, 0x00, 0x07,
0xef, 0x01, 0xc0, 0xc1, 0xc1, 0x01, 0x16, 0x24,
0xe2, 0xc0, 0x01, 0xff, 0xe1, 0xff, 0x00, 0x00,
0x00, 0x70, 0x07, 0x00, 0x0e, 0xf8, 0x00, 0x80,
0xc3, 0xc0, 0xf1, 0x11, 0x24, 0xe4, 0xc0, 0x03,
0xe0, 0xe1, 0x7f, 0x00, 0x00, 0x00, 0x70, 0x07,
0x00, 0x1e, 0x3c, 0x00, 0x80, 0xe3, 0x80, 0x0f,
0x10, 0x24, 0xe4, 0xc0, 0xff, 0xff, 0xff, 0xff,
0xff, 0x01, 0x00, 0xe0, 0x03, 0x00, 0xfc, 0x0f,
0x00, 0x00, 0x63, 0x80, 0x01, 0x08, 0x44, 0xe4,
0xc0, 0xff, 0xff, 0xff, 0xff, 0xff, 0x01, 0x00,
0xe0, 0x03, 0x00, 0xf8, 0x07, 0x00, 0x00, 0x73,
0x80, 0x03, 0x08, 0x44, 0xe4, 0xc0, 0xfc, 0x00,
0x07, 0x0e, 0x00, 0x00, 0x00, 0xc0, 0x03, 0x00,
0xf0, 0x01, 0x00, 0x00, 0x33, 0x00, 0x03, 0x08,
0x44, 0xe4, 0xe0, 0xcc, 0x00, 0x07, 0x0e, 0x00,
```

```
0x00, 0x00, 0xc0, 0x03, 0x00, 0x78, 0x00, 0x00,
0x80, 0x3f, 0x00, 0x07, 0x04, 0x44, 0xe8, 0x70,
0xcc, 0x01, 0x87, 0x0f, 0x00, 0x00, 0x00, 0x80,
0x07, 0x00, 0x3e, 0x00, 0x00, 0x80, 0x1f, 0x00,
0x0e, 0x04, 0x44, 0xe8, 0x38, 0xcc, 0x81, 0xe7,
0x03, 0x00, 0x00, 0x00, 0x00, 0x07, 0x00, 0x0f,
0x00, 0x00, 0x80, 0x0f, 0x00, 0x1c, 0x02, 0x44,
0xf8, 0x1e, 0xcc, 0xe1, 0xff, 0x00, 0x00, 0x00,
0x00, 0x00, 0x0f, 0xc0, 0x23, 0x00, 0x00, 0xc0,
0x07, 0x00, 0x38, 0x01, 0x42, 0xfc, 0x0f, 0xcc,
0xf1, 0x3f, 0x00, 0x00, 0x00, 0x00, 0x00, 0x0e,
0xf0, 0x39, 0x00, 0x00, 0xe0, 0x03, 0x00, 0xf0,
0x00, 0xc2, 0xff, 0x07, 0xcc, 0x7f, 0x0f, 0x00,
0x00, 0x00, 0x00, 0x00, 0x3c, 0x7c, 0x0e, 0x00,
0x00, 0xf0, 0x01, 0x00, 0xe0, 0x03, 0xe2, 0xe7,
0x07, 0xcc, 0x1f, 0x07, 0x00, 0x00, 0x00, 0x00,
0x00, 0xf8, 0xbf, 0x23, 0xe0, 0xff, 0xff, 0x00,
0x00, 0xc0, 0x1f, 0xff, 0x64, 0x06, 0xcc, 0x07,
0x00, 0x00, 0x00, 0x00, 0x00, 0x00, 0xf0, 0xff,
0x3c, 0xf0, 0xff, 0x7f, 0x00, 0x00, 0x00, 0xff,
0x7f, 0x64, 0x06, 0xcc, 0x03, 0x00, 0x00, 0x00,
0x00, 0x00, 0x00, 0x70, 0xf8, 0x1f, 0x78, 0x7c,
0x7f, 0x00, 0x00, 0x00, 0xfc, 0x20, 0x64, 0x06,
0xcc, 0x03, 0x00, 0x00, 0x00, 0x00, 0x00, 0x00,
0x70, 0xf8, 0x33, 0x1c, 0x38, 0x66, 0x00, 0x00,
0x00, 0x0c, 0x20, 0x6c, 0x06, 0xcc, 0x03, 0x00,
0x00, 0x00, 0x00, 0x00, 0x00, 0x30, 0x78, 0x3e,
0x0e, 0x38, 0x76, 0x00, 0x00, 0x00, 0x0c, 0x20,
0x68, 0x06, 0xcc, 0x03, 0x00, 0x00, 0x00, 0x00,
0x00, 0x00, 0x38, 0xf8, 0x87, 0x0f, 0x38, 0x76,
0x00, 0x00, 0x00, 0x0c, 0x20, 0x68, 0x06, 0xcc,
0x07, 0x00, 0x00, 0x00, 0x00, 0x00, 0x00, 0x38,
0x78, 0xf8, 0x0f, 0x38, 0x76, 0x00, 0x00, 0x00,
0x0c, 0x10, 0x68, 0x06, 0xcc, 0x07, 0x00, 0x00,
0x00, 0x00, 0x00, 0x00, 0x18, 0xf8, 0xff, 0x0f,
0x38, 0x76, 0x00, 0x00, 0x00, 0x0c, 0x10, 0x68,
0x06, 0xcc, 0x07, 0x00, 0x00, 0x00, 0x00, 0x00,
0x00, 0x1c, 0xf8, 0xff, 0x0e, 0x38, 0x76, 0x00,
0x00, 0x00, 0x0c, 0x10, 0x68, 0x06, 0xcc, 0x07,
0x00, 0x00, 0x00, 0x00, 0x00, 0x00, 0x1c, 0xf8,
0xe1, 0x0e, 0x38, 0x3e, 0x00, 0x00, 0x00, 0x0c,
0x08, 0x68, 0x06, 0xcc, 0x06, 0x00, 0x00, 0x00,
```

```
0x00, 0x00, 0x00, 0x0c, 0x38, 0xe0, 0x0e, 0x38,
0x3e, 0x00, 0x00, 0x00, 0x0c, 0x08, 0x68, 0x06,
0xcc, 0x06, 0x00, 0x00, 0x00, 0x00, 0x00, 0x00,
0x0e, 0x38, 0xe0, 0x0e, 0x38, 0x3e, 0x00, 0x00,
0x00, 0x0c, 0x04, 0x68, 0x06, 0xcc, 0x0e, 0x00,
0x00, 0x00, 0x00, 0x00, 0x00, 0x0e, 0x38, 0xe0,
0x0e, 0x38, 0x3e, 0x00, 0x00, 0x00, 0x1c, 0x04,
0x68, 0x06, 0xcc, 0x0e, 0x00, 0x00, 0x00, 0x00,
0x00, 0x00, 0x06, 0x38, 0xe0, 0x0e, 0x38, 0x3e,
0x00, 0x00, 0x00, 0x1c, 0x02, 0x68, 0x06, 0xcc,
0x0c, 0x00, 0x00, 0x00, 0x00, 0x00, 0x00, 0x06,
0x38, 0xe0, 0x0e, 0x38, 0x3e, 0x00, 0x00, 0x00,
0x1c, 0x02, 0x68, 0x06, 0xcc, 0x0c, 0x00, 0x00,
0x00, 0x00, 0x00, 0x00, 0x07, 0x38, 0xe0, 0x0e,
0x38, 0x3e, 0x00, 0x00, 0x00, 0x1c, 0x01, 0x68,
0x06, 0xcc, 0x1c, 0x00, 0x00, 0x00, 0x00, 0x00,
0x00, 0x07, 0x38, 0xe0, 0x0e, 0x38, 0x3e, 0x00,
0x00, 0x00, 0x18, 0x01, 0x68, 0x06, 0xcc, 0x1c,
0x00, 0x00, 0x00, 0x00, 0x00, 0x00, 0x03, 0x38,
0xe0, 0x0e, 0x38, 0x3e, 0x00, 0x00, 0x00, 0x98,
0x00, 0x68, 0x06, 0xcc, 0x1c, 0x00, 0x00, 0x00,
0x00, 0x00, 0x80, 0x03, 0x38, 0xe0, 0x0e, 0x38,
0x3e, 0x00, 0x00, 0x00, 0x98, 0x00, 0x68, 0x06,
0xcc, 0x18, 0x00, 0x00, 0x00, 0x00, 0x00, 0x80,
0x03, 0x38, 0xe0, 0x0e, 0x38, 0x1e, 0x00, 0x00,
0x00, 0x58, 0x00, 0x6c, 0x0e, 0xcc, 0x18, 0x00,
0x00, 0x00, 0x00, 0x00, 0x80, 0x01, 0x30, 0xe0,
0x0e, 0x38, 0x1e, 0x00, 0x00, 0x00, 0x38, 0x00,
0x64, 0x0e, 0xcc, 0x18, 0x00, 0x00, 0x00, 0x00,
0x00, 0xc0, 0x01, 0x70, 0xe0, 0x0e, 0x1c, 0x1e,
0x00, 0x00, 0x00, 0x18, 0x00, 0x64, 0x1e, 0xcc,
0x38, 0x00, 0x00, 0x00, 0x00, 0x00, 0xc0, 0x01,
0xe0, 0xe1, 0x0e, 0x0f, 0x1e, 0x00, 0x00, 0x00,
0x18, 0x00, 0x64, 0x3e, 0xcc, 0x38, 0x00, 0x00,
0x00, 0x00, 0x00, 0xc0, 0x00, 0xc0, 0xef, 0xce,
0x07, 0x1e, 0x00, 0x00, 0x00, 0x18, 0x00, 0x64,
0x3e, 0xcc, 0x30, 0x00, 0x00, 0x00, 0x00, 0x00,
0xe0, 0x00, 0x00, 0xff, 0xfe, 0x03, 0x1e, 0x00,
0x00, 0x00, 0x18, 0x00, 0x64, 0x7e, 0xcc, 0x30,
0x00, 0x00, 0x00, 0x00, 0x00, 0xe0, 0x00, 0x00,
0xfc, 0xfe, 0x00, 0x1e, 0x00, 0x00, 0x00, 0x18,
0x00, 0x64, 0x66, 0xcc, 0x30, 0x00, 0x00, 0x00,
```

```
0x00, 0x00, 0xe0, 0x00, 0x00, 0xe0, 0x1e, 0x00,
0x1e, 0x00, 0x00, 0x00, 0x18, 0x00, 0x66, 0x66,
0xcc, 0x70, 0x00, 0x00, 0x00, 0x00, 0x00, 0x60,
0x00, 0x00, 0xe0, 0x0e, 0x00, 0x1e, 0x00, 0x00,
0x00, 0x18, 0x00, 0x62, 0xc6, 0xcd, 0x70, 0x00,
0x00, 0x00, 0x00, 0x00, 0x70, 0x00, 0x00, 0xfe,
0xff, 0x0f, 0x1e, 0x00, 0x00, 0x00, 0x18, 0x00,
0x62, 0xc6, 0xcd, 0x70, 0x00, 0x00, 0x00, 0x00,
0x00, 0x70, 0x00, 0xc0, 0xff, 0xff, 0x0f, 0x0e,
0x00, 0x00, 0x00, 0x38, 0x00, 0x62, 0x86, 0xcf,
0x60, 0x00, 0x00, 0x00, 0x00, 0x00, 0x30, 0x00,
0xf0, 0xff, 0xff, 0x0f, 0x0e, 0x00, 0x00, 0x00,
0x38, 0x00, 0x61, 0x86, 0xcf, 0xe0, 0x00, 0x00,
0x00, 0x00, 0x00, 0x38, 0x00, 0xfc, 0x00, 0x00,
0x0e, 0x0e, 0x00, 0x00, 0x00, 0x38, 0x00, 0x61,
0x8e, 0xcf, 0xe0, 0x00, 0x00, 0x00, 0x00, 0x00,
0x38, 0x00, 0x78, 0x00, 0x00, 0x0e, 0x0e, 0x00,
0x00, 0x00, 0xf8, 0xff, 0x7f, 0xfe, 0xdf, 0xff,
0x00, 0x00, 0x00, 0x00, 0x00, 0x18, 0x00, 0xf0,
0x00, 0x00, 0x0e, 0x0e, 0x00, 0x00, 0x00, 0xf0,
0xff, 0x3f, 0xff, 0xdf, 0xff, 0x00, 0x00, 0x00,
0x00, 0x00, 0x1c, 0x00, 0xe0, 0x01, 0x00, 0x0e,
0x0e, 0x00, 0x00, 0x00, 0xf0, 0xff, 0x8f, 0x07,
0x9e, 0xff, 0x00, 0x00, 0x00, 0x00, 0x00, 0x1c,
0x00, 0xe0, 0x07, 0x00, 0x0e, 0x0f, 0x00, 0x00,
0x00, 0x30, 0x00, 0xc0, 0xff, 0x3f, 0xc0, 0x01,
0x00, 0x00, 0x00, 0x00, 0x1c, 0x00, 0xfe, 0xff,
0xff, 0xff, 0x0f, 0x00, 0x00, 0x00, 0xf0, 0xff,
0xff, 0xff, 0xff, 0xff, 0x01, 0x00, 0x00, 0x00,
0x00, 0x1c, 0x00, 0xfe, 0xff, 0xff, 0xff, 0x07,
0x00, 0x00, 0x00, 0xf0, 0xff, 0xff, 0x00, 0xff,
0xff, 0x01, 0x00, 0x00, 0x00, 0x00, 0xfe, 0xff,
0x3f, 0x00, 0x00, 0x00, 0x06, 0x00, 0x00, 0x00,
0x00, 0x0e, 0x38, 0x00, 0x38, 0xe0, 0x01, 0x00,
0x00, 0x00, 0x00, 0xfe, 0xff, 0x7f, 0x00, 0x00,
0x00, 0x06, 0x00, 0x00, 0x00, 0x00, 0x06, 0x38,
0x00, 0x38, 0xe0, 0x00, 0x00, 0x00, 0x00, 0x00,
0xe0, 0x00, 0x7c, 0x00, 0x00, 0x00, 0x06, 0x00,
0x00, 0x00, 0x00, 0x06, 0x18, 0x00, 0x38, 0xe0,
0x00, 0x00, 0x00, 0x00, 0x00, 0xe0, 0x00, 0xfc,
0x00, 0x00, 0x00, 0x06, 0x00, 0x00, 0x00, 0x00,
0x06, 0x18, 0x00, 0x38, 0xe0, 0x00, 0x00, 0x00,
```

```
0x00, 0x00, 0xe0, 0x00, 0xdc, 0x01, 0x00, 0x00,
0x06, 0x00, 0x00, 0x00, 0x00, 0x06, 0x1c, 0x00,
0x38, 0x60, 0x00, 0x00, 0x00, 0x00, 0x00, 0xe0,
0x00, 0x9c, 0x03, 0x00, 0x00, 0x06, 0x00, 0x00,
0x00, 0x00, 0x06, 0x1c, 0x00, 0x18, 0x70, 0x00,
0x00, 0x00, 0x00, 0x00, 0xe0, 0x00, 0x1c, 0x07,
0x00, 0x00, 0x06, 0x00, 0x00, 0x00, 0x00, 0x07,
0x0c, 0x00, 0x18, 0x70, 0x00, 0x00, 0x00, 0x00,
0x00, 0xe0, 0x00, 0x1c, 0xfe, 0xff, 0xff, 0x07,
0x00, 0x00, 0x00, 0x00, 0x07, 0x0c, 0x00, 0x18,
0x70, 0x00, 0x00, 0x00, 0x00, 0x00, 0xe0, 0x00,
0x1c, 0xfc, 0xff, 0xff, 0x07, 0x00, 0x00, 0x00,
0x00, 0x07, 0x0c, 0x00, 0x18, 0x70, 0x00, 0x00,
0x00, 0x00, 0x00, 0xe0, 0x00, 0x1c, 0x1c, 0x00,
0x80, 0x07, 0x00, 0x00, 0x00, 0x00, 0x07, 0x0e,
0x00, 0x18, 0x70, 0x00, 0x00, 0x00, 0x00, 0x00,
0xe0, 0x00, 0x1c, 0x1c, 0x00, 0x80, 0x03, 0x00,
0x00, 0x00, 0x00, 0x07, 0x0e, 0x00, 0x18, 0x30,
0x00, 0x00, 0x00, 0x00, 0x00, 0xe0, 0x00, 0x1c,
0x1c, 0x00, 0x80, 0x03, 0x00, 0x00, 0x00, 0x00,
0x07, 0x0e, 0x00, 0x18, 0x38, 0x00, 0x00, 0x00,
0x00, 0x00, 0xe0, 0x00, 0x1c, 0x1c, 0x00, 0x80,
0x03, 0x00, 0x00, 0x00, 0x00, 0x07, 0x0e, 0x00,
0x18, 0x38, 0x00, 0x00, 0x00, 0x00, 0x00, 0xe0,
0x00, 0x1c, 0x1c, 0x00, 0x80, 0x03, 0x00, 0x00,
0x00, 0x00, 0x07, 0x06, 0x00, 0x18, 0x38, 0x00,
0x00, 0x00, 0x00, 0x00, 0xe0, 0x00, 0xfc, 0xff,
0xff, 0xff, 0x07, 0x00, 0x00, 0x00, 0x00, 0x07,
0x06, 0x00, 0x18, 0x38, 0x00, 0x00, 0x00, 0x00,
0x00, 0xe0, 0x00, 0xfc, 0xff, 0xff, 0xff, 0x07,
0x00, 0x00, 0x00, 0x00, 0x07, 0x0e, 0x00, 0x18,
0x38, 0x00, 0x00, 0x00, 0x00, 0x00, 0xe0, 0x00,
0x1c, 0x00, 0x00, 0x00, 0x06, 0x00, 0x00, 0x00,
0x00, 0x07, 0x0e, 0x00, 0x18, 0x30, 0x00, 0x00,
0x00, 0x00, 0x00, 0xe0, 0x00, 0x1c, 0x00, 0x00,
0x00, 0x06, 0x00, 0x00, 0x00, 0x00, 0x07, 0x0e,
0x00, 0x18, 0x30, 0x00, 0x00, 0x00, 0x00, 0x00,
0xe0, 0x00, 0x1c, 0x00, 0x00, 0x00, 0x06, 0x00,
0x00, 0x00, 0x00, 0x07, 0x0e, 0x00, 0x18, 0x70,
0x00, 0x00, 0x00, 0x00, 0x00, 0xe0, 0x00, 0x1c,
0x00, 0x00, 0x00, 0x06, 0x00, 0x00, 0x00, 0x00,
0x07, 0x0e, 0x00, 0x18, 0x70, 0x00, 0x00, 0x00,
```

```
0x00, 0x00, 0xe0, 0x00, 0x1e, 0x00, 0x00, 0x00,
0x06, 0x00, 0x00, 0x00, 0x00, 0x06, 0x0c, 0x00,
0x38, 0x70, 0x00, 0x00, 0x00, 0x00, 0x00, 0xe0,
0x00, 0x1e, 0x00, 0x00, 0x00, 0x06, 0x00, 0x00,
0x00, 0x00, 0x06, 0x1c, 0x00, 0x38, 0x70, 0x00,
0x00, 0x00, 0x00, 0x00, 0xe0, 0x00, 0x1e, 0x00,
0x00, 0x00, 0x06, 0x00, 0x00, 0x00, 0x00, 0x06,
0x1c, 0x00, 0x38, 0xe0, 0x00, 0x00, 0x00, 0x00,
0x00, 0xe0, 0x00, 0x1e, 0x00, 0x00, 0x00, 0x06,
0x00, 0x00, 0x00, 0x00, 0x06, 0x18, 0x00, 0x38,
0xe0, 0x00, 0x00, 0x00, 0x00, 0x00, 0xe0, 0x00,
0x1e, 0x00, 0x00, 0x00, 0x06, 0x00, 0x00, 0x00,
0x00, 0x0e, 0x18, 0x00, 0x30, 0xe0, 0x00, 0x00,
0x00, 0x00, 0x00, 0xe0, 0x00, 0x1e, 0x00, 0x00,
0x00, 0x06, 0x00, 0x00, 0x00, 0x00, 0x0e, 0x38,
0x00, 0x30, 0xe0, 0x01, 0x00, 0x00, 0x00, 0x00,
0xf0, 0x01, 0x1f, 0x00, 0x00, 0x00, 0x06, 0x00,
0x00, 0x00, 0x00, 0x0c, 0x3c, 0x00, 0x30, 0xf0,
0x01, 0x00, 0x00, 0x00, 0x00, 0xf8, 0x03, 0x1f,
0x00, 0x00, 0x00, 0x06, 0x00, 0x00, 0x00, 0x00,
0x0c, 0x7e, 0x00, 0x70, 0xf8, 0x03, 0x00, 0x00,
0x00, 0x00, 0x3c, 0x0f, 0x1f, 0x00, 0x00, 0x00,
0x06, 0x00, 0x00, 0x00, 0x00, 0x0c, 0xe7, 0x00,
0x70, 0xbc, 0x03, 0x00, 0x00, 0x00, 0x00, 0x1e,
0x1e, 0x1f, 0x00, 0x00, 0x00, 0x06, 0x00, 0x00,
0x00, 0x00, 0xdc, 0xe3, 0x00, 0x60, 0x1e, 0x07,
0x00, 0x00, 0x00, 0x00, 0x0f, 0xfc, 0x1f, 0x00,
0x00, 0x00, 0x06, 0x00, 0x00, 0x00, 0x00, 0xfc,
0xc1, 0x01, 0xe0, 0x0f, 0x0f, 0x00, 0x00, 0x00,
0x80, 0x07, 0xf0, 0x1f, 0x00, 0x00, 0x00, 0x06,
0x00, 0x00, 0x00, 0x00, 0xf8, 0x80, 0x03, 0xe0,
0x03, 0x1e, 0x00, 0x00, 0x00, 0xc0, 0x03, 0xe0,
0x1b, 0x00, 0x00, 0x00, 0x06, 0x00, 0x00, 0x00,
0x00, 0x78, 0x80, 0x07, 0xe0, 0x01, 0x1c, 0x00,
0x00, 0x00, 0xe0, 0x01, 0xc0, 0x1b, 0x00, 0x00,
0x00, 0x06, 0x00, 0x00, 0x00, 0x00, 0x38, 0x00,
0x0f, 0xe0, 0x01, 0x38, 0x00, 0x00, 0x00, 0xf0,
0x00, 0xc0, 0x19, 0x00, 0x00, 0x00, 0x06, 0x00,
0x00, 0x00, 0x00, 0x30, 0x0e, 0x1e, 0xc0, 0x71,
0xf8, 0x00, 0x00, 0x00, 0x78, 0x00, 0xdc, 0x19,
0x00, 0x00, 0x00, 0x06, 0x00, 0x00, 0x00, 0x00,
0x30, 0x1f, 0x1e, 0xc0, 0xf9, 0xf8, 0x00, 0x00,
```

```
   0x00, 0xfc, 0xff, 0xff, 0xff, 0xff, 0xff,
   0x07, 0x00, 0x00, 0x00, 0x00, 0xf0, 0xff, 0xff,
   0xff, 0xff, 0xff, 0x07, 0x00, 0x00, 0xff, 0xff,
   0xff, 0xff, 0xff, 0xff, 0xff, 0x07, 0x00, 0x00,
   0x00, 0x00, 0xe0, 0xff, 0xff, 0xff, 0xff, 0xff,
   0x0f, 0x00, 0x00, 0x00, 0x00, 0x00, 0x00, 0x00,
   0x00, 0x00, 0x00, 0x00, 0x00, 0x00, 0x00, 0x00,
   0x00, 0x00, 0x00, 0x00, 0x00, 0x00, 0x00, 0x00,
   0x00, 0x00, 0x00, 0x00, 0x00, 0x00, 0x00, 0x00,
   0x00, 0x00, 0x00, 0x00, 0x00, 0x00, 0x00, 0x00,
   0x00, 0x00, 0x00, 0x00, 0x00 };

#define ex9_2_width 32
#define ex9_2_height 32
static char ex9_2_bits[] =
{
   0x00, 0xf8, 0x0f, 0x00, 0x00, 0xf8, 0x0f, 0x00,
   0x00, 0x18, 0x0c, 0x00, 0x00, 0x00, 0x0c, 0x00,
   0x00, 0x00, 0x0c, 0x00, 0x00, 0x00, 0x0c, 0x00,
   0x00, 0x00, 0x0c, 0x00, 0x00, 0x00, 0x0c, 0x00,
   0x00, 0xf8, 0x0f, 0x00, 0x00, 0xf8, 0x0f, 0x00,
   0x00, 0x18, 0x00, 0x00, 0x00, 0x18, 0x00, 0x00,
   0x00, 0x18, 0x00, 0x00, 0x00, 0x18, 0x00, 0x00,
   0x00, 0x18, 0x00, 0x00, 0x00, 0xf8, 0x0f, 0x00,
   0x00, 0xf8, 0x0f, 0x00, 0x00, 0x00, 0x00, 0x00,
   0x00, 0xc0, 0x01, 0x00, 0x00, 0xc0, 0x01, 0x00,
   0x00, 0x00, 0x00, 0x00, 0x00, 0x00, 0x00, 0x00,
   0xfe, 0x8c, 0x99, 0x7f, 0xfe, 0x8c, 0x99, 0x7f,
   0xc6, 0x8c, 0x19, 0x0c, 0xc6, 0x8c, 0x19, 0x0c,
   0xc6, 0x8c, 0x19, 0x0c, 0xc6, 0x8c, 0x19, 0x0c,
   0xfe, 0xfc, 0x19, 0x0c, 0xfe, 0xfd, 0x19, 0x0c,
   0x00, 0x01, 0x00, 0x0c, 0x00, 0x00, 0x00, 0x00
};

#define NUM_ICONS 2
#define BITMAPDEPTH 1
#define BORDER_WIDTH 2
#define FALSE 0
#define TRUE 1

Display      *thedisplay;
Window       thewindow;
```

```
int             thescreen;
Pixmap          pixmap[NUM_ICONS];
char            *w_name;
unsigned long   foreground;
unsigned long   background;
XSizeHints      thehints;
GC              thegc;

void init();
void load_strings_and_icons();
void set_hints();
void create_window_set_properties();
void cleanup();

main(argc, argv)
int argc;
char *argv[];
{
XEvent theevent;
int done = FALSE;
int result;

   init(argv);

   set_hints();

   create_window_set_properties(argc,argv);

   XMapRaised(thedisplay, thewindow);

   XSelectInput(thedisplay, thewindow,
               ButtonPressMask | ExposureMask);

   while (!done)
   {
     XNextEvent(thedisplay, &theevent);

     switch(theevent.type)
     {
       case Expose:
         if (theevent.xexpose.count == 0)
         {
```

```
                   load_strings_and_icons();
             }
         break;

         case ButtonPress:
           done = TRUE;
           cleanup();
           printf("\n Ready to exit ...\n");
         break;
       }
   }  /*  End while  */
} /*  End main  */

void init(argv)
char *argv[];
{

  w_name = argv[0];
  thedisplay = XOpenDisplay("");
  thescreen = DefaultScreen(thedisplay);

  background = WhitePixel(thedisplay, thescreen);
  foreground = BlackPixel(thedisplay, thescreen);
}

void load_strings_and_icons()
{
int index = 0;

  thegc = XCreateGC(thedisplay, thewindow, 0, 0);
  XSetForeground(thedisplay, thegc,
                 BlackPixel(thedisplay, thescreen));
  XSetBackground(thedisplay, thegc,
                 WhitePixel(thedisplay, thescreen));
  XClearWindow(thedisplay, thewindow);
  XDrawString(thedisplay, thewindow, thegc, 210, 50,
              "Point to created window.",
              strlen("Point to created window."));
  XDrawString(thedisplay, thewindow, thegc, 210, 80,
              "Press on mouse button to exit.",
```

```
                   strlen("Press on mouse button to exit."));
   XCopyPlane(thedisplay, pixmap[index], thewindow,
              thegc, 0, 0,
              mensetmanus_width,
              mensetmanus_height,
              0, 0, BITMAPDEPTH);
   index++;
   XCopyPlane(thedisplay, pixmap[index], thewindow,
              thegc, 0, 0,
              ex9_2_width,
              ex9_2_height,
              thehints.min_width/2-ex9_2_width/2,
              thehints.min_height-ex9_2_height,
              BITMAPDEPTH);
}


void create_window_set_properties(argc, argv)
int argc;
char *argv[];
{
int index = 0;

   thewindow = XCreateSimpleWindow(thedisplay,
                        DefaultRootWindow(thedisplay),
                        thehints.x,
                        thehints.y,
                        thehints.width,
                        thehints.height,
                        BORDER_WIDTH,
                        foreground, background);
   thegc = XCreateGC(thedisplay, thewindow, 0, 0);
   XSetSubwindowMode(thedisplay, thegc, IncludeInferiors);
   pixmap[index] = XCreateBitmapFromData(thedisplay,
                        RootWindow(thedisplay, thescreen),
                        mensetmanus_bits, mensetmanus_width,
                        mensetmanus_height);
   index++;
   pixmap[index] = XCreateBitmapFromData(thedisplay,
                        RootWindow(thedisplay, thescreen),
                        ex9_2_bits, ex9_2_width,
                        ex9_2_height);
   XSetStandardProperties(thedisplay, thewindow, w_name,
```

```
                 w_name, None, argv, argc, &thehints);
}

void set_hints()
{
int height;
int width;

  width = DisplayWidth(thedisplay, thescreen);
  height = DisplayHeight(thedisplay, thescreen);
  thehints.flags = PPosition | PSize | PMinSize;
  thehints.height = height/4;
  thehints.width = 430;
  thehints.x =  width/3;
  thehints.y =  height/3;
  thehints.min_height = 145;
  thehints.min_width = 430;
}

void cleanup()
{
int index;

  for(index = 0; index < NUM_ICONS; index++)
  {
    XFreePixmap(thedisplay, pixmap[index]);
  }
    printf("\n Free pixmap  - done\n");

    XFreeGC(thedisplay, thegc);
    printf("\n Free gc  - done\n");

    XDestroyWindow(thedisplay, thewindow);
    printf("\n Destroy window  - done\n");

    XCloseDisplay(thedisplay);
    printf("\n Disconnect from server - done\n");
}
```

Results of running this program are shown in Figure 9-2.

Two pixmaps and an icon

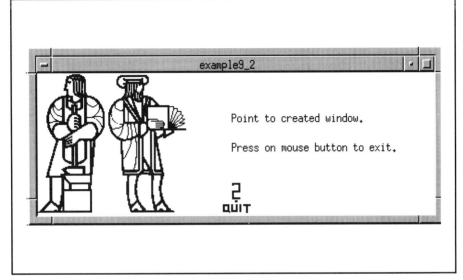

Key Points

Pixmaps

A pixmap is a block of memory associated with the X server that may be used for drawing. Pixmaps are one of the six fundamental categories of server resources.

Pixmaps are closely related to windows. These two drawables share similarities such as having a fixed, positive height and width and employing the same coordinate system (x and y). They both generate images that can contain several bits per pixel and are clipped to the drawable's boundaries.

Pixmaps also are considerably different from windows. Unlike windows, pixmaps do not have background attributes, borders, visual types, or colormap attributes. Pixmaps are not mapped and do not form a hierarchy. Pixmaps are never obscured. Pixmaps appear on the screen only when they are copied to a viewable window.

continues . . .

Pixmap Functions

The **XCreatePixmap** function creates a pixmap. The **XGetGeometry** function is a round-trip request that determines the basic geometrical values for pixmaps and windows. The **XFreePixmap** function releases the storage area associated with a given pixmap.

Bitmaps

A bitmap resource is a pixmap of depth 1. A bitmap file is a text file that can be loaded into a bitmap resource. Bitmap files are read by the **XReadBitmapFile** function. They are written by the **XWriteBitmapFile** function or by the *bitmap* utility program supplied with X Window.

Xlib provides several functions that process bitmap data. The **XCreateBitmapFromData** function applies a bitmap file previously written by the **XWriteBitmapFile** function. The **XCreatePixmap-FromBitmapData** function creates a pixmap and then stores bitmap data in it.

Images

Images are data structures that represent visual data in memory and provide basic operations on this data. These operations include image creation, image destruction, pixel retrieval, pixel setting, sub-image extraction, and addition of a constant to the image. Correct use of the image data structure and image operations simplifies drawing pictures for a wide range of workstations and reduces the volume of data transmitted between the server and the workstation.

continues . . .

Key Points
(continued)

The XCreateImage function allocates memory for an XImage structure for the specified display. The **XSubImage** function creates a rectangular subimage by copying part of an existing image. The **XPutPixel** function sets a pixel value in a specified image. The **XGetPixel** function returns the pixel value from the specified image. The **XAddPixel** function adds a constant value to every pixel in the specified image. The **XPutImage** function draws a memory-resident image into a window or a pixmap. The **XGetImage** and **XGet-SubImage** functions retrieve rectangular pixel arrays from the workstation. The **XDestroyImage** function releases the memory allocated to an image.

Color and Graphics

*T*he previous chapter described how to create and modify groups of pixels by applying three fundamental X Window structures: pixmaps, a server resource that draws off-screen pictures; bitmaps, pixmaps with a depth of 1; and images, data structures that represent visual data in memory and allow basic operations on this data. The chapter concluded by presenting two programs that applied pixmaps and bitmaps.

This chapter discusses at length two features that render applications more informative and easier to use: color and graphics. The world you live in is not black and white, and neither is X Window. This chapter examines how to apply shared color resources and, when necessary, how to develop custom color programs.

An old saying states, "One picture is worth a thousand words." This chapter explores in depth the graphics functions that enable you to draw thousands of pictures. The chapter concludes with a series of programs that illustrate fundamental concepts and functions and review major aspects of Chapter 9, "Pixmaps, Bitmaps, and Images."

Color

Color is more than a luxury for many applications. The appropriate use of color can convey meaning to the user, smoothing the user interface. X Window systems run on a variety of color and monochrome terminals. Special care is required to ensure that applications are portable among nonidentical workstations.

Describing Color Images

Whatever workstation you use, X Window color images have the following characteristics: They are composed of red, green, and blue primary colors. They are displayed in color planes whose depth varies. They belong to one of several visual classes that differ in how they apply colormaps. Each of these features is described in greater detail in the following sections.

RGB: Red, Green, and Blue

Color workstations display all colors as a combination of three primary colors: red, green, and blue. The relative intensity of these colors is expressed in the XColor data structure, shown here:

```
typedef struct {
  unsigned long pixel;                 /* Pixel value */
  unsigned short red, green, blue; /* RGB values */
  char flags;                          /* DoRed, DoGreen,
                                            DoBlue */
  char pad;
} XColor;
```

The red, green, and blue values range from 0 to 65535, no matter what display hardware is used. Black is represented by (0, 0, 0), and white is represented by (65535, 65535, 65535). The *flags* element indicates which of these three primary colors are present. Various color processing functions read or set these flags.

Planes and Pixel Values

Every pixel on a given workstation display has a defined depth—usually 1 for monochrome workstations. The display depth for many color workstations is 8. In this case, the pixmap or window display memory is composed of eight bit planes that may be processed independently. Changing values in one or more bit planes changes the color of any image displayed. Various color and graphics processing functions read or set selected pixels and bit planes. The graphics context contains several components associated with color and graphics processing.

Visual Classes

The X Window system defines six *visual classes*, models for converting pixel values into displayed colors. The header file <X11/X.h> contains symbols representing these visual classes: PseudoColor, DirectColor, GrayScale, StaticColor, TrueColor, and StaticGray. These six visual classes are presented in Table 10-1.

TABLE
10-1

Visual Classes

Visual Class	Signification
PseudoColor	Each pixel value indexes an RGB colormap, which can be changed dynamically. Each pixel indexes a single colormap array.
DirectColor	The pixel value contains distinct bit fields for red, green, and blue. The colormap is three separate arrays for these three primary colors.
GrayScale	Resembles PseudoColor, but displays a single color with shades. Some monochrome monitors have a GrayScale visual type with a depth of 1.
StaticColor	Similar to PseudoColor, except that the StaticColor colormap is predefined and cannot be modified.
TrueColor	Similar to DirectColor, except that the TrueColor colormap is predefined as linear and cannot be modified.
StaticGray	Similar to GrayScale, except that the StaticGray colormap cannot be modified. Most monochrome monitors have a visual class of StaticGray and a depth of 1.

Color Maps

Colormaps, also called *color lookup tables,* translate pixel values into onscreen colors. As shown in Table 10-1, the relationship between the colormap and the associated pixel values depends on the visual class.

A colormap is an array of individual *color cells,* declared with the XColor data structure. Each color cell comprises a combination of red, green, and blue values, designating a single color. Individual color cells change rapidly, whereas colormaps usually do not. Colormaps are one of the six fundamental X server resources that can be shared among applications running on the same workstation.

Applications must decide whether to use a standard or a custom colormap when creating a window. Of course it is simpler to leave color map details to the system. The **XCreateSimpleWindow** function assigns the parent window's color map to the newly created child window. If you create all your windows with this function, they will all apply the default root window color map. If you create windows with the **XCreateWindow** function, you can apply shared color maps by applying functions such as **XAllocColor** that allocate shared color cells. This strategy has the advantage of simplifying bookkeeping, increasing the likelihood that a given application will run on different workstation models and conserve color resources. On the other hand, once allocated, these color cells cannot be changed.

Private color cells can be modified dynamically and can be allocated in groups whose members are mathematically interrelated. For example, it is possible to allocate a series of color cells whose pixel values differ by a single bit (PseudoColor) or by three bits (DirectColor). The applications programmer does not always have the luxury of selecting the color strategy to apply; many workstations are limited to shared color maps.

Color Information Functions

Before you can decide how to manage colors on your workstation, it may be necessary to determine the workstation's specific color capabilities. Xlib provides several such functions. **XDefaultVisual** returns the default visual type for the designated screen. **XDefaultColormap** returns the default color map ID associated with the designated screen. **XDisplayCells** returns the number of entries in the default color map. **XDisplayPlanes** returns the root window depth for the designated screen. **XDefaultDepth** returns the depth of the default window for the designated screen. **XWhitePixel** returns the white-pixel value for the designated screen. **XBlackPixel** returns the black-pixel value for the designated screen. **XMatchVisualInfo** returns the visual information for a visual that matches the designated depth and class for a specified screen.

The **XDefaultVisual** function, shown here, returns the default visual type for the designated screen.

```
Visual *XDefaultVisual(display, screen_number)
   Display *display;            /* Specifies connection
                                   to server */
   int screen_number;          /* Appropriate screen number
                                   on host server */
```

The **XDefaultColormap** function, shown next, returns the default colormap ID associated with the designated screen.

```
Colormap XDefaultColormap(display, screen_number)
   Display *display;            /* Specifies connection
                                   to server */
   int screen_number;          /* Appropriate screen number
                                   on host server */
```

The **XDisplayCells** function, shown next, returns the number of entries in the default colormap.

```
int XDisplayCells(display, screen_number)
   Display *display;            /* Specifies connection
                                   to server */
   int screen_number;          /* Appropriate screen number
                                   on host server */
```

The **XDisplayPlanes** function, shown next, returns the root window depth for the designated screen.

```
int XDisplayPlanes(display, screen_number)
   Display *display;            /* Specifies connection
                                   to server */
   int screen_number;          /* Appropriate screen number
                                   on host server */
```

The **XDefaultDepth** function, shown next, returns the depth of the default window for the designated screen.

```
int XDefaultDepth(display, screen_number)
   Display *display;            /* Specifies connection
                                   to server */
```

```
   int screen_number;        /* Appropriate screen number
                                on host server */
```

The **XWhitePixel** function, shown next, returns the white-pixel value for the designated screen.

```
unsigned long XWhitePixel(display, screen_number)
   Display *display;         /* Specifies connection
                                to server */
   int screen_number;        /* Appropriate screen number
                                on host server */
```

Chapter 2, "Hello World," applied the similar **WhitePixel** macro.

The **XBlackPixel** function, shown next, returns the black-pixel value for the designated screen.

```
unsigned long XBlackPixel(display, screen_number)
   Display *display;         /* Specifies connection
                                to server */
   int screen_number;        /* Appropriate screen number
                                on host server */
```

Chapter 2, "Hello World," applied the similar **BlackPixel** macro.

The **XMatchVisualInfo** function, shown next, returns the visual information for a visual that matches the designated depth and class for a specified screen.

```
Status XMatchVisualInfo(display, screen, depth,
                  class, vinfo_return)
   Display *display;         /* Specifies connection
                                to server */
   int screen;               /* Screen */
   int depth;                /* Screen depth */
   int class;                /* Screen class */
   XVisualInfo *vinfo_return; /* Returns matched
                                visual information */
```

There may be several visuals that match the designated depth and class.

Allocating Shared Color Cells

Xlib provides functions that allocate shared color cells based on pixel values or standard color names. The system returns with the color that best corresponds to the requested color. **XAllocColor** allocates a read-only color cell corresponding to the closest available RGB value for the given hardware. **XAllocNamedColor** allocates a read-only color cell using a color name and returns the closest available color for the given hardware.

The **XAllocColor** function, shown here, allocates a read-only color cell corresponding to the closest available RGB value for the given hardware.

```
Status XAllocColor(display, colormap, screen_in_out)
   Display *display;            /* Specifies connection
                                   to server */
   Colormap colormap;           /* Colormap */
   XColor *screen_in_out;       /* Returns values actually
                                   used in colormap */
```

XAllocColor does not use the flags in the XColor data structure. **XAllocColor** can generate a BadColor error.

The **XAllocNamedColor** function, shown next, allocates a read-only color cell using a color name and returns the closest available color for the given hardware.

```
Status XAllocNamedColor(display, colormap, color_name,
                     screen_def_return, exact_def_return)
   Display *display;            /* Specifies connection
                                   to server */
   Colormap colormap;           /* Colormap */
   char *color_name;            /* Color name string for which
                                   color definition structure
                                   to be returned */
   XColor *screen_def_return;   /* Returns closest RGB values
                                   actually generated
                                   by hardware used */
   XColor *exact_def_return;    /* Returns exact RGB values */
```

The color name is not case sensitive.

XAllocNamedColor can generate a BadColor error.

Allocating Private Color Cells and Color Planes

Xlib provides functions that allocate private color cells and color planes. The function used depends on the visual class. **XAllocColorCells** allocates read/write color cells and color plane combinations for the PseudoColor visual class. **XAllocColorPlanes** allocates read/write color planes and bit masks for the DirectColor visual class.

The **XAllocColorCells** function, shown here, allocates read/write color cells and color plane combinations for the PseudoColor visual class.

```
Status XAllocColorCells(display, colormap, contig,
                    plane_masks_return, nplanes,
                    pixels_return, npixels)
    Display *display;           /* Specifies connection
                                   to server */
    Colormap colormap;          /* Colormap */
    Bool contig;                /* If TRUE, planes must
                                   be contiguous */
    unsigned long plane_masks_return[];
                                /* Returns plane masks array */
    unsigned int nplanes;       /* Number of plane masks
                                   in array */
    unsigned long pixels_return[];
                                /* Returns array of pixel */
    unsigned int npixels;       /* Number of pixel values
                                   in array */
```

When the GrayScale or PseudoColor visual class is used, each mask in the plane masks array has a single bit set to 1. When the DirectColor visual class is used, each mask in the plane masks array has three bits set to 1. **XAllocColorCells** can generate BadColor and BadValue errors.

The **XAllocColorPlanes** function, shown next, allocates read/write color plane and bit masks for the DirectColor visual class.

```
Status XAllocColorPlanes(display, colormap, contig,
            pixels_return, ncolors, nreds, ngreens, nblues,
            rmask_return, gmask_return, bmask_return)
    Display *display;           /* Specifies connection
                                   to server */
```

```
Colormap colormap;          /* Colormap */
Bool contig;                /* If TRUE, planes must
                               be contiguous */
unsigned long pixels_return[];
                            /* Returns array of pixel */
unsigned int ncolors;       /* Number of pixel values
                               in array */
int nreds, ngreens, nblues; /* Number of red, green,
                               and blue planes */
unsigned long rmask_return, gmask_return, bmask_return;
                            /* Returns bit masks for red,
                               green, and blue planes */
```

XAllocColorPlanes can generate BadColor and BadValue errors.

Storing, Querying, and Freeing Color Cells

When you decide to use one or more colors that are not provided by any available colormap, you have a choice of Xlib functions to store these colors in your private color cells. Before storing these colors, you may choose to query which colors you have already stored. It is a good idea to free any color cells that you no longer need. **XStoreColor** stores an RGB value in a single colormap cell. **XStoreColors** stores one or more RGB values in corresponding colormap cells. **XStoreNamedColor** stores a named color in a single colormap cell. **XQueryColor** returns the RGB value of a single colormap cell. **XQueryColors** returns the RGB value of multiple colormap cells. **XFreeColors** releases specified color cells.

The **XStoreColor** function, shown here, stores an RGB value in a single color-map cell.

```
XStoreColor(display, colormap, color)
   Display *display;        /* Specifies connection
                               to server */
   Colormap colormap;       /* Colormap */
   XColor *color;           /* Pixel and RGB values */
```

The pixel value to be stored must be a read/write cell that is a valid index to the colormap.

The color components to be changed are indicated by the DoRed, DoGreen, and DoBlue flags in the XColor data structure. Color changes take place immediately when the colormap is installed. **XStoreColor** can generate BadAccess, BadColor, and BadValue errors.

The **XStoreColors** function, shown next, stores one or more RGB values in corresponding colormap cells.

```
XStoreColors(display, colormap, color, ncolors)
  Display *display;          /* Specifies connection
                               to server */
  Colormap colormap;         /* Colormap */
  XColor color[];            /* Array of color definition
                               structures to store */
  int ncolors;               /* Number of XColor structures
                               in array */
```

The pixel values to be stored must be read/write cells that are valid indexes to the colormap.

The color components to be changed are indicated by the DoRed, DoGreen, and DoBlue flags in the XColor data structure. Color changes take place immediately when the colormap is installed. **XStoreColors** can generate BadAccess, BadColor, and BadValue errors.

The **XStoreNamedColor** function, shown next, stores a named color in a single colormap cell.

```
XStoreNamedColor(display, colormap, color, pixel, flags)
  Display *display;          /* Specifies connection
                               to server */
  Colormap colormap;         /* Colormap */
  char *color;               /* Color name string */
  unsigned long pixel;       /* Colormap entry */
  int flags;                 /* Red, green, and blue
                               components set */
```

The color components to be changed are indicated by the DoRed, DoGreen, and DoBlue flags in the XColor data structure. The color name is not case sensitive. **XStoreNamedColor** can generate BadAccess, BadColor, BadName, and BadValue errors.

The **XQueryColor** function, shown next, returns the RGB value of a single colormap cell.

```
XQueryColor(display, colormap, def_in_out)
  Display *display;          /* Specifies connection
                                to server */
  Colormap colormap;         /* Colormap */
  XColor *def_in_out;        /* Specifies and returns RGB
                                values for designated pixel */
```

XQueryColor sets the DoRed, DoGreen, and DoBlue flags in the XColor data structure. It can generate BadColor and BadValue errors.

The **XQueryColors** function, shown next, returns the RGB value of multiple colormap cells.

```
XQueryColors(display, colormap, def_in_out, ncolors)
  Display *display;          /* Specifies connection
                                to server */
  Colormap colormap;         /* Colormap */
  XColor defs_in_out[];      /* Specifies and returns array
                                of color definition structures
                                for designated pixel */
  int ncolors;               /* Number of XColor structures
                                in color definition array */
```

XQueryColors sets the DoRed, DoGreen, and DoBlue flags in each affected XColor data structure. It can generate BadColor and BadValue errors.

The **XFreeColors** function, shown next, releases those color cells whose pixels are in the *pixels* array.

```
XFreeColors(display, colormap, pixels, npixels, planes)
  Display *display;          /* Specifies connection
                                to server */
  Colormap colormap;         /* Colormap */
  unsigned long pixels[];    /* Array of pixel values mapping
                                to cells in the colormap */
  int npixels;               /* Number of pixels in array */
  unsigned long planes;      /* Planes to be freed */
```

The *planes* argument should not have any bits set to 1 in common with any pixels to be released.

A freed pixel may not be reused until all related pixels are released by all affected clients. **XFreeColors** can generate BadAccess, BadColor, and BadValue errors.

Colormap Processing Functions

The following Xlib functions are useful if you wish to create and apply private colormaps. Many of these functions generate events that should be solicited and tested. **XCreateColormap** creates a colormap for the screen associated with the designated window. **XSetWindowColormap** makes a specified colormap the current colormap for the designated window. **XCopyColormapAndFree** creates a new colormap and frees an existing colormap. **XInstallColormap** installs a colormap for the designated screen. **XUninstallColormap** removes the colormap from the list of colormaps for the designated screen. **XListInstalledColormaps** returns a list of the currently installed colormaps for the screen containing the designated window. **XFreeColormap** frees a colormap, except for the screen's default colormap. **XGetStandardColormap** gets the XStandardColormap data structure associated with the designated atom.

The **XCreateColormap** function, shown here, creates a colormap for the screen associated with the designated window.

```
XCreateColormap(display, w, visual, alloc)
  Display *display;          /* Specifies connection
                                to server */
  Window w;                  /* Window associated with
                                screen for colormap */
  Visual *visual;            /* Visual type supported
                                on screen */
  int alloc;                 /* Colormap entries
                                to be allocated
                                AllocNone or AllocAll */
```

The initial values of the colormap entries are undefined for the DirectColor, GrayScale, and PseudoColor visual classes. The *visual* parameter defines the initial values of the colormap entries for the StaticColor, StaticGray, and TrueColor visual classes.

XCreateColormap can generate BadAlloc, BadMatch, BadValue, and BadWindow errors.

The **XSetWindowColormap** function, shown next, makes a specified colormap the current colormap for the designated window.

```
XSetWindowColormap(display, w, colormap)
    Display *display;          /* Specifies connection
                                  to server */
    Window w;                  /* Window associated with
                                  screen for colormap */
    Colormap colormap;         /* Colormap */
```

XSetWindowColormap generates a ColormapNotify event. It can generate a BadWindow error.

The **XCopyColormapAndFree** function, shown next, creates a new colormap. It is used when a previously shared colormap cannot be allocated.

```
XCopyColormapAndFree(display, colormap)
    Display *display;          /* Specifies connection
                                  to server */
    Colormap colormap;         /* Colormap */
```

XCopyColormapAndFree copies the client's designated colormap to the new colormap, respecting existing color values and read/write or read-only characteristics. It then frees those entries from the original colormap. If the *alloc* parameter of the **XCreateColormap** function creating the original colormap was set to AllocAll, all color values in the original colormap are copied and then freed. If the *alloc* parameter has been set to AllocNone, only pixels and planes allocated by the **XAllocColor**, **XAllocNamedColor**, **XAllocColorCells**, and **XAllocColorPlanes** are copied and then freed. **XCopyColormapAndFree** can generate BadAlloc and BadColor errors.

The **XInstallColormap** function, shown next, installs a colormap for the designated screen.

```
XInstallColormap(display, colormap)
  Display *display;            /* Specifies connection
                                  to server */
  Colormap colormap;           /* Colormap */
```

Windows associated with the installed colormap (by the **XCreateWindow**, **XCreateSimpleWindow**, **XChangeWindowAttributes**, and **XSetWindowColormap** functions) display true colors when the color map is installed. The server generates a ColormapNotify event for windows associated with the designated colormap, if the colormap was not already installed. **XInstallColormap** can generate a BadColor error.

The **XUninstallColormap** function, shown next, removes the color map from the list of colormaps for the designated screen.

```
XUninstallColormap(display, colormap)
  Display *display;            /* Specifies connection
                                  to server */
  Colormap colormap;           /* Colormap */
```

The server generates a ColormapNotify event for windows associated with the designated colormap. **XUninstallColormap** can generate a BadColor error.

The **XListInstalledColormaps** function, shown next, returns a list of the currently installed colormaps for the screen containing the designated window.

```
Colormap *XListInstallColormaps(display, w, num_return)
  Display *display;            /* Specifies connection
                                  to server */
  Window w;                    /* Window associated with
                                  screen for colormap */
  int num_return;              /* Returns number of
                                  installed colormaps */
```

The **XFree** function releases this list. **XListInstalledColormaps** can generate a BadWindow error.

The **XFreeColormap** function, shown next, frees a colormap, except for the screen's default colormap.

```
XFreeColormap(display, colormap)
  Display *display;          /* Specifies connection
                                to server */
  Colormap colormap;         /* Colormap */
```

The **XFreeColormap** function erases the link between the colormap resource ID and the colormap, freeing the colormap storage and uninstalling it, if it was installed. If the designated colormap is associated with a window by the **XCreateWindow**, **XSetWindowColormap**, or **XChangeWindowAttributes** function, **XFreeColormap** changes the colormap to None and generates a ColormapNotify event. **XFreeColormap** can generate a BadColor error.

The **XGetStandardColormap** function, shown next, gets the XStandardColormap data structure associated with the designated atom.

```
Status XGetStandardColormap(display, w,
                            colormap_return, property)
  Display *display;          /* Specifies connection
                                to server */
  Window w;                  /* Window */
  XStandardColormap *colormap_return:
                             /* Returns colormap associated
                                with designated atom */
  Atom property;             /* Property name */
```

XGetStandardColormap can generate BadAtom and BadWindow errors.

Looking Up Color Names

Xlib provides two similar functions for looking up color names. **XParseColor** looks up the string name of a color for the screen associated with the designated colormap and returns exact color values. **XLookupColor** returns the exact color values and the closest available RGB values.

The **XParseColor** function, shown here, maps a color name to its exact RGB value.

```
XParseColor(display, colormap, spec, exact def return)
   Display *display;           /* Specifies connection
                                  to server */
   Colormap colormap;          /* Colormap */
   char spec;                  /* Color name string */
   XColor exact_def_return;    /* Returns exact color value
                                  Sets DoRed, DoGreen,
                                  DoBlue flags */
```

XParseColor can generate a BadColor value.

The **XLookupColor** function, shown next, maps a color name to an RGB value.

```
Status XLookupColor(display, colormap, color_name,
                  exact_def_return, screen_def_return)
   Display *display;           /* Specifies connection
                                  to server */
   Colormap colormap;          /* Colormap */
   char *color_name;           /* Color name string for which
                                  color definition structure
                                  to be returned */
   XColor *exact_def_return;   /* Returns exact RGB values */
   XColor *screen_def_return;  /* Returns closest RGB values
                                  actually generated
                                  by hardware used */
```

XLookupColor can generate a BadColor value.

Graphics

X Window provides extensive graphics processing. The programmer has the choice of applying a wide range of Xlib functions or Xt Intrinsics and OSF/Motif widgets. These functions process information stored in the graphics context.

Graphics Context

The graphics context is one of the fundamental server resources. It contains extensive information describing graphics output. Color, graphics, and text functions reference the graphics context, whose elements are shown here.

```
/* GC attribute value mask bits */
#define GCFunction            (1L<<0)
#define GCPlaneMask           (1L<<1)
#define GCForeground          (1L<<2)
#define GCBackground          (1L<<3)
#define GCLineWidth           (1L<<4)
#define GCLineStyle           (1L<<5)
#define GCCapStyle            (1L<<6)
#define GCJoinStyle           (1L<<7)
#define GCFillStyle           (1L<<8)
#define GCFillRule            (1L<<9)
#define GCTile                (1L<<10)
#define GCStipple             (1L<<11)
#define GCTileStipXOrigin     (1L<<12)
#define GCTileStipYOrigin     (1L<<13)
#define GCFont                (1L<<14)
#define GCSubwindowMode       (1L<<15)
#define GCGraphicsExposures   (1L<<16)
#define GCClipXOrigin         (1L<<17)
#define GCClipYOrigin         (1L<<18)
#define GCClipMask            (1L<<19)
#define GCDashOffset          (1L<<20)
#define GCDashList            (1L<<21)
#define GCArcMode             (1L<<22)
/* Values */
typedef struct {
  int function;                /* Logical operation */
  unsigned long plane_mask;    /* Plane mask */
  unsigned long foreground;    /* Foreground pixel */
  unsigned long background;    /* Background pixel */
  int line_width;              /* Line width in pixels */
  int line_style;              /* LineSolid, LineOnOffDash,
                                  LineDoubleDash */
```

```
    int cap_style;              /* CapNotLast, CapButt,
                                   CapRound, CapProjecting */
    int join_style;             /* JoinMiter, JoinRound,
                                   JoinBevel */
    int fill_style;             /* FillSolid, FillTiled,
                                   FillStippled,
                                   FillOpaqueStippled */
    int fill_rule;              /* EvenOddRule, WindingRule */
    int arc_mode;               /* ArcChord, ArcPieSlice */
    Pixmap tile;                /* Pixmap for tiling */
    Pixmap stipple;             /* Pixmap for stippling */
    int ts_x_origin;            /* Offset for tiling
    int ts_y_origin;               or stippling */
    Font font;                  /* Default text font */
    int subwindow_mode;         /* ClipByChildren,
                                   Include Inferiors */

    Bool graphics_exposures;    /* Generate graphics
                                   exposures or not */
    int clip_x_origin;          /* Origin for clipping */
    int clip_y_origin;
    Pixmap clip_mask;           /* Bitmap clipping */
    int dash_offset;            /* Information for patterned
                                   and dashed lines */

    char dashes;
} XGCValues;
```

Table 10-2 lists the default values for graphics context elements.

Stipples are pixmaps of depth 1 (bitmaps) that serve as a fill pattern. *Tiles* are pixmaps whose depth is equal to the drawable associated with the graphics context. Tiles serve as a fill pattern. The *plane_mask* attribute in the graphics context specifies which bit planes are modified by a given graphics operation. A value of 0 means that the given bit plane may not be altered. The *graphics_exposure* component is a Boolean function indicating whether Exposure events should be generated. The *clip_x_origin* and *clip_y_origin* components indicate the x- and y-origins of the *clip_mask*, a bit mask for clipping graphics output. The *ts_x_origin* and *ts_y_origin* components indicate the x- and y-offset for tiling or stippling.

The following text describes components in the graphics context.

TABLE 10-2   Default Values of the Graphics Context

Element	Default Value
function	GXCopy
plane_mask	All 1s
foreground	0
background	1
line_width	0
line_style	LineSolid
cap_style	CapButt
join_style	JoinMiter
fill_style	FillSolid
fill_rule	EvenOddRule
arc_mode	ArcPieSlice
tile	Defaults to a pixmap whose size is unspecified, filled with the *foreground* pixel; unaffected by later changes to the *foreground* pixel
stipple	Pixmaps of unspecified size filled with 1s
ts_x_origin	0
ts_y_origin	0
font	Depends on implementation
subwindow_mode	ClipByChildren
graphics_exposures	True
clip_x_origin	0
clip_y_origin	0
clip_mask	None
dash_offset	0
dashes	thelist[4,4]

Line_Style Element

The *line_style* element indicates the sections of a line to be drawn:

LineSolid	Draw the line's full path.
LineDoubleDash	Draw the line's full path, but fill even and odd dashes differently (see element *fill_style*). Use CapButt style for junction of odd and even dashes.
LineOnOffDash	Draw only even dashes. Apply *cap_style* element to internal ends of individual dashes. (Treat CapNotDash as CapButt.)

Cap_Style Element

The *cap_style* element indicates how to draw a path's endpoints:

CapNotLast	Equivalent to CapButt, except do not draw final endpoint if line width is 0.
CapButt	Line is square at the endpoint (perpendicular to line slope) and does not project.
CapRound	Line has circular arc whose diameter equals line width. Arc is centered on the endpoint.
CapProjecting	Line is square at end, but path continues beyond endpoint for a distance of half the line width.

Note CapRound and CapProjecting are equivalent to CapButt for a line width of 0.

If a line has coincident endpoints, the *cap_style* element is applied to the two endpoints in the function of the *line_width* element according to the following table.

CapNotLast	thin	Results are device dependent. Ideally, nothing should be drawn.
CapButt	thin	Results are device dependent. Ideally, a single pixel should be drawn.
CapRound	thin	Same as CapButt/thin.
CapProjecting	thin	Same as CapButt/thin.

CapButt	wide	Nothing is drawn.
CapRound	wide	Draws a circle whose center is the endpoint and whose diameter is the line width.
CapProjecting	wide	Draws a square aligned with coordinate axes whose center is the endpoint and whose sides equal the line width.

Join_Style Element

The *join_style* element defines how to draw the corners for wide lines:

JoinMiter	The outer edges of the two lines extend to meet at an angle. If the angle is less than 11 degrees, the JoinBevel is used.
JoinRound	The corner is a circular arc whose diameter equals the line width. The arc is centered on the point of junction.
JoinBevel	The corner has CapButt endpoint styles with the triangular notch filled.

Fill_Style Element

The *fill_style* element defines the source contents for line, text, and fill requests:

FillSolid	Foreground.
FillTiled	Tile.
FillOpaqueStippled	Tile whose width and height equal the stipple, background stipple of 0 and foreground stipple of 1.
FillStippled	Stipple masks the foreground.

Graphics Context Processing Functions

Xlib provides several functions that directly process the graphics context. **XCreateGC** creates a graphics context. **XChangeGC** modifies the components of the designated graphics context, **XCopyGC** copies designated components from the source graphics context to the destination graphics context. **XGetGCValues** returns selected components of the designated graphics context. **XFreeGC** frees the designated graphics context.

The **XCreateGC** function, shown here, creates a graphics context and returns a graphics context ID.

```
GC XCreateGC(display, d, valuemask, values)
   Display *display;          /* Specifies connection
                                 to server */
   Drawable d;                /* Window or pixmap */
   unsigned long valuemask;   /* GC components to be set */
   XGCValues *values;         /* Values specified
                                 by valuemask */
```

The graphics context so created can be used with any drawable that has the same root and depth as the designated drawable. **XCreateGC** can generate BadAlloc, BadDrawable, BadFont, BadMatch, BadPixmap, and BadValue errors.

The **XChangeGC** function, shown next, modifies the components of the designated graphics context.

```
XChangeGC(display, d, valuemask, values)
   Display *display;          /* Specifies connection
                                 to server */
   Drawable d;                /* Window or pixmap */
   unsigned long valuemask;   /* GC components to be changed */
   XGCValues *values;         /* Values specified
                                 by valuemask */
```

The *valuemask* argument is the bitwise inclusive OR of the GC component mask bits to be changed.

Selected components of the graphics context to be modified, even though an error is detected. **XChangeGC** can generate BadAlloc, BadFont, BadGC, BadMatch, BadPixmap, and BadValue errors.

The **XCopyGC** function, shown next, copies designated components from the source graphics context to the destination graphics context.

```
XCopyGC(display, src, dest, valuemask)
  Display *display;            /* Specifies connection
                                  to server */
  GC src, dest;                /* Source and destination
                                  graphics contexts */
  unsigned long valuemask;     /* GC components to be copied */
```

The source graphics context and the destination graphics context must have the same root and depth.

XCopyGC can generate BadAlloc, BadGC, and BadMatch errors.

The **XGetGCValues** function, shown next, returns selected components of the designated graphics context.

```
Status XGetGCValues(display, gc, valuemask, values_return)
  Display *display;            /* Specifies connection
                                  to server */
  GC gc;                       /* Graphics context */
  unsigned long valuemask;     /* GC components to be changed */
  XGCValues *values_return;    /* Returns values specified
                                  by valuemask */
```

The **XGetGCValues** function does not return the clip mask or the dash list. An invalid resource ID is returned for GCFont, GCTile, and GCStipple if the client did not specifically set these components.

The **XFreeGC** function, shown next, frees the designated graphics context.

```
XFreeGC(display, gc)
  Display *display;            /* Specifies connection
                                  to server */
  GC gc;                       /* Graphics context */
```

XFreeGC can generate a BadGC error.

Setting Basic GC Components

Prior to drawing the actual graphics, it may be necessary to set individual graphics context components. Several functions are available.

XSetForeground sets the graphics context foreground. **XSetBackground** sets the graphics context background. **XSetFunction** sets the graphics context display function. **XSetPlaneMask** sets the graphics context plane mask. **XSetState** sets the foreground, background, plane mask, and function components of a given graphics context. **XSetLineAttributes** sets the graphics context line-drawing components. **XSetDashes** sets graphics context parameters defining dashed line styles.

The **XSetForeground** function, shown here, sets the foreground of a given graphics context.

```
XSetForeground(display, gc, foreground)
    Display *display;            /* Specifies connection
                                    to server */
    GC gc;                       /* Graphics context */
    unsigned long foreground;    /* Foreground to set for
                                    specified graphics context */
```

XSetForeground can generate BadAlloc and BadGC errors.

The **XSetBackground** function, shown next, sets the background of a given graphics context.

```
XSetBackground(display, gc, background)
    Display *display;            /* Specifies connection
                                    to server */
    GC gc;                       /* Graphics context */
    unsigned long background;    /* Background to set for
                                    specified graphics context */
```

XSetBackground can generate BadAlloc and BadGC errors.

The **XSetFunction** function, shown next, sets the display function of a given graphics context, as shown in Table 10-3.

```
XSetFunction(display, gc, function)
    Display *display;            /* Specifies connection
                                    to server */
    GC gc;                       /* Graphics context */
    int function;                /* Function to set for
                                    specified graphics context */
```

Boolean Functions Processed by **XSetFunction**

		Source	0	0	1	1
		Destination	0	1	0	1
Boolean Function	**Xlib Option**					
Zero	GXclear		0	0	0	0
Source & Dest	GXand		0	0	0	1
Source & ~Dest	GXandReverse		0	0	1	0
Source	GXcopy		0	0	1	1
~Source & Dest	GXandInverted		0	1	0	0
Dest	GXnoop		0	1	0	1
Source xor Dest	GXxor		0	1	1	0
Source or Dest	GXor		0	1	1	1
~Source & ~Dest	GXnor		1	0	0	0
~Source xor Dest	GXequiv		1	0	0	1
~Dest	GXinvert		1	0	1	0
Source or ~Dest	GXorReverse		1	0	1	1
~Source	GXcopyInverted		1	1	0	0
~Source or Dest	GXorInverted		1	1	0	1
~Source or ~Dest	GXnand		1	1	1	0
One	GXset		1	1	1	1

The source bits are generated by the graphics function. The first two lines of the table present the four possible combinations of the source and destination bits. To use the table, find the desired Boolean function or Xlib option and determine the output bit according to the source and destination bits: for example, the bits displayed prior to execution of the graphics function. Let's examine some of these options. The *GXcopy* option of **XSetFunction** copies the source bits to the output image. It generates bit 1 only when the associated source bit is 1, independent of the destination bit. Another commonly used option is *GXxor*, which generates bit 1 when the source and destination bits are both 0 or both 1 and generates bit 0 otherwise. Drawing twice with this option restores the initial pixel values. This quality of the *GXxor* option makes it useful to draw *rubber-band lines*, indicating the motion of the pointer on the screen.

XSetFunction can generate BadAlloc, BadGC, and BadValue errors.

The **XSetPlaneMask** function, shown next, sets the plane mask of a given graphics context.

```
XSetPlaneMask(display, gc, plane_mask)
  Display *display;          /* Specifies connection
                                to server */
  GC gc;                     /* Graphics context */
  unsigned long plane_mask;  /* Plane mask */
```

XSetPlaneMask can generate BadAlloc and BadGC errors.

The **XSetState** function, shown next, sets the foreground, background, plane mask, and function components of a given graphics context.

```
XSetState(display, gc, foreground, background,
        function, plane_mask)
  Display *display;              /* Specifies connection
                                    to server */
  GC gc;                         /* Graphics context */
  unsigned long foreground, background;
                                 /* Foreground and background
                                    to set for
                                    specified graphics context */
  int function;                  /* Function to set for
                                    specified graphics context */
  unsigned long plane_mask;      /* Plane mask */
```

XSetState can generate BadAlloc, BadGC, and BadValue errors.

The **XSetLineAttributes** function, shown next, sets the line-drawing components of the designated graphics context.

```
XSetLineAttributes(display, gc, line_width, line_style,
                   cap_style, join_style)
  Display *display;           /* Specifies connection
                                 to server */
  GC gc;                      /* Graphics context */
  unsigned int line_width;    /* Line width for
                                 specified graphics context */
  int line_style;             /* Line style for GC
                                 LineSolid, LineOnOffDash,
                                 LineDoubleDash */
  int cap_style;              /* Cap style for GC
                                 CapNotLast, CapButt,
                                 CapRound, CapProjecting */
  int join_style;             /* Line-join style for GC
                                 JoinMiter, JoinRound,
                                 JoinBevel */
```

XSetLineAttributes can generate BadAlloc, BadGC, and BadValue errors.

The **XSetDashes** function, shown next, sets the *dash_offset* and *dash_list* parameters, defining the dashed line styles of a designated graphics context.

```
XSetDashes(display, gc, dash_offset, dash_list, n)
  Display *display;           /* Specifies connection
                                 to server */
  GC gc;                      /* Graphics context */
  int dash_offset;            /* Pattern phase for dashed
                                 line-style for GC */
  char dash_list[];           /* Dash_list for dashed
                                 line-style for GC */
  int n;                      /* Number of elements
                                 in dash_list */
```

XSetDashes can generate BadAlloc, BadGC, and BadValue errors.

Drawing Points

Xlib provides two functions that draw individual points in a drawable. **XDrawPoint** draws a single point, while **XDrawPoints** draws multiple points. Both functions use the following graphics context components: *function, plane_mask, foreground, subwindow_mode, clip_x_origin, clip_y_origin,* and *clip_mask.*

The **XDrawPoint** function, shown here, draws a single point in the designated drawable.

```
XDrawPoint(display, d, gc, x, y)
  Display *display;            /* Specifies connection
                                  to server */
  Drawable d;                  /* Window or pixmap */
  GC gc;                       /* Graphics context */
  int x, y;                    /* Coordinates of point
                                  to be drawn */
```

XDrawPoint can generate BadDrawable, BadGC, and BadMatch errors.

The **XDrawPoints** function, shown next, draws multiple points in the designated drawable.

```
XDrawPoints(display, d, gc, points, npoints, mode)
  Display *display;            /* Specifies connection
                                  to server */
  Drawable d;                  /* Window or pixmap */
  GC gc;                       /* Graphics context */
  XPoint *points;              /* Array of points */
  int npoints;                 /* Number of points in array */
  int mode;                    /* Coordinate mode
                                  CoordModeOrigin or
                                  CoordModePrevious */
```

The CoordModeOrigin value of the *mode* parameter considers all coordinates as relative to the origin. The CoordModePrevious value of the *mode* parameter considers all coordinates except for the first point as relative to the previous point.

XDrawPoints can generate BadDrawable, BadGC, BadMatch, and BadValue errors.

Drawing Lines

Xlib provides three functions that draw lines in a drawable. **XDrawLine** draws a single line. **XDrawLines** draws multiple lines in a drawable. **XDrawSegments** draws multiple unconnected lines in a drawable. These functions use the following graphics context components: *function, plane_mask, line_width, line_style, cap_style, fill_style, sub-window_mode, clip_x_origin, clip_y_origin,* and *clip_mask.* The **XDrawLines** function also uses the *join_style* component. These functions all use the following mode-dependent graphics context components: *foreground, background, tile, stipple, ts_x_origin, ts_y_origin, dash_offset,* and *dash_list.*

The **XDrawLine** function, shown here, draws a single line connecting two points in the designated drawable.

```
XDrawLine(display, d, gc, x1, y1, x2, y2)
   Display *display;          /* Specifies connection
                                 to server */
   Drawable d;                /* Window or pixmap */
   GC gc;                     /* Graphics context */
   int x1, y1, x2, y2;        /* Coordinates of points
                                 (x1, y1) and (x2, y2)
                                 to be connected */
```

XDrawLine does not join two points that coincide. It does not draw a pixel more than once in a given line. It draws intersecting pixels several times, when lines intersect. **XDrawLine** can generate BadDrawable, BadGC, and BadMatch errors.

The **XDrawLines** function, shown next, draws multiple lines in the designated drawable.

```
XDrawLines(display, d, gc, points, npoints, mode)
   Display *display;          /* Specifies connection
                                 to server */
   Drawable d;                /* Window or pixmap */
   GC gc;                     /* Graphics context */
```

```
XPoint *points;              /* Array of points */
int npoints;                 /* Number of points in array */
int mode;                    /* Coordinate mode
                                CoordModeOrigin or
                                CoordModePrevious */
```

XDrawLines draws a line between each pair of points in the order that the points appear in the XPoint array. It joins all pairs of points correctly, including the first and last points, if they coincide. It does not draw a pixel more than once for any given line. Intersecting pixels are drawn multiple times for intersecting lines whose width is 0. Intersecting pixels are drawn only once for intersecting lines whose width is greater than 0.

The CoordModeOrigin value of the *mode* parameter considers all coordinates as relative to the origin. The CoordModePrevious value of the *mode* parameter considers all coordinates except for the first point as relative to the previous point. **XDrawLines** can generate BadDrawable, BadGC, BadMatch, and BadValue errors.

The **XDrawSegments** function, shown next, draws multiple, unconnected lines.

```
XDrawSegments(display, d, gc, segments, nsegments)
  Display *display;          /* Specifies connection
                                to server */
  Drawable d;                /* Window or pixmap */
  GC gc;                     /* Graphics context */
  XSegment *segments;        /* Array of segments */
  int nsegments;             /* Number of segments in array */
```

XDrawSegments draws a line between each pair of points in the order that the points appear in the XSegment array. It does not join coinciding endpoints. It does not draw a pixel more than once for any given line. Intersecting pixels are drawn multiple times for intersecting lines. **XDrawSegments** can generate BadDrawable, BadGC, and BadMatch errors.

Drawing Arcs

Xlib provides two functions that draw circular or elliptical arcs in a drawable. **XDrawArc** draws a single arc, and **XDrawArcs** draws multiple arcs. Both functions use the following graphics context components: *function*, *plane_mask*, *line_width*, *line_style*, *cap_style*, *join_style*, *fill_style*, *subwindow_mode*, *clip_x_origin*, *clip_y_origin*, and *clip_mask*. They use the following graphics context mode-dependent components: *foreground*, *background*, *tile*, *stipple*, *ts_x_origin*, *ts_y_origin*, *dash_offset*, and *dash_list*.

The **XDrawArc** function, shown here, draws a circular or elliptical arc in the designated drawable.

```
XDrawArc(display, d, gc, x, y, width, height, angle1, angle2)
   Display *display;           /* Specifies connection
                                  to server */
   Drawable d;                 /* Window or pixmap */
   GC gc;                      /* Graphics context */
   int x, y;                   /* Coordinates of upper-left
                                  corner of bounding rectangle
                                  relative to drawable origin */
   unsigned int width, height; /* Major and minor axes
                                   of arc */
   int angle1;                 /* Start of arc relative to
                                  three o'clock position
                                  from center
                                  measured in degrees * 64 */
   int angle2;                 /* Path and extent of arc
                                  relative to start of arc
                                  measured in degrees * 64 */
```

Positive angles denote clockwise motion. If *angle2* is greater than 360 degrees, it is truncated to 360 degrees.

XDrawArc does not draw any given pixel more than once for any given arc. If two arcs join correctly, intersect, and have a line width greater than 0, the pixels are drawn only once; otherwise, intersecting pixels are drawn several times. **XDrawArc** can generate BadDrawable, BadGC, and BadMatch errors.

The **XDrawArcs** function, shown next, draws multiple circular or elliptical arcs in the designated drawable.

```
XDrawArcs(display, d, gc, arcs, narcs)
   Display *display;           /* Specifies connection
                                  to server */
```

```
Drawable d;                 /* Window or pixmap */
GC gc;                      /* Graphics context */
XArc *arcs;                 /* Array of arcs */
int narcs;                  /* Number of arcs in array */
```

Positive angles denote clockwise motion. If *angle2* is greater than 360 degrees, it is truncated to 360 degrees.

XDrawArcs does not draw any given pixel more than once for any given arc. If two arcs join correctly, intersect, and have a line width greater than 0, the pixels are drawn only once; otherwise, intersecting pixels are drawn several times. If the last point in an arc coincides with the first point in the next arc, the arcs are joined correctly. If the last point in the last arc coincides with the first point in the first arc, the arcs are joined correctly. **XDrawArcs** can generate BadDrawable, BadGC, and BadMatch errors.

Filling Arcs

Once an arc is drawn, it may be filled. Prior to filling the arc, you may need to invoke the **XSetArcMode** function to set the graphics context component that controls how the arc is filled. **XFillArc** fills a single arc, and **XFillArcs** fills several arcs in the designated drawable. The **XFillArc** and **XFillArcs** functions use the following graphics context components: *function, plane_mask, fill_style, arc_mode, subwindow_mode, clip_x_origin, clip_y_origin,* and *clip_mask.* They use the following graphics context mode-dependent components: *foreground, background, tile, stipple, ts_x_origin,* and *ts_y_origin.*

The **XSetArcMode** function, shown here, sets the arc mode of the designated graphics context.

```
XSetArcMode(display, gc, arc_mode)
    Display *display;       /* Specifies connection
                               to server */
    GC gc;                  /* Graphics context */
    int arc_mode;           /* Arc mode
                               ArcChord or ArcPieSlice */
```

The ArcChord mode denotes that filled arcs are closed by drawing a straight line from the starting point to the ending point. The default ArcPieSlice mode denotes that filled arcs are drawn as pie slices.

XSetArcMode can generate BadAlloc, BadGC, and BadValue errors.

The **XFillArc** function, shown next, fills an arc in the designated drawable.

```
XFillArc(display, d, gc, x, y, width, height, angle1, angle2)
   Display *display;           /* Specifies connection
                                  to server */
   Drawable d;                 /* Window or pixmap */
   GC gc;                      /* Graphics context */
   int x, y;                   /* Coordinates of upper-left
                                  corner of bounding rectangle
                                  relative to drawable origin */
   unsigned int width, height; /* Major and minor axes
                                   of arc */
   int angle1;                 /* Start of arc relative to
                                  three o'clock position
                                  from center
                                  measured in degrees * 64 */
   int angle2;                 /* Path and extent of arc
                                  relative to start of arc
                                  measured in degrees * 64 */
```

XFillArc is similar to the **XFillArcs** function described next. **XFillArc** can generate BadDrawable, BadGC, and BadMatch errors.

The **XFillArcs** function, shown next, fills multiple arcs in the designated drawable.

```
XFillArcs(display, d, gc, arcs, narcs)
   Display *display;           /* Specifies connection
                                  to server */
   Drawable d;                 /* Window or pixmap */
   GC gc;                      /* Graphics context */
   XArc *arcs;                 /* Array of arcs */
   int narcs;                  /* Number of arcs in array */
```

XFillArc and **XFillArcs** fill the region closed by the arc and a single line segment when the *arc_mode* component of the graphics context is ArcChord; they fill the region closed by the arc and two line segments when the *arc_mode* component of the graphics context is ArcPieSlice. For any given arc, these functions do not draw a pixel more than once. If regions intersect, the intersecting pixels are drawn several times. The **XFillArc** functions can generate BadDrawable, BadGC, and BadMatch errors.

Drawing Rectangles

Xlib provides two functions that draw rectangles in a drawable. **XDrawRectangle** draws a single rectangle, and **XDrawRectangles** draws multiple rectangles. They do not draw a pixel more than once for a designated rectangle or rectangles. Both functions use the following graphics context components: *function, plane_mask, line_width, line_style, cap_style, join_style, fill_style, subwindow_mode, clip_x_origin, clip_y_origin,* and *clip_mask.* They use the following graphics context mode-dependent components: *foreground, background, tile, stipple, ts_x_origin, ts_y_origin, dash_offset,* and *dash_list.*

The **XDrawRectangle** function, shown here, draws the outline of a single rectangle in the designated drawable.

```
XDrawRectangle(display, d, gc, x, y, width, height)
  Display *display;              /* Specifies connection
                                    to server */
  Drawable d;                    /* Window or pixmap */
  GC gc;                         /* Graphics context */
  int x, y;                      /* Coordinates of upper-left
                                    corner of the rectangle */
  unsigned int width, height;    /* Dimensions of rectangle */
```

XDrawRectangle can generate BadDrawable, BadGC, and BadMatch errors.

The **XDrawRectangles** function, shown next, draws the outline of multiple rectangles in the designated drawable.

```
XDrawRectangles(display, d, gc, rectangles, rectangles)
  Display *display;              /* Specifies connection
                                    to server */
  Drawable d;                    /* Window or pixmap */
  GC gc;                         /* Graphics context */
  XRectangle rectangles[];       /* Array of rectangles */
  int nrectangles;               /* Number of rectangles
                                    in array */
```

XDrawRectangles draws the rectangles in the order specified in the *rectangles* array. If rectangles intersect, intersecting pixels are drawn several times. **XDrawRectangles** can generate BadDrawable, BadGC, and BadMatch errors.

Filling Rectangles

Xlib provides two functions that fill rectangles in a drawable. **XFillRectangle** fills a single rectangle, and **XFillRectangles** fills multiple rectangles. These functions do not draw a pixel more than once for a designated rectangle or rectangles. Both functions use the following graphics context components: *function, plane_mask, fill_style, subwindow_mode, clip_x_origin, clip_y_origin,* and *clip_mask.* They use the following graphics context mode-dependent components: *foreground, background, tile, stipple, ts_x_origin,* and *ts_y_origin.*

The **XFillRectangle** function, shown here, fills a single rectangular area in a designated drawable.

```
XFillRectangle(display, d, gc, x, y, width, height)
   Display *display;              /* Specifies connection
                                     to server */
   Drawable d;                    /* Window or pixmap */
   GC gc;                         /* Graphics context */
   int x, y;                      /* Coordinates of upper-left
                                     corner of the rectangle */
   unsigned int width, height;    /* Dimensions of rectangle */
```

XFillRectangle can generate BadDrawable, BadGC, and BadMatch errors.

The **XFillRectangles** function, shown next, fills multiple rectangular areas in a designated drawable.

```
XFillRectangles(display, d, gc, rectangles, nrectangles)
   Display *display;              /* Specifies connection
                                     to server */
   Drawable d;                    /* Window or pixmap */
   GC gc;                         /* Graphics context */
   XRectangle rectangles[];       /* Array of rectangles */
   int nrectangles;               /* Number of rectangles
                                     in array */
```

XFillRectangles fills the rectangles in the order specified in the *rectangles* array. If rectangles intersect, intersecting pixels are drawn several times. **XFillRectangles** can generate BadDrawable, BadGC, and BadMatch errors.

Filling a Polygon

The **XSetFillRule** function sets the fill rule in the graphics context accessed by the **XFillPolygon** function. This function fills the polygon.

The **XSetFillRule** function, shown here, sets the fill rule for the designated graphics context.

```
XSetFillRule(display, gc, fill_rule)
   Display *display;              /* Specifies connection
                                     to server */
   GC gc;                         /* Graphics context */
   int fill_rule;                 /* Fill rule for specified GC
                                     EvenOddRule or WindingRule */
```

The fill rule defines the pixels to be drawn when using **XFillPolygon**. The EvenOddRule defines a point to be drawn when an infinite ray whose origin is the given point crosses the polygon an odd number of times. The WindingRule defines a point to be drawn when an infinite ray whose origin is the given point crosses an unequal number of counterclockwise- and clockwise-directed path segments. *Counterclockwise-directed* path segments cross the ray from right to left as seen from the point. *Clockwise-directed* path segments cross the ray from left to right as seen from the point.

The **XFillPolygon** function, shown next, fills a polygon segment of the designated drawable.

```
XFillPolygon((display, d, gc, points, npoints, shape, mode)
   Display *display,              /* Specifies connection
                                     to server */
   Drawable d;                    /* Window or pixmap */
   GC gc;                         /* Graphics context */
   XPoint *points;                /* Array of points */
   int npoints;                   /* Number of points in array */
   int shape;                     /* Shape for server information
```

```
                                  Complex, Convex,
                                  or Nonconvex */
   int mode;                   /* Coordinate mode
                                  CoordModeOrigin or
                                  CoordModePrevious */
```

XFillPolygon fills the segment enclosed by the array of points. If the first and last points do not coincide, the segment is automatically closed. **XFillPolygon** does not draw a pixel more than once.

The CoordModePrevious value of the *mode* parameter considers all coordinates except for the first point as relative to the previous point. **XFillPolygon** uses the following graphics context components: *function, plane_mask, fill_style, fill_rule, subwindow_mode, clip_x_origin, clip_y_origin,* and *clip_mask.* They use the following graphics context mode-dependent components: *foreground, background, tile, stipple, ts_x_origin,* and *ts_y_origin.* **XFillPolygon** can generate BadDrawable, BadGC, BadMatch, and BadValue errors.

Clearing Windows and Areas

The Xlib function **XClearWindow** clears an entire window. The function **XClearArea** clears part of a window. Neither of these functions operates on pixmaps.

The **XClearWindow** function, shown here, clears an entire window.

```
XClearWindow(display, w)
   Display *display;         /* Specifies connection
                                to server */
   Window w;                 /* Window to clear */
```

If the window has a *background* value of None, the window contents are not changed.

XClearWindow can generate BadMatch and BadWindow errors.

The **XClearArea** function, shown next, clears a rectangular area in a designated window.

```
XClearArea(display, w, x, y, width, height, exposures)
   Display *display;         /* Specifies connection
                                to server */
```

```
Window w;                  /* Window to clear */
int x, y;                  /* Coordinates of upper-left
                              corner of the rectangle */
unsigned int width, height; /* Dimensions of rectangle */
Bool exposures;            /* If TRUE
                              generate Expose events */
```

XClearArea fills the rectangular area with the window's background pixel or pixmap. If the window has a *background* value of None, the window contents are not changed. Independent of the window *background* value, if the *exposures* parameter is TRUE, one or more Exposure events are generated for rectangle segments that are visible or stored in a backing store. **XClearArea** can generate BadMatch and BadWindow errors.

Copying Areas and Bitplanes

The Xlib function **XCopyArea** copies an area from one drawable to another. The function **XCopyPlane** copies a single bit plane from one drawable to another.

The **XCopyArea** function, shown here, copies an area from one drawable to another with the same root screen and depth.

```
XCopyArea(display, src, dest, gc, src_x, src_y, width,
        height, dest_x, dest_y)
  Display *display;         /* Specifies connection
                               to server */
  Drawable src, dest;       /* Source and destination
                               rectangles to be combined */
  GC gc;                    /* Graphics context */
  int src_x, src_y;         /* Coordinates of upper-left
                               corner of source rectangle */
  unsigned int width, height; /* Dimensions of source and
                                 destination rectangles */
  int dest_x, dest_y;       /* Coordinates of upper-left
                               corner of
                               destination rectangle */
```

Obscured source rectangle regions are not copied unless they are retained in a backing store. Regions outside the source drawable boundaries are not copied. If the destination is a window whose *background* value is not None, the copied regions are tiled with the background. Independent of any tiling, if the *graphics_exposure* is TRUE, GraphicsExposure events are generated for destination regions in all drawables. If the *graphics_exposure* is TRUE, but no GraphicsExposure events are generated, a NoExpose event is generated.

The function uses the following graphics context components: *function*, *plane_mask*, *subwindow_mode*, *graphics_exposures*, *clip_x_origin*, *clip_y_origin*, and *clip_mask*. **XCopyArea** can generate BadDrawable, BadGC, and BadMatch errors.

The **XCopyPlane** function, shown next, copies a single bit plane of the designated drawable.

```
XCopyPlane(display, src, dest, gc, src_x, src_y, width,
        height, dest_x, dest_y, plane)
  Display *display;          /* Specifies connection
                                to server */
  Drawable src, dest;        /* Source and destination
                                rectangles to be combined */
  GC gc;                     /* Graphics context */
  int src_x, src_y;          /* Coordinates of upper-left
                                corner of source rectangle */
  unsigned int width, height; /* Dimensions of source and
                                 destination rectangles */
  int dest_x, dest_y;        /* Coordinates of upper-left
                                corner of
                                destination rectangle */
  unsigned long plane;       /* Bit plane */
```

XCopyPlane combines a single bit plane of the designated source rectangle with the graphics context to modify the designated destination rectangle. The two rectangles must have the same root, but may differ in depth. The function employs the foreground pixels in the graphics context whenever the source rectangle's bit plane is set to 1; the function employs the background pixels in the graphics context whenever the source rectangle's bit plane is set to 0.

Obscured source rectangle regions are not copied unless they are retained in a backing store. Regions outside the source drawable boundaries are not copied. If the destination is a window whose *background* value is not None, the copied regions are tiled with the background.

Independent of any tiling, if the *graphics exposure* is TRUE, GraphicsExposure events are generated for destination regions in all drawables. If the *graphics_exposure* is TRUE, but no GraphicsExposure events are generated, a NoExpose event is generated.

The **XCopyPlane** function uses the following graphics context components: *function, plane_mask, foreground, background, subwindow_mode, graphics_exposures, clip_x_origin, clip_y_origin,* and *clip_mask*. The **XCopyPlane** function can generate BadDrawable, BadGC, BadMatch, and BadValue errors.

Setting Additional Graphics Context Components

The following functions set graphics context components that are referenced by some graphics functions. **XSetGraphicsExposures** sets the *graphics_exposures* flag. **XSetFillStyle** sets the *fill_style* component. **XSetStipple** sets the stipple in the graphics context. **XSetTile** sets the fill tile. **XSetTSOrigin** sets the tile or stipple origin. **XSetClipMask** sets the *clip_mask* component to a specified pixmap. **XSetClipRectangles** sets the *clip_mask* component to the specified list of rectangles. **XSetClipOrigin** sets the *clip_origin* component. **XSetSubwindowMode** sets the subwindow mode of the designated graphics context.

The **XSetGraphicsExposures** function, shown here, sets the *graphics_exposures* flag of the designated graphics context.

```
XSetGraphicsExposures(display, gc, graphics_exposures)
  Display *display;           /* Specifies connection
                                 to server */
  GC gc;                      /* Graphics context */
  Bool graphics_exposures;    /* If TRUE, generate
                                 GraphicsExpose and
                                 NoExpose events */
```

XSetGraphicsExposures can generate BadAlloc, BadGC, and BadValue errors.

The **XSetFillStyle** function, shown next, sets the *fill_style* component of the designated graphics context.

```
XSetFillStyle(display, gc, fill_style)
   Display *display;            /* Specifies connection
                                   to server */
   GC gc;                       /* Graphics context */
   int fill_style;              /* Fill-style for specified GC
                                   FillSolid, FillTiled,
                                   FillStippled, or
                                   FillOpaqueStippled */
```

XSetFillStyle can generate BadAlloc, BadGC, and BadValue errors.

The **XSetStipple** function, shown next, sets the stipple for the designated graphics context.

```
XSetStipple(display, gc, stipple)
   Display *display;            /* Specifies connection
                                   to server */
   GC gc;                       /* Graphics context */
   Pixmap stipple;              /* Stipple to set for the
                                   graphics context */
```

The stipple depth must be 1.

XSetStipple can generate BadAlloc, BadGC, BadMatch, and BadPixmap errors.

The **XSetTile** function, shown next, sets the fill tile for the designated graphics context.

```
XSetTile(display, gc, tile)
   Display *display;            /* Specifies connection
                                   to server */
   GC gc;                       /* Graphics context */
   Pixmap tile;                 /* File tile to set for the
                                   graphics context */
```

The tile and the graphics context must be of the same depth.

XSetTile can generate BadAlloc, BadGC, BadMatch, and BadPixmap errors.

The **XSetTSOrigin** function, shown next, sets the tile or stipple origin of the designated graphics context.

```
XSetTSOrigin(display, gc, ts_x_origin, ts_y_origin)
  Display *display;            /* Specifies connection
                                  to server */
  GC gc;                       /* Graphics context */
  int ts_x_origin, ts_y_origin; /* X and y coordinates of
                                  tile and stipple origin */
```

The parent's origin is interpreted relative to the destination drawable specified in the graphics request.

XSetTSOrigin can generate BadAlloc and BadGC errors.

The **XSetClipMask** function, shown next, sets the *clip_mask* component of the designated graphics context to a specified pixmap.

```
XSetClipMask(display, gc, pixmap)
  Display *display;            /* Specifies connection
                                  to server */
  GC gc;                       /* Graphics context */
  Pixmap pixmap;               /* Pixmap or None */
```

If the *clip_mask* parameter is set to None, the pixels are always drawn, whatever the value of the *clip_origin* parameter.

XSetClipMask can generate BadAlloc, BadGC, BadMatch, and BadPixmap errors.

The **XSetClipRectangles** function, shown next, sets the *clip_mask* component of the designated graphics context to the specified list of rectangles, thus effectively clipping the output to within the specified rectangles.

```
XSetClipRectangles(display, gc, clip_x_origin, clip_y_origin,
                rectangles, n, ordering)
  Display *display;            /* Specifies connection
                                  to server */
  GC gc;                       /* Graphics context */
  int clip_x_origin, clip_y_origin;
                               /* Coordinates of
                                  clip-mask origin */
  XRectangle rectangles[];     /* Array of rectangles
                                  defining clip-mask */
  int n;                       /* Number of rectangles */
```

```
int ordering;                    /* Ordering relations
                                    on rectangles
                                    Unsorted, YSorted,
                                    YXSorted, YXBanded */
```

The *clip_origin* component is interpreted relative to the destination drawable designated in the graphics function. If the rectangles intersect, graphics results are undefined. The *ordering* argument may increase processing speed. The value Unsorted denotes arbitrary order. The value YSorted denotes that each rectangle's Y origin is equal to or greater than the Y origin of all previous rectangles. YXSorted obeys restrictions for YSorted, but in addition, for rectangles with the same YOrigin, the X origin is equal to or greater than the X origin of previous rectangles. YXBanded obeys the restrictions for YXSorted, but in addition requires that for every Y scan line, rectangles that include that given scan line must have identical Y origins and Y extents.

XSetClipRectangles can generate BadAlloc, BadGC, BadMatch, and BadValue errors.

The **XSetClipOrigin** function, shown next, sets the *clip_origin* component of the designated graphics context.

```
XSetClipOrigin(display, gc, clip_x_origin, clip_y_origin)
   Display *display;             /* Specifies connection
                                    to server */
   GC gc;                        /* Graphics context */
   int clip_x_origin, clip_y_origin; /* X and y coordinates of
                                    clip-mask origin */
```

The *clip_origin* component is interpreted relative to the destination drawable specified in the graphics request.

XSetClipOrigin can generate BadAlloc and BadGC errors.

The **XSetSubwindowMode** function, shown next, sets the subwindow mode of the designated graphics context.

```
XSetSubwindowMode(display, gc, subwindow_mode)
   Display *display;             /* Specifies connection
                                    to server */
   GC gc;                        /* Graphics context */
   int subwindow_mode;           /* Subwindow mode
```

```
                                    ClipByChildren or
                                    IncludeInferiors */
```

The value ClipByChildren designates that both source and destination windows are clipped by all viewable InputOutput child windows. The value IncludeInferiors designates that neither source or destination windows are clipped by child windows.

XSetSubwindowMode can generate BadAlloc, BadGC, and BadValue errors.

Querying the Graphics Context

Xlib provides functions that help the application designer select the stipple and tile for the given workstation. **XQueryBestStipple** returns the stipple size that can be drawn the fastest on the designated drawable. **XQueryBestTile** returns the tile size that can be drawn the fastest on the designated drawable. Note that the returned stipple and tile are drawn the fastest; however, because of compatibility and other reasons, they may not be optimum choices.

The **XQueryBestStipple** function, shown here, returns the stipple size that can be drawn the fastest on the designated drawable.

```
Status XQueryBestStipple(display, which_screen, width,
                height, width_return, height_return)
   Display *display;          /* Specifies connection
                                 to server */
   Drawable which_screen;     /* Any drawable on the screen */
   unsigned int width, height; /* Width and height */
   unsigned int *width_return, *height_return;
                              /* Returns width and height of
                                 best object for the display */
```

The drawable cannot be an InputOnly window.

XQueryBestStipple can generate BadDrawable and BadMatch errors.

The **XQueryBestTile** function, shown next, returns the tile size that can be drawn the fastest on the designated drawable.

```
Status XQueryBestTile(display, which_screen, width,
                height, width_return, height_return)
```

```
Display *display;          /* Specifies connection
                              to server */
Drawable which_screen;     /* Any drawable on the screen */
unsigned int width, height; /* Width and height */
unsigned int *width_return, *height_return;
                           /* Returns width and height of
                              best object for the display */
```

The drawable cannot be an InputOnly window.

XQueryBestTile can generate BadDrawable and BadMatch errors.

Drawing Points and Segments: Example 1

The following example applies graphics functions to draw points and segments on the screen. The **XDrawSegments** function draws multiple, unconnected lines between data points specified in an XSegment data structure. The program declares an array, called *setting*, that contains multiple data points such as

{490, 450, 450, 400}

These values are interpreted as follows:

$x1 = 490$, $y1 = 450$, $x2 = 450$, and $y2 = 400$

The integer variable *num_settings* denotes the number of elements in the *setting* array. Some of the data declarations associated with the XSegment data structure are shown here.

```
XSegment setting[] = {
  {490, 450, 450, 400}
...
  {10, 50, 80, 10}
  }
  int num_settings;
```

The **XDrawPoints** function draws multiple points in the designated drawable. The program declares an array called *points*, which contains multiple data points such as

{0, 0}

These values are interpreted as follows:

$x = 0, y = 0$

The integer variable *num_points* denotes the number of elements in the *points* array. Some of the data declarations associated with the XPoint data structure are shown here.

```
XPoint points[] = {
  {0, 0}
...
  {90, 90}
  }
  int num_points;
```

The C language function **init** performs typical program initialization activities, such as opening the display unit and assigning identifiers to the display unit and the default screen. In addition, it employs the C library function **sizeof** to determine the number of points and number of segments as shown in the following code.

```
num_points = sizeof (points) / sizeof (XPoint);
num_settings = sizeof (setting) / sizeof (XSegment);
```

The heart of this program is the C language function **load_drawings**, which is executed when the count of remaining Expose events becomes 0. This function invokes the Xlib graphics functions that draw the segments and the points. Recall that the CoordModeOrigin value of the *mode* parameter considers all coordinates as relative to the origin, and the CoordModePrevious value of the *mode* parameter considers all coordinates except for the first point as relative to the previous point. The complete **load_drawings** function is shown here.

```
void load_drawings()
{
int num_dashes;

  thegc = XCreateGC(thedisplay, thewindow, 0, 0);
  XSetForeground(thedisplay, thegc,
                 BlackPixel(thedisplay, thescreen));
  XSetBackground(thedisplay, thegc,
                 WhitePixel(thedisplay, thescreen));
  XClearWindow(thedisplay, thewindow);
  XDrawSegments(thedisplay, thewindow, thegc,
                setting, num_settings);
  XDrawPoints(thedisplay, thewindow, thegc,
              points, num_points, CoordModeOrigin);
  XDrawPoints(thedisplay, thewindow, thegc,
              points, num_points, CoordModePrevious);
}
```

The complete program listing is shown here.

```
/* example10_1 */
#include <X11/Xlib.h>
#include <X11/Xutil.h>

#define BORDER_WIDTH 2
#define FALSE 0
#define TRUE 1

Display      *thedisplay;
Window       thewindow;
int          thescreen;
char         *w_name;
XSegment setting[] = {
  {490, 450, 450, 400},
  {470, 430, 400, 380},
  {440, 410, 360, 340},
  {420, 400, 320, 310},
  {390, 370, 290, 250},
  {360, 350, 250, 100},
  {300, 320, 200, 200},
  {240, 230, 200, 180},
  {200, 170, 130, 130},
```

```
  {100, 120, 110, 100},
  {50, 50, 150, 150},
  {370, 360, 280, 280},
  {220, 280, 250, 150},
  {120, 180, 200, 100},
  {50, 150, 150, 50},
  {30, 100, 125, 25},
  {10, 50, 80, 10}
};
int num_settings;
XPoint points[] = {
  {0, 0},
  {120, 120},
  {240, 120},
  {120, 240},
  {240, 240},
  {60, 60},
  {30, 60},
  {60, 30},
  {30, 30},
  {180, 180},
  {180, 90},
  {90, 180},
  {90, 90}
};
int num_points;

unsigned long foreground;
unsigned long background;
XSizeHints    thehints;
GC            thegc;

void init();
void load_drawings();
void set_hints();
void create_window_set_properties();
void cleanup();

main(argc, argv)
int argc;
char *argv[];
{
```

```
XEvent theevent;
int done = FALSE;
int result;

  init(argv);

  set_hints();

  create_window_set_properties(argc,argv);

  XMapRaised(thedisplay, thewindow);

  XSelectInput(thedisplay, thewindow,
               ButtonPressMask | ExposureMask);
  while (!done)
  {
    XNextEvent(thedisplay, &theevent);

    switch(theevent.type)
    {
      case Expose:
        if (theevent.xexpose.count == 0)
        {
          load_drawings();
        }
      break;

      case ButtonPress:
        done = TRUE;
        cleanup();
        printf("\n Ready to exit ...\n");
      break;
    }
  } /*  End while  */
} /*  End main  */

void init(argv)
char *argv[];
{
```

```
    w_name = argv[0];
    thedisplay = XOpenDisplay("");
    thescreen = DefaultScreen(thedisplay);

    background = WhitePixel(thedisplay, thescreen);
    foreground = BlackPixel(thedisplay, thescreen);

    num_points = sizeof (points) / sizeof (XPoint);
    num_settings = sizeof (setting) / sizeof (XSegment);
}

void load_drawings()
{
int num_dashes;

    thegc = XCreateGC(thedisplay, thewindow, 0, 0);
    XSetForeground(thedisplay, thegc,
                   BlackPixel(thedisplay, thescreen));
    XSetBackground(thedisplay, thegc,
                   WhitePixel(thedisplay, thescreen));
    XClearWindow(thedisplay, thewindow);
    XDrawSegments(thedisplay, thewindow, thegc,
                  setting, num_settings);
    XDrawPoints(thedisplay, thewindow, thegc,
                points, num_points, CoordModeOrigin);
    XDrawPoints(thedisplay, thewindow, thegc,
                points, num_points, CoordModePrevious);
}

void create_window_set_properties(argc, argv)
int argc;
char *argv[];
{

    thewindow = XCreateSimpleWindow(thedisplay,
                          DefaultRootWindow(thedisplay),
                          thehints.x, thehints.y,
                          thehints.width, thehints.height,
                          BORDER_WIDTH,
                          foreground, background);
```

```
    XSetStandardProperties(thedisplay, thewindow, w_name, w_name,
                    None, argv, argc, &thehints);
}

void set_hints()
{
int height;
int width;

  width = DisplayWidth(thedisplay, thescreen);
  height = DisplayHeight(thedisplay, thescreen);
  thehints.flags = PPosition | PSize | PMinSize;
  thehints.height = height/4;
  thehints.width = 500;
  thehints.x = width/3;
  thehints.y = height/3;
  thehints.min_height = 400;
  thehints.min_width = 500;
}

void cleanup()
{
  XFreeGC(thedisplay, thegc);
  printf("\n free gc  - done\n");

  XDestroyWindow(thedisplay, thewindow);
  printf("\n Destroy window  - done\n");

  XCloseDisplay(thedisplay);
  printf("\n Disconnect from server - done\n");
}
```

Results of running this program are shown in Figure 10-1.

The following MAKE file was used to process this program using SCO Open Desktop.

```
RM = rm -f
CC = cc
CFLAGS = -O
INCLUDES = -I. -I/usr/include -I/usr/include/X11
LIBS = -lXm -lXt -lX11 -lsocket -lmalloc -lPW
```

```
.c.o:
$(RM) $@
$(CC) -c $(CFFLAGS) $(INCLUDES) $*.c
all:: example10_1
example10_1: example10_1.o
$(RM) $@
$(CC) -o $@ $(CFLAGS) example10_1.o $(LIBS)
@echo makefile for example10_1  - done!
```

Drawing Rectangles: Example 2

The following example draws a series of rectangles on the screen. It is similar to the previous program. For simplicity, only modifications are discussed here. The **XDrawRectangles** function draws the outline of several rectangles for data points specified in an XRectangle data structure. The program declares an array called *rect* that contains multiple data points such as

{180, 130, 200, 180}

Drawing points and line segments

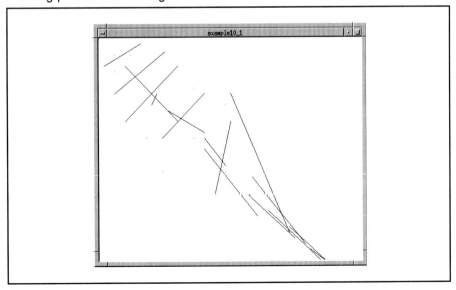

These values are interpreted as follows:

$x = 180$, $y = 130$, $width = 200$, and $height = 180$

The integer variable *num_rect* denotes the number of elements in the *rect* array. Data declarations associated with the XRectangle data structure are shown here.

```
XRectangle rect[] = {
   {180, 130, 200, 180},
   {200, 170, 130, 130},
   {100, 120, 110, 100},
   {50, 50, 150, 150},
   {120, 180, 200, 100},
   {50, 150, 150, 50},
   {20, 10, 15, 25},
   {40, 100, 45, 25},
   {50, 60, 35, 25},
   {90, 10, 75, 25},
   {30, 10, 15, 50},
   {10, 50, 80, 30}
};
int num_rect;
```

The C language function **init** performs typical program initialization activities. It employs the C library function **sizeof** to determine the number of rectangles, as shown in the following code.

```
num_rect = sizeof (rect) / sizeof (XRectangle);
```

The heart of this program is the C language function **load_drawings**, which is executed when the count of remaining Expose events becomes 0. This function invokes the Xlib graphics function **XDrawRectangles**, which draws the rectangle outlines.

```
XDrawRectangles(thedisplay, thewindow, thegc,
                rect, num_rect);
```

The only other differences in this program compared to the program in Example 10-1 are the modified values of the *width, min_height,* and *min_width* hints processed in the C language function **set hints**. The complete listing of this function follows.

```
void set_hints()
{
int height;
int width;

  width = DisplayWidth(thedisplay, thescreen);
  height = DisplayHeight(thedisplay, thescreen);
  thehints.flags = PPosition | PSize | PMinSize;
  thehints.height = height/4;
  thehints.width = 400;
  thehints.x = width/3;
  thehints.y = height/3;
  thehints.min_height = 350;
  thehints.min_width = 400;
}
```

Sample output for this example is shown in Figure 10-2.

Drawing several rectangles

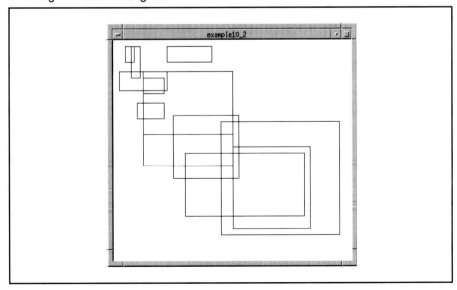

Filling Rectangles: Example 3

The following example fills some of the rectangles drawn on the screen in Example 10-2. It is similar to the previous program. For simplicity, only modifications are discussed here. Data declarations associated with the XRectangle data structure are as follows.

```
XRectangle rect[] = {
  {200, 170, 130, 130},
  {100, 120, 110, 100},
  {50, 50, 150, 150},
  {220, 210, 200, 150},
  {120, 180, 200, 100},
  {50, 150, 150, 50},
  {30, 100, 125, 25},
  {10, 50, 80, 10}
};
int num_rect;
```

The C library function **sizeof** invoked by the C language function **init** assigns the correct value to the variable *num_rect.* The heart of this program is the C language function **load_drawings**, which is executed when the count of remaining Expose events becomes 0. This function invokes the Xlib graphics function **XFillRectangles**, which draws the rectangle outlines.

```
XFillRectangles(thedisplay, thewindow, thegc,
                rect, num_rect);
```

The only other differences in this program compared to the program in Example 10-2 are the modified values of the *width, min_width,* and *min_height* hints processed in the C language function **set_hints**. The complete listing of this function follows.

```
void set_hints()
{
int height;
int width;

  width = DisplayWidth(thedisplay, thescreen);
  height = DisplayHeight(thedisplay, thescreen);
```

```
    thehints.flags = PPosition | PSize | PMinSize;
    thehints.height - height/4;
    thehints.width = 500;
    thehints.x = width/3;
    thehints.y = height/3;
    thehints.min_height = 400;
    thehints.min_width = 500;
}
```

Sample output for this example is shown in Figure 10-3.

Filling Polygons: Example 4

The following example applies the **XFillPolygon** function to fill some of the points on the screen. It is similar to the previous programs. For simplicity, only modifications are discussed here. The program applies the XPoint data structure as in Example 10-1. Data declarations associated with this data structure are shown here.

```
XPoint points[] = {
    {0, 0},
    {120, 120},
    {240, 120},
    {120, 240},
    {240, 240},
    {60, 60},
    {30, 60},
    {60, 30},
    {30, 30},
    {180, 180},
    {180, 90},
    {90, 180},
    {90, 90}
};
int num_points;
```

Filling several rectangles

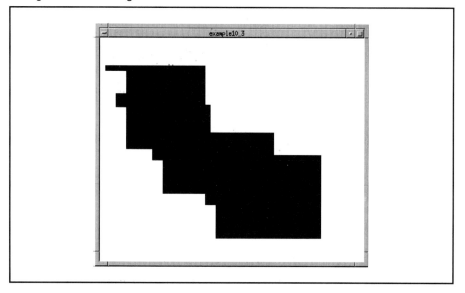

New definitions and declarations include the variable *mod_type*, whose value REGULAR denotes drawing the arcs and whose value FILL denotes filling the arcs. The program name is now *p_name instead of *w_name.

```
#define REGULAR 0
#define FILL 1
...
char        *p_name;
...
int         mod_type = REGULAR;
```

The program includes four variables that determine whether the mouse button was double-clicked, indicating that the user wishes to exit. The *is_button_pressed* variable indicates the first click of the left button. The *clicked* variable indicates the second click of the left button. The *click_time* variable and the *c_t* variable are used to determine whether the two clicks took place within a predetermined period of time: 300 milliseconds. Example 8-2 (in Chapter 8, "Mouse") discusses in greater detail how these variables are employed to process mouse clicks that exit the program.

```
int is_button_pressed = FALSE;
int clicked = FALSE;
```

```
Time click_time = 300;
int c t;
```

The modified C language function **load_drawings** is shown here.

```
void load_drawings()
{

  thegc = XCreateGC(thedisplay, thewindow, 0, 0);
  XSetForeground(thedisplay, thegc,
                BlackPixel(thedisplay, thescreen));
  XSetBackground(thedisplay, thegc,
                WhitePixel(thedisplay, thescreen));
  XClearWindow(thedisplay, thewindow);
  XSetFillRule(thedisplay, thegc, WindingRule);
  XFillPolygon(thedisplay, thewindow, thegc, points,
              num_points, Complex, CoordModeOrigin);
  XFillPolygon(thedisplay, thewindow, thegc, points,
              num_points, Convex, CoordModePrevious);
}
```

The C language function **set_hints** is identical to the one used in Examples 10-1 and 10-3. Sample output from this program is shown in Figure 10-4.

Drawing and Filling Arcs: Example 5

The following example applies Xlib graphics functions to draw and fill arcs on the screen. It is similar to the previous programs. For simplicity, only modifications are discussed here. The program applies the XArc data structure. The program declares an array, called *arcs*, that contains multiple data points such as

{0, 0, 45, 50, 10*04, 50*04}

These values are interpreted as follows:

$x = 0$, $y = 0$, *width* = 45, *height* = 50, *angle1* = 10 degrees, and *angle2* = 50 degrees

FIGURE
10-4

Filling several polygons

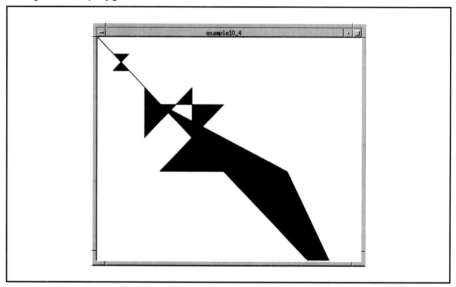

The integer variable *num_arcs* denotes the number of elements in the *arcs* array. Some of the data declarations associated with the XArc data structure are shown here.

```
XArc arcs[] = {
  {0, 0, 45, 50, 10*64, 50*64},
...
  {250, 120, 245, 280, 20*64, 110*64}
};
int num_arcs;
```

The other new data declarations in this program serve two purposes: They control whether the program draws or fills the arcs, and they determine whether the mouse was double-clicked to exit the program. See Example 8-2 for a discussion of processing mouse clicks.

The program solicits ButtonPress, Expose, and ButtonRelease events, creating a font cursor when a mouse putton is pressed. It also solicits MotionNotify events, but implementation of these events is left to the reader.

The complete program listing is shown here.

```
/* example10_5 */
#include <X11/Xlib.h>
#include <X11/Xutil.h>
#include <X11/cursorfont.h>

#define BORDER_WIDTH 2
#define FALSE 0
#define TRUE 1
#define REGULAR 0
#define FILL 1

Display       *thedisplay;
Window        thewindow;
int           thescreen;
Cursor        thecursor;
char          *p_name;
unsigned long foreground;
unsigned long background;
XSizeHints    thehints;
GC            thegc;

XArc arcs[] = {
   {0, 0, 45, 50, 10*64, 50*64},
   {0, 30, 75, 60, 20*64, 70*64},
   {0, 50, 95, 70, 30*64, 80*64},
   {0, 70, 105, 80, 40*64, 90*64},
   {0, 90, 125, 90, 50*64, 100*64},
   {0, 120, 145, 100, 60*64, 110*64},
   {100, 0, 145, 110, 10*64, 30*64},
   {100, 30, 175, 120, 20*64, 50*64},
   {100, 50, 195, 130, 30*64, 80*64},
   {100, 70, 205, 140, 40*64, 90*64},
   {100, 90, 225, 150, 50*64, 100*64},
   {100, 120, 245, 160, 60*64, 110*64},
   {200, 0, 95, 170, 10*64, 50*64},
   {200, 30, 105, 180, 50*64, 70*64},
   {200, 50, 125, 190, 40*64, 80*64},
   {200, 70, 145, 200, 70*64, 90*64},
   {200, 90, 175, 210, 30*64, 100*64},
   {200, 120, 215, 220, 30*64, 110*64},
```

```
        {250, 0, 95, 230, 10*64, 50*64},
        {250, 30, 125, 240, 50*64, 70*64},
        {250, 50, 155, 250, 30*64, 80*64},
        {250, 70, 185, 260, 60*64, 90*64},
        {250, 90, 195, 270, 30*64, 100*64},
        {250, 120, 245, 280, 20*64, 110*64}
};
int num_arcs;
int mod_type = REGULAR;

void init();
void load_drawings();
void set_hints();
void create_window_set_properties();
void cleanup();

main(argc, argv)
int argc;
char *argv[];
{
XEvent theevent;
int done = FALSE;
int is_button_pressed = FALSE;
int clicked = FALSE;
Time click_time = 300;
int c_t;
XTimeCoord *xtc;

    init(argv);

    set_hints();

    create_window_set_properties(argc,argv);

    XSelectInput(thedisplay, thewindow,

    XMapWindow(thedisplay, thewindow);

    while (!done)
    {
      XNextEvent(thedisplay, &theevent);
      switch(theevent.type)
```

```
  {
    case Expose:
      if (theevent.xexpose.count == 0)
      {
        load_drawings();
      }
    break;

    case ButtonPress:
      switch(theevent.xbutton.button)
      {
        case Button1:
          is_button_pressed = TRUE;
          thecursor = XCreateFontCursor(thedisplay,
                                        XC_leftbutton);
          XDefineCursor(thedisplay, thewindow, thecursor);
          mod_type = REGULAR;
          load_drawings();
        break;
        case Button3:
          thecursor = XCreateFontCursor(thedisplay,
                                        XC_rightbutton);
          XDefineCursor(thedisplay, thewindow, thecursor);
          mod_type = FILL;
          load_drawings();
        break;
      }/* End switch */
    break;
    case ButtonRelease:
      XUndefineCursor(thedisplay, thewindow);
      if (clicked)
      {
        is_button_pressed = FALSE;
        clicked = FALSE;
        if ((theevent.xbutton.time - c_t) <= click_time)
          done = TRUE;
      }
      if (is_button_pressed)
      {
        c_t = theevent.xbutton.time;
        clicked = TRUE;
        is_button_pressed = FALSE;
```

```
        }
      break;
      case MotionNotify:
      break;
      }/* End switch */
   }  /*  End while  */
} /*  End main  */

void init(argv)
char *argv[];
{

  p_name = argv[0];
  thedisplay = XOpenDisplay("");
  thescreen = DefaultScreen(thedisplay);

  background = WhitePixel(thedisplay, thescreen);
  foreground = BlackPixel(thedisplay, thescreen);

  num_arcs = sizeof (arcs) / sizeof (XArc);
}
void create_window_set_properties(argc, argv)
int argc;
char *argv[];
{

  thewindow = XCreateSimpleWindow(thedisplay,
                        DefaultRootWindow(thedisplay),
                        thehints.x, thehints.y,
                        thehints.width, thehints.height,
                        BORDER_WIDTH,
                        foreground, background);
  XSetStandardProperties(thedisplay, thewindow,
                    p_name, p_name,
                    None, argv, argc, &thehints);
  thegc = XCreateGC(thedisplay, thewindow, 0, 0);
  XSetForeground(thedisplay, thegc,
              BlackPixel(thedisplay, thescreen));
  XSetBackground(thedisplay, thegc,
  WhitePixel(thedisplay, thescreen));

  }
```

```
void load_drawings()
{

  XClearWindow(thedisplay, thewindow);
  if (mod_type == REGULAR)
    XDrawArcs(thedisplay, thewindow, thegc, arcs, num_arcs);
  else
    XFillArcs(thedisplay, thewindow, thegc, arcs, num_arcs);
}

void set_hints()
{
int height;
int width;

  width = DisplayWidth(thedisplay, thescreen);
  height = DisplayHeight(thedisplay, thescreen);
  thehints.flags = PPosition | PSize | PMinSize;
  thehints.height = height/4;
  thehints.width = 500;
  thehints.x =  width/3;
  thehints.y =  height/3;
  thehints.min_height = 270;
  thehints.min_width = 500;
}

void cleanup()
{
  XUndefineCursor(thedisplay, thewindow);
  printf("\n Undefine cursor - done\n");

  XFreeGC(thedisplay, thegc);
  printf("\n free gc  - done\n");

  XDestroyWindow(thedisplay, thewindow);
  printf("\n Destroy window  - done\n");

  XCloseDisplay(thedisplay);
  printf("\n Disconnect from server - done\n");
}
```

Results of running this program are shown in Figure 10-5.

FIGURE
10-5

Drawing several arcs

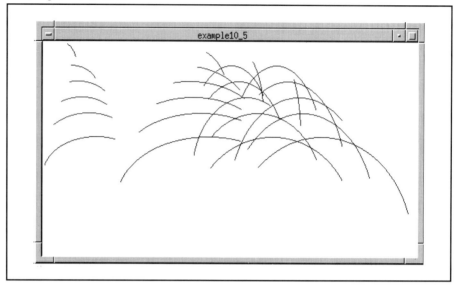

Drawing Bitmaps on the Screen:
Example 6

The final example in this chapter applies several Xlib graphics functions to draw a series of icons on the screen. The example reviews concepts and functions discussed in this chapter and introduced in Chapter 9, "Pixmaps, Bitmaps, and Images."

The program defines four bitmaps: sorceress_bits, xterm_bits, wingdogs_bits, and xlogo64_bits. These bitmaps contain the raw data used in generating the icons displayed on the screen. As discussed in Chapter 9, "Pixmaps, Bitmaps, and Images," these bitmaps could be read into the program from #include files. The program also contains an array *rect*, whose data type is XRectangle. This array contains different values from the *rect* array used in Example 10-2. The heart of the program is composed of two C language functions, **create_window_set_properties** and **load_drawings**.

In the previous examples, the **create_window_set_properties** function creates a simple window, sets standard properties, creates a graphics
context, and sets the foreground and background for the designated
graphics context. This example's **create_window_set_properties** function is more complicated. It creates a simple window and a graphics
context. It sets the *subwindow_mode* for the graphics context. Then it
creates the sorceress bitmap and sets the stipple in the graphics context.
It repeats the bitmap creation and stipple setting process for the three
other icons: xterm, wing_dogs, and xlogo64. The function terminates by
setting standard properties for the window.

The **load_drawings** function clears the window, fills the rectangles,
and calls the **XCopyPlane** function nine times. The first call follows.

```
XCopyPlane(thedisplay, pixmap[0], thewindow,
          thegc, 0, 0,
          sorceress_width,
          sorceress_height,
          0, 0, BITMAPDEPTH);
```

The function parameters are interpreted as follows: *thedisplay* specifies the connection to the server, *pixmap[0]* is the source drawable,
thewindow is the destination drawable, *thegc* is the graphics context, the
values 0, 0 specify the upper-left corner of the source rectangle relative
to the origin, *sorceress_width* and *sorceress_height* specify the width and
height of both the source and the destination rectangles, the values 0, 0
specify the upper-left corner of the destination rectangle relative to the
origin, and *BITMAPDEPTH* specifies the bitplane.

The other **XCopyPlane** function calls employ different source rectangles and copy them to different destination locations.

The complete listing for Example 10-6 follows.

```
/* example10_6 */
#include <X11/Xlib.h>
#include <X11/Xutil.h>

#define BITMAPDEPTH 1
#define NUM_ICONS 4
#define BORDER_WIDTH 2
#define FALSE 0
#define TRUE 1
```

```
#define sorceress_width 75
#define sorceress_height 75
static char sorceress_bits[] = {
  0xfc, 0x7e, 0x40, 0x20, 0x90, 0x00, 0x07, 0x80,
  0x23, 0x00, 0x00, 0xc6, 0xc1, 0x41, 0x98, 0xb8,
  0x01, 0x07, 0x66, 0x00, 0x15, 0x9f, 0x03, 0x47,
  0x8c, 0xc6, 0xdc, 0x7b, 0xcc, 0x00, 0xb0, 0x71,
  0x0e, 0x4d, 0x06, 0x66, 0x73, 0x8e, 0x8f, 0x01,
  0x18, 0xc4, 0x39, 0x4b, 0x02, 0x23, 0x0c, 0x04,
  0x1e, 0x03, 0x0c, 0x08, 0xc7, 0xef, 0x08, 0x30,
  0x06, 0x07, 0x1c, 0x02, 0x06, 0x30, 0x18, 0xae,
  0xc8, 0x98, 0x3f, 0x78, 0x20, 0x06, 0x02, 0x20,
  0x60, 0xa0, 0xc4, 0x1d, 0xc0, 0xff, 0x41, 0x04,
  0xfa, 0x63, 0x80, 0xa1, 0xa4, 0x3d, 0x00, 0x84,
  0xbf, 0x04, 0x0f, 0x06, 0xfc, 0xa1, 0x34, 0x6b,
  0x01, 0x1c, 0xc9, 0x05, 0x06, 0xc7, 0x06, 0xbe,
  0x11, 0x1e, 0x43, 0x30, 0x91, 0x05, 0xc3, 0x61,
  0x02, 0x30, 0x1b, 0x30, 0xcc, 0x20, 0x11, 0x00,
  0xc1, 0x3c, 0x03, 0x20, 0x0a, 0x00, 0xe8, 0x60,
  0x21, 0x00, 0x61, 0x1b, 0xc1, 0x63, 0x08, 0xf0,
  0xc6, 0xc7, 0x21, 0x03, 0xf8, 0x08, 0xe1, 0xcf,
  0x0a, 0xfc, 0x4d, 0x99, 0x43, 0x07, 0x3c, 0x0c,
  0xf1, 0x9f, 0x0b, 0xfc, 0x5b, 0x81, 0x47, 0x02,
  0x16, 0x04, 0x31, 0x1c, 0x0b, 0x1f, 0x17, 0x89,
  0x4d, 0x06, 0x1a, 0x04, 0x31, 0x38, 0x02, 0x07,
  0x56, 0x89, 0x49, 0x04, 0x0b, 0x04, 0xb1, 0x72,
  0x82, 0xa1, 0x54, 0x9a, 0x49, 0x04, 0x1d, 0x66,
  0x50, 0xe7, 0xc2, 0xf0, 0x54, 0x9a, 0x58, 0x04,
  0x0d, 0x62, 0xc1, 0x1f, 0x44, 0xfc, 0x51, 0x90,
  0x90, 0x04, 0x86, 0x63, 0xe0, 0x74, 0x04, 0xef,
  0x31, 0x1a, 0x91, 0x00, 0x02, 0xe2, 0xc1, 0xfd,
  0x84, 0xf9, 0x30, 0x0a, 0x91, 0x00, 0x82, 0xa9,
  0xc0, 0xb9, 0x84, 0xf9, 0x31, 0x16, 0x81, 0x00,
  0x42, 0xa9, 0xdb, 0x7f, 0x0c, 0xff, 0x1c, 0x16,
  0x11, 0x00, 0x02, 0x28, 0x0b, 0x07, 0x08, 0x60,
  0x1c, 0x02, 0x91, 0x00, 0x46, 0x29, 0x0e, 0x00,
  0x00, 0x00, 0x10, 0x16, 0x11, 0x02, 0x06, 0x29,
  0x04, 0x00, 0x00, 0x00, 0x10, 0x16, 0x91, 0x06,
  0xa6, 0x2a, 0x04, 0x00, 0x00, 0x00, 0x18, 0x24,
  0x91, 0x04, 0x86, 0x2a, 0x04, 0x00, 0x00, 0x00,
  0x18, 0x27, 0x93, 0x04, 0x96, 0x4a, 0x04, 0x00,
  0x00, 0x00, 0x04, 0x02, 0x91, 0x04, 0x86, 0x4a,
```

```
0x0c, 0x00, 0x00, 0x00, 0x1e, 0x23, 0x93, 0x04,
0x56, 0x88, 0x08, 0x00, 0x00, 0x00, 0x90, 0x21,
0x93, 0x04, 0x52, 0x0a, 0x09, 0x80, 0x01, 0x00,
0xd0, 0x21, 0x95, 0x04, 0x57, 0x0a, 0x0f, 0x80,
0x27, 0x00, 0xd8, 0x20, 0x9d, 0x04, 0x5d, 0x08,
0x1c, 0x80, 0x67, 0x00, 0xe4, 0x01, 0x85, 0x04,
0x79, 0x8a, 0x3f, 0x00, 0x00, 0x00, 0xf4, 0x11,
0x85, 0x06, 0x39, 0x08, 0x7d, 0x00, 0x00, 0x18,
0xb7, 0x10, 0x81, 0x03, 0x29, 0x12, 0xcb, 0x00,
0x7e, 0x30, 0x28, 0x00, 0x85, 0x03, 0x29, 0x10,
0xbe, 0x81, 0xff, 0x27, 0x0c, 0x10, 0x85, 0x03,
0x29, 0x32, 0xfa, 0xc1, 0xff, 0x27, 0x94, 0x11,
0x85, 0x03, 0x28, 0x20, 0x6c, 0xe1, 0xff, 0x07,
0x0c, 0x01, 0x85, 0x01, 0x28, 0x62, 0x5c, 0xe3,
0x8f, 0x03, 0x4e, 0x91, 0x80, 0x05, 0x39, 0x40,
0xf4, 0xc2, 0xff, 0x00, 0x9f, 0x91, 0x84, 0x05,
0x31, 0xc6, 0xe8, 0x07, 0x7f, 0x80, 0xcd, 0x00,
0xc4, 0x04, 0x31, 0x06, 0xc9, 0x0e, 0x00, 0xc0,
0x48, 0x88, 0xe0, 0x04, 0x79, 0x04, 0xdb, 0x12,
0x00, 0x30, 0x0c, 0xc8, 0xe4, 0x04, 0x6d, 0x06,
0xb6, 0x23, 0x00, 0x18, 0x1c, 0xc0, 0x84, 0x04,
0x25, 0x0c, 0xff, 0xc2, 0x00, 0x4e, 0x06, 0xb0,
0x80, 0x04, 0x3f, 0x8a, 0xb3, 0x83, 0xff, 0xc3,
0x03, 0x91, 0x84, 0x04, 0x2e, 0xd8, 0x0f, 0x3f,
0x00, 0x00, 0x5f, 0x83, 0x84, 0x04, 0x2a, 0x70,
0xfd, 0x7f, 0x00, 0x00, 0xc8, 0xc0, 0x84, 0x04,
0x4b, 0xe2, 0x2f, 0x01, 0x00, 0x08, 0x58, 0x60,
0x80, 0x04, 0x5b, 0x82, 0xff, 0x01, 0x00, 0x08,
0xd0, 0xa0, 0x84, 0x04, 0x72, 0x80, 0xe5, 0x00,
0x00, 0x08, 0xd2, 0x20, 0x44, 0x04, 0xca, 0x02,
0xff, 0x00, 0x00, 0x08, 0xde, 0xa0, 0x44, 0x04,
0x82, 0x02, 0x6d, 0x00, 0x00, 0x08, 0xf6, 0xb0,
0x40, 0x02, 0x82, 0x07, 0x3f, 0x00, 0x00, 0x08,
0x44, 0x58, 0x44, 0x02, 0x93, 0x3f, 0x1f, 0x00,
0x00, 0x30, 0x88, 0x4f, 0x44, 0x03, 0x83, 0x23,
0x3e, 0x00, 0x00, 0x00, 0x18, 0x60, 0xc0, 0x07,
0xe3, 0x00, 0x1e, 0x00, 0x00, 0x00, 0x70, 0x70,
0xe4, 0x07, 0xc7, 0x1b, 0xfe, 0x01, 0x00, 0x00,
0xe0, 0x3c, 0xe4, 0x07, 0xc7, 0xe3, 0xfe, 0x1f,
0x00, 0x00, 0xff, 0x1f, 0xfc, 0x07, 0xc7, 0x03,
0xf8, 0x33, 0x00, 0xc0, 0xf0, 0x07, 0xff, 0x07,
0x87, 0x02, 0xfc, 0x43, 0x00, 0x60, 0xf0, 0xff,
```

```
0xff, 0x07, 0x8f, 0x06, 0xbe, 0x87, 0x00, 0x30,
0xf8, 0xff, 0xff, 0x07, 0x8f, 0x14, 0x9c, 0x8f,
0x00, 0x00, 0xfc, 0xff, 0xff, 0x07, 0x9f, 0x8d,
0x8a, 0x0f, 0x00, 0x00, 0xfe, 0xff, 0xff, 0x07,
0xbf, 0x0b, 0x80, 0x1f, 0x00, 0x00, 0xff, 0xff,
0xff, 0x07, 0x7f, 0x3a, 0x80, 0x3f, 0x00, 0x80,
0xff, 0xff, 0xff, 0x07, 0xff, 0x20, 0xc0, 0x3f,
0x00, 0x80, 0xff, 0xff, 0xff, 0x07, 0xff, 0x01,
0xe0, 0x7f, 0x00, 0xc0, 0xff, 0xff, 0xff, 0x07,
0xff, 0x0f, 0xf8, 0xff, 0x40, 0xe0, 0xff, 0xff,
0xff, 0x07, 0xff, 0xff, 0xff, 0xff, 0x40, 0xf0,
0xff, 0xff, 0xff, 0x07, 0xff, 0xff, 0xff, 0xff,
0x41, 0xf0, 0xff, 0xff, 0xff, 0x07};

#define xterm_width 48
#define xterm_height 48
static char xterm_bits[] = {
0x00, 0x00, 0x00, 0x00, 0x00, 0x00, 0xc0, 0xff,
0xff, 0xff, 0xff, 0x00, 0x20, 0x00, 0x00, 0x00,
0x00, 0x03, 0x20, 0xfe, 0xff, 0xff, 0x1f, 0x05,
0x20, 0x01, 0x00, 0x00, 0x20, 0x09, 0xa0, 0x00,
0x00, 0x00, 0x40, 0x11, 0xa0, 0xfc, 0xff, 0x00,
0x40, 0x21, 0xa0, 0x00, 0x00, 0x00, 0x40, 0x21,
0xa0, 0xfc, 0x01, 0x00, 0x40, 0x21, 0xa0, 0x00,
0x00, 0x00, 0x40, 0x21, 0xa0, 0xfc, 0xff, 0x3f,
0x40, 0x21, 0xa0, 0x00, 0x00, 0x00, 0x40, 0x21,
0xa0, 0xfc, 0x03, 0x00, 0x40, 0x21, 0xa0, 0x00,
0x00, 0x00, 0x40, 0x21, 0xa0, 0xfc, 0xff, 0x01,
0x40, 0x21, 0xa0, 0x00, 0x00, 0x00, 0x40, 0x21,
0xa0, 0xfc, 0x00, 0x00, 0x40, 0x21, 0xa0, 0x00,
0x00, 0x00, 0x40, 0x21, 0xa0, 0x00, 0x00, 0x00,
0x40, 0x21, 0xa0, 0x00, 0x00, 0x00, 0x40, 0x21,
0xa0, 0x00, 0x00, 0x00, 0x40, 0x21, 0xa0, 0x00,
0x00, 0x00, 0x40, 0x21, 0xa0, 0x00, 0x00, 0x00,
0x40, 0x21, 0xa0, 0x00, 0x00, 0x00, 0x40, 0x21,
0xa0, 0x00, 0x00, 0x00, 0x40, 0x21, 0xa0, 0x00,
0x00, 0x00, 0x40, 0x11, 0xa0, 0x00, 0x00, 0x00,
0x40, 0x11, 0xa0, 0x00, 0x00, 0x00, 0x40, 0x09,
0xa0, 0x00, 0x00, 0x00, 0x40, 0x09, 0xa0, 0x00,
0x00, 0x00, 0x40, 0x05, 0x20, 0x01, 0x00, 0x00,
0x20, 0x05, 0x20, 0xfe, 0xff, 0xff, 0x1f, 0x03,
0x20, 0x00, 0x00, 0x00, 0x00, 0x03, 0xc0, 0xff,
```

```
    0xff, 0xff, 0xff, 0x00, 0x00, 0x00, 0x00, 0x00,
    0x00, 0x00, 0x00, 0x00, 0x00, 0x00, 0x00, 0x00,
    0xc0, 0xff, 0xff, 0xff, 0xff, 0x03, 0x20, 0x00,
    0x00, 0x00, 0x00, 0x03, 0xa0, 0xaa, 0xaa, 0xaa,
    0x2a, 0x03, 0x10, 0x00, 0x00, 0x00, 0x80, 0x02,
    0x50, 0x55, 0x55, 0x55, 0x95, 0x02, 0x08, 0x00,
    0x00, 0x00, 0x40, 0x02, 0xa8, 0xaa, 0xaa, 0xaa,
    0x4a, 0x02, 0x04, 0x00, 0x00, 0x00, 0x20, 0x01,
    0xb4, 0xff, 0xff, 0xff, 0xad, 0x00, 0x02, 0x00,
    0x00, 0x00, 0x50, 0x00, 0xfe, 0xff, 0xff, 0xff,
    0x3f, 0x00, 0x00, 0x00, 0x00, 0x00, 0x00, 0x00};

#define wingdogs_width 32
#define wingdogs_height 32
static char wingdogs_bits[] = {
    0x60, 0x00, 0x00, 0x00, 0xc0, 0x00, 0x00, 0x00,
    0x80, 0x03, 0x00, 0x00, 0x20, 0x0f, 0x00, 0x00,
    0x40, 0x3e, 0x00, 0x00, 0xc0, 0x7f, 0x00, 0x80,
    0x84, 0xff, 0x00, 0xc0, 0x86, 0xff, 0x00, 0xc0,
    0x07, 0xff, 0x21, 0xe0, 0x0f, 0xfe, 0x23, 0xf0,
    0x0f, 0xfe, 0x23, 0xfc, 0x1d, 0xfe, 0x13, 0xfe,
    0x39, 0xfc, 0x13, 0xff, 0x3f, 0xfc, 0x83, 0xff,
    0x9f, 0xfc, 0xc1, 0xff, 0x0f, 0xfe, 0xe0, 0xff,
    0xf3, 0xff, 0xff, 0xff, 0xf9, 0xff, 0xff, 0xff,
    0xfc, 0xff, 0xff, 0x7f, 0xf6, 0xff, 0xff, 0x1f,
    0xfb, 0xff, 0xff, 0x07, 0xf8, 0xfd, 0xff, 0x03,
    0xbc, 0xf9, 0xff, 0x01, 0x3c, 0xf9, 0xff, 0x01,
    0x3e, 0xf0, 0xf7, 0x00, 0x1f, 0xe0, 0x77, 0x00,
    0x1f, 0x80, 0x77, 0x00, 0x8f, 0x00, 0x6f, 0x00,
    0xc7, 0x00, 0x6e, 0x80, 0x07, 0x00, 0x7c, 0x80,
    0x0d, 0x00, 0xf8, 0x80, 0x1f, 0x00, 0xf0, 0x01};

#define xlogo64_width 64
#define xlogo64_height 64
static char xlogo64_bits[] = {
    0xff, 0xff, 0x00, 0x00, 0x00, 0x00, 0x00, 0xf8,
    0xfe, 0xff, 0x01, 0x00, 0x00, 0x00, 0x00, 0xf8,
    0xfc, 0xff, 0x03, 0x00, 0x00, 0x00, 0x00, 0x7c,
    0xf8, 0xff, 0x07, 0x00, 0x00, 0x00, 0x00, 0x3e,
    0xf8, 0xff, 0x07, 0x00, 0x00, 0x00, 0x00, 0x1f,
    0xf0, 0xff, 0x0f, 0x00, 0x00, 0x00, 0x80, 0x0f,
    0xe0, 0xff, 0x1f, 0x00, 0x00, 0x00, 0x80, 0x0f,
```

```
0xc0, 0xff, 0x3f, 0x00, 0x00, 0x00, 0xc0, 0x07,
0xc0, 0xff, 0x3f, 0x00, 0x00, 0x00, 0xe0, 0x03,
0x80, 0xff, 0x7f, 0x00, 0x00, 0x00, 0xf0, 0x01,
0x00, 0xff, 0xff, 0x00, 0x00, 0x00, 0xf8, 0x00,
0x00, 0xfe, 0xff, 0x01, 0x00, 0x00, 0xf8, 0x00,
0x00, 0xfe, 0xff, 0x01, 0x00, 0x00, 0x7c, 0x00,
0x00, 0xfc, 0xff, 0x03, 0x00, 0x00, 0x3e, 0x00,
0x00, 0xf8, 0xff, 0x07, 0x00, 0x00, 0x1f, 0x00,
0x00, 0xf0, 0xff, 0x0f, 0x00, 0x80, 0x0f, 0x00,
0x00, 0xf0, 0xff, 0x0f, 0x00, 0xc0, 0x07, 0x00,
0x00, 0xe0, 0xff, 0x1f, 0x00, 0xc0, 0x07, 0x00,
0x00, 0xc0, 0xff, 0x3f, 0x00, 0xe0, 0x03, 0x00,
0x00, 0x80, 0xff, 0x7f, 0x00, 0xf0, 0x01, 0x00,
0x00, 0x80, 0xff, 0x7f, 0x00, 0xf8, 0x00, 0x00,
0x00, 0x00, 0xff, 0xff, 0x00, 0x7c, 0x00, 0x00,
0x00, 0x00, 0xfe, 0xff, 0x01, 0x7c, 0x00, 0x00,
0x00, 0x00, 0xfc, 0xff, 0x03, 0x3e, 0x00, 0x00,
0x00, 0x00, 0xfc, 0xff, 0x03, 0x1f, 0x00, 0x00,
0x00, 0x00, 0xf8, 0xff, 0x87, 0x0f, 0x00, 0x00,
0x00, 0x00, 0xf0, 0xff, 0xcf, 0x07, 0x00, 0x00,
0x00, 0x00, 0xe0, 0xff, 0xcf, 0x07, 0x00, 0x00,
0x00, 0x00, 0xe0, 0xff, 0xe7, 0x03, 0x00, 0x00,
0x00, 0x00, 0xc0, 0xff, 0xf3, 0x01, 0x00, 0x00,
0x00, 0x00, 0x80, 0xff, 0xf9, 0x00, 0x00, 0x00,
0x00, 0x00, 0x00, 0xff, 0xfc, 0x00, 0x00, 0x00,
0x00, 0x00, 0x00, 0x7f, 0xfe, 0x00, 0x00, 0x00,
0x00, 0x00, 0x00, 0x7e, 0xfe, 0x01, 0x00, 0x00,
0x00, 0x00, 0x00, 0x3e, 0xff, 0x03, 0x00, 0x00,
0x00, 0x00, 0x00, 0x9f, 0xff, 0x07, 0x00, 0x00,
0x00, 0x00, 0x80, 0xcf, 0xff, 0x07, 0x00, 0x00,
0x00, 0x00, 0xc0, 0xe7, 0xff, 0x0f, 0x00, 0x00,
0x00, 0x00, 0xc0, 0xe7, 0xff, 0x1f, 0x00, 0x00,
0x00, 0x00, 0xe0, 0xc3, 0xff, 0x3f, 0x00, 0x00,
0x00, 0x00, 0xf0, 0xc1, 0xff, 0x3f, 0x00, 0x00,
0x00, 0x00, 0xf8, 0x80, 0xff, 0x7f, 0x00, 0x00,
0x00, 0x00, 0x7c, 0x00, 0xff, 0xff, 0x00, 0x00,
0x00, 0x00, 0x7c, 0x00, 0xfe, 0xff, 0x01, 0x00,
0x00, 0x00, 0x3e, 0x00, 0xfe, 0xff, 0x01, 0x00,
0x00, 0x00, 0x1f, 0x00, 0xfc, 0xff, 0x03, 0x00,
0x00, 0x80, 0x0f, 0x00, 0xf8, 0xff, 0x07, 0x00,
0x00, 0xc0, 0x07, 0x00, 0xf0, 0xff, 0x0f, 0x00,
0x00, 0xe0, 0x03, 0x00, 0xf0, 0xff, 0x0f, 0x00,
```

```
  0x00, 0xe0, 0x03, 0x00, 0xe0, 0xff, 0x1f, 0x00,
  0x00, 0xf0, 0x01, 0x00, 0xe0, 0xff, 0x3f, 0x00,
  0x00, 0xf8, 0x00, 0x00, 0x80, 0xff, 0x7f, 0x00,
  0x00, 0x7c, 0x00, 0x00, 0x80, 0xff, 0x7f, 0x00,
  0x00, 0x3e, 0x00, 0x00, 0x00, 0xff, 0xff, 0x00,
  0x00, 0x3e, 0x00, 0x00, 0x00, 0xfe, 0xff, 0x01,
  0x00, 0x1f, 0x00, 0x00, 0x00, 0xfc, 0xff, 0x03,
  0x80, 0x0f, 0x00, 0x00, 0x00, 0xfc, 0xff, 0x03,
  0xc0, 0x07, 0x00, 0x00, 0x00, 0xf8, 0xff, 0x07,
  0xe0, 0x03, 0x00, 0x00, 0x00, 0xf0, 0xff, 0x0f,
  0xe0, 0x03, 0x00, 0x00, 0x00, 0xe0, 0xff, 0x1f,
  0xf0, 0x01, 0x00, 0x00, 0x00, 0xe0, 0xff, 0x1f,
  0xf8, 0x00, 0x00, 0x00, 0x00, 0xc0, 0xff, 0x3f,
  0x7c, 0x00, 0x00, 0x00, 0x00, 0x80, 0xff, 0x7f,
  0x3e, 0x00, 0x00, 0x00, 0x00, 0x00, 0xff, 0xff};
Display        *thedisplay;
Window         thewindow;
int            thescreen;

Pixmap         pixmap[NUM_ICONS];
char           *w_name;
XRectangle rect[] = {
  {490, 450, 450, 400},
  {470, 430, 400, 380},
  {440, 410, 360, 340},
  {420, 400, 320, 310},
  {390, 370, 290, 250},
  {360, 350, 250, 100},
  {300, 320, 200, 200},
  {240, 230, 200, 180},
  {200, 170, 130, 130},
  {100, 120, 110, 100},
  {50, 50, 150, 150},
  {370, 360, 280, 280},
  {220, 280, 250, 150},
  {120, 180, 200, 100},
  {50, 150, 150, 50},
  {30, 100, 125, 25},
  {10, 50, 80, 10}
};
int            numrect;
unsigned long foreground;
```

```
unsigned long background;
XSizeHints      thehints;
GC              thegc;

void init();
void load_drawings();
void set_hints();
void create_window_set_properties();
void cleanup();

main(argc, argv)
int argc;
char *argv[];
{
XEvent theevent;
int done = FALSE;
int result;

  init(argv);

  set_hints();

  create_window_set_properties(argc,argv);

  XMapRaised(thedisplay, thewindow);

  XSelectInput(thedisplay, thewindow,
               ButtonPressMask | ExposureMask);
  while (!done)
  {
    XNextEvent(thedisplay, &theevent);

    switch(theevent.type)
    {
      case Expose:
        if (theevent.xexpose.count == 0)
        {
          load_drawings();
        }
        break;

      case ButtonPress:
```

```
            done = TRUE;
            cleanup();
            printf("\n Ready to exit ...\n");
         break;
      }
   } /* End while */
} /* End main */

void init(argv)
char *argv[];
{

  w_name = argv[0];
  thedisplay = XOpenDisplay("");
  thescreen = DefaultScreen(thedisplay);

  background = WhitePixel(thedisplay, thescreen);
  foreground = BlackPixel(thedisplay, thescreen);

  numrect = sizeof (rect) / sizeof (XRectangle);
}

void load_drawings()
{
  XClearWindow(thedisplay, thewindow);
  XFillRectangles(thedisplay, thewindow, thegc,
                  rect, numrect);
  XCopyPlane(thedisplay, pixmap[0], thewindow,
            thegc, 0, 0,
            sorceress_width,
            sorceress_height,
            0, 0, BITMAPDEPTH);
  XCopyPlane(thedisplay, pixmap[1], thewindow,
            thegc, 0, 0,
            xterm_width,
            xterm_heiqht,
            0,
            thehints.min_height/2-xterm_height/2,
            BITMAPDEPTH);
  XCopyPlane(thedisplay, pixmap[3], thewindow,
            thegc, 0, 0,
            xlogo64_width,
```

```
                    xlogo64_height,
                    0,
                    thehints.min_height-xlogo64_height,
                    BITMAPDEPTH);
      XCopyPlane(thedisplay, pixmap[2], thewindow,
                    thegc, 0, 0,
                    wingdogs_width,
                    wingdogs_height,
                    thehints.min_width/2-wingdogs_width/2,
                    0, BITMAPDEPTH);
      XCopyPlane(thedisplay, pixmap[3], thewindow,
                    thegc, 0, 0,
                    xlogo64_width,
                    xlogo64_height,
                    thehints.min_width-xlogo64_width,
                    0, BITMAPDEPTH);
      XCopyPlane(thedisplay, pixmap[2], thewindow,
                    thegc, 0, 0,
                    wingdogs_width,
                    wingdogs_height,
                    thehints.min_width/2-wingdogs_width/2,
                    thehints.min_height/2-wingdogs_height/2,
                    BITMAPDEPTH);
      XCopyPlane(thedisplay, pixmap[3], thewindow,
                    thegc, 0, 0,
                    xlogo64_width,
                    xlogo64_height,
                    thehints.min_width-xlogo64_width,
                    thehints.min_height-xlogo64_height,
                    BITMAPDEPTH);
      XCopyPlane(thedisplay, pixmap[1], thewindow,
                    thegc, 0, 0,
                    xterm_width,
                    xterm_height,
                    thehints.min_width-xterm_width,
                    thehints.min_height/2-xterm_height/2,
                    BITMAPDEPTH);
      XCopyPlane(thedisplay, pixmap[0], thewindow,
                    thegc, 0, 0,
                    sorceress_width,
                    sorceress_height,
                    thehints.min_width/2-sorceress_width/2,
```

```
                  thehints.min height-sorceress height,
                  BITMAPDEPTH);
}


void create_window_set_properties(argc, argv)
int argc;
char *argv[];
{
int index = 0;

  thewindow = XCreateSimpleWindow(thedisplay,
                                  DefaultRootWindow(thedisplay),
                                  thehints.x,
                                  thehints.y,
                                  thehints.width,
                                  thehints.height,
                                  BORDER_WIDTH,
                                  foreground, background);
  thegc = XCreateGC(thedisplay, thewindow, 0, 0);
  XSetSubwindowMode(thedisplay, thegc, IncludeInferiors);
  pixmap[index] = XCreateBitmapFromData(thedisplay,
                    RootWindow(thedisplay, thescreen),
                    sorceress_bits, sorceress_width,
                    sorceress_height);
  XSetStipple(thedisplay, thegc, pixmap[index]);
  index++;
  pixmap[index] = XCreateBitmapFromData(thedisplay,
                    RootWindow(thedisplay, thescreen),
                    xterm_bits, xterm_width,
                    xterm_height);
  XSetStipple(thedisplay, thegc, pixmap[index]);
  index++;
  pixmap[index] = XCreateBitmapFromData(thedisplay,
                    RootWindow(thedisplay, thescreen),
                    wingdogs_bits, wingdogs_width,
                        wingdogs_height);
  XSetStipple(thedisplay, thegc, pixmap[index]);
  index++;
  pixmap[index] = XCreateBitmapFromData(thedisplay,
                    RootWindow(thedisplay, thescreen),
                    xlogo64_bits, xlogo64_width,
                    xlogo64_height);
```

```
    XSetStipple(thedisplay, thegc, pixmap[index]);
    XSetStandardProperties(thedisplay, thewindow, w_name,
              w_name, None, argv, argc, &thehints);
}

void cleanup()
{
int index;

    for (index = 0; index < NUM_ICONS; index++)
    {
      XFreePixmap(thedisplay, pixmap[index]);
    }
    printf("\n Free pixmap  - done\n");

    XFreeGC(thedisplay, thegc);
    printf("\n Free gc  - done\n");

    XDestroyWindow(thedisplay, thewindow);
    printf("\n Destroy window  - done\n");

    XCloseDisplay(thedisplay);
    printf("\n Disconnect from server - done\n");
}

void set_hints()
{
int height;
int width;

    width = DisplayWidth(thedisplay, thescreen);
    height = DisplayHeight(thedisplay, thescreen);
    thehints.flags = PPosition | PSize | PMinSize;
    thehints.height = height/4;
    thehints.width = 500;
    thehints.x =  width/3;
    thehints.y =  height/3;
    thehints.min_height = 400;
    thehints.min_width = 500;
}
```

Selected output from this program is shown in Figure 10-6.

Drawing several bitmaps

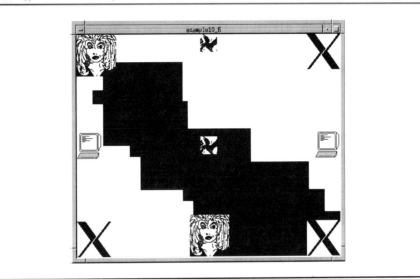

Key Points

Color

Color is more than a luxury for many applications. The appropriate use of color can convey meaning to the user, smoothing the user interface. Color workstations display all colors as a combination of three primary colors: red, green, and blue. The relative intensity of these colors is expressed in the XColor data structure. Every pixel on a given workstation display has a defined depth, usually 1 for monochrome workstations and often 8 for color workstations.

continues . . .

Visual Classes and Colormaps

The X Window system defines six visual classes—models for converting pixel values into displayed colors. The header file <X11/X.h> contains symbols representing these visual classes: PseudoColor, DirectColor, GrayScale, StaticColor, TrueColor, and StaticGray. Colormaps translate pixel values into onscreen colors. The relationship between the colormap and the associated pixel values depends on the visual class.

Color Processing Functions

Xlib provides several groups of color processing functions to help perform the following activities: determine the workstation's specific color capabilities, allocate shared color cells based on pixel values or standard color names, allocate private color cells and color planes, store colors in private color cells, query the colors you have already stored, free color cells no longer needed, create and apply private colormaps, and look up color names.

Graphics

The X Window system provides extensive graphics processing. The programmer has the choice of applying a wide range of Xlib functions or Xt Intrinsics and OSF/Motif widgets. These functions process information stored in the graphics context, one of the fundamental server resources. The graphics context contains extensive information describing graphics output. Color, graphics, and text functions reference the graphics context.

continues . . .

Key Points
(continued)

Graphics Processing Functions

Xlib provides several groups of graphics processing functions to help perform the following activities: set individual graphics context components; draw individual points, lines, circular or elliptical arcs; draw rectangles or polygons in a drawable; fill the drawings according to a specified rule; clear all or part of a window; and copy an area or a bit plane from one drawable to another.

Complete Fundamental Application and Advanced Features

*T*his concluding chapter has two segments. The first segment consists of a complete basic X Window program, integrating Xt Intrinsics, OSF/Motif, C language functions, and UNIX system calls to build a graphical user interface that provides the capabilities of the UNIX operating system to users unfamiliar with UNIX. The second segment presents advanced features of X Window systems. Space considerations have forced us to limit the scope of the programming example and to present these advanced features without applying them in functioning programs. Having reached this point in your X Window system experience, you are ready to address this material.

The Application

The C language function **main** creates and displays the Help menu button and several pulldown menus with their associated callbacks. We will step through two of these menus and their underlying functions to get an idea of how the program works.

The C language function **help_func** describes the program's available features and how to use them, as shown in Figure 11-1. For example, the explanation of the Date/Time function follows.

```
sprintf(h_m, "This program shows a basic implementation of
    UNIX/SHELL-GUI:\n\n\n%s\n%s\n%s\n%s\n%s\n%s\n%s\n%s",
...
    " * Date/Time - You can verify current date and time
                    (updated every minute),
                    to stop, click on Cancel",
...
);
```

Within the C language program **main** that actually drives the application, one call to the **make_menu** function refers to the General menu that creates pulldown menus, one of which is the Date/Time menu. Selecting this menu activates the **date_select** function, shown here:

```
sub_menu = make_menu("General", sub_menu_bar,
            "Date/Time", date_select, (caddr_t) & top_level,
            "Disk Usage", disk_select, (caddr_t) & top_level,
```

```
            "Print", print_select, (caddr_t) & top_level,
            "X Window dump", dump_select,
                            (caddr_t) & top_level,
            NULL);
```

The **date_select** function itself calls the **get_time** function, which uses the UNIX function **popen** (pipe open) to read the UNIX file bin/date, checking for valid file data. If this data is valid, the **get_time** function generates a message indicating the date and time, as shown in Figure 11-2. Then, depending on the button pushed, the function adds one of the two following callbacks:

```
XtAddCallback(time_dialog, XmNcancelCallback,
            time_cancel, (caddr_t) time_dialog);
XtAddCallback(time_dialog, XmNokCallback,
            time_ok, (caddr_t) time_dialog);
```

The **time_cancel** function aborts the time display. The **time_ok** function calls the following **XtAddTimeOut** function, which redisplays the current time at one-minute intervals until the Cancel button is pushed.

FIGURE 11-1   Help text

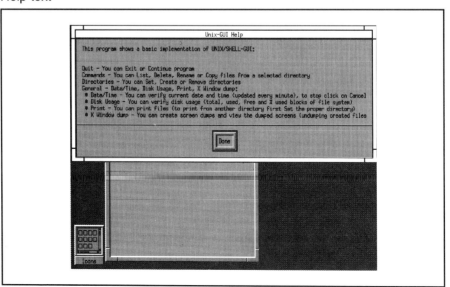

FIGURE 11-2   Date and time message

```
XtAddTimeOut(ONE_MINUTE, get_time, time_dialog);
```

A modified version of the **XtAddTimeOut** function could be added to the program to display any desired function continuously at a requested interval.

This program employs the C language function **scan** to process every directory access. For example, consider the C language function **print_select**, shown here, which prints selected text files. The Mode = SOURCES line selects only source (text) files. The *nums* variable determines the number of source files. If this number equals 0, the program generates a warning message. If there is no error, the program creates buffers for these files and invokes the appropriate print or cancel callback.

```
void print_select(w, client_data, call_data)
Widget w;
caddr_t client_data;
XmAnyCallbackStruct *call_data;
{
int index, nums;
Widget warning_dialog;
```

```
Mode = SOURCES;
nums = scan();
if (nums == 0)
{
  warning_dialog = create_warning(w, 10, 80,
                      "No files for printing");
  XtManageChild(warning_dialog);
}
else
{
  for (index = 0; index < nums; index++) {
    strings[index] =
            (XmString)XmStringCreateLtoR(files[index],
                          XmSTRING_DEFAULT_CHARSET);
  }
  print_dialog = create_selection(0, 0, "Print_Dialog",
                              nums, REGULAR);
  for (index = 0; index < nums; index++) {
    XmStringFree(strings[index]);
  }
  XtAddCallback(print_dialog, XmNcancelCallback,
              print_cancel, (caddr_t) print_dialog);
  XtAddCallback(print_dialog, XmNokCallback, print_ok,
              (caddr_t) print_dialog);
  XtManageChild(print_dialog);
  }
}
```

The C language function **print_ok**, shown next, validates the file to be printed. If the filename is valid, the file is redirected to the appropriate device and printed in the background.

```
void print_ok(w, client_data, call_data)
Widget w;
caddr_t client_data;
XmSelectionBoxCallbackStruct *call_data;
{
char buf[MAX_LEN];

  if (XmStringGetLtoR(call_data->value,
              XmSTRING_DEFAULT_CHARSET, &file_name)) {
    strcpy(buf, "pr ");
```

```
        strcat(buf, file_name);
        strcat(buf, " > /dev/lp0 &");
        system(buf);
/*
This program implements the print operation by redirecting
output to /dev/lp0 because it runs on a PC-based platform
and uses a parallel port. A computer using a serial port
for printing will replace lp0 with one of the tty ports
connected to the printer such as tty1.
*/
        XtFree(file_name);
    }
    else
        printf("Error in file selection \n");
    XtUnmanageChild(print_dialog);
}
```

Other program features include displaying disk usage, shown in
Figure 11-3, directory manipulation, shown in Figures 11-4 and 11-5,
and file manipulation, shown in Figure 11-6.

FIGURE 11-3 Disk usage message

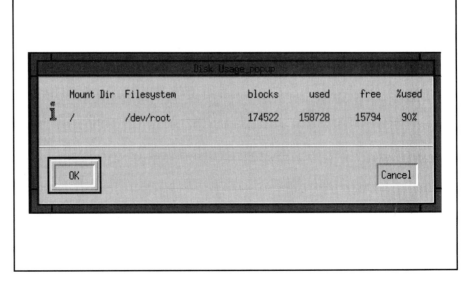

Setting directory command

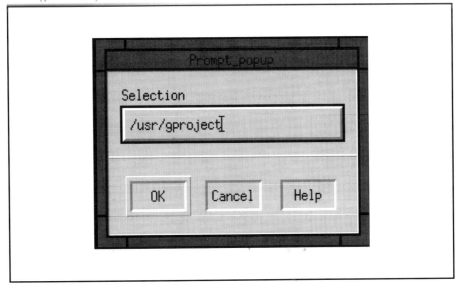

Absent directory message

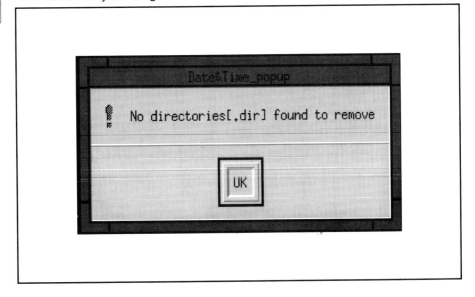

File "info"

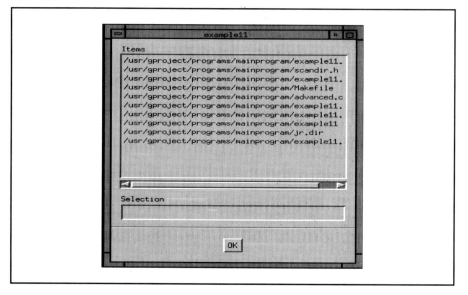

The complete program listing is shown here:

```c
#include <stdio.h>
#include <string.h>
/*
 The following stdarg.h library should be removed on
 BSD UNIX but not on SCO UNIX V
*/
#include <stdarg.h>
#include <sys/types.h>
#include <sys/stat.h>
#include <sys/fcntl.h>

#include <X11/Xlib.h>
#include <X11/Intrinsic.h>
#include <Xm/Xm.h>
#include <Xm/RowColumn.h>
#include <Xm/MainW.h>
#include <Xm/CascadeB.h>
#include <Xm/DrawingA.h>
#include <Xm/BulletinB.h>
```

```c
#include <Xm/FileSB.h>
#include <Xm/ScrollBar.h>
#include <Xm/PushB.h>
#include <Xm/ScrollBar.h>
#include <Xm/SelectioB.h>

#define DWIDTH 300
#define DHEIGHT 400
#define MAX_ELEMENTS 30
#define VISIBLES 2
#define FILES 0
#define DIRS 1
#define ALL 2
#define SOURCES 3
#define REGULAR 0
#define SPECIAL 1
#define FALSE 0
#define TRUE 1
#define ONE_MINUTE 60*1000
#define DIRSIZ 14
#define NAME_MAX 14
#define MAX_LEN 80
#define MAX_PATH_LEN 60
#define MAX_PAGES 200
#define NUM_LINES 2
#define DIR_NAME "."
#define DP_FILE "scrdmp.xwd"
#define DU_FILE "disk_usage"
#define DEF_DIR "def.dir"
#define FILTER "rid."
#define FILTER_1 "c."
#define FILTER_2 "h."

typedef struct {
  ino_t d_ino;
  char d_name[DIRSIZ];
} dirent_1;

typedef struct {
  long ino;
  char d_name[NAME_MAX + 1];
} dirent_2;
```

```
typedef struct {
  int fd;
  dirent_2 d;
} Dir;

/*
 The following two typedef declarations should be removed on
 BSD UNIX but not on SCO UNIX V
*/
typedef char *P_CHAR;

typedef void (*P_FUNC)();

static GC thegc;
XmString strings[MAX_ELEMENTS];
char *file_name = NULL;
char *file_info = NULL;
char *dir_name = NULL;
char *dir_info = NULL;
char *set_info = DIR_NAME;
static char *thename;
static Arg args[MAX_ELEMENTS];
static Cardinal n;
int Mode;
int dump_selected = FALSE;
static char *done_level = "Done";
static char *cancel_level = "Cancel";
char files[MAX_PAGES][MAX_PATH_LEN];
char directory[MAX_PATH_LEN];
char keepname[MAX_PATH_LEN];

Widget top_level, thewindow, menu_bar, sub_menu_bar;
Widget main_menu, sub_menu;
static Widget disk_dialog, time_dialog, info_dialog,
              print_dialog, info_sel_box;
static Widget delete_dialog, select_dialog,
              copy_dialog, rename_dialog;
Widget help_button;
Widget text_widget, text_widget_1;

void help_func();
Widget apply_help();
```

```
void date_select();
void disk_select();
void print_select();
void dump_select();
void dump_ok();
void quit_program();
void continue_program();
void disk_cancel();
void disk_ok();
void time_cancel();
void time_ok();
void get_time();
void print_cancel();
void print_ok();
void info_select();
void info_ok();
void info_cancel();
void delete_file();
void rename_file();
void set_dir();
void create_dir();
void remove_dir();
void create_dir_ok();
void set_dir_ok();
void select_cancel();
void select_ok();
void delete_cancel();
void delete_ok();
void copy_file();
void copy_cancel();
void copy_ok();
void copy_sel_ok();
void rename_cancel();
void rename_ok();
void rename_sel_ok();
Widget get_name();
void create_cascade();
/*
 The following make_menu function declaration should be
 removed on BSD UNIX but not on SCO UNIX V
*/
Widget make_menu();
```

```
Widget create_text();
Widget create_prompt();
Widget create_selection();
Widget create_warning();

int scan();
dirent_2 *read_dir();
Dir *open_dir();
void close_dir();
void mirror();


void main(argc, argv)
int argc;
char **argv;
{
int i;
int foreground, background;
/*
 The following widget declaration is necessary on BSD UNIX
 but not on SCO UNIX V Widget button;
*/
  top_level = XtInitialize(argv[0], "Xexample11", NULL, 0,
                           &argc, argv);

  thename = argv[0];
  n = 0;
  XtSetArg(args[n], XmNwidth, DWIDTH);
  n++;
  XtSetArg(args[n], XmNheight, DHEIGHT);
  n++;
  thewindow = XmCreateMainWindow(top_level, "Main", args, n);
  XtManageChild(thewindow);
  menu_bar = XmCreateMenuBar(thewindow, "menu_bar", NULL, 0);
  XtManageChild(menu_bar);
  sub_menu_bar = XmCreateMenuBar(thewindow, "sub_menu_bar",
                                 NULL, 0);
  XtManageChild(sub_menu_bar);
/*
 The following make_menu function should be
 removed on BSD UNIX but not on SCO UNIX V
*/
```

```
   main_menu = make_menu("Quit", menu_bar,
                "Exit?", quit_program, NULL,
                "Continue", continue_program, NULL,
                NULL);
/*
 The following lines are necessary on BSD UNIX
 but not on SCO UNIX V
  main_menu = XmCreatePulldownMenu(menu_bar, "Quit", NULL, 0);
  button = XmCreatePushButton(main_menu, "Exit?", NULL, 0);
  XtAddCallback(button, XmNactivateCallback,
                quit_program, NULL);
  XtManageChild(button);
  button = XmCreatePushButton(main_menu, "Continue", NULL, 0);
  XtAddCallback(button, XmNactivateCallback,
                continue_program, NULL);
  XtManageChild(button);
*/
  create_cascade(menu_bar, "Quit", main_menu);
/*
 The following make_menu function should be
 removed on BSD UNIX but not on SCO UNIX V
*/

  sub_menu = make_menu("Commands", menu_bar,
                "Info", info_select, (caddr_t) & top_level,
                "Delete", delete_file, (caddr_t) & top_level,
                "Rename", rename_file, (caddr_t)& top_level,
                "Copy", copy_file, (caddr_t) & top_level,
                NULL);
/*
 The following lines are necessary on BSD UNIX
 but not on SCO UNIX V
  sub_menu = XmCreatePulldownMenu(menu_bar, "Commands",
                                  NULL, 0);
  button = XmCreatePushButton(sub_menu, "Info", NULL, 0);
  XtAddCallback(button, XmNactivateCallback,
                info_select, (caddr_t *) top_level);
  XtManageChild(button);
  button = XmCreatePushButton(sub_menu, "Delete", NULL, 0);
  XtAddCallback(button, XmNactivateCallback,
                delete_file, (caddr_t *) top_level);
  XtManageChild(button);
```

```
        button = XmCreatePushButton(sub_menu, "Rename", NULL, 0);
        XtAddCallback(button, XmNactivateCallback,
                        rename_file, (caddr_t *) top_level);
        XtManageChild(button);
        button = XmCreatePushButton(sub_menu, "Copy", NULL, 0);
        XtAddCallback(button, XmNactivateCallback,
                        copy_file, (caddr_t *) top_level);
        XtManageChild(button);
*/
        create_cascade(menu_bar, "Commands", sub_menu);
/*
    BSD UNIX users should replace the following make_menu
    function by applying the previous modifications with the
    appropriate parameters
*/

        sub_menu = make_menu("Directories", menu_bar,
                    "Set", set_dir, (caddr_t) & top_level,
                    "Create", create_dir, (caddr_t) & top_level,
                    "Remove", remove_dir, (caddr_t) & top_level,
                    NULL);
        create_cascade(menu_bar, "Directories", sub_menu);

/*
    BSD UNIX users should replace the following make_menu
    function by applying the previous modifications with the
    appropriate parameters
*/
        sub_menu = make_menu("General", sub_menu_bar,
                    "Date/Time", date_select, (caddr_t) & top_level,
                    "Disk Usage", disk_select, (caddr_t) & top_level,
                    "Print", print_select, (caddr_t) & top_level,
                    "X Window dump", dump_select,
                                        (caddr_t) & top_level,
                    NULL);
        create_cascade(menu_bar, "General", sub_menu);
        n = 0;
        help_button = XmCreateCascadeButton(menu_bar, "Help",
                                                args, n);
        XtManageChild(help_button);
        XtAddCallback(help_button, XmNactivateCallback,
                    help_func, NULL);
```

```
   n=0;
   XtSetArg(args[n], XmNmenuHelpWidget, help_button);
   n++;
   XtSetValues(menu_bar, args, n);
   strcpy(keepname,DIR_NAME);
   XtRealizeWidget(top_level);
   XtMainLoop();
}
/*
 The following make_menu function should be removed on
 BSD UNIX but not on SCO UNIX V
*/

Widget make_menu(name, parent)
char *name;
Widget parent;
{
va_list argp;
Widget main_menu;
char *item;
Widget button;
P_FUNC item_action;
caddr_t action_args;

   main_menu = XmCreatePulldownMenu(parent, name, NULL, 0);
   va_start(argp, parent);
   while ((item = va_arg(argp, P_CHAR)) != NULL) {
     button = XmCreatePushButton(main_menu, item, NULL, 0);
     item_action = va_arg(argp, P_FUNC);
     action_args = va_arg(argp, caddr_t);
     XtAddCallback(button, XmNactivateCallback,
                   item_action, action_args);
     XtManageChild(button);
   }
   va_end(argp);
   return(main_menu);
}

void create_cascade(parent, label, menu)
Widget parent;
char *label;
Widget menu;
```

```
{
Widget cbutton;

  n = 0;
  XtSetArg(args[n], XmNsubMenuId, menu);
  n++;
  cbutton = XmCreateCascadeButton(parent, label, args, n);
  XtManageChild(cbutton);
}


void quit_program(w, client_data, call_data)
Widget w;
caddr_t client_data;
XmAnyCallbackStruct *call_data;
{
  exit(0);
}


void continue_program(w, client_data, call_data)
Widget w;
caddr_t client_data;
XmAnyCallbackStruct *call_data;
{
  printf("\n Continue called \n");
}


void help_func(w, client_data, call_data)
Widget w;
caddr_t client_data;
XmAnyCallbackStruct *call_data;
{
Widget help_box;

  help_box = apply_help(w);
  XtManageChild(help_box);
}


Widget apply_help(w)
Widget w;
{
Widget button;
Widget h_b;
```

```
char h_m[BUFSIZ];
XmString t_s = NULL;
XmString m_s = NULL;
XmString b_s = NULL;

   sprintf(h_m, "This program shows a basic implementation of
     UNIX/SHELL-GUI:\n\n\n%s\n%s\n%s\n%s\n%s\n%s\n%s\n%s",
     "Quit - You can Exit or Continue program",
     "Commands - You can List, Delete, Rename, or Copy files
                 from a selected directory",
     "Directories - You can Set, Create, or Remove directories",
     "General - Date/Time, Disk Usage, Print, X Window dump:",
     " * Date/Time - You can verify current date and time
                     (updated every minute),
                     to stop click on Cancel",
     " * Disk Usage - You can verify disk usage (total, used,
                      free and % used blocks of file system)",
     " * Print - You can print files (to print from another
                 directory, first Set the proper directory)",
     " * X Window dump - You can create screen dumps and view
           the dumped screens (undumping created files)");
   m_s = XmStringCreateLtoR(h_m, XmSTRING_DEFAULT_CHARSET);
   b_s = XmStringCreateLtoR("Done", XmSTRING_DEFAULT_CHARSET);
   t_s = XmStringCreateLtoR("Unix-GUI Help",
                            XmSTRING_DEFAULT_CHARSET);
   n=0;
   XtSetArg(args[n], XmNheight, 200);
   n++;
   XtSetArg(args[n], XmNwidth, 300);
   n++;
   XtSetArg(args[n], XmNdialogTitle, t_s);
   n++;
   XtSetArg(args[n], XmNokLabelString, b_s);
   n++;
   XtSetArg(args[n], XmNmessageString, m_s);
   n++;
   h_b = XmCreateMessageDialog(w, "h_b", args, n);
   button = XmMessageBoxGetChild(h_b, XmDIALOG_CANCEL_BUTTON);
   XtUnmanageChild(button);
   button = XmMessageBoxGetChild(h_b, XmDIALOG_HELP_BUTTON);
   XtUnmanageChild(button);
   if (t_s)
```

```
    XmStringFree(t_s);
  if (m_s)
    XmStringFree(m_s);
  if (b_s)
    XmStringFree(b_s);
  return h_b;
}

void date_select(w, client_data, call_data)
Widget w;
caddr_t client_data;
XmAnyCallbackStruct *call_data;
{
  get_time(w);
}

void get_time(w)
Widget w;
{
XmString d_t;
FILE * fp;
char buf[MAX_LEN];
Widget button;
Widget warning_dialog;

  if ((fp = popen("/bin/date", "r")) == NULL) {
    warning_dialog = create_warning(w, 10, 80,
                                    "Cannot open file date");
    XtManageChild(warning_dialog);
  }
  else
  {
    if (fgets(buf, MAX_LEN, fp) == NULL)
    {
      warning_dialog = create_warning(w, 10, 80,
                              "Cannot read from file date");
      XtManageChild(warning_dialog);
    }
    else
    {
      pclose(fp);
      d_t = (XmString)XmStringCreateLtoR(buf,
```

```
                                    XmSTRING_DEFAULT_CHARSET);
        n = 0;
        XtSetArg(args[n], XmNmessageString, d_t);
        n++;
        time_dialog = XmCreateInformationDialog(thewindow,
                                    "Date&Time", args, n);
        button = XmMessageBoxGetChild(time_dialog,
                            XmDIALOG_HELP_BUTTON);
        XtUnmanageChild(button);
        XmStringFree(d_t);
        XtAddCallback(time_dialog, XmNcancelCallback,
                    time_cancel, (caddr_t) time_dialog);
        XtAddCallback(time_dialog, XmNokCallback,
                    time_ok, (caddr_t) time_dialog);
        XtManageChild(time_dialog);
      }
    }
}


void time_ok(w, client_data, call_data)
Widget w;
caddr_t client_data;
XmSelectionBoxCallbackStruct *call_data;
{
  XtAddTimeOut(ONE_MINUTE, get_time, time_dialog);
}


void time_cancel(w, client_data, call_data)
Widget w;
caddr_t client_data;
XmSelectionBoxCallbackStruct *call_data;
{
  XtUnmanageChild(time_dialog);
}


void disk_select(w, client_data, call_data)
Widget w;
caddr_t client_data;
XmAnyCallbackStruct *call_data;
{
Widget t_widget;
```

```
text_widget = create_prompt(t_widget, 20, 160);
XTAddCallback(text_widget,
    XmNokCallback, disk_ok, (caddr_t) text_widget);
XtManageChild(text_widget);
}


void disk_ok(w, client_data, call_data)
Widget w;
caddr_t client_data;
XmSelectionBoxCallbackStruct *call_data;
{
Widget button, warning_dialog;
XmString d_s;
FILE * fp;
char message [BUFSIZ];
char     buf[NUM_LINES][MAX_LEN];
int      i;

if (XmStringGetLtoR(call_data->value , XmSTRING_DEFAULT_CHARSET,
&file_info))
{
   if (strcmp(file_info,"") == 0)
   {
     file_info = DU_FILE;
     print("No file selected: using default Disk Usage File
     %s\n", file_info);
   }
   else
   {
     printf("Disk Usage File: %s\n", file_info);
   }
}
if ((fp = fopen(file_info, "w")) == NULL) {
   warning_dialog = create_warning(w, 10, 80,
                   "Cannot open Disk Usage File for writing");
   XtUnmanageChild(text_widget);
   XtManageChild(warning_dialog);
} else
 {
       fclose(fp);
       /*The following line should be removed on BSD UNIX and
       replaced with strcpy (buf, "df"); */
```

```
        strcpy(buf, "df -v");
        strcat(buf, "  ");
        strcat(buf, file_info);
        printf("buf is %s\n",buf);
        system(buf);
        if ((fp = fopen(file_info, "r")) == NULL) {
                warning_dialog = create_warning(w, 10, 80,
                    "Cannot open Disk Usage File for reading");
                XtUnmanageChild(text_widget);
                XtManageChild(warning_dialog);
        } else
         {
                for (i = o;  i < NUM_LINES; i++) {
                        fgets(buf[i], MAX_LEN, fp);
                }
                fclose(fp);
                strcpy(message, buf[0]);
                strcat(message,"\n");
                strcat(message, buf[1]);
                d_s = (XmString)XmStringCreateLtoR(message,
                                XmSTRING_DEFAULT_CHARSET);
                n = 0;
                XtSetArg(args[n], XmNmessageString, d_s);
                n++;
                disk_dialog = XmCreateInformationDialog(thewindow,
                    "Disk Usage", args, n);
                button = XmMessageBoxGetChild(disk_dialog,
            XmDIALOG_HELP_BUTTON);
                XtUnmanageChild(button);
                XmStringFree(d_s);
                XtAddCallback(disk_dialog, XmNcancelCallback,
                disk_cancel,
                    (caddr_t) disk_dialog);
                XtUnmanageChild(text_widget);
                XtManageChild(disk_dialog);
         }
}

void disk_cancel(w, client_data, call_data)
Widget w;
caddr_t client_data;
XmSelectionBoxCallbackStruct *call_data;
{
```

```
    XtUnmanageChild(disk_dialog);
}

void print_select(w, client_data, call_data)
Widget w;
caddr_t client_data;
XmAnyCallbackStruct *call_data;
{
int index, nums;
Widget warning_dialog;

  Mode = SOURCES;
  nums = scan();
  if (nums == 0)
  {
    warning_dialog = create_warning(w, 10, 80,
                       "No files for printing");
    XtManageChild(warning_dialog);
  }
  else
  {
    for (index = 0; index < nums; index++) {
      strings[index] =
             (XmString)XmStringCreateLtoR(files[index],
                             XmSTRING_DEFAULT_CHARSET);
    }
    print_dialog = create_selection(0, 0, "Print_Dialog",
                                    nums, REGULAR);
    for (index = 0; index < nums; index++) {
      XmStringFree(strings[index]);
    }
    XtAddCallback(print_dialog, XmNcancelCallback,
                  print_cancel, (caddr_t) print_dialog);
    XtAddCallback(print_dialog, XmNokCallback, print_ok,
                  (caddr_t) print_dialog);
    XtManageChild(print_dialog);
  }
}

void print_ok(w, client_data, call_data)
Widget w;
caddr_t client_data;
```

```
XmSelectionBoxCallbackStruct *call_data;
{
char buf[MAX_LEN];

  if (XmStringGetLtoR(call_data->value,
                 XmSTRING_DEFAULT_CHARSET, &file_name)) {
    strcpy(buf, "pr ");
    strcat(buf, file_name);
    strcat(buf, " > /dev/lp0 &");
    system(buf);
/*
 This program implements the print operation by redirecting
 output to /dev/lp0 because it runs on a PC-based platform
 and uses a parallel port. A computer using a serial port
 for printing will replace lp0 with one of the tty ports
 connected to the printer, such as tty1.
*/
    XtFree(file_name);
  }
  else
    printf("Error in file selection \n");
  XtUnmanageChild(print_dialog);
}

void print_cancel(w, client_data, call_data)
Widget w;
caddr_t client_data;
XmSelectionBoxCallbackStruct *call_data;
{
  XtUnmanageChild(print_dialog);
}

void dump_select(w, client_data, call_data)
Widget w;
caddr_t client_data;
XmAnyCallbackStruct *call_data;
{
Widget t_widget, b_widget;

  text_widget = create_prompt(t_widget, 20, 160);
  XtAddCallback(text_widget, XmNokCallback, dump_ok,
                (caddr_t) text_widget);
```

```
    XtManageChild(text_widget);
}

void dump_ok(w, client_data, call_data)
Widget w;
caddr_t client_data;
XmSelectionBoxCallbackStruct *call_data;
{
char buf[MAX_LEN];

  if (XmStringGetLtoR(call_data->value,
                      XmSTRING_DEFAULT_CHARSET, &file_info))
  if (strcmp(file_info,"") == 0)
  {
    file_info = DP_FILE;
    printf("No file selected: using default file %s\n",
    file_info);
  }
  else
  {
    printf("Screen dump file: %s\n", file_info);
    }
  if (dump_selected == FALSE)
  {
    dump_selected = TRUE;
    strcpy(buf, "xwd -xy -out ");
    strcat(buf, file_info);
    system(buf);
    sleep(15);
    strcpy(buf, "xwud -in ");
    strcat(buf, file_info);
    system(buf);
    XtFree(file_info);
    dump_selected = FALSE;
  }
  XtUnmanageChild(text_widget);
}

void info_select(w, client_data, call_data)
Widget w;
caddr_t client_data;
```

```
XmAnyCallbackStruct *call_data;
{
Widget warning_dialog;
int index, nums;

  Mode = ALL;
  nums = scan();
  if (nums == 0)
  {
    warning_dialog = create_warning(w, 10, 80,
                          "No files found in directory");
    XtManageChild(warning_dialog);
  }
  else
  {
    for (index = 0; index < nums; index++) {
      strings[index] =
              (XmString)XmStringCreateLtoR(files[index],
                          XmSTRING_DEFAULT_CHARSET);
    }
    info_dialog = create_selection(0, 0, "Info_Dialog",
                          nums, SPECIAL);
    for (index = 0; index < nums; index++) {
      XmStringFree(strings[index]);
    }
    XtAddCallback(info_dialog, XmNcancelCallback, info_cancel,
                  (caddr_t) info_dialog);
    XtAddCallback(info_dialog, XmNokCallback, info_ok,
                  (caddr_t) info_dialog);
    XtManageChild(info_dialog);
  }
}


void info_ok(w, client_data, call_data)
Widget w;
caddr_t client_data;
XmSelectionBoxCallbackStruct *call_data;
{
  XtUnmanageChild(info_dialog);
}


void info_cancel(w, client_data, call_data)
```

```
Widget w;
caddr_t client_data;
XmSelectionBoxCallbackStruct *call_data;
{
  XtUnmanageChild(info_dialog);
}

void delete_file(w, client_data, call_data)
Widget w;
caddr_t client_data;
XmAnyCallbackStruct *call_data;
{
Widget warning_dialog;
int index, nums;

  Mode = FILES;
  nums = scan();
  if (nums == 0)
  {
    warning_dialog = create_warning(w, 10, 80,
                          "No file found to delete");
    XtManageChild(warning_dialog);
  }
  else
  {
    for (index = 0; index < nums; index++) {
      strings[index] =
              (XmString)XmStringCreateLtoR(files[index],
                          XmSTRING_DEFAULT_CHARSET);
    }
    delete_dialog = create_selection(0, 0, "Delete_Dialog",
                                    nums, REGULAR);
    for (index = 0; index < nums; index++) {
      XmStringFree(strings[index]);
    }
    XtAddCallback(delete_dialog, XmNcancelCallback,
                  delete_cancel, (caddr_t) delete_dialog);
    XtAddCallback(delete_dialog, XmNokCallback, delete_ok,
                  (caddr_t) delete_dialog);
    XtManageChild(delete_dialog);
  }
}
```

```
void delete_ok(w, client_data, call_data)
Widget w;
caddr_t client_data;
XmSelectionBoxCallbackStruct *call_data;
{
char buf[MAX_LEN];

  if (XmStringGetLtoR(call_data->value,
                       XmSTRING_DEFAULT_CHARSET, &file_name)) {
    strcpy(buf, "rm -f ");
    strcat(buf, file_name);
    system(buf);
    XtFree(file_name);
  }
  else
    printf("Error in file selection \n");
  XtUnmanageChild(delete_dialog);
}

void copy_file(w, client_data, call_data)
Widget w;
caddr_t client_data;
XmAnyCallbackStruct *call_data;
{
Widget warning_dialog;
int index, nums;

  Mode = FILES;
  nums = scan();
  if (nums == 0)
  {
    warning_dialog = create_warning(w, 10, 80,
                                    "No file found to copy");
    XtManageChild(warning_dialog);
  }
  else
  {
    for (index = 0; index < nums; index++) {
      strings[index]
              = (XmString)XmStringCreateLtoR(files[index],
                            XmSTRING_DEFAULT_CHARSET);
    }
```

```
        copy_dialog = create_selection(0, 0, "Copy_Dialog",
                                        nums, REGULAR);
        for (index = 0; index < nums; index++) {
          XmStringFree(strings[index]);
        }
        XtAddCallback(copy_dialog, XmNcancelCallback, copy_cancel,
                      (caddr_t) copy_dialog);
        XtAddCallback(copy_dialog, XmNokCallback, copy_ok,
                      (caddr_t) copy_dialog);
        XtManageChild(copy_dialog);
    }
}

void copy_ok(w, client_data, call_data)
Widget w;
caddr_t client_data;
XmSelectionBoxCallbackStruct *call_data;
{
Widget t_widget;

    if (XmStringGetLtoR(call_data->value,
                        XmSTRING_DEFAULT_CHARSET, &file_info)) {
      printf("file selected: %s \n", file_info);
    }
    else
      printf("Error in file selection \n");
    XtUnmanageChild(copy_dialog);
    text_widget = create_prompt(t_widget, 10, 80);
    XtAddCallback(text_widget, XmNokCallback, copy_sel_ok,
                  (caddr_t) text_widget);
    XtManageChild(text_widget);
}

void copy_sel_ok(w, client_data, call_data)
Widget w;
caddr_t client_data;
XmSelectionBoxCallbackStruct *call_data;
{
char buf[MAX_LEN];

    if (XmStringGetLtoR(call_data->value,
                        XmSTRING_DEFAULT_CHARSET, &file_name)) {
```

```
      strcpy(buf, "cp ");
      strcat(buf, file_info);
      strcat(buf, " ");
      strcat(buf, file_name);
      system(buf);
      XtFree(file_info);
      XtFree(file_name);
    }
    else
      printf("file not selected\n");
    XtUnmanageChild(text_widget);
}


void rename_file(w, client_data, call_data)
Widget w;
caddr_t client_data;
XmAnyCallbackStruct *call_data;
{
Widget warning_dialog;
int index, nums;

    Mode = ALL;
    nums = scan();
    if (nums == 0)
    {
      warning_dialog = create_warning(w, 10, 80,
                            "No file found to rename");
      XtManageChild(warning_dialog);
    }
    else
    {
      for (index = 0; index < nums; index++) {
        strings[index]
               = (XmString)XmStringCreateLtoR(files[index],
                                 XmSTRING_DEFAULT_CHARSET);
      }
      rename_dialog = create_selection(0, 0, "Rename_Dialog",
                                     nums, REGULAR);
      for (index = 0; index < nums; index++) {
        XmStringFree(strings[index]);
      }
      XtAddCallback(rename_dialog, XmNcancelCallback,
```

```
                            rename_cancel, (caddr_t) rename_dialog);
        XtAddCallback(rename_dialog, XmNokCallback, rename_ok,
                        (caddr_t) rename_dialog);
        XtManageChild(rename_dialog);
    }
}

void rename_ok(w, client_data, call_data)
Widget w;
caddr_t client_data;
XmSelectionBoxCallbackStruct *call_data;
{
Widget t_widget;

    if (XmStringGetLtoR(call_data->value,
        XmSTRING_DEFAULT_CHARSET, &file_info))
      printf("file selected: %s \n", file_info);
    else
      printf("Error in file selection \n");
    XtUnmanageChild(rename_dialog);
    text_widget_1 = create_prompt(t_widget, 10, 80);
    XtAddCallback(text_widget_1, XmNokCallback, rename_sel_ok,
                    (caddr_t) text_widget_1);
    XtManageChild(text_widget_1);
}

void rename_sel_ok(w, client_data, call_data)
Widget w;
caddr_t client_data;
XmSelectionBoxCallbackStruct *call_data;
{
char buf[MAX_LEN];

    file_name = XmTextGetString(text_widget_1);
    if (XmStringGetLtoR(call_data->value,
        XmSTRING_DEFAULT_CHARSET, &file_name)) {
      strcpy(buf, "mv ");
      strcat(buf, file_info);
      strcat(buf, " ");
      strcat(buf, file_name);
      system(buf);
      XtFree(file_info);
```

```
    XtFree(file name);
  }
  else
    printf("file not selected\n");
  XtUnmanageChild(text_widget_1);
}

void set_dir(w, client_data, call_data)
Widget w;
caddr_t client_data;
XmAnyCallbackStruct *call_data;
{
Widget t_widget;

  text_widget = create_prompt(t_widget, 20, 160);
  XtAddCallback(text_widget, XmNokCallback, set_dir_ok,
                (caddr_t) text_widget);
  XtManageChild(text_widget);
}

void set_dir_ok(w, client_data, call_data)
Widget w;
caddr_t client_data;
XmSelectionBoxCallbackStruct *call_data;
{
char buf[MAX_LEN];

  if (XmStringGetLtoR(call_data->value,
      XmSTRING_DEFAULT_CHARSET, &set_info)) {
    strcpy(keepname, set_info);
    XtFree(set_info);
  }
  else
    printf("Setting no directory\n");
  XtUnmanageChild(text_widget);
}

void create_dir(w, client_data, call_data)
Widget w;
caddr_t client_data;
XmAnyCallbackStruct *call_data;
{
```

```
Widget t_widget;

  text_widget = create_prompt(t_widget, 10, 80);
  XtAddCallback(text_widget, XmNokCallback, create_dir_ok,
                (caddr_t) text_widget);
  XtManageChild(text_widget);
}

void create_dir_ok(w, client_data, call_data)
Widget w;
caddr_t client_data;
XmSelectionBoxCallbackStruct *call_data;
{
char buf[MAX_LEN];
char *cks;
int result;

  if (XmStringGetLtoR(call_data->value,
      XmSTRING_DEFAULT_CHARSET, &dir_info))
{
  if (strcmp(dir_info,"") == 0)
  {
    dir_info = DEF_DIR;
    printf("No dir selected: using default dir %s\n",
    dir_info);
  }
  else
  {
    printf("Dir: %s", dir_info);
    strcpy(cks,dir_info);
    mirror(cks);
    result = strncmp(cks,FILTER,4);
    if (result |= 0)
      strcat(dir_info,".dir");
    strcpy(buf, "mkdir ");
    strcat(buf, dir_info);
    system(buf);
    XtFree(dir_info);
  }
  else
    printf("No dir selected\n");
  XtUnmanageChild(text_widget);
```

```
}

void remove_dir(w, client_data, call_data)
Widget w;
caddr_t client_data;
XmAnyCallbackStruct *call_data;
{
int index, nums;
Widget warning_dialog;

  Mode = DIRS;
  nums = scan();
  if (nums == 0)
  {
    warning_dialog = create_warning(w, 10, 80,
                      "No directories[.dir] found to remove");
    XtManageChild(warning_dialog);
  }
  else
  {
    for (index = 0; index < nums; index++) {
      strings[index]
             = (XmString)XmStringCreateLtoR(files[index],
                                 XmSTRING_DEFAULT_CHARSET);
    }
    select_dialog = create_selection(0, 0, "Select_Dialog",
                                      nums, REGULAR);
    for (index = 0; index < nums; index++) {
      XmStringFree(strings[index]);
    }
    XtAddCallback(select_dialog, XmNcancelCallback,
                  select_cancel, (caddr_t) select_dialog);
    XtAddCallback(select_dialog, XmNokCallback, select_ok,
                  (caddr_t) select_dialog);
    XtManageChild(select_dialog);
  }
}

void select_ok(w, client_data, call_data)
Widget w;
caddr_t client_data;
XmSelectionBoxCallbackStruct *call_data;
```

```
{
char buf[MAX_LEN];

   if (XmStringGetLtoR(call_data->value,
                       XmSTRING_DEFAULT_CHARSET, &dir_name)) {
     strcpy(buf, "rm-r");
     strcat(buf, dir_name);
     system(buf);
     XtFree(dir_name);
   }
   else
     printf("Error in dir selection \n");
   XtUnmanageChild(select_dialog);
}

void select_cancel(w, client_data, call_data)
Widget w;
caddr_t client_data;
XmSelectionBoxCallbackStruct *call_data;
{
   XtUnmanageChild(select_dialog);
}

void copy_cancel(w, client_data, call_data)
Widget w;
caddr_t client_data;
XmSelectionBoxCallbackStruct *call_data;
{
   XtUnmanageChild(copy_dialog);
}

void rename_cancel(w, client_data, call_data)
Widget w;
caddr_t client_data;
XmSelectionBoxCallbackStruct *call_data;
{
   XtUnmanageChild(rename_dialog);
}

void delete_cancel(w, client_data, call_data)
Widget w;
caddr_t client_data;
```

```
XmSelectionBoxCallbackStruct *call_data;
{
  XtUnmanageChild(delete_dialog);
}

Widget create_warning(w, t_x, t_y, message)
Widget w;
int t_x, t_y;
char *message;
{
Widget w_d, button;
XmString w_s;

  w_s = (XmString)XmStringCreateLtoR(message,
                       XmSTRING_DEFAULT_CHARSET);
  n = 0;
  XtSetArg(args[n], XmNmessageString, w_s);
  n++;
  w_d = XmCreateWarningDialog(w, "Warning", args, n);
  button = XmMessageBoxGetChild(w_d, XmDIALOG_HELP_BUTTON);
  XtUnmanageChild(button);
  button = XmMessageBoxGetChild(w_d, XmDIALOG_CANCEL_BUTTON);
  XtUnmanageChild(button);
  XmStringFree(w_s);
  return w_d;
}

Widget create_prompt(text_widget, t_x, t_y)
Widget text_widget;
int t_x, t_y;
{

  n=0;
  XtSetArg(args[n], XmNx, t_x);
  n++;
  XtSetArg(args[n], XmNy, t_y);
  text_widget = XmCreatePromptDialog(thewindow, "Prompt",
                                     args, n);
  return text_widget;
}

Widget create_selection(s_x, s_y, title, elements, mode)
```

```
int s_x, s_y;
char *title;
int elements;
int mode;
{
Widget d_widget;
Widget button;

  n = 0;
  XtSetArg(args[n], XmNdialogStyle, XmDIALOG_MODELESS);
  n++;
  XtSetArg(args[n], XmNwidth, DWIDTH);
  n++;
  XtSetArg(args[n], XmNheight, DHEIGHT);
  n++;
  XtSetArg(args[n], XmNx, s_x);
  n++;
  XtSetArg(args[n], XmNy, s_y);
  n++;
  XtSetArg(args[n], XmNlistVisibleItemCount, VISIBLES);
  n++;
  XtSetArg(args[n], XmNlistItems, strings);
  n++;
  XtSetArg(args[n], XmNlistItemCount, elements);
  n++;
  XtSetArg(args[n], XmNdialogType, XmDIALOG_SELECTION);
  n++;
  d_widget = XmCreateSelectionBox(thewindow, title, args, n);
  button = XmSelectionBoxGetChild(d_widget,
                                  XmDIALOG_APPLY_BUTTON);
  XtUnmanageChild(button);
  button = XmSelectionBoxGetChild(d_widget,
                                  XmDIALOG_HELP_BUTTON);
  XtUnmanageChild(button);
  if (mode == SPECIAL)
  {
    button = XmSelectionBoxGetChild(d_widget,
                                    XmDIALOG_CANCEL_BUTTON);
    XtUnmanageChild(button);
  }
  return d_widget;
}
```

```
int scan()
{
struct stat stbuf;
int n_f;

  n_f = 0;
  strcpy(directory,keepname);
  if (stat(directory,&stbuf) == -1)
    printf("\n can not access %s\n",directory);
  if ((stbuf.st_mode & S_IFMT) == S_IFDIR)
    n_f = scan_dir(directory);
  return n_f;
}

int scan_dir(dir)
char *dir;
{
char cs[MAX_PATH_LEN];
dirent 2 *dp;
Dir *dfd;
int result;
int result1, result2;
int num_files;

  num_files = 0;
  if ((dfd = open_dir(dir)) == NULL)
  {
    printf("dirscan: can't open %s",dir);
    return;
  }
  printf("\n dirscan activated and opened directory %s\n",
         dir);
  printf("\n      Scanning ...\n",dir);
  while ((dp = read_dir(dfd)) != NULL)
  {
    if ((strcmp(dp->d_name,".") == 0)
        ||
        (strcmp(dp->d_name,"..") == 0))
      continue;
    if (strlen(dir) + strlen(dp->d_name) + 2 >
        sizeof(directory))
      printf("\n dirscan: name %s/%s too long\n",
```

```
              dir,dp->d_name);
      else
      {
        if (Mode == ALL)
        {
          strcpy(files[num_files],dir);
          strcat(files[num_files],"/");
          strcat(files[num_files],dp->d_name);
          ++num_files;
        }
        else
        if ((Mode == SOURCES) || (Mode == DIRS))
        {
          strcpy(cs,dp->d_name);
          mirror(cs);
          if (Mode == DIRS)
            result = strncmp(cs,FILTER,4);
          else
          {
            result1 = strncmp(cs,FILTER_1,2);
            result2 = strncmp(cs,FILTER_2,2);
            result = (result1 && result2);
          }
          if (result == 0)
          {
            strcpy(files[num_files],dir);
            strcat(files[num_files],"/");
            strcat(files[num_files],dp->d_name);
            ++num_files;
          }
        }
        else
        if (Mode == FILES)
        {
          result = strncmp(cs,FILTER,4);
          if (result |= 0)
          {
            strcpy(files[num_files],dir);
            strcat(files[num_files],"/");
            strcat(files[num_files],dp->d_name);
            ++num_files;
          }
```

```
      }
    }
  }
  return num_files;
  close_dir(dfd);
}

void mirror(buf)
char *buf;
{
int c,i,j;

  for (i=0, j=strlen(buf) - 1; i<j; i++,j--)
  {
    c = buf[i];
    buf[i] = buf[j];
    buf[j] = c;
  }
}

dirent_2 *read_dir(dp)
Dir *dp;
{
dirent_1 dirbuf;
static dirent_2 d;
int ssize;

  ssize = sizeof(dirbuf);
  while (read(dp->fd,(char *)&dirbuf, ssize) == ssize)
  {
    if (dirbuf.d_ino == 0)
      continue;
    d.ino = dirbuf.d_ino;
    strncpy(d.d_name,dirbuf.d_name, DIRSIZ);
    d.d_name[DIRSIZ] = '\0';
    return &d;
  }
  return NULL;
}

Dir *open_dir(dirname)
char *dirname;
```

```
{
int fd;
struct stat stbuf;
Dir *dp;

  if ((((fd = open(dirname, O_RDONLY,0)) == -1)
       ||
       (fstat(fd,&stbuf) == -1)
       ||
       ((stbuf.st_mode & S_IFMT) != S_IFDIR)
       ||
       ((dp = (Dir *) malloc(sizeof(Dir))) == NULL))
     return NULL;
  dp->fd = fd;
  return dp;
}

void close_dir(dp)
Dir *dp;
{
  if (dp)
  {
    close(dp->fd);
    free(dp);
  }
}
```

 Note   OSF/Motif often provides a choice of functions to accomplish a given task. For example, the preceding program applies the **XmCreateSelectionBox** function and the C language **scan** function to display the directory contents. Another option is to use the **XmFileSelectionBox** function. The **XmCreateSelectionBox** function affords the programmer greater control over the display output at the cost of being more complicated to program. Mastery of X Window programming implies selecting the appropriate programming level and, in many cases, choosing the optimum toolkit function.

The following MAKE file was used to process this program using SCO Open Desktop:

```
RM = rm - f
CC = cc
```

```
CFLAGS = -O
INCLUDES = -I. -I/usr/include -I/usr/include/X11
LIBS = -lXm -lXt -lX11 -lsocket -lmalloc -lPW
.c.o:
$(RM) $@
$(CC) -c $(CFLAGS) $(INCLUDES) $*.c
all:: example11
example11: example11.o
$(RM) $@
$(CC) -o $@ $(CFLAGS) example11.o $(LIBS)
@echo makefile for example11
```

Advanced Features and Functions

Among the advanced features and functions of the X Window system that have not been discussed in this text because of space limitations are interclient communication, client/window manager communication, device-independent color processing, internationalized text processing, and error processing.

A key aspect of the X Window system is the ability of the server to display output from several applications on the same screen. This chapter introduces diverse mechanisms by which this communication takes place. A special type of interclient communication that occurs even when only a single application is active is client/window manager communication accomplished by special Xlib functions and associated data structures. Chapter 10, "Color and Graphics," examined in detail RGB color processing functions and data structures. While widely used, they have the default of being device dependent. As organizations augment their X Window hardware, they inevitably face the issue of developing color applications that are platform independent. This capability is briefly addressed here. Chapter 6, "Text," discussed general text processing. The present chapter introduces internationalized text processing, an X Window feature that is proving to be particularly useful in a world with ever-shrinking borders in which national particularities and ways of expression are far from disappearing. This chapter concludes with an examination of error processing, a subject, alas, that comes up all too often, whatever the level of the application being developed.

Interclient Communication

One of the key aspects of the X Window system is the ability of the server to display output from several applications on the same screen. It should seem natural that the server may be used to transfer messages and data from one application to another. This can be done in several ways. Before examining these methods let's review relevant terminology.

Recall from Chapter 6, "Text," that an *atom* is a unique 32-bit identifier that replaces a string name. Proper use of atoms reduces the volume of data transmitted between the server and the workstation. Atom names start with the characters XA_. Atoms are often associated with properties.

Properties

A *property* is a name, a type, a data format, or data associated with a window. A property is not interpreted by the X protocol, but is useful for data storage and interclient communication. Chapter 6, "Text," discussed predefined font properties such as the maximum suggested space to leave between words. Other server resources have predefined properties.

The **XGetWindowProperty** function obtains the type, format, and value of a named property for a designated window. The **XListProperties** function lists the properties associated with a designated window. The **XChangeProperty** function changes a property associated with a designated window. The **XRotateWindowProperties** function rotates a window's property list in a circular fashion. The **XDeleteProperty** function deletes a property on the designated window. The **XSetTextProperty** and **XGetTextProperty** functions are discussed later in the text.

The **XGetWindowProperty** function, shown here, obtains the type, format, and value of a named property for a designated window.

```
int XGetWindowProperty(display, w, property, long_offset,
            long_length, delete, req_type,
            actual_type_return, actual_format_return,
            nitems_return, bytes_after_return, prop_return)
    Display *display;           /* Specifies connection
                                    to server */
    Window w;                   /* Window whose property
                                    to be obtained */
```

```
Atom property;                /* Property name */
long long_offset;             /* Property offset
                                 measured in 32-bit units */
long long_length;                /* Data length
                                 measured in 32-bit units
Bool delete;                  /* If TRUE, deleted */
Atom req_type;                /* Atom identifier or
                                 AnyPropertyType */
Atom *actual_type_return;     /* Returns actual
                                 type of property */
int *actual_format_return; /* Returns actual
                                 format of property */
unsigned long *nitems_return; /* Returns actual number
                                    of items in prop_return */
unsigned long *bytes_after_return; /* Returns number of
                                       bytes to be read for
                                       a partial read */
unsigned char **prop_return; /* Returns property data */
```

See your system manual to determine how the return arguments are set, depending on the requested property type. **XGetWindowProperty** can generate BadAtom, BadValue, and BadWindow errors.

The **XListProperties** function, shown next, lists the properties associated with a designated window.

```
Atom *XListProperties(display, w, num_prop_return)
  Display *display;             /* Specifies connection
                                   to server */
  Window w;                     /* Window whose property
                                   list to be obtained */
  int *num_prop_return;         /* Returns number of properties
                                   in array */
```

XListProperties returns a pointer to an array containing the atom properties for the designated window or NULL if no properties were found. **XListProperties** can generate a BadWindow error.

The **XChangeProperty** function, shown next, changes a property associated with a designated window.

```
XChangeProperty(display, w, property, type, format, mode,
            data, nelements)
```

```
Display *display;          /* Specifies connection
                              to server */
Window w;                  /* Window whose property
                              to be changed */
Atom property, type;       /* Property name and type */
int format;                /* Property format
                              8-, 16-, or 32-bit units */
int mode;                  /* PropModeReplace,
                              PropModePrepend, or
                              PropModeAppend */
unsigned char *data;       /* Property data */
int nelements;             /* Number of elements of
                              specified data format */
```

XChangeProperty is responsible for the server generating a PropertyNotify event on the window whose property changed. The *mode* argument determines whether the changed property replaces the original property, or is placed before or after the original data.

Properties continue to exist even after the client storing them has ceased to be active. They terminate when explicitly deleted, when the supporting window is destroyed, or when the server resets. **XChangeProperty** can generate BadAlloc, BadAtom, BadMatch, BadValue, and BadWindow errors.

The **XRotateWindowProperties** function, shown next, rotates a window's property list in a circular fashion.

```
XRotateWindowProperties(display, w, properties,
                 num_prop, npositions)
  Display *display;          /* Specifies connection
                                to server */
  Window w;                  /* Window whose properties
                                to be rotated */
  Atom properties[];         /* Array of properties */
  int num_prop;              /* Length of properties array */
  int npositions;            /* Rotation amount */
```

XRotateWindowProperties is responsible for the server generating a PropertyNotify event on the window whose properties are rotated. **XRotateWindowProperties** can generate BadAtom, BadMatch, and BadWindow errors.

The **XDeleteProperty** function, shown next, deletes a property on the designated window.

```
XDeleteProperty(display, w, property)
    Display *display;            /* Specifies connection
                                    to server */
    Window w;                    /* Window whose property
                                    to be deleted */
    Atom property;               /* Property name */
```

XDeleteProperty deletes the designated property if it was defined on the specified window. It is responsible for the server generating a PropertyNotify event on the window if the property exists. **XDeleteProperty** can generate BadAtom and BadWindow errors.

The server generates PropertyNotify events in response to property changes on a designated window. The client solicits these events by setting the PropertyChangeMask bit in the window's *event_mask* attribute, as shown here in the XPropertyEvent data structure.

```
typedef struct {
    int type;                    /* PropertyNotify */
    unsigned long serial;        /* # of last request processed
                                    by the server */
    Bool send_event;             /* TRUE if event issued by a
                                    SendEvent request */
    Display *display;            /* Display the event read on */
    Window window;               /* Event window */
    Atom atom;                   /* Atom associated with
                                    changed property */
    Time time;                   /* Server time of
                                    property change */
    int state;                   /* PropertyNewValue or
                                    PropertyDelete */
} XPropertyEvent;
```

Processing Cut Buffers

X Window provides a simple mechanism for transferring data from one application to another. *Cut buffers* are eight properties defined on the root window named XA_CUT_BUFFER0 to XA_CUT_BUFFER7. Cut buffers may contain only text, but this text need not be ASCII or NULL-terminated. The following functions process cut buffers.

The **XStoreBytes** function, shown here, stores data in cut buffer 0.

```
XStoreBytes(display, bytes, nbytes)
    Display *display;           /* Specifies connection
                                   to server */
    char *bytes;                /* Bytes to be stored */
    int nbytes;                 /* Number of bytes
                                   to be stored */
```

XStoreBytes can generate a BadAlloc error.

The **XStoreBuffer** function, shown next, stores data in any designated cut buffer.

```
XStoreBuffer(display, bytes, nbytes, buffer)
    Display *display;           /* Specifies connection
                                   to server */
    char *bytes;                /* Bytes to be stored */
    int nbytes;                 /* Number of bytes
                                   to be stored */
    int buffer;                 /* Buffer to store data */
```

XStoreBuffer can generate a BadAlloc error.

The **XFetchBytes** function, shown next, returns data from cut buffer 0.

```
char *XFetchBytes(display, nbytes_return)
    Display *display;           /* Specifies connection
                                   to server */
    int *nbytes_return;         /* Returns number of
                                   stored bytes */
```

The **XFetchBuffer** function, shown next, returns data from any designated cut buffer.

```
char *XFetchBuffer(display, nbytes_return, buffer)
    Display *display;           /* Specifies connection
                                   to server */
    int *nbytes_return;         /* Returns number of
```

```
                                        stored bytes */
    int buffer;                 /* Buffer containing data */
```

The **XRotateBuffers** function, shown next, rotates the cut buffers.

```
XRotateBuffers(display, rotate)
    Display *display;           /* Specifies connection
                                   to server */
    int rotate;                 /* Amount to rotate buffers */
```

All eight cut buffers must be created prior to invoking this function. **XRotateBuffers** can generate a BadMatch error.

Selections

Selections provide a more flexible mechanism of transferring text between applications. In contrast to cut buffers, which contain text only, selections may contain data of any type. The data type can be changed when selection data is exchanged between applications. In addition, selections do not require that data be stored within the server.

The **XSetSelectionOwner** function sets the selection owner and the time. The **XGetSelectionOwner** function determines the selection owner. The **XConvertSelection** function requests conversion of the designated selection from one data type to another.

The **XSetSelectionOwner** function, shown here, sets the selection owner and the time.

```
XSetSelectionOwner(display, selection, owner, time)
    Display *display;           /* Specifies connection
                                   to server */
    Atom selection;             /* Selection atom */
    Window owner;               /* Owner of selection atom
                                   Window or None */
    Time time;                  /* Time of selection
                                   Time stamp or CurrentTime */
```

If the *owner* changes and the current owner is not None, the current owner is sent a SelectionClear event. If the connection to the current owner is cut or the owner window is destroyed, the selection owner becomes None, but the *time* parameter is unchanged.

XSetSelectionOwner can generate BadAtom and BadWindow errors.

The **XGetSelectionOwner** function, shown next, determines the selection owner.

```
XGetSelectionOwner(display, selection)
    Display *display;          /* Specifies connection
                                  to server */
    Atom selection;            /* Selection atom whose
                                  owner to be returned */
```

XGetSelectionOwner returns the window ID for the window that owns the designated selection. **XGetSelectionOwner** can generate a BadAtom error.

The **XConvertSelection** function, shown next, requests conversion of the designated selection from one data type to another.

```
XConvertSelection(display, selection, target, property,
                  requestor, time)
    Display *display;          /* Specifies connection
                                  to server */
    Atom selection, target;    /* Selection and target atoms */
    Atom property;             /* Property name or None */
    Window requestor;          /* Requester window */
    Time time;                 /* Time of selection
                                  Timestamp or CurrentTime */
```

The *selection* atom specifies the selection to be converted. The *target* atom specifies the desired data type. The *property* atom specifies the desired property name.

The server sends a SelectionRequest event to the selection owner, if there is any. Otherwise, the server sends a SelectionNotify event to the requestor with property None. **XConvertSelection** can generate BadAtom and BadWindow errors.

The server reports SelectionRequest events to the owner of a selection. It generates these events when a client calls the **XSelectionConversion** function.

SelectionRequest events inform the interested owner of a selection that a client has requested a selection conversion, changing the type of shared data, if possible. SelectionNotify events are generated by the server in response to a ConvertSelection protocol request when the selection has no owner. SelectionClear events occur when a client loses ownership of a selection.

The data structure associated with SelectionRequest events is shown here:

```
typedef struct {
    int type;                       /* SelectionRequest */
    unsigned long serial;           /* # of last request processed
                                        by the server */
    Bool send_event;                /* TRUE if event issued by a
                                        SendEvent request */
    Display *display;               /* Display the event read on */
    Window owner;                   /* Window specified in
                                        XSetSelectionOwner call */
    Window requester;               /* Window requesting selection */
    Atom selection;                 /* Names selection */
    Atom target;                    /* Designates desired
                                        selection type */
    Atom property;                  /* Property name or None */
    Time time;                      /* Time stamp or CurrentTime set
                                        by ConvertSelection request */
} XSelectionRequestEvent;
```

The selection owner should convert the selection according to the *target* specification and then send the requester a SelectionNotify event as described next.

A SelectionNotify event is generated by the server for **XConvertSelection** functions that access selections without owners. If the selection is owned, the owner should generate a SelectionNotify event with an **XSendEvent** function.

The data structure associated with SelectionNotify events is shown here:

```
typedef struct {
    int type;                       /* SelectionNotify */
    unsigned long serial;           /* # of last request processed
                                        by the server */
    Bool send_event;                /* TRUE if event issued by a
                                        SendEvent request */
```

```
    Display *display;          /* Display the event read on */
    Window requester;          /* Window requesting selection */
    Atom selection;            /* Names selection */
    Atom target;               /* Designates desired
                                  selection type */
    Atom property;             /* Atom or None */
    Time time;                 /* Timestamp or CurrentTime */
} XSelectionEvent;
```

If the **XConvertSelection** function specifies a *property* element of None, the selection owner should choose a property name, store the name with the requester window, and send a SelectionNotify event with that name.

SelectionClear events occur when a client loses ownership of a selection. The data structure associated with a SelectionClear event is shown here:

```
typedef struct {
    int type;                  /* SelectionClear */
    unsigned long serial;      /* # of last request processed
                                  by the server */
    Bool send_event;           /* TRUE if event issued by a
                                  SendEvent request */
    Display *display;          /* Display the event read on */
    Window window;             /* Window specified by current
                                  selection owner */
    Atom selection;            /* Names selection */
    Time time;                 /* Timestamp or CurrentTime */
} XSelectionClearEvent;
```

Sending Events

The **XSendEvent** function, shown here, is used to send an event to a designated window, for example, when processing selections.

```
Status XSendEvent(display, w, propagate,
                  event_mask, event_send)
    Display *display;          /* Specifies connection
                                  to server */
    Window w;                  /* Window to send event to
                                  or PointerWindow
                                  or InputFocus */
```

```
    Bool propagate;            /* If FALSE, event sent to all
                                  clients selecting
                                  destination */
    long event_mask;           /* Event mask */
    XEvent *event_send;        /* Event to be sent */
```

The function processes the *propagate* and *event_mask* arguments to ascertain those clients that receive the events. **XSendEvent** can generate BadValue and BadWindow errors.

The server generates ClientMessage events when the client invokes the **XSendEvent** function. The server makes no attempt to interpret the contents of the *window, message_type,* or *data* components of the data structure, which is shown here:

```
typedef struct {
   int type;                   /* ClientMessage */
   unsigned long serial;       /* # of last request processed
                                  by the server */
   Bool send_event;            /* TRUE if event issued by a
                                  SendEvent request */
   Display *display;           /* Display the event read on */
   Window window;              /* Event window */
   Atom message_type;          /* Indicates how data to
                                  be interpreted */
   int format;                 /* 8 for bytes, 16 for short,
                                  32 for long */
   union {
      char b[20];
      short s[10];
      long l[5];
         } data;
} XClientMessageEvent;
```

Client/Window Manager Communication

Chapter 4, "Windows and Windowing Techniques," introduced the window manager, the X Window application responsible for handling window real estate. This section examines some of the ways in which a client and the window manager may communicate with each other.

Top-Level Window Manipulation Functions

X Window provides several functions that manipulate top-level windows, which are children of the root window. These windows may be processed by the window manager.

The **XIconifyWindow** function, shown here, requests that a top-level window be *iconified*, or reduced in size to a small image or icon.

```
Status XIconifyWindow(display, w, screen_number)
    Display *display;              /* Specifies connection
                                      to server */
    Window w;                      /* Window to iconify */
    int screen_number;             /* Screen number
                                      on host server */
```

XIconifyWindow sends a WM_CHANGE_STATE ClientMessage event and a window *w* to the root window of the designated screen. The event mask is set to SubstructureNotifyMask or SubstructureRedirectMask.

The **XWithdrawWindow** function, shown next, requests that a top-level window be *withdrawn*—disappear entirely from the screen.

```
Status XWithdrawWindow(display, w, screen_number)
    Display *display;              /* Specifies connection
                                      to server */
    Window w;                      /* Window to withdraw */
    int screen_number;             /* Screen number
                                      on host server */
```

XWithdrawWindow unmaps the designated window and sends an UnmapNotify event to the root window of the designated screen. **XWithdrawWindow** can generate a BadWindow error.

The **XReconfigureWMWindow** function, shown next, requests that a top-level window be reconfigured.

```
Status XReconfigureWMWindow(display, w, screen_number,
                            value_mask, values)
    Display *display;              /* Specifies connection
                                      to server */
    Window w;                      /* Window to withdraw */
    int screen_number;             /* Screen number
```

```
                                       on host server */
  unsigned int value_mask;    /* Values to be set
                                  in values structure */
  XWindowChanges *values;     /* Data structure
                                  containing window changes */
```

XReconfigureWMWindow can generate BadValue and BadWindow errors.

Processing Text Properties

The beginning of this chapter described properties and their relevance to interclient communication. This section describes a particular type of property, text properties, and the functions that process them. A window may have four text properties: WM_NAME, the application name; WM_ICON_NAME, the icon name; WM_COMMAND, the command and arguments used to invoke the application; and WM_CLIENT_MACHINE, the string name of the machine running the client application.

The **XSetTextProperty** and **XGetTextProperty** functions set and retrieve any of these text properties. Other functions such as the **XSetWMName** process a single text property. For the sake of brevity, these functions are not described here. They may be found in your system manual.

The **XSetTextProperty** function, shown here, sets one of the four text properties.

```
void XSetTextProperty(display, w, text_prop, property)
  Display *display;           /* Specifies connection
                                 to server */
  Window w;                   /* Window whose
                                 property to set */
  XTextProperty *text_prop;   /* Text property
                                 data structure */
  Atom property;              /* Property name */
```

If the designated property does not exist, the **XSetTextProperty** function sets it. **XSetTextProperty** can generate BadAlloc, BadAtom, BadValue, and BadWindow errors.

The **XGetTextProperty** function, shown next, retrieves one of the four text properties.

```
void XGetTextProperty(display, w, text_prop_return, property)
  Display *display;          /* Specifies connection
                                to server */
  Window w;                  /* Window whose
                                property to set */
  XTextProperty *text_prop_return;
                             /* Returns text property
                                data structure */
  Atom property;             /* Property name */
```

XGetTextProperty can generate BadAtom and BadWindow errors.

The XTextProperty data structure, shown next, contains a text property's value and describes its encoding, type, and length.

```
typedef struct {
  unsigned char *value;      /* Specifies property data */
  Atom encoding;             /* Type of property */
  int format;                /* 8, 16, or 32 bits */
  unsigned long nitems;      /* Number of items */
  }XTextProperty;
```

Processing the WM_NORMAL_HINTS Property

The WM_NORMAL_HINTS property contains size hints to the window manager describing a window in the normal state. This information is included in the XSizeHints data structure, shown here.

```
/* Size hints mask bits */
#define USPosition          (1L<<0)
#define USSize              (1L<<1)
#define PPosition           (1L<<2)
#define PSize               (1L<<3)
#define PMinSize            (1L<<4)
#define PMaxSize            (1L<<5)
#define PResizeInc          (1L<<6)
#define PAspect             (1L<<7)
#define PBaseSize           (1L<<8)
```

```
#define PWinGravity            (1L<<9)
#define PAlltHints             (PPosition | Psize | PMinSize |
                                PMaxSize | PResizeInc | PAspect)
/* Values /*
typedef struct {
  long flags;                  /* Specifies defined fields */
  int x, y;                    /* Obsolete */
  int width, height;           /* Obsolete */
  int min_width, min_height;   /* Minimum useful window size */
  int max_width, max_height;   /* Maximum window size */
  int width_inc, height_inc;   /* Size increments */
  struct {
     int x;                    /* Numerator */
     int y;                    /* Denominator */
        }
  min_aspect, max_aspect;      /* Aspect ratios (x to y) */
  int base_width, base_height; /* Desired window size */
  int win_gravity;             /* Gravity */
} XSizeHints;
```

The two mask bits whose names begin with US are user specified. All other mask bits are program specified.

The **XAllocSizeHints** function, shown here, allocates an XSizeHints data structure.

```
XSizeHints *XAllocSizeHints()
```

The **XSetWMNormalHints** function, shown next, sets a window's WM_NORMAL_HINTS property.

```
Status XSetWMNormalHints(display, w, hints)
  Display *display;            /* Specifies connection
                                  to server */
  Window w;                    /* Window with hints */
  XSizeHints *hints;           /* Size hints */
```

XSetWMNormalHints can generate BadAlloc and BadWindow errors.

The **XGetWMNormalHints** function, shown next, reads a window's WM_NORMAL_HINTS property.

```
Status XGetWMNormalHints(display, w,
                         hints_return, supplied_return)
   Display *display;            /* Specifies connection
                                   to server */
   Window w;                    /* Window with hints */
   XSizeHints *hints_return;    /* Returns size hints */
   long *supplied_return;       /* Returns user-supplied hints */
```

XGetWMNormalHints can generate a BadWindow error.

The **XSetWMSizeHints** function, shown next, sets a specific atom in the window's WM_NORMAL_HINTS property.

```
Status XSetWMSizeHints(display, w, hints, property)
   Display *display;            /* Specifies connection
                                   to server */
   Window w;                    /* Window with hints */
   XSizeHints *hints;           /* Size hints */
   Atom property;               /* Property name */
```

XSetWMSizeHints can generate BadAlloc, BadAtom, and BadWindow errors.

The **XGetWMSizeHints** function, shown next, reads a specific atom in a window's WM_NORMAL_HINTS property.

```
Status XGetWMSizeHints(display, w, hints_return,
                       supplied_return, property)
   Display *display;            /* Specifies connection
                                   to server */
   Window w;                    /* Window with hints */
   XSizeHints *hints_return;    /* Returns size hints */
   long *supplied_return;       /* Returns user-supplied hints */
   Atom property;               /* Property name */
```

XGetWMSizeHints can generate BadAtom and BadWindow errors.

Processing the WM_HINTS Property

The WM_HINTS property contains nonsize hints about a window for the window manager. This information is included in the XWMHints data structure, shown here:

```
/* Window manager hints mask bits */
#define InputHint          (1L<<0)
#define StateHint          (1L<<1)
#define IconPixmapHint     (1L<<2)
#define IconWindowHint     (1L<<3)
#define IconPositionHint   (1L<<4)
#define IconMaskHint       (1L<<5)
#define WindowGroupHint    (1L<<6)
#define AlltHints          (InputHint | StateHint |
                           IconPixmapHint | IconWindowHint |
                           IconPositionHint | IconMaskHint |
                           WindowGroupHint)
/* Values */
typedef struct {
  long flags;                     /* Specifies defined fields */
  Bool input;                     /* If TRUE, application gets
                                     keyboard input from
                                     window manager */
  int initial_state;              /* WithdrawnState 0
                                     NormalState    1
                                     IconicState    3 */
  Pixmap icon_pixmap;             /* Pixmap used as icon */
  Window icon_window;             /* Window used as icon */
  int icon_x, icon_y;             /* Icon's initial position */
  Pixmap icon_mask;               /* Mask for icon pixmap */
  XID window_group;               /* ID of related window group */
                                  /* Data structure subject to
                                     future extension */
} XWMHints;
```

The **XAllocWMHints** function, shown here, allocates an XWMHints data structure.

```
XWMHints *XAllocWMHints()
```

The **XSetWMHints** function, shown next, sets a window's WM_HINTS property.

```
XSetWMHints(display, w, hints)
  Display *display;               /* Specifies connection
                                     to server */
```

```
Window w;                    /* Window with hints */
XSizeHints *hints;           /* Size hints */
```

XSetWMHints can generate BadAlloc and BadWindow errors.

The **XGetWMHints** function, shown next, reads a window's WM_HINTS property.

```
XWMHints *XGetWMHints(display, w)
  Display *display;          /* Specifies connection
                                to server */
  Window w;                  /* Window with hints */
```

The **XGetWMHints** function returns NULL if no WM_HINTS property was set for the designated window. Otherwise it returns a pointer to the XWMHints data structure. **XGetWMHints** can generate a BadWindow error.

Device-Independent Color Processing

Chapter 10, "Color and Graphics," described the RGB (red, green, and blue) color data structure and functions. These RGB colors are device dependent—such colors appear differently on different display units. The XcmsColorFormat data structure and the associated color processing functions are device independent.

The **XcmsAllocColor** function allocates a read-only color cell in arbitrary format corresponding to the closest available RGB value for the given hardware.

Device-Independent Color Data Structures

The XcmsColorFormat data structure, shown here, is used by functions that operate on all color space values. It contains a union of substructures that support color specification for a particular color space.

```
typedef unsigned long XcmsColorFormat;
                              /* Color Specification Format */
typedef struct{
  union{
      XcmsRGB RBG;
```

```
        XcmsRGBi RGBi;
        XcmsCIEXYZ CIEXYZ;
        XcmsCIEuvY CIEuvY;
        XcmsCIExyY CIExyY;
        XcmsCIELab CIELab;
        XcmsCIELuv CIELuv;
        XcmsTekHVC TekHVC;
        XcmsPad Pad;
    } spec;
        XcmsColorFormat format;
        unsigned long pixel;
} XcmsColor;                   /* Xcms Color Structure */
```

The XcmsRGB data structure, shown here, contains red, green, and blue values associated with the designated output device. These values range from 0 to FFFF hexadecimal or, equivalently, from 0 to 65535 decimal, and are interchangeable with the RGB values in an XColor data structure.

```
typodof otruct {
  unsigned short red;        /* 0x0000 to 0xffff */
  unsigned short green;      /* 0x0000 to 0xffff */
  unsigned short blue;       /* 0x0000 to 0xffff */
} XcmsRGB;                    /* RGB Device */
```

The XcmsRGB data structure, shown next, contains red, green, and blue linear intensity values ranging from 0.0 (absent) to 1.0 (full intensity).

```
typedef struct {
  XcmsFloat red;             /* 0.0 to 1.0 */
  XcmsFloat green;           /* 0.0 to 1.0 */
  XcmsFloat blue;            /* 0.0 to 1.0 */
} XcmsRGB;                    /* RGB Intensity */
```

See your systems manual for the other Xcms data structures.

Device-Independent Color Functions

The **XcmsAllocColor** function, shown here, allocates a read-only color cell in arbitrary format corresponding to the closest available RGB value for the given hardware.

```
Status XcmsAllocColor(display, colormap,
                      color_in_out, result_format)
    Display *display;          /* Specifies connection
                                  to server */
    Colormap colormap;         /* Color map */
    XcmsColor *color_in_out;   /* Returns values actually
                                  used in color map */
    XcmsColorFormat result_format;
                               /* Returns color format for the
                                  color specification */
```

XcmsAllocColor converts the designated color to an RGB value and then invokes the device-dependent **XAllocColor** function described in Chapter 10, "Color and Graphics." **XcmsAllocColor** can generate a BadColor error.

The following table summarizes the relationship between X color functions and Xcms color functions.

X Color and Xcms Color Functions

XAllocColor	**XcmsAllocColor**
3 parameters including	4 parameters including
1 return parameter	2 return parameters
XLookupColor	**XcmsLookupColor**
5 parameters including	6 parameters including
2 return parameters	3 return parameters
XAllocNamedColor	**XcmsAllocNamedColor**
5 parameters including	6 parameters including
2 return parameters	3 return parameters
XStoreColor	**XcmsStoreColor**
3 parameters	3 parameters
XStoreColors	**XcmsStoreColors**
4 parameters	5 parameters including
	1 return parameter
XQueryColor	**XcmsQueryColor**
3 parameters including	4 parameters including
1 return parameter	2 return parameters

X Color and Xcms Color Functions

XQueryColors

4 parameters including

1 return parameter

XcmsQueryColors

4 parameters including

2 return parameters

Internationalized Text Processing

Internationalized applications meet the needs of different languages, local customs, and character sets. Successful localization allows a program to run in different international environments without modifying the source code or recompiling the program. A *locale* defines the localized behavior of a program at execution. It includes encoding and processes input method text, encoding of resource values and files, encoding and imaging of text strings, and encoding and decoding for interclient text communication. This chapter introduces Xlib functions and associated data structures used in processing internationalized applications.

XCreateFontSet Function

The **XCreateFontSet** function, shown here, creates an international text-drawing font set.

```
XFontSet XCreateFontSet (display, base_font_name_list,
                        missing_charset_list_return,
                        missing_charset_count_return,
                        def_string_return)
  Display *display;                    /* Display structure */
  char *base_font_name_list;           /* Base font names */
  char **missing_charset_list_return;  /* Missing charsets */
  int *missing_charset_count_return;   /* Count of missing
                                          charsets */
  char **def_string_return;            /* Returns string
                                          drawn for
                                          missing charsets */
```

If the function cannot create the font set, it returns the value NULL, sets the parameter *missing_charset_list_return* to NULL, and sets the parameter *missing_charset_count_return* to 0. If fonts exist for all charsets required by the current locale, the function returns a valid XFontSet, sets the parameter *missing_charset_list_return* to NULL, and sets the parameter *missing_charset_count_return* to 0.

See your systems manual for additional information and functions related to internationalized font sets.

Drawing Functions

The following functions draw various types of text in the designated drawable. The **XmbDrawText** function draws text using multiple font sets. The **XwcDrawText** function draws wide-character text font sets. The **XmbDrawString** function draws text using a single font set. The **XwcDrawString** function draws wide-character text using a single font set. The **XmbDrawImageString** function draws the background and foreground bits of text characters using a single font set. The **XwcDrawImageString** function draws the background and foreground bits of wide-character text using a single font set.

The **XmbDrawText** function, shown here, draws text using multiple font sets in a designated drawable. This function corresponds to the **XDrawText** function discussed in Chapter 6, "Text."

```
void XmbDrawText(display, d, gc, x, y, items, nitems)
  Display *display;           /* Specifies connection
                                 to the server */
  Drawable d;                 /* Window or pixmap */
  GC gc;                      /* Graphics context */
  int x, y;                   /* Coordinates defining origin
                                 of first character relative
                                 to window or pixmap origin */
  XmbTextItem *items;         /* Array of text items */
  int nitems;                 /* Number of text items
                                 in above array */
```

XmbDrawText allows complex spacing and font set shifts between text strings. It accesses the XmbTextItem data structure defined here:

```
typedef struct {
  char *chars;                /* Specifies pointer to
```

```
                              string to draw */
  int nchars;                 /* Number of characters to draw */
  int delta;                  /* Gap between strings */
  XFontSet font_set;          /* Font to use for string
                                 If None, don't change */
} XmbTextItem;
```

The **XwcDrawText** function, shown next, draws wide-character text using multiple font sets in a designated drawable. This function corresponds to the **XDrawText16** function discussed in Chapter 6, "Text."

```
void XwcDrawText(display, d, gc, x, y, items, nitems)
  Display *display;           /* Specifies connection
                                 to the server */
  Drawable d;                 /* Window or pixmap */
  GC gc;                      /* Graphics context */
  int x, y;                   /* Coordinates defining origin
                                 of first character relative
                                 to window or pixmap origin */
  XwcTextItem *items;         /* Array of wide-character
                                 text items */
  int nitems;                 /* Number of text items
                                 in above array */
```

XwcDrawText allows complex spacing and font set shifts between wide-character text strings. It accesses the XwcTextItem data structure defined next:

```
typedef struct {
  wchar_t *chars;             /* Specifies pointer to
                                 wide string to draw */
  int nchars;                 /* Number of wide characters
                                 to draw */
  int delta;                  /* Gap between strings */
  XFontSet font_set;          /* Font to use for string
                                 If None don't change */
} XwcTextItem;
```

The **XmbDrawString** function, shown next, draws text using a single font set in a designated drawable. This function corresponds to the **XDrawString** function discussed in Chapter 6, "Text."

```
void XmbDrawString(display, d, font_set, gc, x, y,
                   string, num_bytes)
   Display *display;            /* Specifies connection
                                   to the server */
   Drawable d;                  /* Window or pixmap */
   XFontSet font_set;           /* Font set */
   GC gc;                       /* Graphics context */
   int x, y;                    /* Coordinates defining origin
                                   of first character relative
                                   to window or pixmap origin */
   char *string;                /* Character string to draw */
   int num_bytes;               /* Number of characters in the
                                   string to draw */
```

The **XwcDrawString** function draws wide-character text using a single font set in a designated drawable. In the interest of brevity, it is not shown.

The **XmbDrawImageString** function, shown next, draws the background and foreground bits of text characters using a single font set. This function corresponds to the **XDrawImageString** function discussed in Chapter 6, "Text."

```
XmbDrawImageString(display, d, font_set, gc, x, y,
                   string, num_bytes)
   Display *display;            /* Specifies connection
                                   to the server */
   Drawable d;                  /* Window or pixmap */
   XFontSet font_set;           /* Font set */
   GC gc;                       /* Graphics context */
   int x, y;                    /* Coordinates defining origin
                                   of first character relative
                                   to window or pixmap origin */
   char *string;                /* Character string to draw */
   int num_bytes;               /* Number of characters in the
                                   string to draw */
```

This function makes extensive use of the graphics context. Drawing both the foreground and the background bits tends to reduce flicker.

The **XwcDrawImageString** function draws both the foreground and background bits of wide-character text using a single font set in a designated drawable. In the interest of brevity, it is not shown.

Internationalizing the Keyboard

Chapter 7, "Keyboard," presented the **XLookupString** function, which converts the key pressed into a character string and supplies the string's length. The **XLookupString** function translates a key event to a keysym and a string. If the keysym has been rebound by the **XRebindKeysym** function, the bound string is stored in the buffer. If not, the keysym may be mapped to an ISO Latin-1 character or an ASCII control character, and is stored in the designated buffer.

The **XmbLookupString** function, shown here, gets internationalized byte text input from the keyboard. The **XwcLookupString** function gets internationalized wide-character text input from the keyboard. In the interest of brevity, it is not shown.

```
int XmbLookupString(ic, event, buffer_return, bytes_buffer,
              keysym_return, status_return)
  XIC ic;                      /* Specifies input context */
  XKeyPressedEvent *event;     /* Key event to be used */
  char *buffer_return;         /* Returns translated
                                  characters */
  int bytes_buffer;            /* Buffer length */
  KeySym *keysym_return;       /* Returns computer keysym
                                  if argument not NULL */
  Status *status_return;       /* Returns value indicating
                                  type of data returned */
```

XmbLookupString and the **XwcLookupString** react to KeyPress events. Their behavior is undefined for KeyRelease events.

An *input context* contains any data required by an input method and the information required to display the data. The **XCreateIC** function, shown next, creates an input context. See your system manual for more details on input contexts and the Xlib functions that process them.

```
XIC XCreateIC(im, ...)
  XIM im;                      /* Specifics input method */
  ...                          /* Variable length argument
                                  list to set XIC values */
```

XCreateIC can generate BadAtom, BadColor, BadPixmap, and BadWindow errors.

Error Processing

Given the complexity of programming for the X Window system, it should come as no suprise that this system provides several functions that aid debugging. Chapter 2, "Hello World," discussed the **XSynchronize** function, which allows the programmer to receive information about errors as they occur. The **XSetErrorHandler** function sets the user-specified or default error handler. The **XGetErrorText** function obtains the textual description associated with a given error code. The **XGetErrorDatabaseText** function obtains error messages from the error database. The **XDisplayName** function reports an error for an absent display unit. The **XSetIOErrorHandler** function processes fatal Input/Output errors. The error format and XErrorEvent data structure were described in Chapter 3, "Basic Concepts and Terminology."

The **XSynchronize** function, shown here, turns on or off synchronization, which reports errors as they occur.

```
int(*XSynchronize(display, onoff))()
  Display *display;          /* Specifies connection
                                to server */
  Bool onoff;                /* If TRUE, enable
                                synchronization */
```

The **XSetErrorHandler** function, shown next, sets the error handler.

```
*XSetErrorHandler(handler)
  int (*handler)(Display*, XErrorEvent*)
                             /* Specifies program's
                                supplied error handler */
```

Default error handlers generate an error message and terminate the program. This function enables applications to access custom error handlers that may invoke sophisticated error processing.

The **XGetErrorText** function, shown next, obtains the textual description associated with a given error code.

```
XGetErrorText(display, code, buffer_return, length)
  Display *display;          /* Specifies connection
```

```
                                     to server */
   int code;                /* Error code whose description
                               is required */
   char *buffer_return;     /* Returns error description */
   int length;              /* Buffer size */
```

XGetErrorText copies a NULL-terminated string describing the designated error code into the specified buffer.

The **XGetErrorDatabaseText** function, shown next, obtains error messages from the error database.

```
XGetErrorDatabaseText(display, name, message, default_string,
                  buffer_return, length)
   Display *display;        /* Specifies connection
                               to server */
   char *name;              /* Application name */
   char *message;           /* Error message type */
   char *default_string;    /* Default error message */
   char *butter_return;     /* Returns error description */
   int length;              /* Buffer size */
```

XGetErrorDatabaseText returns a NULL-terminated message from the error message database.

The **XDisplayName** function, shown next, reports an error for an absent display unit.

```
char *XDisplayName(string)
   char *string             /* Specifies display name */
```

XDisplayName returns the display unit name associated with the **XOpenDisplay** function. If you specify NULL, the function obtains the display unit name from the appropriate environment variable.

The **XSetIOErrorHandler** function, shown next, processes fatal Input/Output errors.

```
*XSetIOErrorHandler(handler)
   int(*handler)(Display*) /* Specifies program's
                              supplied error handler */
```

Key Points

Interclient Communication

The server may be used to transfer messages and data from one application to another. Interclient communication may involve atoms, unique 32-bit identifiers that replace a string name; properties, a name, a type, a data format, and data associated with a window; cut buffers, one of the eight properties containing text only defined on the root window; and selections, data of any type that may be passed from one application to another.

Events associated with interclient communication include PropertyNotify events generated by the server in response to property changes on the designated window, SelectionRequest events informing the interested owner of a selection that a client has requested a selection conversion, SelectionNotify events generated by the server in response to a ConvertSelection protocol request when the selection has no owner, and SelectionClear events that occur when a client loses ownership of a selection. A wide variety of Xlib functions accompany interclient communication.

Client/Window Manager Communication

Client/window manager communication is a special case of interclient communication. It may involve Xlib functions that manipulate top-level windows or process one of four text properties associated with the window manager. The WM_NORMAL_HINTS property contains size hints to the window manager describing a window in the normal state. The WM_HINTS property contains nonsize hints about a window to the window manager. Xlib functions process these properties.

continues . . .

Device-Independent Color Processing

RGB (red, green, and blue) colors described in Chapter 10, "Color and Graphics," are device dependent; such colors appear differently on different display units. The XcmsColorFormat data structure and the associated color-processing functions are device independent. The **Xcms-AllocColor** function allocates a read-only color cell in arbitrary format corresponding to the closest available RGB value for the given hardware.

Internationalized Text Processing

Internationalized applications meet the needs of different languages, local customs, and character sets. Successful localization allows a program to run in different international environments without modifying the source code or recompiling the program. Xlib functions create an internationalized text-drawing font set and draw this text using byte or wide-character internationalized text. Different functions use single and multiple font sets and draw both the foreground and background bits. Xlib functions get internationalized byte or wide-character text input from the keyboard, applying an input context.

Error Processing

The X Window system provides several functions that aid debugging. The **XSynchronize** function allows the programmer to receive information about errors as they occur. The **XSetErrorHandler** function sets the user-specified or default error handler. The **XGetErrorText** function obtains the textual description associated with a given error code. The **XGetErrorDatabaseText** function obtains error messages from the error database. The **XDisplayName** function reports an error for an absent display unit. The **XSetIOErrorHandler** function processes fatal Input/Output errors.

APPENDIX

Xlib

*T*he file <X11/Xlib.h> is the main header file for Xlib. Place this file at the top of your program to include the majority of the symbolic constants, data types, and data structure declarations required by Xlib. To conserve space, Xlib functions and data structures presented in the text are referenced by chapter number.

```
/*
 * Xlib.h - Header definition and support file for the C
 * subroutine interface library (Xlib) to the X Window System
 * Protocol (V11). Structures and symbols starting with "_"
 * are private to the library.
 */
#ifndef _XLIB_H_
#define _XLIB_H_

#ifdef SCO_SHLIB
#include "imports.h"    /* for sco shared libs S000 */
#endif

#ifdef USG
#ifndef __TYPES__
#include <sys/types.h>   /* forgot to protect it... */
#define __TYPES__
#endif /* __TYPES__ */
#else
#include <sys/types.h>
#endif /* USG */

#include <X11/X.h>

#ifndef NeedFunctionPrototypes
#if defined(FUNCPROTO) || defined(__STDC__) ||
 defined(__cplusplus) || defined(c_plusplus)
#define NeedFunctionPrototypes 1
#else
#define NeedFunctionPrototypes 0
#endif /* __STDC__ */
#endif /* NeedFunctionPrototypes */

#ifndef NeedWidePrototypes
#if defined(NARROWPROTO)
#define NeedWidePrototypes 0
```

```
#else
#define NeedWidePrototypes 1  /* default to make
                                  interrupt easier */
#endif
#endif

#ifdef __cplusplus   /* do not leave open across #includes */
extern "C" {       /* for C++ V2.0 */
#endif

#define Bool int
#define Status int
#define True  1
#define False 0

#define QueuedAlready        0
#define QueuedAfterReading 1
#define QueuedAfterFlush    2

#define ConnectionNumber(dpy)  ((dpy)->fd)
#define RootWindow(dpy, scr)  (((dpy)->screens[(scr)]).root)
#define DefaultScreen(dpy)  ((dpy)->default_screen)
#define DefaultRootWindow(dpy)
        (((dpy)->screens[(dpy)->default_screen]).root)
#define DefaultVisual(dpy, scr)
        (((dpy)->screens[(scr)]).root_visual)
#define DefaultGC(dpy, scr)
                 (((dpy)->screens[(scr)]).default_gc)
#define BlackPixel(dpy, scr)
                 (((dpy)->screens[(scr)]).black_pixel)
#define WhitePixel(dpy, scr)
                 (((dpy)->screens[(scr)]).white_pixel)
#define AllPlanes   (~0)
#define QLength(dpy)  ((dpy)->qlen)
#define DisplayWidth(dpy, scr)
                    (((dpy)->screens[(scr)]).width)
#define DisplayHeight(dpy, scr)
                    (((dpy)->screens[(scr)]).height)
#define DisplayWidthMM(dpy, scr)
                    (((dpy)->screens[(scr)]).mwidth)
#define DisplayHeightMM(dpy, scr)
                    (((dpy)->screens[(scr)]).mheight)
```

```
#define DisplayPlanes(dpy, scr)
                        (((dpy)->screens[(scr)]).root_depth)
#define DisplayCells(dpy, scr)
                        (DefaultVisual((dpy), (scr))->map_entries)
#define ScreenCount(dpy)   ((dpy)->nscreens)
#define ServerVendor(dpy)   ((dpy)->vendor)
#define ProtocolVersion(dpy)   ((dpy)->proto_major_version)
#define ProtocolRevision(dpy)   ((dpy)->proto_minor_version)
#define VendorRelease(dpy)   ((dpy)->release)
#define DisplayString(dpy)   ((dpy)->display_name)
#define DefaultDepth(dpy, scr)
                        (((dpy)->screens[(scr)]).root_depth)
#define DefaultColormap(dpy, scr)
                        (((dpy)->screens[(scr)]).cmap)
#define BitmapUnit(dpy)   ((dpy)->bitmap_unit)
#define BitmapBitOrder(dpy)   ((dpy)->bitmap_bit_order)
#define BitmapPad(dpy)   ((dpy)->bitmap_pad)
#define ImageByteOrder(dpy)   ((dpy)->byte_order)
#define NextRequest(dpy) ((dpy)->request + 1)
#define LastKnownRequestProcessed(dpy)
                                    ((dpy)->last_request_read)

/* macros for screen oriented applications (toolkit) */
#define ScreenOfDisplay(dpy, scr)(&((dpy)->screens[(scr)]))
#define DefaultScreenOfDisplay(dpy)
                (&((dpy)->screens[(dpy)->default_screen]))
#define DisplayOfScreen(s) ((s)->display)
#define RootWindowOfScreen(s) ((s)->root)
#define BlackPixelOfScreen(s) ((s)->black_pixel)
#define WhitePixelOfScreen(s) ((s)->white_pixel)
#define DefaultColormapOfScreen(s)((s)->cmap)
#define DefaultDepthOfScreen(s) ((s)->root_depth)
#define DefaultGCOfScreen(s) ((s)->default_gc)
#define DefaultVisualOfScreen(s)((s)->root_visual)
#define WidthOfScreen(s) ((s)->width)
#define HeightOfScreen(s) ((s)->height)
#define WidthMMOfScreen(s) ((s)->mwidth)
#define HeightMMOfScreen(s) ((s)->mheight)
#define PlanesOfScreen(s) ((s)->root_depth)
#define CellsOfScreen(s)
                (DefaultVisualOfScreen((s))->map_entries)
#define MinCmapsOfScreen(s) ((s)->min_maps)
```

```
#define MaxCmapsOfScreen(s) ((s)->max_maps)
#define DoesSaveUnders(s) ((s)->save_unders)
#define DoesBackingStore(s) ((s)->backing_store)
#define EventMaskOfScreen(s) ((s)->root_input_mask)

/*
 * Extensions need a way to hang private data on
 * some structures.
 */
typedef struct _XExtData {
 int number;  /* number returned by XRegisterExtension */
 struct _XExtData *next; /* next item on list of data
                            for structure */
 int (*free_private)(); /* called to free private storage */
 char *private_data; /* data private to this extension. */
} XExtData;

/*
 * This file contains structures used by the
 * extension mechanism.
 */
typedef struct { /* public to extension, cannot be changed */
 int extension;    /* extension number */
 int major_opcode; /* major op-code assigned by server */
 int first_event;  /* first event number for the extension */
 int first_error;  /* first error number for the extension */
} XExtCodes;

/*
 * This structure is private to the library.
 */
typedef struct _XExten { /* private to extension mechanism */
 struct _XExten *next;   /* next in list */
 XExtCodes codes;        /* public information,
                            all extension told */
 int (*create_GC)();     /* routine to call when GC created */
 int (*copy_GC)();       /* routine to call when GC copied */
 int (*flush_GC)();      /* routine to call when GC flushed */
 int (*free_GC)();       /* routine to call when GC freed */
 int (*create_Font)();   /* routine to call when
                            Font created */
 int (*free_Font)();     /* routine to call when Font freed */
```

```
    int (*close_display)(); /* routine to call when
                                connection closed */
    int (*error)();         /* who to call when an
                                error occurs */
    char *(*error_string)(); /* routine to supply error string */
    char *name;             /* name of this extension */
} _XExtension;

/*
 * Data structure for retrieving info about pixmap formats.
 */

typedef struct {
    int depth;
    int bits_per_pixel;
    int scanline_pad;
} XPixmapFormatValues;


/*
 * Data structure for setting graphics context.
 */
typedef struct {

/* see Chapter 10, "Color and Graphics" */

} XGCValues;

/*
 * Graphics context. All Xlib routines deal in this rather
 * than in raw protocol GContext IDs. This is so that the
 * library can keep a "shadow" set of values, and thus avoid
 * passing values over the wire that are not in
 * fact changing.
 */

typedef struct _XGC {
    XExtData *ext_data; /* hook for extension to hang data */
    GContext gid;       /* protocol ID for graphics context */
    Bool rects;         /* Boolean: TRUE if clipmask is list
                           of rectangles */
    Bool dashes;        /* Boolean: TRUE if dash-list is
```

```
                                really a list */
    unsigned long dirty; /* cache dirty bits */
    XGCValues values;     /* shadow structure of values */
} *GC;



/*
 * Visual structure; contains information about
 * colormapping possible.
 */
typedef struct {
 XextData *ext_data; /* hook for extension to hang data */
 VisualID visualid; /* visual ID of this visual */
#if defined(__cplusplus) || defined(c_plusplus)
 int c_class;   /* C++ class of screen (monochrome, etc.) */
#else
 int class;   /* class of screen (monochrome, etc.) */
#endif
 unsigned long red_mask, green_mask, blue_mask;
                      /* mask values */
 int bits_per_rgb;   /* log base 2 of distinct color values */
 int map_entries;    /* color map entries */
} Visual;


/*
 * Depth structure; contains information for each
 * possible depth.
 */
typedef struct {
 int depth;       /* this depth (Z) of the depth */
 int nvisuals;    /* number of Visual types at this depth */
 Visual *visuals; /* list of visuals possible at this depth */
} Depth;


/*
 * Information about the screen.
 */
typedef struct {
 XExtData *ext_data;  /* hook for extension to hang data */
 struct _XDisplay *display; /* back pointer to
                                display structure */
 Window root;                /* Root window ID */
```

```
    int width, height;          /* width and height of screen */
    int mwidth, mheight;        /* width and height
                                   in millimeters */

    int ndepths;                /* number of depths possible */
    Depth *depths;              /* list of allowable depths on
                                   the screen */

    int root_depth;             /* bits per pixel */
    Visual *root_visual;        /* root visual */
    GC default_gc;              /* GC for the root visual */
    Colormap cmap;              /* default color map */
    unsigned long white_pixel;
    unsigned long black_pixel;  /* White and Black pixel values */
    int max_maps, min_maps;     /* max and min color maps */
    int backing_store;          /* Never, WhenMapped, Always */
    Bool save_unders;
    long root_input_mask;       /* initial root input mask */
} Screen;

/*
 * Format structure; describes ZFormat data the
 * screen will understand.
 */
typedef struct {
 XExtData *ext_data; /* hook for extension to hang data */
 int depth;             /* depth of this image format */
 int bits_per_pixel; /* bits/pixel at this depth */
 int scanline_pad;    /* scanline must be padded to
                          this multiple */
} ScreenFormat;

#if NeedFunctionPrototypes /* prototypes require
                              event type definitions */
#undef _XSTRUCT_
#endif
#ifndef _XSTRUCT_           /* hack to reduce symbol load
                              in Xlib routines */
/*
 * Data structure for setting window attributes.
 */
typedef struct {

/* see Chapter 4, "Windows and Windowing Techniques" */
```

```
    } XSetWindowAttributes;

    typedef struct {
        int x, y;               /* location of window */
        int width, height;      /* width and height of window */
        int border_width;       /* border width of window */
        int depth;              /* depth of window */
        Visual *visual;         /* the associated visual structure */
        Window root;            /* root of screen containing window */
#if defined(__cplusplus) || defined(c_plusplus)
        int c_class;            /* C++ InputOutput, InputOnly*/
#else
        int class;              /* InputOutput, InputOnly*/
#endif
        int bit_gravity;        /* one of the bit gravity values */
        int win_gravity;        /* one of the window gravity values */
        int backing_store;      /* NotUseful, WhenMapped, Always */
        unsigned long backing_planes; /* planes to be preserved
                                        if possible */
        unsigned long backing_pixel;  /* value to be used when
                                        restoring planes */
        Bool save_under;                /* Boolean, should bits
                                        under be saved? */
        Colormap colormap;              /* colormap to be
                                        associated with window */
        Bool map_installed;             /* Boolean, is colormap
                                        currently installed*/
        int map_state;  /* IsUnmapped, IsUnviewable, IsViewable */
        long all_event_masks;           /* set of events all people
                                        have interest in*/
        long your_event_mask;   /* my event mask */
        long do_not_propagate_mask;     /* set of events that
                                        should not propagate */
        Bool override_redirect;         /* Boolean value for
                                        override-redirect */
        Screen *screen;  /* back pointer to correct screen */
    } XWindowAttributes;

    /*
     * Data structure for host setting; getting routines.
```

```
 *
 */

typedef struct {
 int family;       /* for example AF_DNET */
 int length;       /* length of address, in bytes */
 char *address;    /* pointer to where to find the bytes */
} XHostAddress;

/*
 * Data structure for "image" data, used by image
 * manipulation routines.
 */
typedef struct _XImage {
    int width, height;  /* size of image */
    int xoffset;   /* number of pixels offset in X direction */
    int format;          /* XYBitmap, XYPixmap, ZPixmap */
    char *data;          /* pointer to image data */
    int byte_order;  /* data byte order, LSBFirst, MSBFirst */
    int bitmap_unit;     /* quant. of scanline 8, 16, 32 */
    int bitmap_bit_order; /* LSBFirst, MSBFirst */
    int bitmap_pad;      /* 8, 16, 32 either XY or ZPixmap */
    int depth;           /* depth of image */
    int bytes_per_line;  /* accelerator to next line */
    int bits_per_pixel;  /* bits per pixel (ZPixmap) */
    unsigned long red_mask; /* bits in z arrangement */
    unsigned long green_mask;
    unsigned long blue_mask;
    char *obdata;          /* hook for the object routines
                             to hang on */
    struct funcs {  /* image manipulation routines */
 struct _XImage *(*create_image)();
#if NeedFunctionPrototypes
 int (*destroy_image)          (struct _XImage *);
 unsigned long (*get_pixel)  (struct _XImage *, int, int);
 int (*put_pixel)             (struct _XImage *, int, int,
                                unsigned long);
 struct _XImage *(*sub_image)
    (struct _XImage *, int, int, unsigned int, unsigned int);
 int (*add_pixel)             (struct _XImage *, long);
#else
 int (*destroy_image)();
```

```
 unsigned long (*get_pixel)();
 int (*put_pixel)();
 struct _XImage *(*sub_image)();
 int (*add_pixel)();
#endif
 } f;
} XImage;

/*
 * Data structure for XReconfigureWindow
 */
typedef struct {
    int x, y;
    int width, height;
    int border_width;
    Window sibling;
    int stack_mode;
} XWindowChanges;

/*
 * Data structure used by color operations
 */
typedef struct {

/* see Chapter 10, "Color and Graphics" */

} XColor;

/*
 * Data structures for graphics operations. On most machines,
 * these are congruent with the wire protocol structures, so
 * reformatting the data can be avoided on these
 * architectures.
 */
typedef struct {
    short x1, y1, x2, y2;
} XSegment;

typedef struct {
    short x, y;
} XPoint;
```

```
typedef struct {
    short x, y;
    unsigned short width, height;
} XRectangle;

typedef struct {
    short x, y;
    unsigned short width, height;
    short angle1, angle2;
} XArc;


/* Data structure for XChangeKeyboardControl */

typedef struct {
        int key_click_percent;
        int bell_percent;
        int bell_pitch;
        int bell_duration;
        int led;
        int led_mode;
        int key;
        int auto_repeat_mode;    /* On, Off, Default */
} XKeyboardControl;

/* Data structure for XGetKeyboardControl */

typedef struct {
        int key_click_percent;
 int bell_percent;
 unsigned int bell_pitch, bell_duration;
 unsigned long led_mask;
 int global_auto_repeat;
 char auto_repeats[32];
} XKeyboardState;

/* Data structure for XGetMotionEvents. */

typedef struct {
        Time time;
        short x, y;
} XTimeCoord;
```

```
/* Data structure for X{Set,Get}ModifierMapping */

typedef struct {
    int max_keypermod;      /* The server's max # of keys
                               per modifier */
    KeyCode *modifiermap;   /* An 8 by max_keypermod array
                               of modifiers */
} XModifierKeymap;

#endif /* _XSTRUCT_ */




/*
 * internal atoms used for ICCCM things;
 * not to be used by client
 */

struct _DisplayAtoms {
    Atom text;
    Atom wm_state;
    Atom wm_protocols;
    Atom wm_save_yourself;
    Atom wm_change_state;
    Atom wm_colormap_windows;
    /* add new atoms to end of list */
};




/*
 * Display datatype maintaining display specific data.
 */
typedef struct _XDisplay {
 XExtData *ext_data; /* hook for extension to hang data */
 struct _XDisplay *next; /* next open Display on list */
 int fd;                /* Network socket */
 int lock;              /* is someone in critical section? */
 int proto_major_version;  /* major version of server's
                              X protocol */
 int proto_minor_version;  /* minor version of server's
                              X protocol */
 char *vendor;             /* vendor of the server hardware */
```

```
long resource_base;        /* resource ID base */
long resource_mask;        /* resource ID mask bits */
long resource_id;          /* allocator current ID */
int resource_shift;     /* allocator shift to correct bits */
XID (*resource_alloc)();   /* allocator function */
int byte_order;  /* screen byte order, LSBFirst, MSBFirst */
int bitmap_unit; /* padding and data requirements */
int bitmap_pad;  /* padding requirements on bitmaps */
int bitmap_bit_order; /* LeastSignificant
                            or MostSignificant */
int nformats;           /* number of pixmap formats in list */
ScreenFormat *pixmap_format; /* pixmap format list */
int vnumber;  /* Xlib's X protocol version number */
int release;  /* release of the server */
struct _XSQEvent *head, *tail; /* Input event queue */
int qlen;  /* Length of input event queue */
unsigned long last_request_read; /* seq number of
                                     last event read */
unsigned long request; /* sequence number of last request */
char *last_req;  /* beginning of last request, or dummy */
char *buffer;  /* Output buffer starting address */
char *bufptr;  /* Output buffer index pointer */
char *bufmax;  /* Output buffer maximum+1 address */
unsigned max_request_size; /* maximum number 32-bit words
                              in request*/
struct _XrmHashBucketRec *db;
int (*synchandler)(); /* Synchronization handler */
char *display_name;  /* "host:display" string used
                        on this connect*/
int default_screen;  /* default screen for operations */
int nscreens;           /* number of screens on this server*/
Screen *screens;      /* pointer to list of screens */
unsigned long motion_buffer; /* size of motion buffer */
Window current;   /* for use internally for Keymap notify */
int min_keycode;  /* minimum defined keycode */
int max_keycode;  /* maximum defined keycode */
KeySym *keysyms;  /* This server's keysyms */
XModifierKeymap *modifiermap;  /* This server's
                                 modifier keymap */
int keysyms_per_keycode;      /* number of rows */
char *xdefaults; /* contents of defaults from server */
char *scratch_buffer; /* place to hang scratch buffer */
```

```
unsigned long scratch_length; /* length of scratch buffer */
int ext_number;  /* extension number on this display */
_XExtension *ext_procs; /* extensions initialized
                                on this display */
/*
 * The following can be fixed size, as the protocol defines
 * how much address space is available.
 * While this could be done using the extension vector, there
 * may be MANY events processed, so a search through the
 * extension list to find the right procedure for each event
 * might be expensive if many extensions are being used.
 */
Bool (*event_vec[128])();  /* vector for wire to event */
Status (*wire_vec[128])(); /* vector for event to wire */
KeySym lock_meaning;        /* for XLookupString */
struct XKeytrans *key_bindings; /* for XLookupString */
Font cursor_font;           /* for XCreateFontCursor */
/*
 * ICCCM information, version 1
 */
struct _DisplayAtoms *atoms;
struct { /* for XReconfigureWMWindow */
    long sequence_number;
    int (*old_handler)();
    Bool succeeded;
} reconfigure_wm_window;
/*
 * additional connection info
 */
unsigned long flags;        /* internal connection flags */
unsigned int mode_switch;  /* keyboard group modifiers */
} Display;

#if NeedFunctionPrototypes /s* prototypes require
                                event type definitions */
#undef _XEVENT_
#endif
#ifndef _XEVENT_
/*
 * An "XEvent" structure always has type as the first entry.
 * This uniquely identifies what kind of event it is.
 * The second entry is always a pointer to the display the
```

```
 * event was read from. The third entry is always a window
 * of one type or another, carefully selected to be useful
 * to toolkit dispatchers (except for keymap events, which
 * have no window). You must not change the order of the
 * three elements or toolkits will break! The pointer to
 * the generic event must be cast before use to access any
 * other information in the structure. */

/*
 * Definitions of specific events.
 */
typedef struct {

/* see Chapter 7, "Keyboard" */

} XKeyEvent;
typedef XKeyEvent XKeyPressedEvent;
typedef XKeyEvent XKeyReleasedEvent;

typedef struct {

/* see Chapter 8, "Mouse" */

} XButtonEvent;
typedef XButtonEvent XButtonPressedEvent;
typedef XButtonEvent XButtonReleasedEvent;

typedef struct {

/* see Chapter 8, "Mouse" */

} XMotionEvent;
typedef XMotionEvent XPointerMovedEvent;

typedef struct {

/* see Chapter 8, "Mouse" */

} XCrossingEvent;
typedef XCrossingEvent XEnterWindowEvent;
typedef XCrossingEvent XLeaveWindowEvent;
```

```
typedef struct {

/* see Chapter 7, "Keyboard" */

} XFocusChangeEvent;
typedef XFocusChangeEvent XFocusInEvent;
typedef XFocusChangeEvent XFocusOutEvent;

/* generated on EnterWindow and FocusIn when
   KeyMapState selected */
typedef struct {

/* see Chapter 7, "Keyboard" */

} XKeymapEvent;

typedef struct {

/* see Chapter 4, "Windows and Windowing Techniques" */

} XExposeEvent;

typedef struct {
 int type;
 unsigned long serial; /* # of last request
                          processed by server */
 Bool send_event;      /* true if this came from a
                          SendEvent request */
 Display *display;      /* Display the event was read from */
 Drawable drawable;
 int x, y;
 int width, height;
 int count;            /* if non-zero, at least this
                          many more */
 int major_code;       /* core is CopyArea or CopyPlane */
 int minor_code;       /* not defined in the core */
} XGraphicsExposeEvent;

typedef struct {
 int type;
 unsigned long serial; /* # of last request processed
                          by server */
```

```
    Bool send_event;      /* true if this came from a
                             SendEvent request */
    Display *display;     /* Display the event was read from */
    Drawable drawable;
    int major_code;       /* core is CopyArea or CopyPlane */
    int minor_code;       /* not defined in the core */
} XNoExposeEvent;

typedef struct {

/* see Chapter 4, "Windows and Windowing Techniques" */

} XVisibilityEvent;

typedef struct {

/* see Chapter 4, "Windows and Windowing Techniques" */

} XCreateWindowEvent;

typedef struct {

/* see Chapter 4, "Windows and Windowing Techniques" */

} XDestroyWindowEvent;

typedef struct {

/* see Chapter 4, "Windows and Windowing Techniques" */

} XUnmapEvent;

typedef struct {

/* see Chapter 4, "Windows and Windowing Techniques" */

} XMapEvent;

typedef struct {
 int type;
 unsigned long serial; /* # of last request processed
```

```
                                        by server */
   Bool send_event;       /* true if this came from a
                              SendEvent request */
   Display *display;       /* Display the event was read from */
   Window parent;
   Window window;
} XMapRequestEvent;

typedef struct {

/* see Chapter 4, "Windows and Windowing Techniques" */

} XReparentEvent;

typedef struct {

/* see Chapter 4, "Windows and Windowing Techniques" */

} XConfigureEvent;

typedef struct {

/* see Chapter 4, "Windows and Windowing Techniques" */

} XGravityEvent;

typedef struct {
  int type;
  unsigned long serial; /* # of last request processed
                           by server */
  Bool send_event;       /* true if this came from a
                             SendEvent request */
  Display *display;       /* Display the event was read from */
  Window window;
  int width, height;
} XResizeRequestEvent;

typedef struct {
  int type;
  unsigned long serial; /* # of last request processed
                           by server */
  Bool send_event;       /* true if this came from a
```

```
                                      SendEvent request */
        Display *display;      /* Display the event was read from */
        Window parent;
        Window window;
        int x, y;
        int width, height;
        int border_width;
        Window above;
        int detail;  /* Above, Below, TopIf, BottomIf, Opposite */
        unsigned long value_mask;
        } XConfigureRequestEvent;


typedef struct {

/* see Chapter 4, "Windows and Windowing Techniques" */

} XCirculateEvent;

typedef struct {
 int type;
 unsigned long serial; /* # of last request processed
                              by server */
 Bool send_event;        /* true if this came from a
                              SendEvent request */
 Display *display;       /* Display the event was read from */
 Window parent;
 Window window;
 int place;  /* PlaceOnTop, PlaceOnBottom */
} XCirculateRequestEvent;

typedef struct {

/* see Chapter 11, "Complete Fundamental Application and
   Advanced Features" */

} XPropertyEvent;

typedef struct {

/* see Chapter 11, "Complete Fundamental Application and
   Advanced Features" */
```

```
} XSelectionClearEvent;

typedef struct {

/* see Chapter 11, "Complete Fundamental Application and
   Advanced Features" */

} XSelectionRequestEvent;

typedef struct {

/* see Chapter 11, "Complete Fundamental Application and
   Advanced Features" */

} XSelectionEvent;

typedef struct {
 int type;
 unsigned long serial; /* # of last request processed
                          by server */
 Bool send_event;      /* true if this came from a
                          SendEvent request */
 Display *display;     /* Display the event was read from */
 Window window;
 Colormap colormap;    /* COLORMAP or None */
#if defined(__cplusplus) || defined(c_plusplus)
 Bool c_new;  /* C++ */
#else
 Bool new;
#endif
 int state;  /* ColormapInstalled, ColormapUninstalled */
} XColormapEvent;

typedef struct {

/* see Chapter 11, "Complete Fundamental Application and
                    Advanced Features" */

} XClientMessageEvent;

typedef struct {
```

```
/* see Chapter 4, "Windows and Windowing Techniques" */

} XMappingEvent;

typedef struct {
 int type;
 Display *display;       /* Display the event was read from */
 XID resourceid;         /* resource ID */
 unsigned long serial;   /* serial number of failed request */
 unsigned char error_code; /* error code of failed request */
 unsigned char request_code; /* Major op-code of
                                    failed request */
 unsigned char minor_code;   /* Minor op-code of
                                    failed request */
} XErrorEvent;

typedef struct {

/* see Chapter 3, "Basic Concepts and Terminology" */

} XAnyEvent;

/*
 * This union is defined so Xlib can always use the same sized
 * event structure internally, to avoid memory fragmentation.
 */
typedef union _XEvent {

/* see Chapter 3, "Basic Concepts and Terminology" */

} XEvent;
/*
 * _QEvent datatype for use in input queueing.
 */
typedef struct _XSQEvent {
    struct _XSQEvent *next;
    XEvent event;
} _XQEvent;
#endif
#define XAllocID(dpy) ((*(dpy)->resource_alloc)((dpy)))
#ifndef _XSTRUCT_
```

```
/*
 * per character font metric information.
 */
typedef struct {

/* see Chapter 6, "Text" */

} XCharStruct;

/*
 * To allow arbitrary information with fonts, there are
 * additional properties returned.
 */
typedef struct {
    Atom name;
    unsigned long card32;
} XFontProp;

typedef struct {

/* see Chapter 6, "Text" */

} XFontStruct;

/*
 * PolyText routines take these as arguments.
 */
typedef struct {

/* see Chapter 6, "Text" */

} XTextItem;

typedef struct { /* normal 16-bit characters are two bytes */
    unsigned char byte1;
    unsigned char byte2;
} XChar2b;

typedef struct {

/* see Chapter 6, "Text" */
```

```
} XTextItem16;


typedef union { Display *display;
  GC gc;
  Visual *visual;
  Screen *screen;
  ScreenFormat *pixmap_format;
  XFontStruct *font; } XEDataObject;

extern XFontStruct *XLoadQueryFont(
/* see Chapter 6, "Text" */
);

extern XFontStruct *XQueryFont(
/* see Chapter 6, "Text" */
);

extern XTimeCoord *XGetMotionEvents(
/* see Chapter 8, "Mouse" */
);

extern XModifierKeymap *XDeleteModifiermapEntry(
#if NeedFunctionPrototypes
    XModifierKeymap* /* modmap */,
#if NeedWidePrototypes
    unsigned int     /* keycode_entry */,
#else
    KeyCode          /* keycode_entry */,
#endif
    int              /* modifier */
#endif
);

extern XModifierKeymap *XGetModifierMapping(
#if NeedFunctionPrototypes
    Display*  /* display */
#endif
);

extern XModifierKeymap *XInsertModifiermapEntry(
#if NeedFunctionPrototypes
```

```
    XModifierKeymap* /* modmap */,
#if NeedWidePrototypes
    unsigned int      /* keycode_entry */,
#else
    KeyCode           /* keycode_entry */,
#endif
    int               /* modifier */
#endif
);

extern XModifierKeymap *XNewModifiermap(
#if NeedFunctionPrototypes
    int    /* max_keys_per_mod */
#endif
);

extern XImage *XCreateImage(
/* see Chapter 9, "Pixmaps, Bitmaps, and Images" */
);

extern XImage *XGetImage(
/* see Chapter 9, "Pixmaps, Bitmaps, and Images" */
);

extern XImage *XGetSubImage(
/* see Chapter 9, "Pixmaps, Bitmaps, and Images" */
);

#endif /* _XSTRUCT_ */
/*
 * X function declarations.
 */
extern Display *XOpenDisplay(
#if NeedFunctionPrototypes
    const char*  /* display_name */
#endif
);

extern void XrmInitialize(
#if NeedFunctionPrototypes
    void
```

```
#endif
);

extern char *XFetchBytes(
/* see Chapter 11, "Complete Fundamental Application and
   Advanced Features" */
);

extern char *XFetchBuffer(
/* see Chapter 11, "Complete Fundamental Application and
   Advanced Features" */
);

extern char *XGetAtomName(
#if NeedFunctionPrototypes
    Display*  /* display */,
    Atom      /* atom */
#endif
);
extern char *XGetDefault(
#if NeedFunctionPrototypes
    Display*     /* display */,
    const char*  /* program */,
    const char*  /* option */
#endif
);
extern char *XDisplayName(
#if NeedFunctionPrototypes
    const char*  /* string */
#endif
);
extern char *XKeysymToString(
/* see Chapter 7, Keyboard" */
);

extern int (*XSynchronize(
#if NeedFunctionPrototypes
    Display*     /* display */,
    Bool         /* onoff */
#endif
))();
extern int (*XSetAfterFunction(
#if NeedFunctionPrototypes
```

```
    Display*     /* display */,
    int (*) ( Display*   /* display */
          )              /* procedure */
#endif
))();
extern Atom XInternAtom(
#if NeedFunctionPrototypes
    Display*     /* display */,
    const char*  /* atom_name */,
    Bool         /* only_if_exists */
#endif
);
extern Colormap XCopyColormapAndFree(
/* see Chapter 10, "Color and Graphics" */
);

extern Colormap XCreateColormap(
/* see Chapter 10, "Color and Graphics" */
);

extern Cursor XCreatePixmapCursor(
/* see Chapter 8, "Mouse" */
);

extern Cursor XCreateGlyphCursor(
/* see Chapter 8, "Mouse" */
);

extern Cursor XCreateFontCursor(
/* see Chapter 8, "Mouse" */
);

extern Font XLoadFont(
/* see Chapter 6, "Text" */
);

extern GC XCreateGC(
/* see Chapter 10, "Color and Graphics" */
);

extern GContext XGContextFromGC(
#if NeedFunctionPrototypes
```

```
      GC    /* gc */
#endif
);
extern Pixmap XCreatePixmap(
/* see Chapter 9 "Pixmaps, Bitmaps, and Images" */
);

extern Pixmap XCreateBitmapFromData(
/* see Chapter 9 "Pixmaps, Bitmaps, and Images" */
);

extern Pixmap XCreatePixmapFromBitmapData(
/* see Chapter 9 "Pixmaps, Bitmaps, and Images" */
);

extern Window XCreateSimpleWindow(
/* see Chapter 4 "Windows and Windowing Techniques" */
);

extern Window XGetSelectionOwner(
/* see Chapter 11, "Complete Fundamental Application and
    Advanced Features" */
);

extern Window XCreateWindow(
/* see Chapter 4 "Windows and Windowing Techniques" */
);

extern Colormap *XListInstalledColormaps(
/* see Chapter 10, "Color and Graphics" */
);

extern char **XListFonts(
/* see Chapter 6, "Text" */
);

extern char **XListFontsWithInfo(
/* see Chapter 6, "Text" */
);
```

```
extern char **XGetFontPath(
/* see Chapter 6, "Text" */
);


extern char **XListExtensions(
#if NeedFunctionPrototypes
    Display*  /* display */,
    int*      /* nextensions_return */
#endif
);
extern Atom *XListProperties(
#if NeedFunctionPrototypes
    Display*  /* display */,
    Window    /* w */,
    int*      /* num_prop_return */
#endif
);
extern XHostAddress *XListHosts(
#if NeedFunctionPrototypes
    Display*  /* display */,
    int*      /* nhosts_return */,
    Bool*     /* state_return */
#endif
);
extern KeySym XKeycodeToKeysym(
/* see Chapter 7 "Keyboard" */
);


extern KeySym XLookupKeysym(
/* see Chapter 7 "Keyboard" */
);


extern KeySym *XGetKeyboardMapping(
/* see Chapter 7 "Keyboard" */
);


extern KeySym XStringToKeysym(
/* see Chapter 7 "Keyboard" */
);
```

```
extern long XMaxRequestSize(
#if NeedFunctionPrototypes
    Display*  /* display */
#endif
);
extern char *XResourceManagerString(
#if NeedFunctionPrototypes
    Display*  /* display */
#endif
);
extern unsigned long XDisplayMotionBufferSize(
#if NeedFunctionPrototypes
    Display*  /* display */
#endif
);
extern VisualID XVisualIDFromVisual(
#if NeedFunctionPrototypes
    Visual*  /* visual */
#endif
);


/* routines for dealing with extensions */

extern XExtCodes *XInitExtension(
#if NeedFunctionPrototypes
    Display*     /* display */,
    const char*  /* name */
#endif
);


extern XExtCodes *XAddExtension(
#if NeedFunctionPrototypes
    Display*  /* display */
#endif
);
extern XExtData *XFindOnExtensionList(
#if NeedFunctionPrototypes
    XExtData**  /* structure */,
    int         /* number */
#endif
);
extern XExtData **XEHeadOfExtensionList(
```

```
#if NeedFunctionPrototypes
    XEDataObject /* object */
#endif
);

/* these are routines for which there are also macros */
extern Window XRootWindow(
#if NeedFunctionPrototypes
    Display*  /* display */,
    int       /* screen_number */
#endif
);
extern Window XDefaultRootWindow(
#if NeedFunctionPrototypes
    Display*  /* display */
#endif
);
extern Window XRootWindowOfScreen(
#if NeedFunctionPrototypes
    Screen*  /* screen */
#endif
);
extern Visual *XDefaultVisual(
#if NeedFunctionPrototypes
    Display*  /* display */,
    int       /* screen_number */
#endif
);
extern Visual *XDefaultVisualOfScreen(
#if NeedFunctionPrototypes
    Screen*  /* screen */
#endif
);
extern GC XDefaultGC(
#if NeedFunctionPrototypes
    Display*  /* display */,
    int       /* screen_number */
#endif
);
extern GC XDefaultGCOfScreen(
#if NeedFunctionPrototypes
    Screen*  /* screen */
```

```
#endif
);
extern unsigned long XBlackPixel(
/* see Chapter 10, "Color and Graphics" */
);

extern unsigned long XWhitePixel(
/* see Chapter 10, "Color and Graphics" */
);

extern unsigned long XAllPlanes(
#if NeedFunctionPrototypes
    void
#endif
);
extern unsigned long XBlackPixelOfScreen(
#if NeedFunctionPrototypes
    Screen*  /* screen */
#endif
);
extern unsigned long XWhitePixelOfScreen(
#if NeedFunctionPrototypes
    Screen*  /* screen */
#endif
);
extern unsigned long XNextRequest(
#if NeedFunctionPrototypes
    Display*  /* display */
#endif
);
extern unsigned long XLastKnownRequestProcessed(
#if NeedFunctionPrototypes
    Display*  /* display */
#endif
);
extern char *XServerVendor(
#if NeedFunctionPrototypes
    Display*  /* display */
#endif
);
extern char *XDisplayString(
#if NeedFunctionPrototypes
```

```
    Display*  /* display */
#endif
);
extern Colormap XDefaultColormap(
/* see Chapter 10, "Color and Graphics" */
);


extern Colormap XDefaultColormapOfScreen(
#if NeedFunctionPrototypes
    Screen*  /* screen */
#endif
);
extern Display *XDisplayOfScreen(
#if NeedFunctionPrototypes
    Screen*  /* screen */
#endif
);
extern Screen *XScreenOfDisplay(
#if NeedFunctionPrototypes
    Display*  /* display */,
    int       /* screen_number */
#endif
);
extern Screen *XDefaultScreenOfDisplay(
#if NeedFunctionPrototypes
    Display*  /* display */
#endif
);
extern long XEventMaskOfScreen(
#if NeedFunctionPrototypes
    Screen*  /* screen */
#endif
);


extern int XScreenNumberOfScreen(
#if NeedFunctionPrototypes
    Screen*  /* screen */
#endif
);


typedef int (*XErrorHandler)
    (/* WARNING, this type not in Xlib spec */
```

```
#if NeedFunctionPrototypes
    Display*     /* display */,
    XErrorEvent* /* error_event */
#endif
);

extern XErrorHandler XSetErrorHandler (
/* see Chapter 11, "Complete Fundamental Application
    and Advanced Features" */
);

typedef int (*XIOErrorHandler)
    (/* WARNING, this type not in Xlib spec */
#if NeedFunctionPrototypes
    Display*  /* display */
#endif
);

extern XIOErrorHandler XSetIOErrorHandler (
/* see Chapter 11, "Complete Fundamental Application
    and Advanced Features" */
);

extern XPixmapFormatValues *XListPixmapFormats(
#if NeedFunctionPrototypes
    Display*  /* display */,
    int*      /* count_return */
#endif
);
extern int *XListDepths(
#if NeedFunctionPrototypes
    Display*  /* display */,
    int       /* screen_number */,
    int*      /* count_return */
#endif
);

/* ICCCM routines for things that don't require special
    include files; */
/* other declarations are given in Xutil.h */
extern Status XReconfigureWMWindow(
#if NeedFunctionPrototypes
```

```
    Display*        /* display */,
    Window          /* w */,
    int             /* screen_number */,
    unsigned int    /* mask */,
    XWindowChanges* /* changes */
#endif
);

extern Status GetWMProtocols(
#if NeedFunctionPrototypes
    Display*  /* display */,
    Window    /* w */,
    Atom**    /* protocols_return */,
    int*      /* count_return */
#endif
);
extern Status XSetWMProtocols(
#if NeedFunctionPrototypes
    Display*  /* display */,
    Window    /* w */,
    Atom*     /* protocols */,
    int       /* count */
#endif
);
extern Status XIconifyWindow(
/* see Chapter 11, "Complete Fundamental Application and
                    Advanced Features" */
);

extern Status XWithdrawWindow(
/* see Chapter 11, "Complete Fundamental Application and
                    Advanced Features" */
);

extern Status XGetCommand(
#if NeedFunctionPrototypes
    Display*  /* display */,
    Window    /* w */,
    char***   /* argv_return */,
    int*      /* argc_return */
#endif
);
```

```
extern Status XGetWMColormapWindows(
#if NeedFunctionPrototypes
    Display*  /* display */,
    Window    /* w */,
    Window**  /* windows_return */,
    int*      /* count_return */
#endif
);
extern Status XSetWMColormapWindows(
#if NeedFunctionPrototypes
    Display*  /* display */,
    Window    /* w */,
    Window*   /* colormap_windows */,
    int       /* count */
#endif
);
extern void XFreeStringList(
#if NeedFunctionPrototypes
    char**    /* list */
#endif
);
extern XSetTransientForHint(
#if NeedFunctionPrototypes
    Display*  /* display */,
    Window    /* w */,
    Window    /* prop_window */
#endif
);


/* The following are given in alphabetical order */

extern XActivateScreenSaver(
#if NeedFunctionPrototypes
    Display*  /* display */
#endif
);

extern XAddHost(
#if NeedFunctionPrototypes
    Display*        /* display */,
    XHostAddress*   /* host */
```

```
#endif
);

extern XAddHosts(
#if NeedFunctionPrototypes
    Display*      /* display */,
    XHostAddress* /* hosts */,
    int           /* num_hosts */
#endif
);

extern XAddToExtensionList(
#if NeedFunctionPrototypes
    struct _XExtData** /* structure */,
    XExtData*          /* ext_data */
#endif
);

extern XAddToSaveSet(
#if NeedFunctionPrototypes
    Display* /* display */,
    Window   /* w */
#endif
);

extern Status XAllocColor(
/* see Chapter 10, "Color and Graphics " */
);

extern Status XAllocColorCells(
/* see Chapter 10, "Color and Graphics " */
);

extern Status XAllocColorPlanes(
/* see Chapter 10, "Color and Graphics " */
);

extern Status XAllocNamedColor(
/* see Chapter 10, "Color and Graphics " */
);
```

```
extern XAllowEvents(
#if NeedFunctionPrototypes
    Display*  /* display */,
    int       /* event_mode */,
    Time      /* time */
#endif
);

extern XAutoRepeatOff(
#if NeedFunctionPrototypes
    Display*  /* display */
#endif
);

extern XAutoRepeatOn(
#if NeedFunctionPrototypes
    Display*  /* display */
#endif
);

extern XBell(
/* see Chapter 7, "Keyboard" */
);

extern int XBitmapBitOrder(
#if NeedFunctionPrototypes
    Display*  /* display */
#endif
);

extern int XBitmapPad(
#if NeedFunctionPrototypes
    Display*  /* display */
#endif
);

extern int XBitmapUnit(
#if NeedFunctionPrototypes
    Display*  /* display */
#endif
);
```

```
extern int XCellsOfScreen(
#if NeedFunctionPrototypes
    Screen*    /* screen */
#endif
);

extern XChangeActivePointerGrab(
#if NeedFunctionPrototypes
    Display*      /* display */,
    unsigned int /* event_mask */,
    Cursor        /* cursor */,
    Time          /* time */
#endif
);

extern XChangeGC(
/* see Chapter 10, "Color and Graphics " */
);

extern XChangeKeyboardControl(
/* see Chapter 7, "Keyboard" */
);

extern XChangeKeyboardMapping(
/* see Chapter 7, "Keyboard" */
);

extern XChangePointerControl(
/* see Chapter 8, "Mouse" */
);

extern XChangeProperty(
/* see Chapter 11, "Complete Fundamental Application and
                    Advanced Features" */
);

extern XChangeSaveSet(
#if NeedFunctionPrototypes
    Display* /* display */,
    Window    /* w */,
    int       /* change_mode */
```

```
#endif
);

extern XChangeWindowAttributes(
/* see Chapter 4, "Windows and Windowing Techniques" */
);

extern Bool XCheckIfEvent(
#if NeedFunctionPrototypes
    Display*   /* display */,
    XEvent*    /* event_return */,
    Bool (*)   ( Display*   /* display */,
                 XEvent*    /* event */,
                 char*    /* arg */
               ) /* predicate */,
    char*      /* arg */
#endif
);

extern Bool XCheckMaskEvent(
#if NeedFunctionPrototypes
    Display*   /* display */,
    long       /* event_mask */,
    XEvent*    /* event_return */
#endif
);

extern Bool XCheckTypedEvent(
#if NeedFunctionPrototypes
    Display*   /* display */,
    int        /* event_type */,
    XEvent*    /* event_return */
#endif
);

extern Bool XCheckTypedWindowEvent(
#if NeedFunctionPrototypes
    Display*   /* display */,
    Window     /* w */,
    int        /* event_type */,
    XEvent*    /* event_return */
```

```
#endif
);

extern Bool XCheckWindowEvent(
#if NeedFunctionPrototypes
    Display*  /* display */,
    Window    /* w */,
    long      /* event_mask */,
    XEvent*   /* event_return */
#endif
);

extern XCirculateSubwindows(
/* see Chapter 4, "Windows and Windowing Techniques" */
);

extern XCirculateSubwindowsDown(
/* see Chapter 4, "Windows and Windowing Techniques" */
);

extern XCirculateSubwindowsUp(
/* see Chapter 4, "Windows and Windowing Techniques" */
);

extern XClearArea(
/* see Chapter 10, "Color and Graphics" */
);

extern XClearWindow(
/* see Chapter 10, "Color and Graphics" */
);

extern XCloseDisplay(
#if NeedFunctionPrototypes
    Display*  /* display */
#endif
);

extern XConfigureWindow(
/* see Chapter 4, "Windows and Windowing Techniques" */
);
```

```
extern int XConnectionNumber(
#if NeedFunctionPrototypes
    Display*  /* display */
#endif
);

extern XConvertSelection(
/* see Chapter 11, "Complete Fundamental Application and
                    Advanced Features" */
);

extern XCopyArea(
/* see Chapter 10, "Color and Graphics" */
);

extern XCopyGC(
/* see Chapter 10, "Color and Graphics" */
);

extern XCopyPlane(
/* see Chapter 10, "Color and Graphics" */
);

#if NeedFunctionPrototypes

extern int XDefaultDepth(
#if NeedFunctionPrototypes
    Display*  /* display */,
    int       /* screen_number */
#endif
);

extern int XDefaultDepthOfScreen(
#if NeedFunctionPrototypes
    Screen*   /* screen */
#endif
);

extern int XDefaultScreen(
#if NeedFunctionPrototypes
    Display*  /* display */
```

```
#endif
);

extern XDefineCursor(
#if NeedFunctionPrototypes
    Display*  /* display */,
    Window    /* w */,
    Cursor    /* cursor */
#endif
);

extern XDeleteProperty(
/* see Chapter 11, "Complete Fundamental Application and
                    Advanced Features" */
);

extern XDestroyWindow(
/* see Chapter 4, "Windows and Windowing Techniques" */
);

extern XDestroySubwindows(
/* see Chapter 4, "Windows and Windowing Techniques" */
);

extern int XDoesBackingStore(
#if NeedFunctionPrototypes
    Screen*   /* screen */
#endif
);

extern Bool XDoesSaveUnders(
#if NeedFunctionPrototypes
    Screen*   /* screen */
#endif
);

extern XDisableAccessControl(
#if NeedFunctionPrototypes
    Display*  /* display */
#endif
);
```

```
extern int XDisplayCells(
/* see Chapter 10, "Color and Graphics" */
);

extern int XDisplayHeight(
#if NeedFunctionPrototypes
    Display*  /* display */,
    int       /* screen_number */
#endif
);

extern int XDisplayHeightMM(
#if NeedFunctionPrototypes
    Display*  /* display */,
    int       /* screen_number */
#endif
);

extern XDisplayKeycodes(
#if NeedFunctionPrototypes
    Display*  /* display */,
    int*      /* min_keycodes_return */,
    int*      /* max_keycodes_return */
#endif
);

extern int XDisplayPlanes(
/* see Chapter 10, "Color and Graphics" */
);

extern int XDisplayWidth(
#if NeedFunctionPrototypes
    Display*  /* display */,
    int       /* screen_number */
#endif
);

extern int XDisplayWidthMM(
#if NeedFunctionPrototypes
    Display*  /* display */,
    int       /* screen_number */
```

```
#endif
);

extern XDrawArc(
/* see Chapter 10, "Color and Graphics" */
);

extern XDrawArcs(
/* see Chapter 10, "Color and Graphics" */
);

extern XDrawImageString(
/* see Chapter 6, "Text" */
);

extern XDrawImageString16(
/* see Chapter 6, "Text" */
);

extern XDrawLine(
/* see Chapter 10, "Color and Graphics" */
);

extern XDrawLines(
/* see Chapter 10, "Color and Graphics" */
);

extern XDrawPoint(
/* see Chapter 10, "Color and Graphics" */
);

extern XDrawPoints(
/* see Chapter 10, "Color and Graphics" */
);

extern XDrawRectangle(
/* see Chapter 10, "Color and Graphics" */
);

extern XDrawRectangles(
/* see Chapter 10, "Color and Graphics" */
);
```

```
extern XDrawSegments(
/* see Chapter 10, "Color and Graphics" */
);

extern XDrawString(
/* see Chapter 6, "Text" */
);

extern XDrawString16(
/* see Chapter 6, "Text" */
);

extern XDrawText(
/* see Chapter 6, "Text" */
);

extern XDrawText16(
/* see Chapter 6, "Text" */
);

extern XEnableAccessControl(
#if NeedFunctionPrototypes
    Display*  /* display */
#endif
);

extern int XEventsQueued(
#if NeedFunctionPrototypes
    Display*  /* display */,
    int       /* mode */
#endif
);

extern Status XFetchName(
#if NeedFunctionPrototypes
    Display*  /* display */,
    Window    /* w */,
    char**    /* window_name_return */
#endif
);
```

```
extern XFillArc(
/* see Chapter 10, "Color and Graphics" */
);

extern XFillArcs(
/* see Chapter 10, "Color and Graphics" */
);

extern XFillPolygon(
/* see Chapter 10, "Color and Graphics" */
);

extern XFillRectangle(
/* see Chapter 10, "Color and Graphics" */
);

extern XFillRectangles(
/* see Chapter 10, "Color and Graphics" */
);

extern XFlush(
#if NeedFunctionPrototypes
    Display*  /* display */
#endif
);

extern XForceScreenSaver(
#if NeedFunctionPrototypes
    Display*  /* display */,
    int       /* mode */
#endif
);

extern XFree(
#if NeedFunctionPrototypes
    char*     /* data */
#endif
);
```

```
extern XFreeColormap(
/* see Chapter 10, "Color and Graphics" */
);

extern XFreeColors(
/* see Chapter 10, "Color and Graphics" */
);

extern XFreeCursor(
/* see Chapter 8, "Mouse" */
);

extern XFreeExtensionList(
#if NeedFunctionPrototypes
    char**     /* list */
#endif
);

extern XFreeFont(
/* see Chapter 6, "Text" */
);

extern XFreeFontInfo(
/* see Chapter 6, "Text" */
);

extern XFreeFontNames(
/* see Chapter 6, "Text" */
);

extern XFreeFontPath(
/* see Chapter 6, "Text" */
);

extern XFreeGC(
/* see Chapter 10, "Color and Graphics" */
);

extern XFreeModifiermap(
#if NeedFunctionPrototypes
    XModifierKeymap* /* modmap */
```

```
#endif
);

extern XFreePixmap(
/* see Chapter 9, "Pixmaps, Bitmaps, and Images" */
);

extern int XGeometry(
#if NeedFunctionPrototypes
    Display*   /* display */,
    int        /* screen */,
    const char*  /* position */,
    const char*  /* default_position */,
    unsigned int /* bwidth */,
    unsigned int /* fwidth */,
    unsigned int /* fheight */,
    int          /* xadder */,
    int          /* yadder */,
    int*         /* x_return */,
    int*         /* y_return */,
    int*         /* width_return */,
    int*         /* height_return */
#endif
);

extern XGetErrorDatabaseText(
/* see Chapter 11, "Complete Fundamental Application and
                    Advanced Features" */
);

extern XGetErrorText(
/* see Chapter 11, "Complete Fundamental Application and
                    Advanced Features" */
);

extern Bool XGetFontProperty(
/* see Chapter 6, "Text" */
);

extern Status XGetGCValues(
/* see Chapter 10, "Color and Graphics" */
);
```

```
extern Status XGetGeometry(
/* see Chapter 9, "Pixmaps, Bitmaps, and Images" */
);

extern Status XGetIconName(
#if NeedFunctionPrototypes
    Display*  /* display */,
    Window    /* w */,
    char**    /* icon_name_return */
#endif
);

extern XGetInputFocus(
/* see Chapter 7, "Keyboard" */
);

extern XGetKeyboardControl(
/* see Chapter 7, "Keyboard" */
);

extern XGetPointerControl(
/* see Chapter 8, "Mouse" */
);

extern int XGetPointerMapping(
/* see Chapter 8, "Mouse" */
);

extern XGetScreenSaver(
#if NeedFunctionPrototypes
    Display*  /* display */,
    int*      /* timeout_return */,
    int*      /* interval_return */,
    int*      /* prefer_blanking_return */,
    int*      /* allow_exposures_return */
#endif
);

extern Status XGetTransientForHint(
#if NeedFunctionPrototypes
    Display*  /* display */,
    Window    /* w */,
```

```
      Window*    /* prop_window_return */
#endif
);

extern int XGetWindowProperty(
/* see Chapter 11, "Complete Fundamental Application and
                     Advanced Features" */
);

extern Status XGetWindowAttributes(
#if NeedFunctionPrototypes
    Display*  /* display */,
    Window    /* w */,
    XWindowAttributes* /* window_attributes_return */
#endif
);

extern XGrabButton(
/* see Chapter 8, "Mouse" */
);

extern XGrabKey(
/* see Chapter 7, "Keyboard" */
);

extern int XGrabKeyboard(
/* see Chapter 7, "Keyboard" */
);

extern int XGrabPointer(
/* see Chapter 8, "Mouse" */
);

extern XGrabServer(
#if NeedFunctionPrototypes
    Display*  /* display */
#endif
);

extern int XHeightMMOfScreen(
#if NeedFunctionPrototypes
    Screen*   /* screen */
```

```
#endif
);

extern int XHeightOfScreen(
#if NeedFunctionPrototypes
    Screen*   /* screen */
#endif
);

extern XIfEvent(
#if NeedFunctionPrototypes
    Display*  /* display */,
    XEvent*   /* event_return */,
    Bool (*) ( Display*   /* display */,
               XEvent*   /* event */,
               char*   /* arg */
             ) /* predicate */,
    char*      /* arg */
#endif
);

extern int XImageByteOrder(
#if NeedFunctionPrototypes
    Display*  /* display */
#endif
);

extern XInstallColormap(
/* see Chapter 10, "Color and Graphics" */
);

extern KeyCode XKeysymToKeycode(
/* see Chapter 7, "Keyboard" */
);

extern XKillClient(
#if NeedFunctionPrototypes
    Display*  /* display */,
    XID       /* resource */
#endif
);
```

```
extern unsigned long XLastKnownRequestProcessed(
#if NeedFunctionPrototypes
    Display*  /* display */
#endif
);

extern Status XLookupColor(
/* see Chapter 10, "Color and Graphics" */
);

extern XLowerWindow(
/* see Chapter 4, "Windows and Windowing Techniques" */
);

extern XMapRaised(
/* see Chapter 4, "Windows and Windowing Techniques" */
);

extern XMapSubwindows(
/* see Chapter 4, "Windows and Windowing Techniques" */
);

extern XMapWindow(
/* see Chapter 4, "Windows and Windowing Techniques" */
);

extern XMaskEvent(
#if NeedFunctionPrototypes
    Display*  /* display */,
    long      /* event_mask */,
    XEvent*   /* event_return */
#endif
);

extern int XMaxCmapsOfScreen(
#if NeedFunctionPrototypes
    Screen*   /* screen */
#endif
);

extern int XMinCmapsOfScreen(
#if NeedFunctionPrototypes
```

```
    Screen*   /* screen */
#endif
);

extern XMoveResizeWindow(
/* see Chapter 4, "Windows and Windowing Techniques" */
);

extern XMoveWindow(
/* see Chapter 4, "Windows and Windowing Techniques" */
);

extern XNextEvent(
#if NeedFunctionPrototypes
    Display*  /* display */,
    XEvent*   /* event_return */
#endif
);

extern XNoOp(
#if NeedFunctionPrototypes
    Display*  /* display */
#endif
);

extern Status XParseColor(
/* see Chapter 10, "Color and Graphics" */
);

extern int XParseGeometry(
#if NeedFunctionPrototypes
    const char*   /* parsestring */,
    int*          /* x_return */,
    int*          /* y_return */,
    unsigned int* /* width_return */,
    unsigned int* /* height_return */
#endif
);

extern XPeekEvent(
#if NeedFunctionPrototypes
```

```
    Display*  /* display */,
    XEvent*   /* event_return */
#endif
);

extern XPeekIfEvent(
#if NeedFunctionPrototypes
    Display*  /* display */,
    XEvent*   /* event_return */,
    Bool (*) ( Display*  /* display */,
               XEvent*  /* event */,
               char*  /* arg */
             ) /* predicate */,
    char*     /* arg */
#endif
);

extern int XPending(
#if NeedFunctionPrototypes
    Display*  /* display */
#endif
);

extern int XPlanesOfScreen(
#if NeedFunctionPrototypes
    Screen*   /* screen */

#endif
);

extern int XProtocolRevision(
#if NeedFunctionPrototypes
    Display*  /* display */
#endif
);

extern int XProtocolVersion(
#if NeedFunctionPrototypes
    Display*  /* display */
#endif
);
```

```
extern XPutBackEvent(
#if NeedFunctionPrototypes
    Display*  /* display */,
    XEvent*   /* event */
#endif
);

extern XPutImage(
/* see Chapter 9 "Pixmaps, Bitmaps, and Images" */
);

extern int XQLength(
#if NeedFunctionPrototypes
    Display*  /* display */
#endif
);

extern Status XQueryBestCursor(
/* see Chapter 8, "Mouse" */
);

extern Status XQueryBestSize(
#if NeedFunctionPrototypes
    Display*  /* display */,
    int       /* class */,
    Drawable  /* which_screen */,
    unsigned int  /* width */,
    unsigned int  /* height */,
    unsigned int* /* width_return */,
    unsigned int* /* height_return */
#endif
);

extern Status XQueryBestStipple(
/* see Chapter 10, "Color and Graphics" */
);

extern Status XQueryBestTile(
/* see Chapter 10, "Color and Graphics" */
);
```

```
extern XQueryColor(
/* see Chapter 10, "Color and Graphics" */
);

extern XQueryColors(
/* see Chapter 10, "Color and Graphics" */
);

extern Bool XQueryExtension(
#if NeedFunctionPrototypes
    Display*      /* display */,
    const char*  /* name */,
    int*  /* major_opcode_return */,
    int*  /* first_event_return */,
    int*  /* first_error_return */
#endif
);

extern XQueryKeymap(
/* see Chapter 7, "Keyboard" */
);

extern Bool XQueryPointer(
/* see Chapter 8, "Mouse" */
);

extern XQueryTextExtents(
/* see Chapter 6, "Text" */
);

extern XQueryTextExtents16(
/* see Chapter 6, "Text" */
);

extern Status XQueryTree(
#if NeedFunctionPrototypes
    Display*  /* display */,
    Window     /* w */,
    Window*    /* root_return */,
    Window*    /* parent_return */,
```

```
    Window**  /* children_return */,
    unsigned int* /* nchildren_return */
#endif
);

extern XRaiseWindow(
/* see Chapter 4, "Windows and Windowing Techniques" */
);

extern int XReadBitmapFile(
/* see Chapter 9, "Pixmaps, Bitmaps, and Images" */
);

extern XRebindKeysym(
/* see Chapter 7, "Keyboard" */
);

extern XRecolorCursor(
/* see Chapter 8, "Mouse" */
);

extern XRefreshKeyboardMapping(
/* see Chapter 7, "Keyboard" */
);

extern XRemoveFromSaveSet(
#if NeedFunctionPrototypes
    Display*  /* display */,
    Window    /* w */
#endif
);

extern XRemoveHost(
#if NeedFunctionPrototypes
    Display*      /* display */,
    XHostAddress* /* host */
#endif
);

extern XRemoveHosts(
#if NeedFunctionPrototypes
    Display*      /* display */,
```

```
    XHostAddress* /* hosts */,
    int           /* num_hosts */
#endif
);

extern XReparentWindow(
/* see Chapter 4, "Windows and Windowing Techniques" */
);

extern XResetScreenSaver(
#if NeedFunctionPrototypes
    Display*  /* display */
#endif
);

extern XResizeWindow(
/* see Chapter 4, "Windows and Windowing Techniques" */
);

extern XRestackWindows(
/* see Chapter 4, "Windows and Windowing Techniques" */
);

extern XRotateBuffers(
/* see Chapter 11, "Complete Fundamental Application and
                    Advanced Features" */
);

extern XRotateWindowProperties(
/* see Chapter 11, "Complete Fundamental Application and
                    Advanced Features" */
);

extern int XScreenCount(
#if NeedFunctionPrototypes
    Display*  /* display */
#cndif
);

extern XSelectInput(
#if NeedFunctionPrototypes
    Display*  /* display */,
```

```
    Window     /* w */,
    long       /* event_mask */
#endif
);

extern Status XSendEvent(
#if NeedFunctionPrototypes
    Display*   /* display */,
    Window     /* w */,
    Bool       /* propagate */,
    long       /* event_mask */,
    XEvent*    /* event_send */
#endif
);

extern XSetAccessControl(
#if NeedFunctionPrototypes
    Display*   /* display */,
    int        /* mode */
#endif
);

extern XSetArcMode(
/* see Chapter 10, "Color and Graphics" */
);

extern XSetBackground(
/* see Chapter 10, "Color and Graphics" */
);

extern XSetClipMask(
/* see Chapter 10, "Color and Graphics" */
);

extern XSetClipOrigin(
/* see Chapter 10, "Color and Graphics" */
);

extern XSetClipRectangles(
/* see Chapter 10, "Color and Graphics" */
);
```

```
extern XSetCloseDownMode(
#if NeedFunctionPrototypes
    Display*   /* display */,
    int        /* close_mode */
#endif
);

extern XSetCommand(
#if NeedFunctionPrototypes
    Display*   /* display */,
    Window     /* w */,
    char**     /* argv */,
    int        /* argc */
#endif
);

extern XSetDashes(
/* see Chapter 10, "Color and Graphics" */
);

extern XSetFillRule(
/* sce Chapter 10, "Color and Graphics" */
);

extern XSetFillStyle(
/* see Chapter 10, "Color and Graphics" */
);

extern XSetFont(
/* see Chapter 6, "Text" */
);

extern XSetFontPath(
/* see Chapter 6, "Text" */
);

extern XSetForeground(
/* see Chapter 10, "Color and Graphics" */
);
```

```
extern XSetFunction(
/* see Chapter 10, "Color and Graphics" */
);

extern XSetGraphicsExposures(
/* see Chapter 10, "Color and Graphics" */
);

extern XSetIconName(
#if NeedFunctionPrototypes
    Display*  /* display */,
    Window    /* w */,
    const char*  /* icon_name */
#endif
);

extern XSetInputFocus(
/* see Chapter 7, "Keyboard" */
);

extern XSetLineAttributes(
/* see Chapter 10, "Color and Graphics" */
);

extern int XSetModifierMapping(
#if NeedFunctionPrototypes
    Display*  /* display */,
    XModifierKeymap* /* modmap */
#endif
);

extern XSetPlaneMask(
/* see Chapter 10, "Color and Graphics" */
);

extern int XSetPointerMapping(
/* see Chapter 8, "Mouse" */
);

extern XSetScreenSaver(
#if NeedFunctionPrototypes
```

```
    Display*  /* display */,
    int       /* timeout */,
    int       /* interval */,
    int       /* prefer_blanking */,
    int       /* allow_exposures */
#endif
);

extern XSetSelectionOwner(
/* see Chapter 11, "Complete Fundamental Application and
                   Advanced Features" */
);

extern XSetState(
/* see Chapter 10, "Color and Graphics" */
);

extern XSetStipple(
/* see Chapter 10, "Color and Graphics" */
);

extern XSetSubwindowMode(
/* see Chapter 10, "Color and Graphics" */
);

extern XSetTSOrigin(
/* see Chapter 10, "Color and Graphics" */
);

extern XSetTile(
/* see Chapter 10, "Color and Graphics" */
);

extern XSetWindowBackground(
/* see Chapter 4, "Windows and Windowing Techniques" */
);

extern XSetWindowBackgroundPixmap(
/* see Chapter 4, "Windows and Windowing Techniques" */
);
```

```
extern XSetWindowBorder(
/* see Chapter 4, "Windows and Windowing Techniques" */
);

extern XSetWindowBorderPixmap(
/* see Chapter 4, "Windows and Windowing Techniques" */
);

extern XSetWindowBorderWidth(
/* see Chapter 4, "Windows and Windowing Techniques" */
);

extern XSetWindowColormap(
/* see Chapter 10, "Color and Graphics" */
);

extern XStoreBuffer(
/* see Chapter 11 "Complete Fundamental Application and
                  Advanced Features" */
);

extern XStoreBytes(
/* see Chapter 11 "Complete Fundamental Application and
                  Advanced Features" */
);

extern XStoreColor(
/* see Chapter 10, "Color and Graphics" */
);

extern XStoreColors(
/* see Chapter 10, "Color and Graphics" */
);

extern XStoreName(
#if NeedFunctionPrototypes
    Display*    /* display */,
    Window      /* w */,
    const char* /* window_name */
#endif
);
```

```
extern XStoreNamedColor(
/* see Chapter 10, "Color and Graphics" */
);

extern XSync(
#if NeedFunctionPrototypes
    Display*  /* display */,
    Bool      /* discard */
#endif
);

extern XTextExtents(
/* see Chapter 6, "Text" */
);

extern XTextExtents16(
/* see Chapter 6, "Text" */
);

extern int XTextWidth(
/* see Chapter 6, "Text" */
);

extern int XTextWidth16(
/* see Chapter 6, "Text" */
);

extern Bool XTranslateCoordinates(
/* see Chapter 8, "Mouse" */
);

extern XUndefineCursor(
#if NeedFunctionPrototypes
    Display*  /* display */,
    Window    /* w */
#endif
);

extern XUngrabButton(
/* see Chapter 8, "Mouse" */
);
```

```
extern XUngrabKey(
#if NeedFunctionPrototypes
    Display*  /* display */,
    int       /* keycode */,
    unsigned int /* modifiers */,
    Window    /* grab_window */
#endif
);

extern XUngrabKeyboard(
/* see Chapter 7, "Keyboard" */
);

extern XUngrabPointer(
/* see Chapter 8, "Mouse" */
);

extern XUngrabServer(
#if NeedFunctionPrototypes
    Display*  /* display */
#endif
);

extern XUninstallColormap(
/* see Chapter 10, "Color and Graphics" */
);

extern XUnloadFont(
/* see Chapter 6, "Text" */
);

extern XUnmapSubwindows(
/* see Chapter 4, "Windows and Windowing Techniques" */
);

extern XUnmapWindow(
/* see Chapter 4, "Windows and Windowing Techniques" */
);

extern int XVendorRelease(
#if NeedFunctionPrototypes
    Display*  /* display */
```

```
#endif
);

extern XWarpPointer(
/* see Chapter 8, "Mouse" */
);

extern int XWidthMMOfScreen(
#if NeedFunctionPrototypes
    Screen*    /* screen */
#endif
);

extern int XWidthOfScreen(
#if NeedFunctionPrototypes
    Screen*    /* screen */
#endif
);

extern XWindowEvent(
#if NeedFunctionPrototypes
    Display*  /* display */,
    Window    /* w */,
    long      /* event_mask */,
    XEvent*   /* event_return */
#endif
);

extern int XWriteBitmapFile(
/* see Chapter 9, "Pixmaps, Bitmaps, and Images" */
);

#ifdef __cplusplus
} /* for C++ V2.0 */
#endif

#endif /* _XLIB_H_ */
```

APPENDIX

Xutil

The <X11/Xutil.h> header file declares various functions, types, and symbols used for interclient communication and application utility functions. You must include <X11/Xlib.h> before including this file.

```
#ifndef _XUTIL_H_
#define _XUTIL_H_

#ifdef __cplusplus
extern "C" { /* for C++ V2.0 */
#endif

#ifndef NeedFunctionPrototypes
#if defined(FUNCPROTO) || defined(__STDC__) ||
    defined(__cplusplus) || defined(c_plusplus)
#define NeedFunctionPrototypes 1
#else
#define NeedFunctionPrototypes 0
#endif /* __STDC__ */
#endif /* NeedFunctionPrototypes */

/*
 * Bitmask returned by XParseGeometry(). Each bit tells
 * if the corresponding value (x, y, width, height)
 * was found in the parsed string.
 */

#define NoValue 0x0000
#define XValue  0x0001
#define YValue 0x0002
#define WidthValue  0x0004
#define HeightValue  0x0008
#define AllValues 0x000F
#define XNegative 0x0010
#define YNegative 0x0020

/*
 * New version containing base_width, base_height,
 * and win_gravity fields; used with WM_NORMAL_HINTS.
 */

typedef struct {
    long flags;/* marks which fields in this structure
```

```
                    are defined */
int x, y; /* obsolete for new window mgrs, but clients */
int width, height; /* should set so old wm's don't mess up */
int min_width, min_height;
int max_width, max_height;
int width_inc, height_inc;
struct {
int x; /* numerator */
int y; /* denominator */
} min_aspect, max_aspect;
int base_width, base_height;  /* added by ICCCM version 1 */
int win_gravity; /* added by ICCCM version 1 */
} XSizeHints;

/*
 * The next block of definitions are for window manager
 * properties that clients and applications use
 * for communication.
 */

/* flags argument in size hints */
#define USPosition (1L << 0) /* user-specified x, y */
#define USSize (1L << 1) /* user-specified width, height */

#define PPosition  (1L << 2) /* program-specified position */
#define PSize   (1L << 3) /* program-specified size */
#define PMinSize (1L << 4) /* program-specified minimum size */
#define PMaxSize (1L << 5) /* program-specified maximum size */
#define PResizeInc (1L << 6) /* program-specified
                              resize increments */
#define PAspect (1L << 7) /* program-specified min and max
                            aspect ratios */
#define PBaseSize (1L << 8) /* program-specified base
                             for incrementing */
#define PWinGravity (1L << 9) /* program-specified
                               window gravity */

/* obsolete */
#define PAllHints (PPosition|PSize|PMinSize|PMaxSize|
                   PResizeInc|PAspect)
```

```
typedef struct {
long flags; /* marks which fields in this structure
                are defined */
Bool input; /* does this application rely on the
                window manager to get keyboard input? */
int initial_state; /* see below */
Pixmap icon_pixmap; /* pixmap to be used as icon */
Window icon_window;  /* window to be used as icon */
int icon_x, icon_y; /* initial position of icon */
Pixmap icon_mask; /* icon mask bitmap */
XID window_group; /* ID of related window group */
/* this structure may be extended in the future */
} XWMHints;

/* definition for flags of XWMHints */
#define InputHint          (1L << 0)
#define StateHint          (1L << 1)
#define IconPixmapHint     (1L << 2)
#define IconWindowHint     (1L << 3)
#define IconPositionHint   (1L << 4)
#define IconMaskHint       (1L << 5)
#define WindowGroupHint    (1L << 6)
#define AllHints (InputHint|StateHint|
                  IconPixmapHint|IconWindowHint| \
IconPositionHint|IconMaskHint|WindowGroupHint)

/* definitions for initial window state */
#define WithdrawnState 0 /* for windows that are not mapped */
#define NormalState    1 /* most applications want to start
                            this way */
#define IconicState    3 /* application wants to start as
                            an icon */

/*
 * Obsolete states no longer defined by ICCCM.
 */
#define DontCareState 0 /* don't know or care */
#define ZoomState 2 /* application wants to start zoomed */
#define InactiveState 4 /* application believes it
                            is seldom used; */
   /* some wm's may put it on inactive menu */
```

```
/*
 * New structure for manipulating TEXT properties; used with
 * WM_NAME, WM_ICON_NAME, WM_CLIENT_MACHINE, and WM_COMMAND.
 */

typedef struct {
    unsigned char *value;  /* same as Property routines */
    Atom encoding;    /* prop type */
    int format;     /* prop data format: 8, 16, or 32 */
    unsigned long nitems;  /* number of data items in value */
} XTextProperty;


typedef struct {
 int min_width, min_height;
 int max_width, max_height;
 int width_inc, height_inc;
} XIconSize;

typedef struct {
 char *res_name;
 char *res_class;
} XClassHint;

/*
 * These macros are used to give some sugar to the image
 * routines so that naive people are more comfortable
 * with them.
 */

#define XDestroyImage(ximage) \
 ((*((ximage)->f.destroy_image))((ximage)))
#define XGetPixel(ximage, x, y) \
 ((*((ximage)->f.get_pixel))((ximage), (x), (y)))
#define XPutPixel(ximage, x, y, pixel) \
 ((*((ximage)->f.put_pixel))((ximage), (x), (y), (pixel)))
#define XSubImage(ximage, x, y, width, height) \
 ((*((ximage)->f.sub_image))((ximage), (x), (y),
   (width), (height)))
#define XAddPixel(ximage, value) \
 ((*((ximage)->f.add_pixel))((ximage), (value)))
```

```
/*
 * Compose sequence status structure, used in
 * calling XLookupString.
 */

typedef struct _XComposeStatus {
    char *compose_ptr;  /* state table pointer */
    int chars_matched;  /* match state */
} XComposeStatus;

/*
 * Keysym macros, used on Keysyms to test for classes
 * of symbols.
 */

#define IsKeypadKey(keysym) \
  (((unsigned)(keysym) >= XK_KP_Space) && \
   ((unsigned)(keysym) <= XK_KP_Equal))

#define IsCursorKey(keysym) \
  (((unsigned)(keysym) >= XK_Home) && \
   ((unsigned)(keysym) <  XK_Select))

#define IsPFKey(keysym) \
  (((unsigned)(keysym) >= XK_KP_F1) && \
   ((unsigned)(keysym) <= XK_KP_F4))

#define IsFunctionKey(keysym) \
  (((unsigned)(keysym) >= XK_F1) && \
   ((unsigned)(keysym) <= XK_F35))

#define IsMiscFunctionKey(keysym) \
  (((unsigned)(keysym) >= XK_Select) && \
   ((unsigned)(keysym) <  XK_KP_Space))

#define IsModifierKey(keysym) \
  (((unsigned)(keysym) >= XK_Shift_L) && \
   ((unsigned)(keysym) <= XK_Hyper_R))

/*
 * opaque reference to Region data type
```

```
 */
typedef struct _XRegion *Region;

/* Return values from XRectInRegion(). */

#define RectangleOut   0
#define RectangleIn    1
#define RectanglePart  2


/*
 * Information used by the visual utility routines to find
 * desired visual type from the many visuals a display
 * may support.
 */

typedef struct {
  Visual *visual;
  VisualID visualid;
  int screen;
  int depth;
#if defined(__cplusplus) || defined(c_plusplus)
  int c_class;        /* C++ */
#else
  int class;
#endif
  unsigned long red_mask;
  unsigned long green_mask;
  unsigned long blue_mask;
  int colormap_size;
  int bits_per_rgb;
} XVisualInfo;

#define VisualNoMask          0x0
#define VisualIDMask          0x1
#define VisualScreenMask      0x2
#define VisualDepthMask       0x4
#define VisualClassMask       0x8
#define VisualRedMaskMask     0x10
#define VisualGreenMaskMask   0x20
#define VisualBlueMaskMask    0x40
#define VisualColormapSizeMask 0x80
```

```
#define VisualBitsPerRGBMask    0x100
#define VisualAllMask           0x1FF


/*
 * This defines a window manager property that clients may
 * use to share standard color maps of type RGB_COLOR_MAP.
 */

typedef struct {
 Colormap colormap;
 unsigned long red_max;
 unsigned long red_mult;
 unsigned long green_max;
 unsigned long green_mult;
 unsigned long blue_max;
 unsigned long blue_mult;
 unsigned long base_pixel;
 VisualID visualid;  /* added by ICCCM version 1 */
 XID killid;    /* added by ICCCM version 1 */
} XStandardColormap;

#define ReleaseByFreeingColormap ((XID) 1L)  /* for killid
                                                field above */



/*
 * Return codes for XReadBitmapFile and XWriteBitmapFile.
 */
#define BitmapSuccess       0
#define BitmapOpenFailed    1
#define BitmapFileInvalid   2
#define BitmapNoMemory      3
/*
 * Declare the routines that don't return int.
 */

/**********************************************************
 *
 * Context Management
 *
 **********************************************************/
```

```
/* Associative lookup table return codes */

#define XCSUCCESS 0    /* No error */
#define XCNOMEM   1    /* Out of memory */
#define XCNOENT   2    /* No entry in table */

typedef int XContext;

#define XUniqueContext()        ((XContext) XrmUniqueQuark())
#define XStringToContext(string)  ((XContext)
                                   XrmStringToQuark(string))

extern int XSaveContext(
#if NeedFunctionPrototypes
    Display*  /* display */,
    Window  /* w */,
    XContext  /* context */,
    const void*  /* data */
#endif
);

extern int XFindContext(
#if NeedFunctionPrototypes
    Display*  /* display */,
    Window  /* w */,
    XContext  /* context */,
    caddr_t*  /* data_return */
#endif
);

extern int XDeleteContext(
#if NeedFunctionPrototypes
    Display*  /* display */,
    Window    /* w */,
    XContext  /* context */
#endif
);


extern XWMHints *XGetWMHints(
#if NeedFunctionPrototypes
```

```
    Display*  /* display */,
    Window    /* w */
#endif
);
extern Region XCreateRegion(
#if NeedFunctionPrototypes
    void
#endif
);
extern Region XPolygonRegion(
#if NeedFunctionPrototypes
    XPoint*  /* points */,
    int      /* n */,
    int      /* fill_rule */
#endif
);

extern XVisualInfo *XGetVisualInfo(
#if NeedFunctionPrototypes
    Display*     /* display */,
    long         /* vinfo_mask */,
    XVisualInfo* /* vinfo_template */,
    int*         /* nitems_return */
#endif
);

/* Allocation routines for properties that may get longer */
extern XSizeHints *XAllocSizeHints (
#if NeedFunctionPrototypes
    void
#endif
);
extern XStandardColormap *XAllocStandardColormap (
#if NeedFunctionPrototypes
    void
#endif
);
extern XWMHints *XAllocWMHints (
#if NeedFunctionPrototypes
    void
#endif
);
```

```
extern XClassHint *XAllocClassHint (
#if NeedFunctionPrototypes
    void
#endif
);
extern XIconSize *XAllocIconSize (
#if NeedFunctionPrototypes
    void
#endif
);


/* ICCCM routines for data structures defined in this file */
extern Status XGetWMSizeHints(
#if NeedFunctionPrototypes
    Display*        /* display */,
    Window          /* w */,
    XSizeHints*     /* hints_return */,
    long*           /* supplied_return */,
    Atom            /* property */
#endif
);
extern Status XGetWMNormalHints(
#if NeedFunctionPrototypes
    Display*        /* display */,
    Window          /* w */,
    XSizeHints*     /* hints_return */,
    long*           /* supplied_return */
#endif
);
extern Status XGetRGBColormaps(
#if NeedFunctionPrototypes
    Display*            /* display */,
    Window              /* w */,
    XStandardColormap** /* stdcmap_return */,
    int*                /* count_return */,
    Atom                /* property */
#endif
);
extern Status XGetTextProperty(
#if NeedFunctionPrototypes
    Display*        /* display */,
    Window          /* window */,
```

```
    XTextProperty* /* text_prop_return */,
    Atom           /* property */
#endif
);
extern Status XGetWMName(
#if NeedFunctionPrototypes
    Display*       /* display */,
    Window         /* w */,
    XTextProperty* /* text_prop_return */
#endif
);
extern Status XGetWMIconName(
#if NeedFunctionPrototypes
    Display*       /* display */,
    Window         /* w */,
    XTextProperty* /* text_prop_return */
#endif
);
extern Status XGetWMClientMachine(
#if NeedFunctionPrototypes
    Display*       /* display */,
    Window         /* w */,
    XTextProperty* /* text_prop_return */
#endif
);
extern void XSetWMProperties(
#if NeedFunctionPrototypes
    Display*       /* display */,
    Window         /* w */,
    XTextProperty* /* window_name */,
    XTextProperty* /* icon_name */,
    char**         /* argv */,
    int            /* argc */,
    XSizeHints*    /* normal_hints */,
    XWMHints*      /* wm_hints */,
    XClassHint*    /* class_hints */
#endif
);
extern void XSetWMSizeHints(
#if NeedFunctionPrototypes
    Display*    /* display */,
    Window      /* w */,
```

```
    XSizeHints*  /* hints */,
    Atom         /* property */
#endif
);
extern void XSetWMNormalHints(
#if NeedFunctionPrototypes
    Display*     /* display */,
    Window       /* w */,
    XSizeHints*  /* hints */
#endif
);
extern void XSetRGBColormaps(
#if NeedFunctionPrototypes
    Display*            /* display */,
    Window              /* w */,
    XStandardColormap*  /* stdcmaps */,
    int                 /* count */,
    Atom                /* property */
#endif
);
extern void XSetTextProperty(
#if NeedFunctionPrototypes
    Display*      /* display */,
    Window        /* w */,
    XTextProperty* /* text_prop */,
    Atom          /* property */
#endif
);
extern void XSetWMName(
#if NeedFunctionPrototypes
    Display*      /* display */,
    Window        /* w */,
    XTextProperty* /* text_prop */
#endif
);
extern void XSetWMIconName(
#if NeedFunctionPrototypes
    Display*      /* display */,
    Window        /* w */,
    XTextProperty* /* text_prop */
#endif
);
```

```
extern void XSetWMClientMachine(
#if NeedFunctionPrototypes
    Display*       /* display */,
    Window         /* w */,
    XTextProperty* /* text_prop */
#endif
);
extern Status XStringListToTextProperty(
#if NeedFunctionPrototypes
    char**         /* list */,
    int            /* count */,
    XTextProperty* /* text_prop_return */
#endif
);
extern Status XTextPropertyToStringList(
#if NeedFunctionPrototypes
    XTextProperty* /* text_prop */,
    char***        /* list_return */,
    int*           /* count_return */
#endif
);

/* The following declarations are alphabetized. */

extern XClipBox(
#if NeedFunctionPrototypes
    Region         /* r */,
    XRectangle*    /* rect_return */
#endif
);

extern XDestroyRegion(
#if NeedFunctionPrototypes
    Region  /* r */
#endif
);

extern XEmptyRegion(
#if NeedFunctionPrototypes
    Region  /* r */
#endif
);
```

```
extern XEqualRegion(
#if NeedFunctionPrototypes
    Region  /* r1 */,
    Region  /* r2 */
#endif
);

extern Status XGetClassHint(
#if NeedFunctionPrototypes
    Display*     /* display */,
    Window       /* w */,
    XClassHint*  /* class_hints_return */
#endif
);

extern Status XGetIconSizes(
#if NeedFunctionPrototypes
    Display*     /* display */,
    Window       /* w */,
    XIconSize**  /* size_list_return */,
    int*         /* count_return */
#endif
);

extern Status XGetNormalHints(
#if NeedFunctionPrototypes
    Display*     /* display */,
    Window       /* w */,
    XSizeHints*  /* hints_return */
#endif
);

extern Status XGetSizeHints(
#if NeedFunctionPrototypes
    Display*     /* display */,
    Window       /* w */,
    XSizeHints*  /* hints_return */,
    Atom         /* property */
#endif
);
```

```
extern Status XGetStandardColormap(
#if NeedFunctionPrototypes
    Display*           /* display */,
    Window             /* w */,
    XStandardColormap* /* colormap_return */,
    Atom               /* property */
#endif
);

extern Status XGetZoomHints(
#if NeedFunctionPrototypes
    Display*     /* display */,
    Window       /* w */,
    XSizeHints*  /* zhints_return */
#endif
);

extern XIntersectRegion(
#if NeedFunctionPrototypes
    Region  /* sra */,
    Region  /* srb */,
    Region  /* dr_return */
#endif
);

extern int XLookupString(
#if NeedFunctionPrototypes
    XKeyEvent*       /* event_struct */,
    char*            /* buffer_return */,
    int              /* bytes_buffer */,
    KeySym*          /* keysym_return */,
    XComposeStatus*  /* status_in_out */
#endif
);

extern Status XMatchVisualInfo(
#if NeedFunctionPrototypes
    Display*     /* display */,
    int          /* screen */,
    int          /* depth */,
    int          /* class */,
    XVisualInfo* /* vinfo_return */
```

```
#endif
);

extern XOffsetRegion(
#if NeedFunctionPrototypes
    Region /* r */,
    int     /* dx */,
    int     /* dy */
#endif
);

extern Bool XPointInRegion(
#if NeedFunctionPrototypes
    Region /* r */,
    int     /* x */,
    int     /* y */
#endif
);

extern Region XPolygonRegion(
#if NeedFunctionPrototypes
    XPoint*  /* points */,
    int      /* n */,
    int      /* fill_rule */
#endif
);

extern int XRectInRegion(
#if NeedFunctionPrototypes
    Region      /* r */,
    int         /* x */,
    int         /* y */,
    unsigned int /* width */,
    unsigned int /* height */
#endif
);

extern XSetClassHint(
#if NeedFunctionPrototypes
    Display*    /* display */,
    Window      /* w */,
    XClassHint*  /* class_hints */
```

```
#endif
);

extern XSetIconSizes(
#if NeedFunctionPrototypes
    Display*    /* display */,
    Window      /* w */,
    XIconSize*  /* size_list */,
    int         /* count */
#endif
);

extern XSetNormalHints(
#if NeedFunctionPrototypes
    Display*    /* display */,
    Window      /* w */,
    XSizeHints* /* hints */
#endif
);

extern XSetSizeHints(
#if NeedFunctionPrototypes
    Display*    /* display */,
    Window      /* w */,
    XSizeHints* /* hints */,
    Atom        /* property */
#endif
);

extern XSetStandardProperties(
#if NeedFunctionPrototypes
    Display*    /* display */,
    Window      /* w */,
    const char* /* window_name */,
    const char* /* icon_name */,
    Pixmap      /* icon_pixmap */,
    char**      /* argv */,
    int         /* argc */,
    XSizeHints* /* hints */
#endif
);
```

```
extern XSetWMHints(
#if NeedFunctionPrototypes
    Display*   /* display */,
    Window     /* w */,
    XWMHints*  /* wm_hints */
#endif
);

extern XSetRegion(
#if NeedFunctionPrototypes
    Display*  /* display */,
    GC        /* gc */,
    Region    /* r */
#endif
);

extern void XSetStandardColormap(
#if NeedFunctionPrototypes
    Display*           /* display */,
    Window             /* w */,
    XStandardColormap* /* colormap */,
    Atom               /* property */
#endif
);

extern XSetZoomHints(
#if NeedFunctionPrototypes
    Display*    /* display */,
    Window      /* w */,
    XSizeHints* /* zhints */
#endif
);

extern XShrinkRegion(
#if NeedFunctionPrototypes
    Region /* r */,
    int    /* dx */,
    int    /* dy */
#endif
);
```

```
extern XSubtractRegion(
#if NeedFunctionPrototypes
    Region  /* sra */,
    Region  /* srb */,
    Region  /* dr_return */
#endif
);

extern XUnionRectWithRegion(
#if NeedFunctionPrototypes
    XRectangle*  /* rectangle */,
    Region       /* src_region */,
    Region       /* dest_region_return */
#endif
);

extern XUnionRegion(
#if NeedFunctionPrototypes
    Region  /* sra */,
    Region  /* srb */,
    Region  /* dr_return */
#endif
);

extern int XWMGeometry(
#if NeedFunctionPrototypes
    Display*      /* display */,
    int           /* screen_number */,
    const char*   /* user_geometry */,
    const char*   /* default_geometry */,
    unsigned int  /* border_width */,
    XSizeHints*   /* hints */,
    int*          /* x_return */,
    int*          /* y_return */,
    int*          /* width_return */,
    int*          /* height_return */,
    int*          /* gravity_return */
#endif
);

extern XXorRegion(
#if NeedFunctionPrototypes
```

```
    Region  /* sra */,
    Region  /* srb */,
    Region  /* dr_return */
#endif
);

#ifdef __cplusplus
}       /* for C++ V2.0 */
#endif

#endif /* _XUTIL_H_ */
```

APPENDIX

Intrinsic.h

*T*he <X11/Intrinsic.h> header file defines all data types and data structures required by the application for toolkit calls. It also includes many Xlib calls and declarations for toolkit procedures used by applications.

```
#ifndef _XtIntrinsic_h
#define _XtIntrinsic_h

#include <X11/Xlib.h>
#include <X11/Xutil.h>
#include <X11/Xresource.h>
#include <X11/Xos.h>

#define XtSpecificationRelease 4

#ifdef XTFUNCPROTO
#undef NeedFunctionPrototypes
#define NeedFunctionPrototypes 1
#else
#undef NeedFunctionPrototypes
#define NeedFunctionPrototypes 0
#undef NeedWidePrototypes
#define NeedWidePrototypes 0
#endif

#ifndef NeedFunctionPrototypes
#if defined(FUNCPROTO) || defined(__STDC__) ||
 defined(__cplusplus) || defined(c_plusplus)
#define NeedFunctionPrototypes 1
#else
#define NeedFunctionPrototypes 0
#endif /* __STDC__ */
#endif /* NeedFunctionPrototypes */

/* NeedVarargsPrototypes is temporary until function
   prototypes work everywhere */
#ifndef NeedVarargsPrototypes
#if defined(FUNCPROTO) || defined(__STDC__) ||
 defined(__cplusplus) || defined(c_plusplus) ||
 NeedFunctionPrototypes
#define NeedVarargsPrototypes 1
#else
```

```
#define NeedVarargsPrototypes 0
#endif /* __STDC__ */
#endif /* NeedVarargsPrototypes */


typedef char *String;

#if defined(__cplusplus) || defined(c_plusplus)
#define CONST const
/* make const String do the right thing */
#define String char*
#else
#define CONST
#endif /* __cplusplus */


#ifndef NeedWidePrototypes
#if defined(NARROWPROTO)
#define NeedWidePrototypes 0
#else
#define NeedWidePrototypes 1  /* default to make
                                  interrupt. easier */
#endif
#endif

#ifndef NULL
#define NULL 0
#endif


#ifdef VMS
#define externalref globalref
#define externaldef(psect) globaldef {"psect"} noshare
#else
#define externalref extern
#define externaldef(psect)
#endif /* VMS */

#ifndef FALSE
#define FALSE 0
#define TRUE 1
#endif

#define XtNumber(arr)
                ((Cardinal) (sizeof(arr) / sizeof(arr[0])))
```

```
typedef struct _WidgetRec *Widget;
typedef Widget *WidgetList;
typedef struct _WidgetClassRec *WidgetClass;
typedef struct _CompositeRec *CompositeWidget;
typedef struct _XtActionsRec *XtActionList;
typedef struct _XtEventRec *XtEventTable;
typedef struct _XtBoundAccActionRec *XtBoundAccActions;

typedef struct _XtAppStruct *XtAppContext;
typedef unsigned long XtValueMask;
typedef unsigned long XtIntervalId;
typedef unsigned long XtInputId;
typedef unsigned long XtWorkProcId;
typedef unsigned int XtGeometryMask;
typedef unsigned long XtGCMask;    /* Mask of values that are
                                      used by widget */
typedef unsigned long Pixel;       /* Index into colormap */
typedef int  XtCacheType;
#define   XtCacheNone         0x001
#define   XtCacheAll          0x002
#define   XtCacheByDisplay    0x003
#define   XtCacheRefCount     0x100


/************************************************************
 *
 * System Dependent Definitions; see spec for specific range
 * requirements. Do not assume every implementation uses the
 * same base types!
 *
 *
 * XtArgVal ought to be a union of XtPointer, char *, long,
 * int *, and proc * but casting to union types is not
 * really supported.
 * So the typedef for XtArgVal should be chosen such that
 *
 * sizeof (XtArgVal) >= sizeof(XtPointer)
 *     sizeof(char *)
 *     sizeof(long)
 *     sizeof(int *)
 *     sizeof(proc *)
 *
```

```
 * ArgLists rely heavily on the above typedef.
 *
 ************************************************************/
#ifdef CRAY
typedef long   Boolean;
typedef char*  XtArgVal;
typedef long   XtEnum;
#else
typedef unsigned char Boolean;
typedef long   XtArgVal;
typedef unsigned char XtEnum;
#endif

typedef unsigned int Cardinal;
typedef unsigned short Dimension;  /* Size in pixels   */
typedef short  Position;   /* Offset from 0 coordinate  */

#ifdef __STDC__
typedef void*  XtPointer;
#else
typedef char*  XtPointer;
#endif

typedef XtPointer Opaque;

#include <X11/Core.h>
#include <X11/Composite.h>
#include <X11/Constraint.h>
#include <X11/Object.h>
#include <X11/RectObj.h>

typedef struct _TranslationData *XtTranslations;
typedef struct _TranslationData *XtAccelerators;
typedef unsigned int Modifiers;

typedef void (*XtActionProc)(
#if NeedFunctionPrototypes
    Widget   /* widget */,
    XEvent*  /* event */,
    String*  /* params */,
    Cardinal*  /* num_params */
```

```
#endif
);

typedef XtActionProc* XtBoundActions;

typedef struct _XtActionsRec{
    String  string;
    XtActionProc proc;
} XtActionsRec;

typedef enum {
/* address mode   parameter representation    */
/* ------------   ------------------------    */
    XtAddress,          /* address      */
    XtBaseOffset,       /* offset       */
    XtImmediate,        /* constant      */
    XtResourceString,   /* resource name string    */
    XtResourceQuark,    /* resource name quark     */
    XtWidgetBaseOffset, /* offset from ancestor     */
    XtProcedureArg      /* procedure to invoke     */
} XtAddressMode;

typedef struct {
    XtAddressMode   address_mode;
    XtPointer       address_id;
    Cardinal        size;
} XtConvertArgRec, *XtConvertArgList;

typedef void (*XtConvertArgProc)(
#if NeedFunctionPrototypes
    Widget      /* widget */,
    Cardinal*   /* size */,
    XrmValue*   /* value */
#endif
);

typedef struct {
    XtGeometryMask request_mode;
    Position x, y;
    Dimension width, height, border_width;
    Widget sibling;
    int stack_mode;     /* Above, Below, TopIf, BottomIf,
```

```
                          Opposite, DontChange */
} XtWidgetGeometry;

/* Additions to Xlib geometry requests: ask what would
   happen, don't do it */
#define XtCWQueryOnly (1 << 7)

/* Additions to Xlib stack modes: don't change stack order */
#define XtSMDontChange 5

typedef void (*XtConverter)(
#if NeedFunctionPrototypes
    XrmValue*  /* args */,
    Cardinal*  /* num_args */,
    XrmValue*  /* from */,
    XrmValue*  /* to */
#endif
);

typedef Boolean (*XtTypeConverter)(
#if NeedFunctionPrototypes
    Display*    /* dpy */,
    XrmValue*   /* args */,
    Cardinal*   /* num_args */,
    XrmValue*   /* from */,
    XrmValue*   /* to */,
    XtPointer*  /* converter_data */
#endif
);

typedef void (*XtDestructor)(
#if NeedFunctionPrototypes
    XtAppContext /* app */,
    XrmValue*    /* to */,
    XtPointer    /* converter_data */,
    XrmValue*    /* args */,
    Cardinal*    /* num_args */
#endif
);

typedef Opaque XtCacheRef;
```

```
typedef Opaque XtActionHookId;

typedef void (*XtActionHookProc)(
#if NeedFunctionPrototypes
    Widget      /* w */,
    XtPointer  /* client_data */,
    String     /* action_name */,
    XEvent*    /* event */,
    String*    /* params */,
    Cardinal*  /* num_params */
#endif
);

typedef void (*XtKeyProc)(
#if NeedFunctionPrototypes
    Display*  /* dpy */,
#if NeedWidePrototypes
    /* KeyCode */ int /* keycode */,
#else
    KeyCode   /* keycode */,
#endif /* NeedWidePrototypes */
    Modifiers   /* modifiers */,
    Modifiers*  /* modifiers_return */,
    KeySym*     /* keysym_return */
#endif
);

typedef void (*XtCaseProc)(
#if NeedFunctionPrototypes
    Display*  /* display */,
    KeySym    /* keysym */,
    KeySym*   /* lower_return */,
    KeySym*   /* upper_return */
#endif
);

typedef void (*XtEventHandler)(
#if NeedFunctionPrototypes
    Widget      /* widget */,
    XtPointer  /* closure */,
    XEvent*    /* event */,
    Boolean*    /* continue_to_dispatch */
```

```
#endif
);
typedef unsigned long EventMask;

typedef enum {XtListHead, XtListTail } XtListPosition;

typedef unsigned long XtInputMask;
#define XtInputNoneMask    0L
#define XtInputReadMask    (1L<<0)
#define XtInputWriteMask   (1L<<1)
#define XtInputExceptMask  (1L<<2)

typedef void (*XtTimerCallbackProc)(
#if NeedFunctionPrototypes
    XtPointer     /* closure */,
    XtIntervalId* /* id */
#endif
);

typedef void (*XtInputCallbackProc)(
#if NeedFunctionPrototypes
    XtPointer   /* closure */,
    int*        /* source */,
    XtInputId*  /* id */
#endif
);

typedef struct {
    String name;
    XtArgVal value;
} Arg, *ArgList;

typedef XtPointer XtVarArgsList;

typedef void (*XtCallbackProc)(
#if NeedFunctionPrototypes
    Widget      /* widget */,
    XtPointer   /* closure */, /* data the
                                  application registered */
    XtPointer   /* call_data */ /* callback specific data */
#endif
);
```

```
typedef struct _XtCallbackRec {
    XtCallbackProc   callback;
    XtPointer        closure;
} XtCallbackRec, *XtCallbackList;

typedef enum {
 XtCallbackNoList,
 XtCallbackHasNone,
 XtCallbackHasSome
} XtCallbackStatus;

typedef enum  {
    XtGeometryYes,      /* Request accepted. */
    XtGeometryNo,       /* Request denied. */
    XtGeometryAlmost,   /* Request denied, but willing
                            to take replyBox. */
    XtGeometryDone      /* Request accepted and done. */
} XtGeometryResult;

typedef enum {XtGrabNone, XtGrabNonexclusive, XtGrabExclusive}
         XtGrabKind;

typedef struct {
    Widget  shell_widget;
    Widget  enable_widget;
} XtPopdownIDRec, *XtPopdownID;

typedef struct _XtResource {
    String resource_name;      /* Resource name */
    String resource_class;     /* Resource class */
    String resource_type;      /* Representation
                                  type desired */
    Cardinal resource_size;    /* Size in bytes
                                  of representation */
    Cardinal resource_offset; /* Offset from base to put
                                  resource value */
    String default_type;       /* representation type of
                                  specified default */
    XtPointer default_addr;     /* Address of
                                  default resource */
} XtResource, *XtResourceList;
```

```
typedef void (*XtResourceDefaultProc)(
#if NeedFunctionPrototypes
    Widget      /* widget */,
    int         /* offset */,
    XrmValue* /* value */
#endif
);

typedef void (*XtErrorMsgHandler)(
#if NeedFunctionPrototypes
    String      /* name */,
    String      /* type */,
    String      /* class */,
    String      /* defaultp */,
    String*     /* params */,
    Cardinal*   /* num_params */
#endif
);

typedef void (*XtErrorHandler)(
#if NeedFunctionPrototypes
  String   /* msg */
#endif
);

typedef Boolean (*XtWorkProc)(
#if NeedFunctionPrototypes
    XtPointer   /* closure */ /* data the
                                 application registered */
#endif
);

typedef struct {
    char match;
    String substitution;
} SubstitutionRec, *Substitution;

typedef Boolean (*XtFilePredicate)( /* String filename */ );

typedef XtPointer XtRequestId;
```

```
/*
 * Routine to get the value of a selection as a given type.
 * Returns TRUE if it successfully got the value as requested,
 * FALSE otherwise. selection is the atom describing the type
 * of selection (e.g., primary or secondary). value is set to
 * the pointer of the converted value, with length elements
 * of data, each of size indicated by format.
 * (This pointer will be freed using XtFree when the
 * selection has been delivered to the requester.)  target is
 * the type that the conversion should use if possible;
 * type is returned as the actual type returned.
 * format should be either 8, 16, or 32, and specifies the
 * word size of the selection, so that Xlib and the server
 * can convert it between different machine types. */

typedef Boolean (*XtConvertSelectionProc)(
#if NeedFunctionPrototypes
    Widget          /* widget */,
    Atom*           /* selection */,
    Atom*           /* target */,
    Atom*           /* type_return */,
    XtPointer*      /* value_return */,
    unsigned long* /* length_return */,
    int*            /* format_return */
#endif
);


/*
 * Routine to inform a widget that it no longer owns
 * the given selection.
 */

typedef void (*XtLoseSelectionProc)(
#if NeedFunctionPrototypes
    Widget   /* widget */,
    Atom*   /* selection */
#endif
);


/*
 * Routine to inform the selection owner when a selection
```

```
 * requester has successfully retrieved the selection value.
 */

typedef void (*XtSelectionDoneProc)(
#if NeedFunctionPrototypes
    Widget    /* widget */,
    Atom*     /* selection */,
    Atom*     /* target */
#endif
);


/*
 * Routine to call back when a requested value has been
 * obtained for a selection.
 */

typedef void (*XtSelectionCallbackProc)(
#if NeedFunctionPrototypes
    Widget          /* widget */,
    XtPointer       /* closure */,
    Atom*           /* selection */,
    Atom*           /* type */,
    XtPointer       /* value */,
    unsigned long* /* length */,
    int*            /* format */
#endif
);

typedef void (*XtLoseSelectionIncrProc)(
#if NeedFunctionPrototypes
    Widget     /* widget */,
    Atom*      /* selection */,
    XtPointer  /* client_data */
#endif
);

typedef void (*XtSelectionDoneIncrProc)(
#if NeedFunctionPrototypes
    Widget          /* widget */,
    Atom*           /* selection */,
    Atom*           /* target */,
```

```
    XtRequestId* /* receiver_id */,
    XtPointer    /* client_data */
#endif
);

typedef Boolean (*XtConvertSelectionIncrProc)(
#if NeedFunctionPrototypes
    Widget        /* widget */,
    Atom*         /* selection */,
    Atom*         /* target */,
    Atom*         /* type */,
    XtPointer*    /* value */,
    unsigned long* /* length */,
    int*          /* format */,
    unsigned long* /* max_length */,
    XtPointer     /* client_data */,
    XtRequestId*  /* receiver_id */
#endif
);

typedef void (*XtCancelConvertSelectionProc)(
#if NeedFunctionPrototypes
    Widget        /* widget */,
    Atom*         /* selection */,
    Atom*         /* target */,
    XtRequestId* /* receiver_id */,
    XtPointer     /* client_data */
#endif
);

/*************************************************************
 *
 * Exported Interfaces
 *
 *************************************************************/

#ifdef __cplusplus   /* do not leave open across includes */
  extern "C" {    /* for C++ V2.0 */
#endif

extern Boolean XtConvertAndStore(
#if NeedFunctionPrototypes
```

```
    Widget          /* widget */,
    CONST String    /* from_type */,
    XrmValue*       /* from */,
    CONST String    /* to_type */,
    XrmValue*       /* to_in_out */
#endif
);

extern Boolean XtCallConverter(
#if NeedFunctionPrototypes
    Display*         /* dpy */,
    XtTypeConverter  /* converter */,
    XrmValuePtr      /* args */,
    Cardinal         /* num_args */,
    XrmValuePtr      /* from */,
    XrmValue*        /* to_return */,
    XtCacheRef*      /* cache_ref_return */
#endif
);

extern Boolean XtDispatchEvent(
#if NeedFunctionPrototypes
    XEvent*   /* event */
#endif
);

extern Boolean XtCallAcceptFocus(
#if NeedFunctionPrototypes
    Widget   /* widget */,
    Time*    /* t */
#endif
);

extern Boolean XtPeekEvent(
#if NeedFunctionPrototypes
    XEvent*  /* event */
#endif
);

extern Boolean XtAppPeekEvent(
#if NeedFunctionPrototypes
    XtAppContext  /* appContext */,
```

```
    XEvent*        /* event */
#endif
);

extern Boolean XtIsSubclass(
#if NeedFunctionPrototypes
    Widget       /* widget */,
    WidgetClass  /* widgetClass */
#endif
);

extern Boolean XtIsObject(
#if NeedFunctionPrototypes
    Widget   /* object */
#endif
);

extern Boolean _XtCheckSubclassFlag(
                        /* implementation-private */
#if NeedFunctionPrototypes
    Widget  /* object */,
#if NeedWidePrototypes
    /* XtEnum */ int /* type_flag */
#else
    XtEnum  /* type_flag */
#endif /* NeedWidePrototypes */
#endif
);

extern Boolean _XtIsSubclassOf(
                    /* implementation-private */
#if NeedFunctionPrototypes
    Widget       /* object */,
    WidgetClass  /* widget_class */,
    WidgetClass  /* flag_class */,
#if NeedWidePrototypes
    /* XtEnum */ int /* type_flag */
#else
    XtEnum  /* type_flag */
#endif /* NeedWidePrototypes */
#endif
);
```

```
extern Boolean XtIsManaged(
#if NeedFunctionPrototypes
    Widget   /* rectobj */
#endif
);

extern Boolean XtIsRealized(
#if NeedFunctionPrototypes
    Widget   /* widget */
#endif
);

extern Boolean XtIsSensitive(
#if NeedFunctionPrototypes
    Widget   /* widget */
#endif
);

/*
 * Set the given widget to own the selection. The convertProc
 * should be called when someone wants the current value of
 * the selection. If it is not NULL, the losesSelection gets
 * called whenever the window no longer owns the selection
 * (because someone else took it). If it is not NULL, the
 * doneProc gets called when the widget has provided the
 * current value of the selection to a requester and the
 * requester has indicated that it has succeeded in reading
 * it by deleting the property.
 */

extern Boolean XtOwnSelection(
#if NeedFunctionPrototypes
    Widget                  /* widget */,
    Atom                    /* selection */,
    Time                    /* time */,
    XtConvertSelectionProc  /* convert */,
    XtLoseSelectionProc     /* lose */,
    XtSelectionDoneProc     /* done */
#endif
);

/* incremental selection interface */
```

```
extern Boolean XtOwnSelectionIncremental(
#if NeedFunctionPrototypes
    Widget                      /* widget */,
    Atom                        /* selection */,
    Time                        /* time */,
    XtConvertSelectionIncrProc  /* convert_callback */,
    XtLoseSelectionIncrProc     /* lose_callback */,
    XtSelectionDoneIncrProc     /* done_callback */,
    XtCancelConvertSelectionProc /* cancel_callback */,
    XtPointer                   /* client_data */
#endif
);


extern XtGeometryResult XtMakeResizeRequest(
#if NeedFunctionPrototypes
    Widget  /* widget */,
#if NeedWidePrototypes
    /* Dimension */ int /* width */,
    /* Dimension */ int /* height */,
#else
    Dimension   /* width */,
    Dimension   /* height */,
#endif /* NeedWidePrototypes */
    Dimension*  /* replyWidth */,
    Dimension*  /* replyHeight */
#endif
);


extern void XtTranslateCoords(
#if NeedFunctionPrototypes
    Widget  /* widget */,
#if NeedWidePrototypes
    /* Position */ int /* x */,
    /* Position */ int /* y */,
#else
    Position  /* x */,
    Position  /* y */,
#endif /* NeedWidePrototypes */
    Position*  /* rootx_return */,
    Position*  /* rooty_return */
#endif
);
```

```
extern KeySym* XtGetKeysymTable(
#if NeedFunctionPrototypes
    Display*  /* dpy */,
    KeyCode*  /* min_keycode_return */,
    int*      /* keysyms_per_keycode_return */
#endif
);

extern void XtKeysymToKeycodeList(
#if NeedFunctionPrototypes
    Display*   /* dpy */,
    KeySym     /* keysym */,
    KeyCode**  /* keycodes_return */,
    Cardinal*  /* keycount_return */
#endif
);

/* %%% Caution: don't declare any functions past this point
 * that return one of the following types or take a pointer
 * to one of the following types.
 */

#if NeedWidePrototypes
#define Boolean    int
#define Dimension  int
#define KeyCode    int
#define Position   int
#define XtEnum     int
#endif /* NeedWidePrototypes */

extern void XtStringConversionWarning(
#if NeedFunctionPrototypes
    CONST String /* from */, /* String attempted
                                to convert. */
    CONST String /* toType */ /* Type attempted to
                                 convert it to. */
#endif
);

extern void XtDisplayStringConversionWarning(
#if NeedFunctionPrototypes
    Display*   /* dpy */,
```

```
        CONST String /* from */, /* String attempted
                                    to convert. */
        CONST String /* toType */ /* Type attempted to
                                    convert it to. */
#endif
);


#if defined(__STDC__)
externalref XtConvertArgRec const colorConvertArgs[];
externalref XtConvertArgRec const screenConvertArg[];
#else
externalref XtConvertArgRec colorConvertArgs[];
externalref XtConvertArgRec screenConvertArg[];
#endif

extern void XtAppAddConverter( /* obsolete */
#if NeedFunctionPrototypes
    XtAppContext     /* app */,
    CONST String     /* from_type */,
    CONST String     /* to_type */,
    XtConverter      /* converter */,
    XtConvertArgList /* convert_args */,
    Cardinal         /* num_args */
#endif
);


extern void XtAddConverter( /* obsolete */
#if NeedFunctionPrototypes
    CONST String     /* from_type */,
    CONST String     /* to_type */,
    XtConverter      /* converter */,
    XtConvertArgList /* convert_args */,
    Cardinal         /* num_args */
#endif
);


extern void XtSetTypeConverter(
#if NeedFunctionPrototypes
    CONST String      /* from_type */,
    CONST String      /* to_type */,
```

```
    XtTypeConverter    /* converter */,
    XtConvertArgList   /* convert_args */,
    Cardinal           /* num_args */,
    XtCacheType        /* cache_type */,
    XtDestructor       /* destructor */
#endif
);

extern void XtAppSetTypeConverter(
#if NeedFunctionPrototypes
    XtAppContext       /* app_context */,
    CONST String       /* from_type */,
    CONST String       /* to_type */,
    XtTypeConverter    /* converter */,
    XtConvertArgList   /* convert_args */,
    Cardinal           /* num_args */,
    XtCacheType        /* cache_type */,
    XtDestructor       /* destructor */
#endif
);

extern void XtConvert(
#if NeedFunctionPrototypes
    Widget         /* widget */,
    CONST String   /* from_type */,
    XrmValue*      /* from */,
    CONST String   /* to_type */,
    XrmValue*      /* to_return */
#endif
);

extern void XtDirectConvert(
#if NeedFunctionPrototypes
    XtConverter   /* converter */,
    XrmValuePtr   /* args */,
    Cardinal      /* num_args */,
    XrmValuePtr   /* from */,
    XrmValue*     /* to_return */
#endif
);
```

```
/*************************************************************
 *
 * Translation Management
 *
 *************************************************************/

extern XtTranslations XtParseTranslationTable(
#if NeedFunctionPrototypes
    CONST String /* source */
#endif
);

extern XtAccelerators XtParseAcceleratorTable(
#if NeedFunctionPrototypes
    CONST String /* source */
#endif
);

extern void XtOverrideTranslations(
#if NeedFunctionPrototypes
    Widget           /* widget */,
    XtTranslations  /* new */
#endif
);

extern void XtAugmentTranslations(
#if NeedFunctionPrototypes
    Widget           /* widget */,
    XtTranslations  /* new */
#endif
);

extern void XtInstallAccelerators(
#if NeedFunctionPrototypes
    Widget   /* destination */,
    Widget   /* source */
#endif
);

extern void XtInstallAllAccelerators(
#if NeedFunctionPrototypes
    Widget   /* destination */,
```

```
        Widget    /* source */
#endif
);

extern void XtUninstallTranslations(
#if NeedFunctionPrototypes
    Widget    /* widget */
#endif
);

extern void XtAppAddActions(
#if NeedFunctionPrototypes
    XtAppContext   /* app */,
    XtActionList   /* actions */,
    Cardinal       /* num_actions */
#endif
);

extern void XtAddActions(
#if NeedFunctionPrototypes
    XtActionList   /* actions */,
    Cardinal       /* num_actions */
#endif
);

extern XtActionHookId XtAppAddActionHook(
#if NeedFunctionPrototypes
    XtAppContext      /* app */,
    XtActionHookProc  /* proc */,
    XtPointer         /* client_data */
#endif
);

extern void XtRemoveActionHook(
#if NeedFunctionPrototypes
    XtActionHookId  /* id */
#endif
);

extern void XtCallActionProc(
#if NeedFunctionPrototypes
    Widget        /* widget */,
```

```
    CONST String /* action */,
    XEvent*       /* event */,
    String*       /* params */,
    Cardinal      /* num_params */
#endif
);

extern void XtRegisterGrabAction(
#if NeedFunctionPrototypes
    XtActionProc  /* action_proc */,
    Boolean       /* owner_events */,
    unsigned int  /* event_mask */,
    int           /* pointer_mode */,
    int           /* keyboard_mode */
#endif
);

extern void XtSetMultiClickTime(
#if NeedFunctionPrototypes
    Display*  /* dpy */,
    int       /* milliseconds */
#endif
);

extern int XtGetMultiClickTime(
#if NeedFunctionPrototypes
    Display*  /* dpy */
#endif
);

extern KeySym XtGetActionKeysym(
#if NeedFunctionPrototypes
    XEvent*      /* event */,
    Modifiers*   /* modifiers_return */
#endif
);

/************************************************************
 *
 * KeyCode and KeySym procedures for translation management
 *
 ************************************************************/
```

```
extern void XtTranslateKeycode(
#if NeedFunctionPrototypes
    Display*     /* dpy */,
    KeyCode      /* keycode */,
    Modifiers    /* modifiers */,
    Modifiers*   /* modifiers_return */,
    KeySym*      /* keysym_return */
#endif
);

extern void XtTranslateKey(
#if NeedFunctionPrototypes
    Display*     /* dpy */,
    KeyCode      /* keycode */,
    Modifiers    /* modifiers */,
    Modifiers*   /* modifiers_return */,
    KeySym*      /* keysym_return */
#endif
);

extern void XtSetKeyTranslator(
#if NeedFunctionPrototypes
    Display*     /* dpy */,
    XtKeyProc    /* proc */
#endif
);

extern void XtRegisterCaseConverter(
#if NeedFunctionPrototypes
    Display*     /* dpy */,
    XtCaseProc   /* proc */,
    KeySym       /* start */,
    KeySym       /* stop */
#endif
);

extern void XtConvertCase(
#if NeedFunctionPrototypes
    Display*   /* dpy */,
    KeySym     /* keysym */,
    KeySym*    /* lower_return */,
    KeySym*    /* upper_return */
```

```
#endif
);


/************************************************************
 *
 * Event Management
 *
 ************************************************************/


/* XtAllEvents is valid only for XtRemoveEventHandler and
 * XtRemoveRawEventHandler; don't use it to select events!
 */
#define XtAllEvents ((EventMask) -1L)

extern void XtInsertEventHandler(
#if NeedFunctionPrototypes
    Widget          /* widget */,
    EventMask       /* eventMask */,
    Boolean         /* nonmaskable */,
    XtEventHandler  /* proc */,
    XtPointer       /* closure */,
    XtListPosition  /* position */
#endif
);

extern void XtInsertRawEventHandler(
#if NeedFunctionPrototypes
    Widget          /* widget */,
    EventMask       /* eventMask */,
    Boolean         /* nonmaskable */,
    XtEventHandler  /* proc */,
    XtPointer       /* closure */,
    XtListPosition  /* position */
#endif
);

extern void XtAddEventHandler(
#if NeedFunctionPrototypes
    Widget          /* widget */,
    EventMask       /* eventMask */,
    Boolean         /* nonmaskable */,
    XtEventHandler  /* proc */,
```

```
    XtPointer        /* closure */
#endif
);

extern void XtRemoveEventHandler(
#if NeedFunctionPrototypes
    Widget           /* widget */,
    EventMask        /* eventMask */,
    Boolean          /* nonmaskable */,
    XtEventHandler   /* proc */,
    XtPointer        /* closure */
#endif
);

extern void XtAddRawEventHandler(
#if NeedFunctionPrototypes
    Widget           /* widget */,
    EventMask        /* eventMask */,
    Boolean          /* nonmaskable */,
    XtEventHandler   /* proc */,
    XtPointer        /* closure */
#endif
);

extern void XtRemoveRawEventHandler(
#if NeedFunctionPrototypes
    Widget           /* widget */,
    EventMask        /* eventMask */,
    Boolean          /* nonmaskable */,
    XtEventHandler   /* proc */,
    XtPointer        /* closure */
#endif
);

extern void XtInsertEventHandler(
#if NeedFunctionPrototypes
    Widget           /* widget */,
    EventMask        /* eventMask */,
    Boolean          /* nonmaskable */,
    XtEventHandler   /* proc */,
    XtPointer        /* closure */,
    XtListPosition   /* position */
```

```
#endif
);

extern void XtInsertRawEventHandler(
#if NeedFunctionPrototypes
    Widget         /* widget */,
    EventMask      /* eventMask */,
    Boolean        /* nonmaskable */,
    XtEventHandler /* proc */,
    XtPointer      /* closure */,
    XtListPosition /* position */
#endif
);

extern EventMask XtBuildEventMask(
#if NeedFunctionPrototypes
    Widget  /* widget */
#endif
);

extern void XtAddGrab(
#if NeedFunctionPrototypes
    Widget  /* widget */,
    Boolean /* exclusive */,
    Boolean /* spring_loaded */
#endif
);

extern void XtRemoveGrab(
#if NeedFunctionPrototypes
    Widget  /* widget */
#endif
);

extern void XtProcessEvent(
#if NeedFunctionPrototypes
    XtInputMask  /* mask */
#endif
);

extern void XtAppProcessEvent(
#if NeedFunctionPrototypes
```

```
        XtAppContext  /* app */,
        XtInputMask   /* mask */
#endif
);

extern void XtMainLoop(
#if NeedFunctionPrototypes
    void
#endif
);


extern void XtAppMainLoop(
#if NeedFunctionPrototypes
    XtAppContext  /* app */
#endif
);

extern void XtAddExposureToRegion(
#if NeedFunctionPrototypes
    XEvent*  /* event */,
    Region   /* region */
#endif
);

extern void XtSetKeyboardFocus(
#if NeedFunctionPrototypes
    Widget  /* subtree */,
    Widget  /* descendant */
#endif
);

extern Time XtLastTimestampProcessed(
#if NeedFunctionPrototypes
    Display*  /* dpy */
#endif
);

/**********************************************************
 *
 * Event Gathering Routines
 *
 **********************************************************/
```

```
extern XtIntervalId XtAddTimeOut(
#if NeedFunctionPrototypes
    unsigned long         /* interval */,
    XtTimerCallbackProc /* proc */,
    XtPointer             /* closure */
#endif
);


extern XtIntervalId XtAppAddTimeOut(
#if NeedFunctionPrototypes
    XtAppContext          /* app */,
    unsigned long         /* interval */,
    XtTimerCallbackProc /* proc */,
    XtPointer             /* closure */
#endif
);


extern void XtRemoveTimeOut(
#if NeedFunctionPrototypes
    XtIntervalId  /* timer */
#endif
);


extern XtInputId XtAddInput(
#if NeedFunctionPrototypes
    int                   /* source */,
    XtPointer             /* condition */,
    XtInputCallbackProc /* proc */,
    XtPointer             /* closure */
#endif
);


extern XtInputId XtAppAddInput(
#if NeedFunctionPrototypes
    XtAppContext          /* app */,
    int                   /* source */,
    XtPointer             /* condition */,
    XtInputCallbackProc /* proc */,
    XtPointer             /* closure */
#endif
);
```

```
extern void XtRemoveInput(
#if NeedFunctionPrototypes
    XtInputId   /* id */
#endif
);

extern void XtNextEvent(
#if NeedFunctionPrototypes
    XEvent*    /* event */
#endif
);

extern void XtAppNextEvent(
#if NeedFunctionPrototypes
    XtAppContext  /* appContext */,
    XEvent*       /* event */
#endif
);

#define XtIMXEvent  1
#define XtIMTimer   2
#define XtIMAlternateInput 4
#define XtIMAll (XtIMXEvent | XtIMTimer | XtIMAlternateInput)

extern XtInputMask XtPending(
#if NeedFunctionPrototypes
    void
#endif
);

extern XtInputMask XtAppPending(
#if NeedFunctionPrototypes
    XtAppContext  /* appContext */
#endif
);

/************************************************************
 *
 * Random utility routines
 *
 ************************************************************/
```

```
#define XtIsRectObj(object)
        (_XtCheckSubclassFlag(object, (XtEnum)0x02))
#define XtIsWidget(object)
        (_XtCheckSubclassFlag(object, (XtEnum)0x04))
#define XtIsComposite(widget)
        (_XtCheckSubclassFlag(widget, (XtEnum)0x08))
#define XtIsConstraint(widget)
        (_XtCheckSubclassFlag(widget, (XtEnum)0x10))
#define XtIsShell(widget)
        (_XtCheckSubclassFlag(widget, (XtEnum)0x20))
#define XtIsOverrideShell(widget) \
        (_XtIsSubclassOf(widget,
        (WidgetClass)overrideShellWidgetClass, \
        (WidgetClass)shellWidgetClass, (XtEnum)0x20))
#define XtIsWMShell(widget)
        (_XtCheckSubclassFlag(widget, (XtEnum)0x40))
#define XtIsVendorShell(widget) \
        (_XtIsSubclassOf(widget,
        (WidgetClass)vendorShellWidgetClass, \
        (WidgetClass)wmShellWidgetClass, (XtEnum)0x40))
#define XtIsTransientShell(widget) \
        (_XtIsSubclassOf(widget,
        (WidgetClass)transientShellWidgetClass, \
        (WidgetClass)wmShellWidgetClass, (XtEnum)0x40))
#define XtIsTopLevelShell(widget)
        (_XtCheckSubclassFlag(widget, (XtEnum)0x80))
#define XtIsApplicationShell(widget) \
        (_XtIsSubclassOf(widget,
        (WidgetClass)applicationShellWidgetClass, \
        (WidgetClass)topLevelShellWidgetClass, (XtEnum)0x80))

extern void XtRealizeWidget(
#if NeedFunctionPrototypes
    Widget   /* widget */
#endif
);

void XtUnrealizeWidget(
#if NeedFunctionPrototypes
    Widget   /* widget */
#endif
);
```

```
extern void XtDestroyWidget(
#if NeedFunctionPrototypes
    Widget    /* widget */
#endif
);

extern void XtSetSensitive(
#if NeedFunctionPrototypes
    Widget    /* widget */,
    Boolean   /* sensitive */
#endif
);

extern void XtSetMappedWhenManaged(
#if NeedFunctionPrototypes
    Widget    /* widget */,
    Boolean   /* mappedWhenManaged */
#endif
);

extern Widget XtNameToWidget(
#if NeedFunctionPrototypes
    Widget       /* root */,
    CONST String /* name */
#endif
);

extern Widget XtWindowToWidget(
#if NeedFunctionPrototypes
    Display*  /* display */,
    Window    /* window */
#endif
);

/****************************************************************
 *
 * Arg lists
 *
 ****************************************************************/

#define XtSetArg(arg, n, d) \
    ((void)( (arg).name = (n), (arg).value = (XtArgVal)(d) ))
```

```
extern ArgList XtMergeArgLists(
#if NeedFunctionPrototypes
    ArgList     /* args1 */,
    Cardinal    /* num_args1 */,
    ArgList     /* args2 */,
    Cardinal    /* num_args2 */
#endif
);


/************************************************************
 *
 * Vararg lists
 *
 ************************************************************/

#define XtVaNestedList    "XtVaNestedList"
#define XtVaTypedArg      "XtVaTypedArg"

extern XtVarArgsList XtVaCreateArgsList(
#if NeedVarargsPrototypes
    XtPointer   /*unused*/, ...
#endif
);


/************************************************************
 *
 * Information routines
 *
 ************************************************************/

#ifndef _XtIntrinsicP_h

/* We're not included from the private file,
   so define these */

extern Display *XtDisplay(
#if NeedFunctionPrototypes
    Widget    /* widget */
#endif
);
```

```
extern Display *XtDisplayOfObject(
#if NeedFunctionPrototypes
    Widget   /* object */
#endif
);

extern Screen *XtScreen(
#if NeedFunctionPrototypes
    Widget   /* widget */
#endif
);

extern Screen *XtScreenOfObject(
#if NeedFunctionPrototypes
    Widget   /* object */
#endif
);

extern Window XtWindow(
#if NeedFunctionPrototypes
    Widget   /* widget */
#endif
);

extern Window XtWindowOfObject(
#if NeedFunctionPrototypes
    Widget   /* object */
#endif
);

extern String XtName(
#if NeedFunctionPrototypes
    Widget   /* object */
#endif
);

extern WidgetClass XtSuperclass(
#if NeedFunctionPrototypes
    Widget   /* object */
#endif
);
```

```
extern WidgetClass XtClass(
#if NeedFunctionPrototypes
    Widget    /* object */
#endif
);

extern Widget XtParent(
#if NeedFunctionPrototypes
    Widget    /* widget */
#endif
);

#endif /*_XtIntrinsicP_h*/

#define XtMapWidget(widget) XMapWindow(XtDisplay(widget),
                                      XtWindow(widget))
#define XtUnmapWidget(widget) \
  XUnmapWindow(XtDisplay(widget), XtWindow(widget))

extern void XtAddCallback(
#if NeedFunctionPrototypes
    Widget         /* widget */,
    CONST String   /* callback_name */,
    XtCallbackProc /* callback */,
    XtPointer      /* closure */
#endif
);

extern void XtRemoveCallback(
#if NeedFunctionPrototypes
    Widget         /* widget */,
    CONST String   /* callback_name */,
    XtCallbackProc /* callback */,
    XtPointer      /* closure */
#endif
);

extern void XtAddCallbacks(
#if NeedFunctionPrototypes
    Widget         /* widget */,
    CONST String   /* callback_name */,
    XtCallbackList /* callbacks */
```

```
#endif
);

extern void XtRemoveCallbacks(
#if NeedFunctionPrototypes
    Widget          /* widget */,
    CONST String    /* callback_name */,
    XtCallbackList  /* callbacks */
#endif
);

extern void XtRemoveAllCallbacks(
#if NeedFunctionPrototypes
    Widget          /* widget */,
    CONST String    /* callback_name */
#endif
);


extern void XtCallCallbacks(
#if NeedFunctionPrototypes
    Widget          /* widget */,
    CONST String    /* callback_name */,
    XtPointer       /* call_data */
#endif
);

extern void XtCallCallbackList(
#if NeedFunctionPrototypes
    Widget          /* widget */,
    XtCallbackList  /* callbacks */,
    XtPointer       /* call_data */
#endif
);

extern XtCallbackStatus XtHasCallbacks(
#if NeedFunctionPrototypes
    Widget          /* widget */,
    CONST String    /* callback_name */
#endif
);
```

```
/*************************************************************
 *
 * Geometry Management
 *
 *************************************************************/


extern XtGeometryResult XtMakeGeometryRequest(
#if NeedFunctionPrototypes
    Widget           /* widget */,
    XtWidgetGeometry* /* request */,
    XtWidgetGeometry* /* reply_return */
#endif
);


extern XtGeometryResult XtQueryGeometry(
#if NeedFunctionPrototypes
    Widget           /* widget */,
    XtWidgetGeometry* /* intended */,
    XtWidgetGeometry* /* reply_return */
#endif
);


extern Widget XtCreatePopupShell(
#if NeedFunctionPrototypes
    CONST String /* name */,
    WidgetClass  /* widgetClass */,
    Widget       /* parent */,
    ArgList      /* args */,
    Cardinal     /* num_args */
#endif
);


extern Widget XtVaCreatePopupShell(
#if NeedVarargsPrototypes
    CONST String /* name */,
    WidgetClass  /* widgetClass */,
    Widget       /* parent */,
    ...
#endif
);
```

```c
extern void XtPopup(
#if NeedFunctionPrototypes
    Widget          /* widget */,
    XtGrabKind      /* grab_kind */
#endif
);

extern void XtPopupSpringLoaded(
#if NeedFunctionPrototypes
    Widget    /* widget */
#endif
);

extern void XtCallbackNone(
#if NeedFunctionPrototypes
    Widget          /* widget */,
    XtPointer       /* closure */,
    XtPointer       /* call_data */
#endif
);

extern void XtCallbackNonexclusive(
#if NeedFunctionPrototypes
    Widget          /* widget */,
    XtPointer       /* closure */,
    XtPointer       /* call_data */
#endif
);

extern void XtCallbackExclusive(
#if NeedFunctionPrototypes
    Widget          /* widget */,
    XtPointer       /* closure */,
    XtPointer       /* call_data */
#endif
);

extern void XtPopdown(
#if NeedFunctionPrototypes
    Widget    /* widget */
#endif
);
```

```
extern void XtCallbackPopdown(
#if NeedFunctionPrototypes
    Widget        /* widget */,
    XtPointer    /* closure */,
    XtPointer    /* call_data */
#endif
);

extern void XtMenuPopupAction(
#if NeedFunctionPrototypes
    Widget        /* widget */,
    XEvent*      /* event */,
    String*      /* params */,
    Cardinal*    /* num_params */
#endif
);

extern Widget XtCreateWidget(
#if NeedFunctionPrototypes
    CONST String  /* name */,
    WidgetClass   /* widget_class */,
    Widget        /* parent */,
    ArgList       /* args */,
    Cardinal      /* num_args */
#endif
);

extern Widget XtCreateManagedWidget(
#if NeedFunctionPrototypes
    CONST String  /* name */,
    WidgetClass   /* widget_class */,
    Widget        /* parent */,
    ArgList       /* args */,
    Cardinal      /* num_args */
#endif
);

extern Widget XtVaCreateWidget(
#if NeedVarargsPrototypes
    CONST String  /* name */,
    WidgetClass   /* widget */,
    Widget        /* parent */,
```

```
    ...
#endif
);

extern Widget XtVaCreateManagedWidget(
#if NeedVarargsPrototypes
    CONST String  /* name */,
    WidgetClass   /* widget_class */,
    Widget        /* parent */,
    ...
#endif
);

extern Widget XtCreateApplicationShell(
#if NeedFunctionPrototypes
    CONST String  /* name */,
    WidgetClass   /* widget_class */,
    ArgList       /* args */,
    Cardinal      /* num_args */
#endif
);

extern Widget XtAppCreateShell(
#if NeedFunctionPrototypes
    CONST String  /* name */,
    CONST String  /* class */,
    WidgetClass   /* widget_class */,
    Display*      /* display */,
    ArgList       /* args */,
    Cardinal      /* num_args */
#endif
);

extern Widget XtVaAppCreateShell(
#if NeedVarargsPrototypes
    CONST String  /* name */,
    CONST String  /* class */,
    WidgetClass   /* widget_class */,
    Display*      /* display */,
    ...
#endif
);
```

```
/**************************************************************
 *
 * Toolkit initialization
 *
 **************************************************************/

extern void XtToolkitInitialize(
#if NeedFunctionPrototypes
    void
#endif
);

extern void XtDisplayInitialize(
#if NeedFunctionPrototypes
    XtAppContext            /* appContext */,
    Display*                /* dpy */,
    CONST String            /* name */,
    CONST String            /* class */,
    XrmOptionDescRec*       /* options */,
    Cardinal                /* num_options */,
    Cardinal*               /* argc */,
    char**                  /* argv */
#endif
);

extern Widget XtAppInitialize(
#if NeedFunctionPrototypes
    XtAppContext*           /* app_context_return */,
    CONST String            /* application_class */,
    XrmOptionDescList       /* options */,
    Cardinal                /* num_options */,
    Cardinal*               /* argc_in_out */,
    String*                 /* argv_in_out */,
    CONST String*           /* fallback_resources */,
    ArgList                 /* args */,
    Cardinal                /* num_args */
#endif
);

extern Widget XtVaAppInitialize(
#if NeedVarargsPrototypes
    XtAppContext*           /* app_context_return */,
```

```
    CONST String        /* application_class */,
    XrmOptionDescList   /* options */,
    Cardinal            /* num_options */,
    Cardinal*           /* argc_in_out */,
    String*             /* argv_in_out */,
    CONST String*       /* fallback_resources */,
    ...
#endif
);

extern Widget XtInitialize(
#if NeedFunctionPrototypes
    CONST String        /* name */,
    CONST String        /* class */,
    XrmOptionDescRec*   /* options */,
    Cardinal            /* num_options */,
    Cardinal*           /* argc */,
    char**              /* argv */
#endif
);

extern Display *XtOpenDisplay(
#if NeedFunctionPrototypes
    XtAppContext        /* appContext */,
    CONST String        /* displayName */,
    CONST String        /* applName */,
    CONST String        /* className */,
    XrmOptionDescRec*   /* urlist */,
    Cardinal            /* num_urs */,
    Cardinal*           /* argc */,
    char**              /* argv */
#endif
);

extern XtAppContext XtCreateApplicationContext(
#if NeedFunctionPrototypes
    void
#endif
);

extern void XtAppSetFallbackResources(
#if NeedFunctionPrototypes
```

```
    XtAppContext   /* app_context */,
    CONST String*  /* specification_list */
#endif
);

extern void XtDestroyApplicationContext(
#if NeedFunctionPrototypes
    XtAppContext  /* appContext */
#endif
);

extern void XtInitializeWidgetClass(
#if NeedFunctionPrototypes
    WidgetClass  /* widget_class */
#endif
);

extern XtAppContext XtWidgetToApplicationContext(
#if NeedFunctionPrototypes
    Widget   /* widget */
#endif
);

extern XtAppContext XtDisplayToApplicationContext(
#if NeedFunctionPrototypes
    Display*  /* dpy */
#endif
);

extern XrmDatabase XtDatabase(
#if NeedFunctionPrototypes
    Display*  /* dpy */
#endif
);

extern void XtCloseDisplay(
#if NeedFunctionPrototypes
    Display*  /* dpy */
#endif
);
```

```
extern void XtCopyFromParent(
#if NeedFunctionPrototypes
    Widget      /* widget */,
    int         /* offset */,
    XrmValue*   /* value */
#endif
);

extern void XtCopyDefaultDepth(
#if NeedFunctionPrototypes
    Widget      /* widget */,
    int         /* offset */,
    XrmValue*   /* value */
#endif
);

extern void XtCopyDefaultColormap(
#if NeedFunctionPrototypes
    Widget      /* widget */,
    int         /* offset */,
    XrmValue*   /* value */
#endif
);

extern void XtCopyAncestorSensitive(
#if NeedFunctionPrototypes
    Widget      /* widget */,
    int         /* offset */,
    XrmValue*   /* value */
#endif
);

extern void XtCopyScreen(
#if NeedFunctionPrototypes
    Widget      /* widget */,
    int         /* offset */,
    XrmValue*   /* value */
#endif
);
```

```
extern void XrmCompileResourceList(
#if NeedFunctionPrototypes
    XtResourceList  /* resources */,
    Cardinal        /* num_resources */
#endif
);

extern void XtGetApplicationResources(
#if NeedFunctionPrototypes
    Widget          /* widget */,
    XtPointer       /* base */,
    XtResourceList  /* resources */,
    Cardinal        /* num_resources */,
    ArgList         /* args */,
    Cardinal        /* num_args */
#endif
);

extern void XtVaGetApplicationResources(
#if NeedVarargsPrototypes
    Widget          /* widget */,
    XtPointer       /* base */,
    XtResourceList  /* resources */,
    Cardinal        /* num_resources */,
    ...
#endif
);

extern void XtGetSubresources(
#if NeedFunctionPrototypes
    Widget          /* widget */,
    XtPointer       /* base */,
    CONST String    /* name */,
    CONST String    /* class */,
    XtResourceList  /* resources */,
    Cardinal        /* num_resources */,
    ArgList         /* args */,
    Cardinal        /* num_args */
#endif
);
```

```
extern void XtVaGetSubresources(
#if NeedVarargsPrototypes
    Widget           /* widget */,
    XtPointer        /* base */,
    CONST String     /* name */,
    CONST String     /* class */,
    XtResourceList   /* resources */,
    Cardinal         /* num_resources */,
    ...
#endif
);

extern void XtSetValues(
#if NeedFunctionPrototypes
    Widget    /* widget */,
    ArgList   /* args */,
    Cardinal  /* num_args */
#endif
);

extern void XtVaSetValues(
#if NeedVarargsPrototypes
    Widget  /* widget */,
    ...
#endif
);

extern void XtGetValues(
#if NeedFunctionPrototypes
    Widget    /* widget */,
    ArgList   /* args */,
    Cardinal  /* num_args */
#endif
);

extern void XtVaGetValues(
#if NeedVarargsPrototypes
    Widget  /* widget */,
    ...
#endif
);
```

```
extern void XtSetSubvalues(
#if NeedFunctionPrototypes
    XtPointer        /* base */,
    XtResourceList   /* resources */,
    Cardinal         /* num_resources */,
    ArgList          /* args */,
    Cardinal         /* num_args */
#endif
);

extern void XtVaSetSubvalues(
#if NeedVarargsPrototypes
    XtPointer        /* base */,
    XtResourceList   /* resources */,
    Cardinal         /* num_resources */,
    ...
#endif
);

extern void XtGetSubvalues(
#if NeedFunctionPrototypes
    XtPointer        /* base */,
    XtResourceList   /* resources */,
    Cardinal         /* num_resources */,
    ArgList          /* args */,
    Cardinal         /* num_args */
#endif
);

extern void XtVaGetSubvalues(
#if NeedVarargsPrototypes
    XtPointer        /* base */,
    XtResourceList   /* resources */,
    Cardinal         /* num_resources */,
    ...
#endif
);

extern void XtGetResourceList(
#if NeedFunctionPrototypes
    WidgetClass      /* widget_class */,
    XtResourceList*  /* resources_return */,
```

```
    Cardinal*         /* num_resources_return */
#endif
);


extern void XtGetConstraintResourceList(
#if NeedFunctionPrototypes
    WidgetClass       /* widget_class */,
    XtResourceList*   /* resources_return */,
    Cardinal*         /* num_resources_return */
#endif
);


#define XtUnspecifiedPixmap ((Pixmap)2)
#define XtUnspecifiedShellInt (-1)
#define XtUnspecifiedWindow ((Window)2)
#define XtUnspecifiedWindowGroup ((Window)3)
#define XtDefaultForeground "XtDefaultForeground"
#define XtDefaultBackground "XtDefaultBackground"
#define XtDefaultFont "XtDefaultFont"

#if defined(CRAY) || defined(__arm)
#ifdef CRAY2

#define XtOffset(p_type,field) \
  (sizeof(int)*((unsigned int)&(((p_type)NULL)->field)))

#else /* !CRAY2 */

#define XtOffset(p_type,field) \
  ((unsigned int)&(((p_type)NULL)->field))

#endif /* !CRAY2 */
#else /* ! (CRAY || __arm) */

#define XtOffset(p_type,field) \
 ((Cardinal) (((char *)
 (&(((p_type)NULL)->field))) - ((char *) NULL)))

#endif /* !CRAY */


#define XtOffsetOf(s_type,field) XtOffset(s_type*,field)
```

```
#ifdef notdef
/* this doesn't work on picky compilers */
#define XtOffset(p_type,field)
 ((unsigned int)&(((p_type)NULL)->field))
#endif


/************************************************************
 *
 * Error Handling
 *
 ************************************************************/

extern XtErrorMsgHandler XtAppSetErrorMsgHandler(
#if NeedFunctionPrototypes
    XtAppContext          /* app */,
    XtErrorMsgHandler    /* handler */
#endif
);

extern void XtSetErrorMsgHandler(
#if NeedFunctionPrototypes
    XtErrorMsgHandler    /* handler */
#endif
);

extern XtErrorMsgHandler XtAppSetWarningMsgHandler(
#if NeedFunctionPrototypes
    XtAppContext          /* app */,
    XtErrorMsgHandler    /* handler */
#endif
);

extern void XtSetWarningMsgHandler(
#if NeedFunctionPrototypes
    XtErrorMsgHandler    /* handler */
#endif
);

extern void XtAppErrorMsg(
#if NeedFunctionPrototypes
    XtAppContext    /* app */,
    CONST String    /* name */,
```

```
    CONST String   /* type */,
    CONST String   /* class */,
    CONST String   /* defaultp */,
    String*        /* params */,
    Cardinal*      /* num_params */
#endif
);

extern void XtErrorMsg(
#if NeedFunctionPrototypes
    CONST String   /* name */,
    CONST String   /* type */,
    CONST String   /* class */,
    CONST String   /* defaultp */,
    String*        /* params */,
    Cardinal*      /* num_params */
#endif
);

extern void XtAppWarningMsg(
#if NeedFunctionPrototypes
    XtAppContext   /* app */,
    CONST String   /* name */,
    CONST String   /* type */,
    CONST String   /* class */,
    CONST String   /* defaultp */,
    String*        /* params */,
    Cardinal*      /* num_params */
#endif
);

extern void XtWarningMsg(
#if NeedFunctionPrototypes
    CONST String   /* name */,
    CONST String   /* type */,
    CONST String   /* class */,
    CONST String   /* defaultp */,
    String*        /* params */,
    Cardinal*      /* num_params */
#endif
);
```

```
extern XtErrorHandler XtAppSetErrorHandler(
#if NeedFunctionPrototypes
    XtAppContext    /* app */,
    XtErrorHandler  /* handler */
#endif
);

extern void XtSetErrorHandler(
#if NeedFunctionPrototypes
    XtErrorHandler  /* handler */
#endif
);

extern XtErrorHandler XtAppSetWarningHandler(
#if NeedFunctionPrototypes
    XtAppContext    /* app */,
    XtErrorHandler  /* handler */
#endif
);

extern void XtSetWarningHandler(
#if NeedFunctionPrototypes
    XtErrorHandler  /* handler */
#endif
);

extern void XtAppError(
#if NeedFunctionPrototypes
    XtAppContext  /* app */,
    CONST String  /* message */
#endif
);

extern void XtError(
#if NeedFunctionPrototypes
    CONST String  /* message */
#endif
);

extern void XtAppWarning(
#if NeedFunctionPrototypes
    XtAppContext  /* app */,
```

```
    CONST String   /* message */
#endif
);

extern void XtWarning(
#if NeedFunctionPrototypes
    CONST String   /* message */
#endif
);

extern XrmDatabase *XtAppGetErrorDatabase(
#if NeedFunctionPrototypes
    XtAppContext  /* app */
#endif
);

extern XrmDatabase *XtGetErrorDatabase(
#if NeedFunctionPrototypes
    void
#endif
);

extern void XtAppGetErrorDatabaseText(
#if NeedFunctionPrototypes
    XtAppContext   /* app */,
    CONST String   /* name */,
    CONST String   /* type */,
    CONST String   /* class */,
    CONST String   /* defaultp */,
    String         /* buffer */,
    int            /* nbytes */,
    XrmDatabase    /* database */
#endif
);

extern void XtGetErrorDatabaseText(
#if NeedFunctionPrototypes
    CONST String   /* name */,
    CONST String   /* type */,
    CONST String   /* class */,
    CONST String   /* defaultp */,
    String         /* buffer */,
```

```
        int              /* nbytes */
#endif
);


/*************************************************************
 *
 * Memory Management
 *
 *************************************************************/

#define XtNew(type) ((type *) XtMalloc((unsigned)
                                        sizeof(type)))
#define XtNewString(str) \
    ((str) != NULL ?
    (strcpy(XtMalloc((unsigned)strlen(str) + 1), str)) : NULL)

extern char *XtMalloc(
#if NeedFunctionPrototypes
    Cardinal   /* size */
#endif
);

extern char *XtCalloc(
#if NeedFunctionPrototypes
    Cardinal  /* num */,
    Cardinal  /* size */
#endif
);

extern char *XtRealloc(
#if NeedFunctionPrototypes
    char*      /* ptr */,
    Cardinal   /* num */
#endif
);

extern void XtFree(
#if NeedFunctionPrototypes
    char*  /* ptr */
#endif
);
```

```
/************************************************************
 *
 *  Work procs
 *
 ************************************************************/

extern XtWorkProcId XtAddWorkProc(
#if NeedFunctionPrototypes
    XtWorkProc  /* proc */,
    XtPointer   /* closure */
#endif
);

extern XtWorkProcId XtAppAddWorkProc(
#if NeedFunctionPrototypes
    XtAppContext  /* app */,
    XtWorkProc    /* proc */,
    XtPointer     /* closure */
#endif
);

extern void  XtRemoveWorkProc(
#if NeedFunctionPrototypes
    XtWorkProcId  /* id */
#endif
);



/************************************************************
 *
 * Graphic Context Management
 *
 ************************************************************/

extern GC XtGetGC(
#if NeedFunctionPrototypes
    Widget     /* widget */,
    XtGCMask   /* valueMask */,
    XGCValues* /* values */
#endif
);
```

```
extern void XtDestroyGC(
#if NeedFunctionPrototypes
    GC      /* gc */
#endif
);

extern void XtReleaseGC(
#if NeedFunctionPrototypes
    Widget  /* object */,
    GC      /* gc */
#endif
);

extern void XtReleaseCacheRef(
#if NeedFunctionPrototypes
    XtCacheRef*  /* cache_ref */
#endif
);

extern void XtCallbackReleaseCacheRef(
#if NeedFunctionPrototypes
    Widget     /* widget */,
    XtPointer  /* closure */, /* XtCacheRef */
    XtPointer  /* call_data */
#endif
);

extern void XtCallbackReleaseCacheRefList(
#if NeedFunctionPrototypes
    Widget     /* widget */,
    XtPointer  /* closure */, /* XtCacheRef* */
    XtPointer  /* call_data */
#endif
);

extern void XtSetWMColormapWindows(
#if NeedFunctionPrototypes
    Widget    /* widget */,
    Widget*   /* list */,
    Cardinal  /* count */
#endif
);
```

```
extern String XtFindFile(
#if NeedFunctionPrototypes
    CONST String       /* path */,
    Substitution       /* substitutions */,
    Cardinal           /* num_substitutions */,
    XtFilePredicate    /* predicate */
#endif
);

extern String XtResolvePathname(
#if NeedFunctionPrototypes
    Display*           /* dpy */,
    CONST String       /* type */,
    CONST String       /* filename */,
    CONST String       /* suffix */,
    CONST String       /* path */,
    Substitution       /* substitutions */,
    Cardinal           /* num_substitutions */,
    XtFilePredicate    /* predicate */
#endif
);


/*************************************************************
 *
 * Selections
 *
 *************************************************************/


#define XT_CONVERT_FAIL (Atom)0x80000001


/*
 * The given widget no longer wants the selection. If it
 * still owns it, then the selection owner is cleared,
 * and the window's losesSelection is called.
 */

extern void XtDisownSelection(
#if NeedFunctionPrototypes
    Widget /* widget */,
    Atom   /* selection */,
```

```
      Time    /* time */
#endif
);


/*
 * Get the value of the given selection.
 */

extern void XtGetSelectionValue(
#if NeedFunctionPrototypes
    Widget                  /* widget */,
    Atom                    /* selection */,
    Atom                    /* target */,
    XtSelectionCallbackProc /* callback */,
    XtPointer               /* closure */,
    Time                    /* time */
#endif
);

extern void XtGetSelectionValues(
#if NeedFunctionPrototypes
    Widget                  /* widget */,
    Atom                    /* selection */,
    Atom*                   /* targets */,
    int                     /* count */,
    XtSelectionCallbackProc /* callback */,
    XtPointer*              /* closures */,
    Time                    /* time */
#endif
);


/* Set the selection timeout value,
   in units of milliseconds */

extern void XtAppSetSelectionTimeout(
#if NeedFunctionPrototypes
    XtAppContext   /* app */,
    unsigned long  /* timeout */
#endif
);
```

```
extern void XtSetSelectionTimeout(
#if NeedFunctionPrototypes
    unsigned long  /* timeout */
#endif
);

 /* Return the selection timeout value,
    in units of milliseconds */

extern unsigned int XtAppGetSelectionTimeout(
#if NeedFunctionPrototypes
    XtAppContext  /* app */
#endif
);

extern unsigned int XtGetSelectionTimeout(
#if NeedFunctionPrototypes
    void
#endif
);

extern XSelectionRequestEvent *XtGetSelectionRequest(
#if NeedFunctionPrototypes
    Widget        /* widget */,
    Atom          /* selection */,
    XtRequestId   /* request_id */
#endif
);

extern void XtGetSelectionValueIncremental(
#if NeedFunctionPrototypes
    Widget                   /* widget */,
    Atom                     /* selection */,
    Atom                     /* target */,
    XtSelectionCallbackProc  /* selection_callback */,
    XtPointer                /* client_data */,
    Time                     /* time */
#endif
);

extern void XtGetSelectionValuesIncremental(
#if NeedFunctionPrototypes
```

```
        Widget                  /* widget */,
        Atom                    /* selection */,
        Atom*                   /* targets */,
        int                     /* count */,
        XtSelectionCallbackProc /* callback */,
        XtPointer*              /* client_data */,
        Time                    /* time */
#endif
);

extern void XtGrabKey(
#if NeedFunctionPrototypes
    Widget     /* widget */,
    KeyCode    /* keycode */,
    Modifiers  /* modifiers */,
    Boolean    /* owner_events */,
    int        /* pointer_mode */,
    int        /* keyboard_mode */
#endif
);

extern void XtUngrabKey(
#if NeedFunctionPrototypes
    Widget     /* widget */,
    KeyCode    /* keycode */,
    Modifiers  /* modifiers */
#endif
);

extern int XtGrabKeyboard(
#if NeedFunctionPrototypes
    Widget   /* widget */,
    Boolean  /* owner_events */,
    int      /* pointer_mode */,
    int      /* keyboard_mode */,
    Time     /* time */
#endif
);

extern void XtUngrabKeyboard(
#if NeedFunctionPrototypes
    Widget  /* widget */,
```

```
    Time    /* time */
#endif
);

extern void XtGrabButton(
#if NeedFunctionPrototypes
    Widget        /* widget */,
    int           /* button */,
    Modifiers     /* modifiers */,
    Boolean       /* owner_events */,
    unsigned int  /* event_mask */,
    int           /* pointer_mode */,
    int           /* keyboard_mode */,
    Window        /* confine_to */,
    Cursor        /* cursor */
#endif
);

extern void XtUngrabButton(
#if NeedFunctionPrototypes
    Widget        /* widget */,
    unsigned int  /* button */,
    Modifiers     /* modifiers */
#endif
);

extern int XtGrabPointer(
#if NeedFunctionPrototypes
    Widget        /* widget */,
    Boolean       /* owner_events */,
    unsigned int  /* event_mask */,
    int           /* pointer_mode */,
    int           /* keyboard_mode */,
    Window        /* confine_to */,
    Cursor        /* cursor */,
    Time          /* time */
#endif
);

extern void XtUngrabPointer(
#if NeedFunctionPrototypes
    Widget  /* widget */,
```

```
        Time      /* time */
#endif
);

extern void XtGetApplicationNameAndClass(
#if NeedFunctionPrototypes
    Display*   /* dpy */,
    String*    /* name_return */,
    String*    /* class_return */
#endif
);

#ifdef __cplusplus
}        /* for C++ V2.0 */
#endif

#if NeedWidePrototypes
#undef Boolean
#undef Dimension
#undef KeyCode
#undef Position
#undef XtEnum
#endif /* NeedWidePrototypes */

#undef String
#undef CONST

#endif /*_XtIntrinsic_h*/
/* DON'T ADD STUFF AFTER THIS #endif */
```

APPENDIX

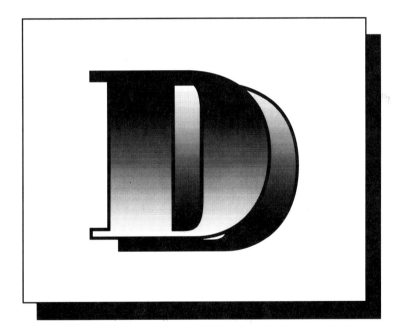

OSF/Motif Widgets

*T*his appendix presents widgets that are provided with the OSF/Motif proprietary toolkit.

Shell Widgets

Shell widgets provide communication between the window manager and an application's widgets. Motif provides three Shell widgets: XmDialogShell, XmMenuShell, and VendorShell.

The DialogShell widget class is a subclass of the Xt Intrinsics Shell class TransientShell, associated with Shell windows that cannot be iconified. The DialogShell furnishes communication with the Motif window manager.

The MenuShell widget class is a subclass of the Xt Intrinsics Shell class OverrideShell, associated with Shell windows that bypass the window manager. Instances of the MenuShell widget class are employed as the parents of menu panes.

The VendorShell widget class is a subclass of the Xt Intrinsics Shell class WMShell, which contains resources necessary for the common window manager protocol. The VendorShell widget class provides information necessary for window manager visible shells.

Display Widgets

Motif defines 11 classes of display widgets that manage the screen display, in addition to the Core widget class discussed in Chapter 5, "Toolkit Concepts and Techniques." These classes are XmPrimitive, XmArrowButton, XmDrawnButton, XmLabel, XmList, XmPushButton, XmScrollBar, XmSeparator, XmText, XmTextField, and XmToggleButton.

The XmPrimitive class is a supporting superclass for other widget classes. It provides resources for border drawing, highlighting, and so on.

The ArrowButton widget consists of an arrow surrounded by a border shadow. When the widget is selected, the shadow moves and gives the appearance that the arrow button has been pressed.

The DrawnButton widget consists of an empty widget window surrounded by a shadow border. It provides the application developer with a graphics area that works like a pushbutton.

The Label widget consists of either text or graphics. It can be used as a superclass for button widgets. Label widgets do not accept any input except help buttons.

The List widget allows a selection from a list of items, which may be selected by a scroll bar.

The PushButton widget consists of a text label or pixmap surrounded by a border shadow. To select the pushbutton, place the mouse cursor on it and press the first mouse button. Selecting the pushbutton changes the widget colors and invokes an action.

The ScrollBar widget displays a portion of data that is too large to be viewed in its entirety. Scroll bars are used in conjunction with a widget containing the data to be viewed. Horizontal scroll bars are placed at the bottom edge of the work area. Vertical scroll bars are placed at the right edge of the work area.

The Separator widget is a primitive widget used to separate items in a display. This separation may be horizontal or vertical and can involve different line drawing styles.

The Text widget provides a single or multiline text editor with a customizable user interface. It can be used for form-based data entry with extensive data validation.

The TextField widget is similar to the text widget but is restricted to single-line text editing.

The ToggleButton widget consists of a graphics or text button face with a square- or diamond-shaped selection box to the left of the graphics or text. Use the mouse cursor to activate or deactivate the selection box, changing its color.

Container Widgets

Container widgets are Composite widgets furnishing applications with general layout functionality. Motif provides eight classes of container widgets: XmManager, XmDrawingArea, XmFrame, XmMainWindow, XmPanedWindow, XmRowColumn, XmScale, and XmScrolledWindow.

The XmManager widget class is a metaclass, a class for organizing widgets that may not be instantiated. It provides the required visual resources and graphics contexts. It is built from the Core, Composite, and Constraint widget classes.

The DrawingArea widget is an empty widget that may be incorporated in a variety of applications. Except for callbacks, it does not define any behavior.

The Frame widget is a manager used to enclose a single child within a border that it draws. This widget is often used to enclose other manager widgets to enforce a uniform border appearance.

The MainWindow widget provides a standard layout for the primary window of an application. The layout may include a menu bar, a command window, a work region, and scroll bars.

The PanedWindow manager widget is a Composite widget that lays out children in a vertically tiled format, with children appearing from top to bottom. All children are set to the same width and may have constraints.

The RowColumn widget is a general-purpose RowColumn manager that can contain any widget type as a child. This widget can arrange its children in rows, columns, or closely packed.

Scale widgets are used by an application to indicate a value within a range of values and allow a user to input or modify a value from this range. A scale has a long rectangular region similar to a scroll bar, containing a slider to indicate the current value.

The ScrolledWindow widget combines one or more ScrollBar widgets and a viewing area to implement a visible window onto another, usually larger, data display. The scrolled window may be set up to function automatically.

Dialog Widgets

Dialog widgets are container widgets that accompany user-application activities including displaying messages, setting properties, and selecting from a list of items. Motif provides six categories of Dialog widgets:

XmBulletinBoard, XmCommand, XmFileSelectionBox, XmForm, XmMessageBox, and XmSelectionBox.

The BulletinBoard widget is a Composite widget that provides simple geometry management for children widgets without imposing positioning. This widget is often used as the base for other dialog widgets.

The Command widget is a subclass of SelectionBox widgets that includes a command input region and a command history region. The history region scrolls when required.

The FileSelectionBox widget is a subclass of SelectionBox widgets that selects from a list of choices. It includes an editable text file for the directory mask and selected file and a scrolling list of filenames and directories.

The Form widget is a Container widget that places constraints on its children. The relationships among the Form widget's children are maintained when the form changes size, when new children appear on the form, or when existing children are modified.

The MessageBox widget is a subclass of the BulletinBoard widget that provides the user with information. A message box includes a symbol and a message.

The SelectionBox widget is a subclass of the BulletinBoard widget, which enables the user to select an item from a list of choices. A selection box includes a message, an editable text field, and a scrolled list of choices.

APPENDIX

Common X Window Programming Errors

As you surely realize by now, programming X Window systems is an error-prone process. This appendix describes several common errors and how to avoid them. Take a close look, and you can save yourself hours of debugging.

X Window programming errors can be divided into four major classifications: design errors, syntax errors, usage errors, and compatibility errors.

Design Errors

As is the case with any other programming language, system design oversights inevitably lead to programming errors. You can reduce the frequency of design errors by applying the appropriate level of X Window programming and the correct loop structure, such as the Xlib event loop or the Motif applications structure.

Avoiding the Toolkits

Correct use of Xt Intrinsics and a proprietary toolkit such as OSF/Motif greatly reduces the programming burden. A single reusable widget may replace multiple Xlib function calls. The programming example presented in Chapter 11, "Complete Fundamental Application and Advanced Features," illustrates a practical, relatively sophisticated application coded without using any Xlib functions. An Xlib program with the same functionality would be much longer and harder to code without offering any concrete advantages.

Event Mishandling

Event processing is the central focus of the X Window system. Every activity that affects input or output, and many additional activities as well, generates one or more events. The application must choose to solicit or ignore individual event types. The easiest way to handle events is to apply the toolkits, which automatically generate event loops. If Xlib functions are required, reduce event-handling errors by designing such programs around a single event loop as in Chapter 2, "Hello World," and the other Xlib programs in Chapters 5 to 10.

Two common event-handling errors are forgetting to solicit the desired event type and improperly processing exposure events. Except for keyboard-mapping events, all event types must be selected, or the event in question is not reported to the application. On the other hand, selecting a given event type can be an error, depending on the application. In general, a program with an active mouse should not select motion notify events lest it be forced to process literally hundreds of events, most of which are irrelevant.

Syntax Errors

As you have probably noticed by now, the syntax of X Window systems tends to be heavy. The programmer must choose among hundreds of functions. Spelling is rarely intuitive, and parameters abound.

Toolkit Syntax Errors

Because many widgets set the default window width and height to 0, the program must verify the window size to avoid generating meaningless results. Parameter coding errors are discussed in this syntax section.

Xlib Syntax Errors

Errors occur when exceeding system limits. For example, the fill functions **XFillArc**, **XFillArcs**, **XFillPolygon**, **XFillRectangle**, and **XFillRectangles** may process a limited amount of data in a single call. The allowed maximum depends on the implementation. Some implementations subdivide such function calls to permit processing of voluminous data. Xlib functions are usually limited to 16-bit size (signed or unsigned), so errors may occur when drawing large windows.

Parameter Errors

When using either toolkit or Xlib functions, it is easy to code the arguments in the wrong order or omit one or more arguments. If the C compiler does not perform extensive parameter checking, the function will generate unpredictable results that may be very difficult to track down. Chapter 3, "Basic Concepts and Terminology," discusses Xlib naming and argument conventions in detail. Keep this information as a ready reference until it becomes second nature.

Resource Specification Errors

Resource spelling errors can be particularly pernicious because the compiler does not report them but uses default values. When you consider that the full resource class of a widget instance's field is obtained by concatenating the application class, the widget class names of all the widget's ancestors up to the top of the widget tree, the widget's own class name, and the resource class of the specified field, you know why judicious use of wildcards and defaults is highly suggested. The resource specification order and resource naming conventions are discussed in detail in Chapter 5, "Toolkit Concepts and Techniques." Watch your spelling and don't forget that capitalization is significant.

Usage Errors

It is easy to apply both Xlib and toolkit functions incorrectly. Among the common errors are display errors and incomplete operations.

Display Errors

X Window does not immediately update the display to reflect all changes. Consider a change in an existing window's background attributes. This change becomes visible only after an Expose event is generated. You may, for example, invoke the **XClear** function, which repaints the window and its background. Other display errors occur when relying on default graphics contexts. On the other hand, sharing of graphics contexts may be necessary when running several applications simultaneously on limited hardware.

The **XSetFunction** selects among 16 Boolean functions that combine pixels generated by graphics functions with existing pixels to display the final output. It is easy to apply the wrong Boolean function and generate incorrect results that may be close to the desired results, thus complicating the debugging process. For example, in three of the four possible combinations of source and destination bits, the widely used GXxor option generates the same results as the GXor option. Once again, watch your spelling.

Incomplete Operations

The window and widget display processes are both multistep operations. It is not sufficient to create a window with a function such as **XCreateSimpleWindow**. An Xlib function such as **XMapRaised** is also required. In much the same way, displaying a widget requires a toolkit function such as **XtVaCreateManagedWidget**, followed by registering any appropriate callbacks and event handlers. The process is completed with a single call to a function such as **XtRealizeWidget**. Once again, the sample programs in Chapter 2, "Hello World," and Chapter 5, "Toolkit Concepts and Techniques," provide templates for Xlib and toolkit programs.

Other Usage Errors

Among the many other usage errors associated with X Window are input focus problems and the lack of synchronization. Recall that unless specifically commanded otherwise, X Window system is asynchronous. Xlib buffers request and process them in groups. Thus an error message may not appear immediately, which renders debugging more difficult. The **XSynchronize** function is available for debugging, but it slows down system performance drastically.

Compatibility Errors

X Window was designed to be hardware independent. However, when your X Window applications make extensive use of C language functions or UNIX system calls, as in the program of Chapter 11, "Complete Fundamental Application and Advanced Features," you may expect compatibility problems between different platforms. Furthermore, in spite of the objectives of X Window systems, several compatibility issues can arise when developing applications to run on multiple platforms.

Hardware Incompatibility

Problems that may occur when porting an application from one system to another include the number of buttons on the mouse, the maximum cursor size, and the screen size and depth (number of pixels per image). Make liberal use of the appropriate Xlib functions to query these values before coding the application.

Color Processing

Chapter 10, "Color and Graphics," discussed six different color models. Not all color models are available on all workstations, even color workstations. Changing the color model may impact the application. Not all workstations accept the same range of color names. Furthermore, as many developers can testify, not all workstations interpret a given color name exactly the same. The use of device-independent color-processing functions introduced in Chapter 11, "Complete Fundamental Application and Advanced Features," may alleviate this problem. Other techniques are required to address the problem of the server's limited capacity to process multiple colors simultaneously.

Font Processing

Not all X servers support the same fonts. The **XQueryFont** function informs you whether the given font is available on your server. If possible, determine the fonts to use before coding the application. Compatibility problems are likely to arise when using foreign language character sets or older versions of X Window systems.

GLOSSARY

Active grab   An application's attempt to grab the pointer for its exclusive use. Also called an *active keyboard grab.*

Active keyboard grab   An application's attempt to obtain exclusive control of the keyboard. Also called a *keyboard grab.*

Ancestor   A given window's parent, grandparent, and so on.

Application   A toolkit-based program.

Application context   A pointer to a data structure that contains toolkit-designated data for the application.

Application programmers   In the context of X Window systems, programmers who employ existing widgets.

Atom   A unique 32-bit identifier that replaces a string name.

Attributes   A window's features that can be changed.

Backing store   The stored pixels for an X Window implementation in which the X server itself maintains window contents.

Bit gravity   Repositioning a window image relative to a resized window.

Bitmap   A pixmap whose pixels are each represented by a single bit.

Bitmap file   A text file that can be loaded into a bitmap resource.

Callback list   A series of functions to be performed when a callback procedure is invoked.

Callback procedure   An application-dependant function called by a widget that requires information from the application. Also known as a *callback*.

Characteristics   A window's permanent features.

Child window   A window created with reference to an existing window. Also called a *subwindow*.

Class   An object's type defining the legal operations for that object.

Class hierarchy   The formal relationship among classes.

Client   In X Window systems, the application program.

Client/server architecture   The X Window system model by which *clients*, or application programs, communicate with *servers*, or display units, over a network.

Clipped   Window contents may be *clipped* by their parents—an image does not extend beyond the window's edges.

Color cell   A combination of red, green, and blue values designating a single color.

Colormap   A map associating a pixel value to a color. Also called a *color lookup table*.

Colormap state notification events   Events that inform interested clients when the colormap changes and when a colormap is installed or removed.

Cursor   A small visible object that points to a specific screen location.

Cut buffers   Eight properties defined in root windows XA_CUT_BUFFER0 to XA_CUT_BUFFER7.

Define directive   A program statement that associates a meaningful programmer-defined name with a C language construct.

Depth   The number of bits per pixel in a window's pixel values.

Descendants   A given window's children, grandchildren, and so on.

Dialog box   An onscreen box that requests user input, displays a message, or both.

Drawables   Windows and pixmaps.

Dyadic key   A key with two keysyms.

Event   An indication that something of interest has happened.

Event mask   An object defined in the standard header library whose bits are set to solicit given event types.

Exposure events   Events that express interference between multiple windows on a single screen.

Font   An object that describes the size and shape of each character within a unified collection of characters.

Font properties   Descriptions of a font's characteristics. They often take the form of suggested values to maintain a font's visual appeal.

Geometry   A window's size, shape, and position within its parent window.

Graphical user interface   A computer/user interface that runs in graphics mode.

Graphics contexts   Data structures that manage graphics features, including line style and width, foreground and background color, and fill patterns.

Hints   An application's suggestions to the window manager, often describing window size, window placement, and window decorations.

Icon   A symbolic representation of an object, such as a garbage can to signify file deletion.

Images   Data structures that represent visual data in memory and provide basic operations on this data.

Include directive   A program statement that accesses a predefined set of declarations and constants in a named header file.

Inferiors   A given window's children, grandchildren, and so on.

Inheritance   The ability to implement specific operations (methods) from the instance's superclass.

Input context   Any data required by an input method and the information required to display the data.

Input focus   The window associated with the keyboard. Also called *keyboard focus*.

Instance   A given occurrence of a particular object, such as a widget.

Intrinsics   The X Window programming layer that defines standard functions and data types applied in creating widgets and implementing them in user applications.

Keyboard event   An event that indicates when a key is pressed or released.

Keyboard focus   The window associated with the keyboard. Also called the *input focus*.

Keyboard grab An application's attempt to obtain exclusive control of the keyboard. Also called an *active keyboard grab*.

Keycodes Integers between 8 and 255 assigned to a workstation's physical keys.

Keymap An array of bytes containing one bit per keycode.

Keysyms Standard mnemonic codes for keycap symbols.

Locale The localized behavior of a program at execution.

Managed widget A widget whose geometry is handled by the parent widget.

Mapped A precondition for displaying a window.

Mapping a window Making the window visible on the display.

Mask A group of bits that specifies the elements to be selected in an accompanying data structure.

Metaclass A class for organizing widget classes, not for organizing widgets themselves.

Method A procedure implementing a given operation supported by the widget class.

Monospaced font A font in which character widths are the same, independent of the character used. Computer listings in this text are set in a monospaced font.

MotionNotify event An event that indicates that the pointer has moved.

Object A self-contained unit including data and the operations defined for this data. Widgets are the major objects supported by the toolkit.

Obscures   Window Y *obscures* window Z if window Y is higher in the stacking order and the rectangle defined by the outside edges of window Y intersects the rectangle defined by the outside edges of window Z. The contents of an obscured window are not visible.

Occludes   Window I *occludes* window J if both windows are mapped, if I is higher in the stacking order than J, and if the rectangle defined by I's outer edges (the window including the border) intersects the rectangle defined by J's outer edges. Window occlusion is similar to, but not exactly the same as, window obscuring.

One-way protocol request message   X protocol requests that do not require a system reply.

Opaque   An object, such as an application context, that cannot be read by clients.

Parent window   An existing window for which a child window is created.

Passive keyboard grab   An activity alerting the system to look for three conditions related to keys that the user pressed. When these three conditions all occur, the passive grab issues an active keyboard grab.

Pixel   An addressable point on a graphical computer display unit.

Pixmap   A block of memory associated with the X server that can be used for drawing.

Pointer events   Events associated with a pointer, typically the mouse pointer.

Popups   Transient widgets that appear on the screen for a short time.

Propagation   The process by which, if a given event is not selected for a window, the event is passed to the window's ancestors until the event reaches a window for which the event has been selected or the event is blocked by the *do_not_propagate* mask.

Property   A name, a type, a data format, and data associated with a window, often used for interclient communication.

Proportional font   A font in which character widths vary, such as the body of this text.

Proprietary toolkits   Commercially available X Window software, such as OSF/Motif, with custom features that promise attractive output, ease of use, and rapid application development.

Public header file   A file supplied by X Window in a predefined directory that contains required information for a given widget class.

Quantum   The bitmap unit indicating the number of bits in each scanline unit.

Rebinding   Associating a predefined character string with a selected key.

Request   A block of data sent by an application to inform the server that it requires a service.

Resource classes   Groups of related resources that can be assigned a common value.

Resource specification   An indication of the resource value for one widget or a related group of widgets.

Resources   Objects stored on the X server. These include windows, graphics contexts, fonts, cursors, color maps, and pixmaps.

Root window   The window that consists of the entire screen. It cannot be moved, resized, or destroyed.

Round-trip protocol request message   X Protocol requests in which processing resumes only when the server returns the required information to the application.

Rubber-band line A line that indicates the motion of the pointer on the screen.

Save-unders Processes by which some servers preserve the contents of selected windows under other windows.

Scanline A row of pixels across the display screen.

Scroll bar A visual onscreen element that allows the user to scroll data appearing in a window.

Selection A special type of buffer used to move data from one application to another.

Server The display unit in X Window systems.

Shell widget The widget tree root.

Siblings Child windows with the same parent window.

Stacking order A description of the relationship among siblings.

Stipple A pixmap of depth 1 (bitmap) that serves as a fill pattern.

Structure control events Four types of events usually handled by the window manager: CirculateRequest, ConfigureRequest, MapRequest, and ResizeRequest events.

Subclass A class below (within) another class in the class hierarchy.

Subwindow A window created with reference to an existing window. Also called a *child window*.

Superclass A class above another class in the class hierarchy.

Symbolic name A widget's resource name preceded by the string "XtN". The compiler can detect spelling errors in the symbolic name.

Synchronization The separate processing of each Xlib function, often used when debugging a program.

Tile A pixmap, the depth of which is equal to the drawable associated with the graphics context.

Tiled windows Windows placed side by side.

Toolkit resource A named widget attribute that can be set by the programmer or, perhaps, by the user. Toolkit resources are similar to, but distinct from, Xlib resources.

Unmapping The process of rendering a window and all its descendents invisible on the screen.

Unrealizing The destruction of windows for a specified widget and its descendants without destroying its popup windows.

Viewable A window whose ancestors are all mapped.

Visual A workstation's pixel-value format.

Visual class A model for converting pixel values into displayed colors.

Widget class The widget type defining the attributes and operations available for a related group of widgets.

Widget geometry The widget's size, border width, position on the screen, and stacking order.

Widget programmers In the context of X Window systems, programmers who create widgets for sale.

Widgets Standard onscreen building blocks such as menus, scroll bars, buttons, and dialog boxes.

Window creation   The process of defining the window's relationship to its parent and, implicitly, to its siblings. This process sets the window geometry, characteristics, and attributes.

Window destruction   The process of removing a window and returning its resources to the system.

Window gravity   Repositioning a child window relative to its parent window is called applying *window gravity*.

Window hierarchy   The vertical relationships among windows. The window hierarchy roughly corresponds to a family tree.

Window manager   A special client responsible for manipulating windows on the screen.

Window state notification events   Events generated by the server whenever a window moves, changes its size or changes its place in the stacking order.

Window-crossing events   Events that indicate pointer motion or window hierarchy changes.

Windows   Generally, rectangular display areas that appear on the screen.

Workstations   Desktop computers whose computational and graphics facilities are more powerful than high-end microcomputers.

X protocol   The network protocol that defines the exact bytes required to perform all X Window operations.

X terminal   A diskless graphical computer terminal that runs a single program, the X Window server program.

X Toolkit Intrinsics   A standard part of the X Window system that enables programmers to create and use standard onscreen building blocks called *widgets*: for instance, menus, scroll bars, buttons, and dialog boxes. Also known as *Xt Intrinsics*.

X Window system The standard hardware-independent windowing system for workstations.

Xlib A library of over 300 C language functions used to generate X protocol.

Xt Intrinsics A standard part of the X Window system that enables programmers to create and use standard onscreen building blocks called *widgets*: for instance, menus, scroll bars, buttons, and dialog boxes. Also known as *X Toolkit Intrinsics*.

Index